INDIVIDUALITY INCO[...]

INDIVIDUALITY INCORPORATED

Indians and the Multicultural Modern

Joel Pfister

Duke University Press Durham and London 2004

For my dear friend and mother, Elizabeth Pfister. . . .
It's okay to wake up laughing.

Contents

List of Illustrations

Acknowledgments

It gives me great pleasure to acknowledge the collective dimensions of an effort that was never solely individual. This book originated as a term-paper-in-progress in Jean-Christophe Agnew's first American studies graduate seminar—in cultural history and theory—at Yale in spring, 1981. My ever-expanding work on it seemed endless. At last I had to bag it to do something doable. But the archives were too fascinating, disturbing, eye-opening, haunting. Stubbornly I kept teaching material pertaining to this term paper that never got written. Even so, it took me fourteen years to revive the project. Jean-Christophe, a gifted teacher, wry and laid-back, was always good about accepting stuff a bit late.

My debts—institutional, intellectual, and personal—are legion. Wesleyan University generously provided me with several sabbaticals and leaves—not to mention research funds for books—that gave me the time to conceptualize, research, and write this project along with two other book projects. Brian Fay, Dean of the Social Sciences, went above and beyond by helping subsidize this book's publication. I am grateful to the Rockefeller Foundation for awarding me a fellowship that allowed me to complete a key draft of *Individuality Incorporated* at the enchanting and intellectually intoxicating Villa Serbelloni in Bellagio, Italy, in 2000. I came back to the U.S. from Bellagio to be a visiting research fellow in the American Studies Program at Yale for a term and polished the edit.

My dear friend Sarah Winter read the first premature draft—in some parts, more a detailed sketch of what was to come—in spring 1997. She made a multitude of suggestions. Years later she re-read versions of the introduction and conclusion. Sarah is a magnificent theorist and editor.

As usual, she has helped me expand my thinking and tighten my argument. Elizabeth Pfister, otherwise known as mom, read the post-Bellagio draft in 2000 and proposed emendations. She is now 82 and I dedicate this work with love and admiration to her. Lisa Wyant, my beloved consort, edited the introduction and has had an ongoing powerful artistic and intellectual influence on my work in our daily exchanges and adventures. Her smart and creative support for this project—in Paris, New York, New Haven, and Branford—has made a difference in so many ways.

Back in 1981 I consulted George Miles, curator of the Western Americana Collection at Yale's Beinecke Rare Book and Manuscript Library, and he told me much more than I thought I needed to know about the Richard Henry Pratt archives and related resources. George also steered me to the John Collier papers in Yale's Manuscripts and Archives, where Judith Schiff has been so helpful. I re-appeared in his office in 1995, and, sometimes in two hour meetings, George shared his knowledge, advice, and enthusiasm. George himself is a rich archive. The skilled and imaginative librarians of Wesleyan and Yale have been indispensable in making this book possible.

My appendix ruptured on Labor Day, 1997, after a summer of hard labor, just as I was about to write the afterword to an advanced version of the book. That fall, on medical leave, I struggled in slow motion to finish that draft and Richard Slotkin, one of the most sagacious and decent American studies colleagues anyone could ever hope to work with, read and improved the entire manuscript. My internal combustion, however, was jarring enough to make me put aside writing this particular book for a spell and turn to another project not associated with the episode. I did not return to it wholeheartedly till the summer of 1999. Rich's interest in my work helped me resume my labors on it with renewed vigor and ideas.

Near the end of that challenging autumn in 1997, two days before a final surgery, I gave my first talk on the book at the Yale Americanist Colloquium. I thank the wonderful graduate students, especially Scott Saul, Joseph Entin, Leigh Raiford, and Robert Perkinson, for inviting me. Two years earlier Alan Trachtenberg had given me good bibliographic counsel when I recommended my work on this project. His warm introduction to my talk at the Yale colloquium contributed much to my resolve. I owe much of my ability as an editor—and scholar—to Alan. Over the past few years we have swapped ideas about and references to Native-White history over long lunches in New Haven.

Bryan Wolf, another old friend and teacher, read the 1997 burst-appendix edition of the manuscript and gave me inspired feedback. Arnold Krupat also read it at this time and later met me for lunch in Greenwich Village to share his remarkable expertise and critical acumen with me. Both Arnold and Bryan made it a better book. Joseph Entin, a talented critic and political thinker, scrutinized part of chapter 3 and all of the afterword when those sections were in need of theoretical clarification in 2000 and helped elevate them to a new level.

My savvy ally David Lubin, in response to two talks I gave on the book in 1998, at the University of London and at the American Studies Association conference in Seattle, taught me much about my presentation of this material. In particular, I want to thank Clive Bush for his hospitality and critical engagement at London. It was a thrill to be on the Seattle panel with my buddies Richard Lowry and Angela Miller.

Helle Porsdam and Dale Bauer were instrumental in keeping me connected to this project when I had put my work on it in brackets. Helle invited me to lecture at the University of Odense, her institution, and at a conference at Aarhus University in 1998. Meeting Carl Pedersen at Odense and Dale Carter at Aarhus made this Danish trip even more special. Dale Bauer kindly persuaded me to present some of my research on a panel with her at the Narrative conference held at Northwestern University in 1998. Both experiences were illuminating, restorative, and fun. Khachig Tölölyan, esteemed Wesleyan colleague, founder-editor of *Diaspora*, and theorist extraordinaire, claims he knows nothing about Indians and Indian schools, but kept sending me books on these subjects.

For three semesters, from 1996 to 1998, I benefited from teaching an advanced American studies and English seminar, "Constructing 'Individuals': Toward a Cultural History of the 'Individual.' " In these classes my students and I explored much material I cover in the book, more so than I had been able to do in other seminars. My stellar Wesleyan students relentlessly broadened my horizons, sharpened my formulations, gave me new ideas, and animated my spirits. We've learned and unlearned much together.

Several years ago Barbara Landis, Indian School Research Specialist at the Cumberland County Historical Society, sent me an email asking if I would like to receive her weekly transcriptions of all the Carlisle publications. I had read the Carlisle newspapers in Richard Henry Pratt's collection at Beinecke at that point, but I agreed and have profited from re-reading selections. Barbara's occasional notes about them also have been useful. Her transcriptions, perused by people in many walks of life, including many Indian school graduates and survivors, are invaluable.

Since then I have visited her and Genevieve Bell's outstanding website on Carlisle. Barbara and her colleague Richard L. Tritt helped identify some Pratt papers photographs I am reproducing. Not long ago I had the gumption to ask Barbara to read chapters 1 and 2. She did so and strengthened my work on Carlisle. Martha Viehmann also read these two chapters very carefully and responded with good questions, ideas, and emendations.

It has been a joy to work with Reynolds Smith, Executive Editor, and his colleagues at Duke University Press. I have appreciated their good humor as well as their professionalism throughout the process of making this book. To note that I am contributing my royalties to the American Indian College Fund does not begin to pay back my primary and permanent debt to the Native peoples whose writings, courage, strategies, and resilience have rewired my brain.

INDIVIDUALITY INCORPORATED

Introduction

Lessons Indians Can Teach American Studies about

the Rule of Individuality

The chief preoccupation of the state-builders in America was to establish institutions in their new country which would allow each citizen enough elbow room to grow into individuality. . . . Protection of the individual's happiness—the assurance of the elbow room he needed to reach his full stature—was the reason for the state's existence. . . . [The Founding Fathers'] passion for individuality instead of conformity was unique in all the world. What the generation of 1776 did was to organize those traditions into a new system.

—John Dos Passos, "A Question of Elbow Room," 1958

Individualist. It will open your eyes.

—Estée Lauder, Individualist mascara advertisement, 1990s

Don't let it get easy.

—Wendy Rose (Hopi and Miwok), "What My Father Said," 1985[1]

I confess that it gives me wicked delight to fantasize how John Dos Passos, in his conservative postwar phase, might have responded to Monty Python's film *Life of Brian* (1979). In the British comedy troupe's spoof on the messiah business, Brian, an unwilling ersatz-Christ figure, entreats the yea-saying multitudes, who follow him everywhere, not to follow anyone anywhere. Brian beseeches them: "You're all *individuals.*" The masses intone in unison: "Yes, we're all individuals." He insists, frustrated: "You're all *different.*" They chant, mesmerized: "Yes, we're all different." In the ensuing pause, deep in the shoulder-to-shoulder horde, a sole dissenter mutters: "I'm not."[2] Perhaps Dos Passos would have grumbled dismissively: "how un-American." Yet, as much that follows suggests, American Indians who survived schools that tried to train them to parrot "We're all individuals" might have retorted, "how American."

These Indians, many of whom were taken from their tribes and families and forced to attend government boarding schools, might have asked Dos Passos to pause to reflect on what was at stake in drilling thousands of Indian children to drown something named the *Indian* in them so they could be reborn and redeemed as "individuals" and "Americans." Savoring the Monty Python satire about the gospel of individuality as a spellbinding form of mass management, they might have dared Dos Passos to consider the irony that the rule of "individuality" had been imposed on them. The continent's indigenous tribal cultures had their own ways of imagining, enhancing, and motivating the self. I will begin to elaborate the details and lessons of this enlightening Native-White history of what was termed *individualizing* after surveying some of the premises that Dos Passos hoped all Americans and everyone everywhere would accept without question, for the implications of this history are legion.

For most Americans it has been easy to convert to *individuality*, the word Dos Passos extolled in 1958 with sacred significance as the defining American trait—what one critic terms America's "civil religion."[3] Certainly some American studies scholars in the early Cold War period, through their publications, teaching, and lecturing abroad, served as apostles of an American "individuality." They presented this ideal of individualism as evidence of American political, economic, cultural, spiritual, and psychological freedom. In the early decades of the Cold War, American literature, psychology, television, and film helped make dominant concepts of individuality seem like the human essence that naturally called forth America's democratic capitalist system.

Of course, this ideological reverence flourished long before the Cold War. In 1922, for example, in the wake of the Red Scare, Herbert Hoover glorified giant American corporations as institutional expressions of "rugged individualism" and demonized Russia as a destroyer of "self-interest." American individualism, he affirmed, prevents "frozen strata of classes," guarantees "equality of opportunity" for individuals of unequal "intelligence, character, ability, and ambition," preserves "pioneer" initiative, and guards against socialism by advocating service.[4] In Hoover's rendition of America, individuals—not classes—are rich. Hoover and Dos Passos hail America's *homo nationalis* as *homo individualis.* For them American exceptionalism relies on America's cultural, economic, and psychological nurturance of individual exceptionalism. Hence America had to win the Cold War because "human nature"—socially suppressed "individuality"—would eventually surface even in the enemy.[5]

Dos Passos commenced "A Question of Elbow Room," his Sputnik–space race paean to free world individuality, by assuring his reader that "individuality is freedom lived." He presented this as literary, not only political and economic, wisdom. The greatest authors, he rhapsodized, were driven by their "appetite . . . for elbow room" and rejection of conformity. He tried to give literary distinction to the stock claim that modern America—not any form of socialism, communism, cooperative-planned economy, or welfare state—has "come nearest to producing a classless society."[6]

This evangelical essay is intriguing for numerous reasons. The piece seems uncannily familiar the first time one reads it, even in the new millennium, because it is so adept at voicing ideologies many Americans take for granted. Students of American culture will know it before they have read it. It conveys how effectively the word *individuality* evokes not just nationality but humanity—human agency, human potential, making up one's own mind, the emotional need for don't-fence-me-in elbow room. In America the state derives a good measure of its ideological power by representing itself as a service enterprise. It supposedly exists by and for the people—the "individuals"—not for itself.

While Dos Passos occasionally represents individuality as a natural condition ("No two men are alike any more than two snowflakes are alike"), he also depicts it as a socially developmental process (one "grows into individuality").[7] Thus one might ask, how do these two readings work, or fail to work, in concert with one another?

The snowflake assertion has immense argumentative appeal. After all, no one is wholly like anyone else, even when two or more persons have been raised in similar conditions. Humans are not like the eugenic Epsilon clones in Aldous Huxley's *Brave New World* (1931). Some *singularity*—in taste, preference, psychological specificity, defining characteristics, idiosyncracies of expression—seems to persist in small or large ways even when ideological unanimity or social conditioning appears to hold sway. Early- and mid-nineteenth-century German romantics celebrated *Individualität* to signify the snowflake subjectivity that modern psychology industries purport to analyze.[8] "All the societal generalizations in the world tell us nothing about this one concrete individual," avers Joel Kovel, an American marxist psychoanalyst. "In the individual, tendencies and probabilities that belong to history are crystallized into a single imaginative resolution." History is never "exactly reproduced in any given person."[9] Singularity is often associated with spontaneity. "Individuality is at first spontaneous and unshaped"; John Dewey believed, shortly before the Great Crash of 1929, "it is a potentiality, a capacity of development." If individuality has become synonymous with singularity and spontaneity, it is also synonymous with choice. In Dos Passos's mythic America, systematized by nonconformist Founding Fathers, you choose to be yourself. Americanism is *be-yourselfism*.

Dos Passos saw America as the guarantor not only of snowflake singularity but of *difference*. In 1917 the German social theorist Georg Simmel wrote of modernity's "individualism of difference, with the deepening of individuality to the point of the individual's incomparability."[10] If social power often tries to reproduce itself by homogenizing peoples' ideas, feelings, and expectations, then how could one be suspicious of an American democratic social power whose reason for being is seemingly to allow difference, singularity, nonconformity, spontaneity, and choice?

To call into question the idea of snowflake singularity, of underlying uniqueness, of individual difference, is to invite censure or ridicule—for repudiating what seems so incontestable, for implicitly advocating social standardization, for sounding anti-American. In part, individuality's political appeal is its promise of relative autonomy. American citizenship is linked ideologically to the assertion of individual rights, a publicly recognized defense one can invoke to challenge what one takes to be abuses of the state or other forms of social and economic power. One may claim that one's individuality and its inherent rights predate laws that violate those rights. Therefore, though often not without risk, one may refuse to play, or play at refusing to play, citizen—as did the civilly disobedient Henry David Thoreau.[11] Many political philosophers since John Locke and Jean-Baptiste Rousseau have assumed that individual rights exist no matter what form of society reigns (nineteenth-century American anarchists dubbed this the "sovereignty of the individual").[12]

The extraordinary subjective appeal of snowflake singularity in part is its validation of psychological or spiritual relative autonomy.[13] Dos Passos's essay addresses a long-standing historically and socially produced American need to think of oneself as one's own property ("self-possessed").[14] Hoover, Dos Passos, and countless Americans—and American businesses—have been indebted to Ralph Waldo Emerson, who devised some of the most enduring advertisements for snowflake individuality and imperial nonconformity.[15] In 1841 he pleaded, "Insist on yourself; never imitate," well before postmodern sneaker, jeans, beer, cologne, and mascara advertisements slavishly and profitably mimicked his exhortation. Motown soul stars famously counseled Americans to "do your thing," though it was Emerson who first popularized the saying. His jingle-like hooks have done much to elevate individual realization and the idea of the inner self into sacrosanct preoccupations: "We but half express ourselves." In an era when class lines were hardening and industrialization's impact on power, people, space, time, and desire was difficult to ignore, Emerson's individualism recharged Americans' spiritual and psychological sense of agency and meaningfulness and bolstered their beliefs in the existence of an unmediated, untainted inner self: "It is only as a man puts off from himself all external support, and stands alone, that I see him to be strong and to prevail." Emerson's soul-stirring sentiments, however, could add up to a Scrooge-like individual declaration of independence from social responsibility and involvement: "Do not tell me, as a good man did to-day, of my obligation to put all poor men in good situations," he commanded. "Are they my poor?"[16]

The tactical value of the snowflake assertion—for Dos Passos, Hoover, and others who argue within this ideological space—resides in the way in which the invocations of singularity and of difference help make the cultural category of individuality appear fundamentally human even when other ideological (sometimes represented as psychological) characteristics—such as assumptions about "human" competitiveness, possessiveness, repressiveness, or evil—are assigned to individuality. Dos Passos's snowflake might be revisualized as a sticky web to which an assortment of ideological values or characteristics (rights, instincts, needs, desires) are adhered, and made to seem like givens, so that anyone questioning these values and characteristics may well get stuck in the web. The assertion of snowflake singularity can function to shield individuality from the charge that it is an ideological contrivance implicated in social structures of power, domination, and stratification. Those who wish to criticize an individualism that smuggles in assumptions about economic relations and political structure may find themselves up against more than they expected. For such a social critique may be dismissed as tantamount to an assault on individuality, singularity, psychological specificity, variety within human nature (Hoover's unequal "intelligence, character, ability, and ambition").

Distinctions can be made between constructions of the category of "individualism" and that of "individuality," but it is the interaction of the two, as what Arthur O. Lovejoy termed *compounds*, that gives each category much of its ideological scope and potency.[17] Dos Passos employs "individuality" more than "individualism" in his praise of elbow room. When it works effectively, the assertion of inborn singularity can even guard constructions of individuality from those who might want to investigate whether historically specific ideas about individuality have operated not as weapons against conformity but rather as ideological systems of conformity—training, forcing, persuading, or bribing persons to act as "individuals" in certain social molds beneficial to some and perhaps detrimental to others. The critical challenge is to sort out what— say, ideas about economic systems, politics, class, race, gender, sexuality—is being made to seem self-evidently "individual" by being linked with attestations of snowflake singularity.

Dos Passos shrewdly has it both ways: he makes individuality the distinctive snowflake truth of the idiosyncratic self, but he also sees it as having some social content. He suggests that one achieves individuality: it is a socially responsible maturity, a phase of civic as well as psychological and spiritual growth. This social perspective admits history, institutions, and cultural machineries of influence into the definitional picture but still views individuality as an inner development—one grows from snowflake infant "individual" to a more socially elaborated snowflake adult "individual." Dos Passos's somewhat historical approach becomes more complex, however, if one begins to examine when, how, and why Americans have "grown into" particular social types of "individuality."

What happens, for instance, when Dos Passos's common sense about elbow-room individuality is reconsidered within the context of America's long history of elbowing? Dos Passos's reverence for elbow room takes no notice of those who were elbowed out to provide elbow room for others. One might inquire: what did having been elbowed out do to their individuality? Did dominant groups perceive those who were elbowed out as having individuality—or as subindividual, subsingular? Did those who got elbowed want to view themselves as having what was defined as individuality in the first place? Has America achieved a classless society, where we can all rub elbows together as equal individuals; or has it produced a class- and race-stratified society in which some Americans' wealth and social position permit them to experience themselves as—and to be treated as—more individual than others?

During Joseph McCarthy's reign of terror C. L. R. James, the great Jamaican social critic, disturbed by these kinds of questions, studied the American history of individuality. James's research, influenced by critiques of corporate individualism outlined years before by the likes of Charles Beard and Theodore Dreiser, probed the history of systemic elbowing. He argued that although the conditions of the Revolutionary period were propitious for the making of "bourgeois individualism" (partly underwritten by slavery) and although this contributed to the tendency of Americans to picture themselves as restless, striving, sometimes rebellious individuals rather than members of sedimented classes (as in Europe), certainly by the late nineteenth century the very corporations that claimed their individual rights to do as they pleased with workers and resources had done much to elbow smash American individuality's more emancipatory social possibilities.[18]

Francis Otto Matthiessen, like Beard, Dreiser, and James, was concerned about the ways in which individuality had been assigned the ideological capacity to ratify elbowing as an expression of inner potential and inherent right. A builder of progressive American studies and casualty of McCarthyism, this Harvard socialist was no Cold War missionary of "individuality." Matthiessen was bitterly disappointed by Dos Passos's reactionary retreat.[19] One of his favorite quotations is from Dreiser's play *The Hand of the Potter* (1918) and novel *An American Tragedy* (1925): "After all, you didn't make yourself, did you?"[20] He was unremittingly critical of how Emersonian individualism came to mean pitting oneself "against the mass" rather than "finding the fulfillment of [one's] nature with [one's] fellow man." Matthiessen assaulted irresponsible literary justifications of the individual as a "law unto himself"—an idea upheld by "money-grabbers" who "have performed travesties of freedom in the name of free enterprise." He gravitated toward "[Nathaniel] Hawthorne's dark sense of the individual's insufficiency" and Walt Whitman's ethos of "solidarity," which "moved steadily, if by no straight course, towards socialism." Reflecting on the history of cultural "allegories of the inner life," he asked: "Don't we have to undo the mistakes of our anarchic nineteenth century and . . . conceive again of inner freedom as something gained, not in isolation, but through an enriching sense of co-operation?"[21] In America, he well knew, social cooperation, unlike individuality, has too rarely been endowed with romantic, glamorous, or literary value; more often it has been distorted as conformity. He may have lived just long enough to see how postwar America's well-funded anxieties about gray-flannel conformity helped sustain its Cold War image of the Soviet bloc as the nightmare of choiceless conformity.

Matthiessen would have appreciated Lawrence Levine's admonition not to "Flintstoniz[e] the past"—the American tendency to project widely held contemporary notions of human nature or social attitudes back on the past to justify the present.[22] The 1960s attraction and humor of the cartoon Flintstone family was that the Flintstones lived in a Stone Age that resembled postwar America (jobs, cars, domesticity). A Flintstone reading of the concept of the individual would never suspect that the earliest recorded uses of *individual* meant indivisible, unity, and connection—not separation, singularity, or being unique—and that the word had a long, varied journey through the often interrelated histories of industrialization, the family, politics, science, and aesthetic practices before it came to mean what Dos Passosesque celebrations of American individualism assume it has naturally and self-evidently always meant.[23]

Although the word *individualize* dates back to the seventeenth century, it was not until the nineteenth century—the era of the rise of industrial capitalism, of the White middle-class cult of sentimentalized domesticity, of romanticism, and of Manifest Destiny—that it came into wider use. By midcentury it referred both to the rendering of someone or something as distinctively "individual" and to the establishment of individually owned land.[24] "When we speak of 'the individual' and of 'society,'" Raymond Williams wrote in 1961, three years after Dos Passos published his piece, "we are using descriptions which embody particular interpretations of the experience to which they refer: interpretations which gained currency at a particular point in history, yet which have now virtually established themselves in our minds as absolutes."[25] The truism that the individual is inherently at odds with society, patent in Emerson's writing, was elaborated by a nineteenth-century transatlantic middle class that wanted to set itself off, on the one hand, from an aristocracy that assigned social, cultural, and subjective merit according to blood and inheritance rather than according to individual ability, and, on the other hand, from a web of capitalist marketplace dependencies that it was striving to extend and profit from but which also made it anxious about its own ongoing capacity to assert its free will, agency, "individuality."

Even beginning to imagine what cross-cultural, intellectual, economic, political, colonial, postcolonial, and national histories of forms of "individuality" might look like—all the while taking into account the intersecting class, ethnoracial, and gender dimensions of these "individuality" productions—is daunting. "It is not any easy task," the systems theorist Niklas Luhmann confesses, "we must travel back at least two hundred years if we want to survey the full array of theories."[26] Individualism, writes Steven Lukes, "is variously traced to the Reformation, the Renaissance, the Enlightenment, the [French] Revolution, to the decline of the aristocracy or the Church or traditional religion, to the Industrial Revolution, to the growth of capitalism and democracy." National differences in notions of individualism and individuality abound. As Lukes generalizes, post-Revolution French intellectuals developed a strong tradition of criticizing individualism as socially destructive (Claude Henri de Saint-Simon, Alexis de Tocqueville, Louis Blanc, Emile Durkheim); in Germany individuality has long been associated with subjective realization, at times national destiny, and in Karl Marx's work with a state of creative being that socialism would truly bring about; in England individualism has signified, among other things, middle-class self-reliance and liberalism, religious nonconformity, and (as in Germany) romantic interiority; and in the United States individualism, natural rights, capitalist free enterprise, laissez-faire, contractualism, free expression, and psychological singularity have been ideologically linked.[27]

In 1905 Max Weber went back more than two centuries to study complex relationships between Protestant conceptualizations of an individual, personal relationship to God (enacted through prayer, piety, Bible reading) and Protestant beliefs in a divinely sanctioned work ethic. These entwined notions simultaneously cultivated capitalist producer individualism (working in order to hope, without certainty, that one would receive God's grace as one of the "elect") and intensely introspective "psychological" subjectivities (fretting about individual salvation). Puritan beliefs in collective obligation (John Winthrop's "Wee must be knitt together"), in divinely established social hierarchies of rich and poor, in innate depravity (necessitating vigilant social rule), in God-ordained inherent differences in talents, and in the importance of interminable spiritual self-monitoring coexisted.[28] Peter Stallybrass has focused attention on the English Puritan revolution as a moment when Puritans nominated themselves individuals rather than subjects of King Charles. The "individual," he clarifies, "is a laborious construction in the political defeat of absolutism, when political freedom is gained at the expense of the occlusion of economic dependence." He uses his historical observation that in the seventeenth century the idea of "the [royal] subject *precedes* [the idea of] the individual" to invert Louis Althusser's oft-quoted ahistorical formulation that " 'ideology interpellates [hails] individuals as subjects.' " Althusser imagines "the individual" as unsubjected by ideology, as a "center of freed consciousness and independent judgment." Puritan history emends this: "Within a capitalist mode of production, ideology interpellated, not the individual as a subject, but the subject as an individual."[29] So being "individual" became the hallmark of a historically specific group identity.

Colin Morris prefaces *The Discovery of the Individual, 1050–1200* (1972) with cross-cultural perspectives on individuality and inwardness and concludes: "Western individualism is . . . far from expressing the common experience of humanity. Taking a world view, one might almost regard it as an eccentricity among cultures." Morris traces early signs of an emerging culture of individuality in self-reflexive sermons, the rise of autobiography, and more personalized portraiture—trends that lost momentum just after 1200.[30] Medieval religious and political ideologies placed greater emphasis on law, order, and collective identity than on "individuality." Generally, authors did not seem to think of themselves as expressing their individuality, originality, or inner life in their writing, but rather as representing their culture's beliefs—plagiarism was not a hot issue.[31] Lee Patterson argues that Geoffrey Chaucer has been valued by modern critics over John Gower and William Langland partly because of his unusual move toward individualizing: "Chaucer begins by posing his opposition to the dominant ideology in terms of class antagonism, but then retreats by setting up his privileged category of subjectivity per se, the free-floating individual whose needs and satisfactions stand outside any social structure—in short, the transhistorical being that criticism has traditionally taken Chaucer himself to be."[32] Stallybrass contends that even in the early seventeenth century, William Shakespeare "was not in the business of producing individuals," nor was "life itself." Whereas John Milton and the Puritan revolution he backed battled to make certain forms of individuality commonsensical.[33]

Taking account of these much debated historical developments, and sundry others, one could not help but find what Weber discovered a century ago—*individualism* is a term that "includes the most heterogeneous things imaginable."[34] Thus to study dimensions of the history of "the individual" in America—my aim in this book—it is judicious not to employ commonsensical notions of individuality to read history, however natural that may seem, but rather to contribute historical perspectives on the social making of that common sense. As Marx contended, "Man is *the human world*, the state, society."[35]

Individuality Incorporated scrutinizes "the individual" as a historically constituted *abstraction* often used to fabricate a sense of national identity (for example, the idea, reiterated by Dos Passos, that being American means being "individual"); a *category* sometimes invoked by groups of Americans to distinguish themselves from "others" (for instance, when members of the White middle class see themselves as more complexly "individual" than members of the working class or various racial gropus); and a changing *definition* of self designed to serve historically generated emotional and ideological needs (as when the industrial era's sentimental ideology helps one "feel" that "inner" "individuality" is most truly "expressed" at home). Individuality becomes a powerful social reality when humans are convinced or compelled—

through property laws, workplace controls, familial socialization, advice books, literature, films, and so on—to imagine themselves within certain notions of what "individuality" has been made to mean.[36] This is why Dos Passos entered the ideological contest to manage what it means. As Raymond Williams argued in the thick of the Cold War, individuality is a social form of subjectivity production that must itself be explained historically and politically. The cultural category of individuality does not exist, or exist in the same way, in all cultures—at least not yet. I am interested not only in how vocabularies, narratives, theories, and uniforms of individuality have changed over time, but in asking why they have existed at all. This approach rubs against the grain of my own cultural and affective socialization. I will often place the category in quotation marks to help myself as well as readers gain critical distance from this quotidian word as an invention that actively shapes social and "psychological" reality.

As I have been suggesting, the politics of making "individuals" is in no way monolithic. Notwithstanding his historical critique of the Puritan formation of "individuals," Stallybrass concludes that there are many "areas where one can't simply dump the [idea of the] individual." For instance: "To be deprived of legal individuality is something that, in this society, is often devastating." Despite his concurrence with socialist critiques of "the individual," Lukes attests, "There is no doubt that historically the abstract conception of the individual represented a major moral advance. It was a decisive step in the direction of a universalist ethics when human beings first came to be regarded as the possessors of certain rights and claims, simply in virtue of being human." The category of individuality has been deployed to support numerous progressive causes and positions: resistances to oppressive gender and sexual norms; greater tolerance of a range of cultural, social, and political actions and attitudes; the idea that everyone should have opportunities to develop her or his abilities; the premise that humans are the ends, not the means, of the social order; the questioning of social authority that shirks from questioning itself (judging the judges).

Yet the concerns I have sketched suggest that the complex history of the category of individuality is critical to recover not just to celebrate its more benign uses. The very idea of individuality has been invested with the ideological power to efface its multifaceted history, so that "individuality" is transmuted into "psychology" or "human nature." Stallybrass, influenced by cultural theories of subjectivity formation, urges "individuals" to contemplate what it means "to be haunted, to be inhabited by other people."[37] What and who haunts, inhabits, and speaks through diverse twenty-first-century American "individuals"? What histories haunt the fabrication of "individuals"? It is crucial to reflect self-critically on what is at stake in being trained to identify oneself as an "individual," one's interests as "individual" interests, and one's rights as "individual" rights—in part because the social uses of the idea of individuality have by no means always been unambiguously humanitarian. Indeed, as the chapters ahead demonstrate, the American history of the rule of individuality has been an important, albeit sometimes subtle, dimension of American imperial history.

As suggested above, the idea that American "individuals" are culturally made and not simply born would have been no news to the many Natives in the late nineteenth and early twentieth centuries who were the subjects of crusades mounted by White reformers and schools to "individualize" them. Indian schools stated plainly that their mission was to "civilize," "Americanize," "citizenize," and "individualize" students. These nouns—*civilization, American, citizen*, and *individual*—were popularized as verbs in this period precisely because some Americans who held socioeconomic, political, and cultural power well understood that what these nouns represented were socializing processes: only by being individualized in accord with dominant definitions of individuality were humans made to fit certain molds of "individuals." The transformative tactics of late-nineteenth- and early-twentieth-century individualizing processes were distinctive and focused on altering selfhood in ideological ways not as emphasized by related processes like civilizing, Americanizing, and citizenizing.[38] Those who sought to "individualize" Indians, we will see, developed strategies of subjectivity and emotion production that aimed to prescribe how an "individual" should properly pursue happiness, meaningfulness, and work—for example, by desiring an affectively intensified romantic bond, having a sentimentally privatized family, and being willing to work at just about any job to possess goods and own property.

Anyone interested in the institutional, industrial, and mass-cultural production of forms of American "individuality" would find the history of the campaigns to individualize Natives illuminating because they were so remarkably brazen in specifying the brand of "individuality" they wanted to impress on Native students. White reformers and educators of Natives were explicit about the social goals "individuality" was expected to help achieve. Assimilationist reformers used the category of individuality to reencode relations of dependence, such as routinized daily work, not just as desirable but as relations signifying independence. They were interested in deploying the ostensible appeal of possessive and sentimental "individuality" as an incentive—to produce worker-individuals who would labor even if they did not like it or felt that they were being exploited. Moreover, they saw the ideological importance of making cultural, sentimental, and romantic individualism seem like the solution to, or at least the compensation for, the anxieties and alienation caused by competitive economic individualism (a closed circuit of options limited to forms of individualism). Their efforts to individualize Indian minds, emotions, and bodies were directed at making Indians not only worker-individuals but "individual" landowners. Appropriately, the government's often coercive division of tribal property into individual plots in this era was termed *individualizing.* Tribal property left over after land was "individualized" was classified as "surplus land" and sold. The "Americanizing" and "civilizing" gift of "individuality" to Indians was intended to legitimate, among other things, the nonmilitary acquisition of Indian real estate.

I will explore these ideological constructions and uses of individualizing as well as many others in the chapters that follow. This study brings together genres of history (American cultural history and Native history) and genres of literary history (canonical and noncanonical American literature, Native literature and autobiography) in one broadly conceived historical critique that contributes to the formation of a field: the American cultural and literary history of "individuality." One of my premises is that the history of Natives casts a great deal of light on the economic, political, cultural, and literary history of American individualizing.

I offer two case studies in two parts, each of which is divided into two chapters: Part 1 is on the Carlisle Industrial School for Indians and part 2 is on connections between the early-twentieth-century Taos White bohemians (focusing on D. H. Lawrence, Mabel Dodge Luhan, and John Collier) and Collier's protomulticultural Indian New Deal. I have chosen the detailed case study rather than the survey approach for several reasons. My interest in this material is critical as well as historical: the voluminous Carlisle school publications and the literary, autobiographical, and political writings of the Taos and Indian New Deal groups are my main texts. These texts are expansive, yet I have given them the sort of nuanced textual analysis that engages and brings out their historical and ideological multidimensionality. When I first studied Carlisle's publications more than two decades ago, I was taken aback by the school's rhetoric of individuality. It was my close reading of the language and tone of the material in these archives which made me realize that the making of "individuals" was not only a provocative but an extremely complex enterprise and that Natives played significant roles in it, as critical agents, by no means just as victims.

Both case studies feature important figures in the history of Native-Euramerican relations. They draw on many rich archival materials that have been underused, thereby making it possible for me to present much original historical research and fresh critical readings of literary works in new historical frameworks. I examine writings by many late-nineteenth- and early-twentieth-century Natives—Charles Eastman [Ohiyesa], Gertrude Bonnin [Zitkala-Ša], Luther Standing Bear, Black Elk, Christine Quintasket [Mourning Dove], Ella Deloria, John Joseph Mathews, D'Arcy McNickle—and non-Natives—Helen Hunt Jackson, Marion Burgess, Frances Sparhawk, Hamlin Garland, Zane Grey, Edgar Rice Burroughs, D. H. Lawrence, Mabel Dodge Luhan, Mary Austin, Oliver La Farge, Langston Hughes. The insights of contemporary Native authors—including N. Scott Momaday, Leslie Marmon Silko, Simon Ortiz, James Welch, Gerald Vizenor, Wendy Rose, Jimmie Durham, Hanay Geiogamah, Joy Harjo, Louise Erdrich, Sherman Alexie, Linda Hogan—appear in my epigraphs, chapters, and notes. These writers often help illuminate the concerns and understandings of earlier Native authors I discuss and suggest the continued relevance of their history to the situation of contemporary Natives.

Broadly, the two case studies—moving from Carlisle to Taos and the Indian New Deal—chart the uneven and often contradictory ideological passage from the nineteenth century's industrial-producer-sentimental culture and its styles of individuality (which value character, the work ethos, self-control, respectability) to the twentieth century's corporate-consumer-therapeutic culture and its styles of individuality (which value personality, the psychological self, impression management, sex appeal). This is a crucial cultural shift—and subjectivity formations shift—that historians of Native-White relations and critics of Native autobiography seldom discuss.[39] The causes, dynamics, and ramifications of this momentous cultural transformation form a historical narrative that does much to clarify the changing ideological significance of Natives within the history of the category of "the individual."

It is this theme—the history of individualizing—that is the theoretical and historical core of the book's study of Native schooling. I will explicate how intensively the education of Natives foregrounded the production of "individuality" as one of its major ideological goals. Nevertheless, *Individuality Incorporated* is not a study of Native education. The four chapters explore how ideological education in "individuality" can also take place outside the school—in the family, in the community, in the process of reading literature, the Bible, or self-help books, in psychoanalytic therapy, in the Euramerican bohemian experience of dancing in deserts with Indians, and in many other circumstances. An emphasis on educational institutions alone would occlude one's larger vision of complex cultural changes taking place in the category of "the individual" and of the roles Natives played in those changes. My study of the Taos literati shows not Whites who wanted to "kill" Indians ideologically in order to resurrect them as American "individuals" (to quote Carlisle rhetoric), but Whites who hoped to resurrect their repressed "individuality" through their imagined therapeutic relationships with Indians. "Individuality" was defined and deployed in manifold ways and contexts around Indians.

Little historical or critical scholarship has staked out the relationship between Natives and dominant constructions of American individuality as a fertile field for investigation. One of the most theoretically sophisticated collections of essays on mass-cultural representations—often misrepresentations—of Natives is *Dressing in Feathers: The Construction of the Indian in American Popular Culture* (1996). In her introductory essay, S. Elizabeth Bird, thinking of films like *Dances With Wolves* (1990) and *Pocahontas* (1995), concludes: "The current wave of Indian images might seem benign—who would not want to be presented as perfect, beautiful, and all-knowing? But this benign image is deeply impersonal and distanced, once again ignoring Indian people as individuals and allowing real Indian people no subjectivity."[40] Bird's commonsense meaning is clear and merits readers' sympathetic responses. Similarly, one can appreciate the force of Devon Mihesuah's (Choctaw) assertion in her penetrating study of the Cherokee Female Seminary (1851–1909), "Cherokee women are especially complex individuals different from one another and from women of other tribes."[41] Natives have long had to contend with racisms that have denied their multifaceted singularity (as persons, clans, bands, tribes, nations) as a justification for their exploitation and oppression. Bird and Mihesuah are responding to the literature, art, films, television shows, schools, and episodes in daily life that have cast Natives, to quote Laura Wexler, as "human [or not so human] scenery" for White individuals' enactments of their fears, fantasies, and therapeutic needs.[42] All this might prompt one to assert that Natives too are "individuals."

Still, one must not forget that words like *individuals* and *subjectivity* have extensive ideological histories linked with exploitation and oppression—histories that have enmeshed Natives, altered their national image, and in many cases affected their self-image and self-regard. Just as Vine Deloria, Jr. (Dakota Sioux) and Clifford M. Lytle have helped readers establish a critical distance from New Deal constructions of (U.S. government-controlled) Native "self-government," it is equally important to study how concepts of individuality have been deployed in Native-White power struggles. "Self-determination and self-government," they explain, "are not equivalent terms" (more on this in chapter 4).[43] Neither are "self-determination" and "individuality" equivalent terms (more on this in the afterword). In describing how Southwestern Native artists were affected by buyers and markets who demanded that Native artwork exhibit ostensibly traditional Indianness rather than individuality, Leah Dilworth is especially careful not to universalize Euramerican ideas of individuality as that which Natives were compelled to suppress (in reference to the potter Nampeyo): "I am not suggesting that Western individualism was the only (or even a viable) alternative for Nampeyo and other Native American artisans."[44] Nor was "individualism" or Euramerican aesthetic "individuality" necessarily even a desirable alternative for them.[45]

The theoretical clarity one must bring to the study of Native-White relations, I suggest, must include a historical awareness that the word *individual* was invested with particular ideological meanings by dominant groups and was used by these groups both to dominate and to "give" certain kinds of opportunities to Natives and others. In some respects, to say that Natives have been ignored as "individuals" manifests a historical irony. Some of the Natives who were not only allowed to but schooled and coerced to act like "individuals" might object to this label with zeal. It is imperative to grasp not only the "construction of the Indian" (something I will address below) but also the construction of "the individual" in U.S. culture if one is to comprehend U.S. history.

Some scholarship on Indian schools points to individualizing as part of the pedagogical rhetoric and agenda, but the far-reaching implications of this process have not previously been worked out. In his seminal studies of Native autobiography, Arnold Krupat has emphasized that autobiography in the nineteenth century's romantic era was based on concepts of individuality not extant in traditional Native cultures. His recent work that seeks to conceptualize "ethnocriticism" has developed some of the theoretical implications of these cultural differences and further complicates ahistorical, universalizing, commonsensical notions about the "self."[46] He has criticized the "modern" premises and values that Marcel Mauss brought to his pathbreaking effort to theorize an anthropology of the person. In 1938 Mauss problematically depicted selfhood within an "evolutionary narrative" in which "primitive" "persons" (*personnages*) with highly social "self-conceptions," evident in Native cultures, had not yet attained a "modern" "egocentric/individualist" idea and expression of the introspective "*moi*" and its psychological interiority. The "modern" bourgeois "moi" tends to envision selfhood within the romantic era's Emersonian individual-versus-society model rather than foregrounding the person's social connectedness and the person's natural connoctedness to the nonhuman.[47] Globalization (the universalization of capitalism) may be globalizing forms of consumer individualism and interiority, but, as anthropologist Clifford Geertz notes, such constructions are by no means universal, inherently human, or decisively "modern": "The Western conception of the person as a bounded, unique, more or less integrated motivational and cognitive universe, a dynamic center of awareness, emotion, judgment, and action organized into a distinctive whole and set contrastively both against other such wholes and against its social and natural background, is . . . a rather peculiar idea within the context of the world's cultures."[48]

Jace Weaver (Cherokee) characterizes Native subjectivities as "I am We." He contrasts dominant notions of bounded (I cannot help but think of barbed-wire) individualism with Native "communitism"—a concept that conjoins the words " 'community' and 'activism' or 'activist.' " In the next four chapters we will see that Native constructions of community and kinship values—embracing notions of family, clan, the communal distribution of affection, land use—threatened many nineteenth- and twentieth-century Euramerican "individuals" who demonized these values as manifestations of communism or socialism. What Weaver terms "communitism" permeates many traditional Native notions of what constitutes survival, art, love, achievement. "There is generally," he observes, "no concept of 'salvation' beyond the continuance of the community."[49] Along these lines Louis Owens (Choctaw and Cherokee) contributes to the historical understanding of much Euramerican literature as an imperialist machinery of "individuality": "The privileging of the individual necessary for the conception of the modern novel . . . is a more radical departure for American Indian cultures than for the Western world as a whole, for Foucault's 'moment of individualization' represents an experience forced harshly, and rather unsuccessfully, upon Native Americans."[50]

First Person, First Peoples (1997), a collection of thirteen autobiographical essays by Native graduates of Dartmouth College (1970s through 1990s), lends greater specificity to some of what Owens, Weaver, and Krupat have sketched. Several writers stressed that some of the tribal social values and modes of relating they brought to the Ivy League—cooperative adaptation, humility, not striving to stand out, quiet attentiveness, privacy, strong feelings of connection to tribe, family, kin, and nonhuman creatures—conflicted dramatically with some of the values and habits of some of their Euramerican peers and some of their institution's expectations. At college they encountered competitive individualism, a widespread desire to perform in the spotlight, inquisitiveness, cultural relativism, and a comfortable professional-managerial class independence from home and region.[51] Some Native students imported traditional nonegoistic concepts of their accomplishments: "I would be a fool to believe that I made it this far by myself," Marianne Chamberlain (Assiniboin and Sioux) acknowledged gratefully. And some held onto traditional concepts of success that focused more on helping Natives than on using college as a stepping stone for self-aggrandizement.[52] In her foreword, Louise Erdrich (Chippewa), herself a Dartmouth graduate, underlines "how many [of the autobiographers] have returned to work in their communities. . . . Remarkable in a capitalist society, and yet not amazing given the sources, not a single narrative is about the wish to attain status, the ambition to make large amounts of money, or the desire to become famous."[53]

Many Natives' traditional concepts of art, artists, and artistic meaningfulness differ from the extreme individualizing of artistic identity and aesthetic value that has predominated in Europe and the United States, especially since the romantic era. "There was always some kind of artistic endeavor that people set themselves to, although they did not necessarily articulate it as 'art' in the sense of western civilization," writes poet Simon Ortiz (Acoma). "One lived and expressed an artful life, whether it was in ceremonial singing and dancing, architecture, painting, speaking, or in the way one's social-cultural life was structured."[54] Similarly, Gary Witherspoon contrasts Navajo art—the creation of "beautiful conditions" and the practice of "a way of living"—with so-called Western aesthetics that are often predicated on self versus nature and mind versus body binary oppositions. Most Navajos are artists; they may stand out as marginal if they are not. If they sell their creations, many do so anonymously.[55]

Yet recently I spoke with a Navajo poet who, though proud of these collective values, practices, and creations, also noted that dancing in line can be restricting. She felt that something, perhaps what some might term *individuality*, seemed to be submerged in this highly formal and collective dancing. Effort to bring knowledge of the history of "Western" "individuality" to the study of Natives' social production of consciousness and, conversely, attempts to bring work on Native formations of subjectivities and epistemologies to scholarship on "Western" fabrications of "individuality" are still too unusual. This knowledge should be central in the economic, political, and cultural history of Native-White relations and should contribute much to the critical advancement of American studies.

My initial emphasis, which considered this book as a contribution to the history of the cultural making of humans induced to call themselves individuals, soon expanded to encompass another major historical concern: the cultural making of people impelled to categorize themselves as Indians. In the first centuries of the European–North American imperialist era, Natives kept discovering Europeans who assumed that they were discovering "Indians."[56] Christopher Columbus, a lost and confused sailor, misidentified the indigenous people he sought to enslave in the Caribbean in 1492 as *los Indios*, and the homogenizing name stuck. (In 1900 Francis La Flesche [Omaha] recounted an amusing school scene in which Euramericans quizzed him and other Native students on who discovered America.) Since this momentous "discovery," Eric Mottram observes, " 'Indians' have been a bank of resources for mythical living for whites, and that bank a major control of white dominance of Amerindian life."[57] Robert Berkhofer stresses that the pre-Columbus North American tribes were anything but monolithic and "spoke at least two hundred mutually unintelligible languages."[58] Yet historians have noted that standard forms of the "white man's Indian" were being mass-produced in print by several European nations long before the Pilgrims and Puritans set up shop. The indigenous inhabitants of what the British labelled New England voiced their bafflement when some of the early colonists confidently addressed them with alien names: "They have often asked me," Roger Williams pondered, "why we call them *Indians Natives*, & c."[59]

The naming problem persists: historians and critics usually feel the need to explain why they chose to call their subjects of study either Indians (often because that imperialist word is the self-description commonly used and resignified by Indians nowadays) or Native Americans (this name, often employed in titles of academic programs, may evoke tribal plurality, but its combination of words remains ideologically inflected with troublesome primitivist and nationalist associations).[60] Historians and critics are often acutely aware that they run the risk of perpetuating colonizing practices when they use everyday words like *Indian, Native American, New World, discovery, wild, wilderness, civili-*

zation, Western (as in Western civilization vs. indigenous cultures of the Western Hemisphere), *progress, development, the environment* (that humans "develop" and preserve), *savage, primitive, prehistory, preindustrial*, and *modern* to discuss Native-White relations (although, as I have said, this caution does not often extend to the use of the ideological abstraction "individual").[61] Obviously, culturally contrived labels for persons or groups who did not originally classify themselves as one group eventually become real and influential when their social circulation is pervasive and meanings assigned to them are accepted as commonsensical. However, meanings ascribed to such labels can be altered to fit new struggles and circumstances.

The nineteenth-century White ideological meanings of *Indian* shifted as genocidal military strategies to remove Natives from their land gradually gave way to cultural tactics to transform them into "individual" workers and landowners, many of whom would also be cleared off much of their land. This change in meaning is registered in a statement of educational and cultural purpose made by Carlisle's superintendent Richard Henry Pratt in 1892: "A great general has said that the only good Indian is a dead one, and that high sanction of his destruction has been an enormous factor in promoting Indian massacres. In a sense, I agree with the sentiment, but only in this: that all the Indian there is in the race should be dead. Kill the Indian in him, and save the man."[62] Before pupils from dozens of tribal cultures underwent attempts to transform them into "individuals" they were first lumped together as "Indians," a category that defined them as deficient in the desires, character, ambitions, and morality that constituted American "individuality." Put differently, Carlisle first *Indianized* its diverse students so that their *individualizing* could be sanctioned—the two ideological classifications worked in unison.[63]

Yet it was in the twentieth century that Natives from many tribes self-consciously Indianized themselves in the process of redefining the White category of *Indian* through such means as the formation of pan-Indian political organizations, the publication of pan-Indian political magazines, the founding of schools, the writing of fiction and autobiographies, and the creation of music and art. The challenge some of these Natives took up was to reimagine Indian as an identity that myriad Native tribes and bands would want to adopt. Some Natives repudiated prevalent ideas of Indians and Indianness altogether. Others tried to invest *Indian* with different class, racial, or ethnic meanings that were both respectful of tribal traditions and partly assimilationist in objective. Still others embraced the word *Indian* to celebrate traditional in-

digenous cultures and criticize the dominant White capitalist culture—
as can be seen in some of the writing of the radical American Indian
Movement (AIM). At times in their lives more than a few Natives cap-
italized on the commercial value of playing "Indians" on stage, on
screen, and on horseback in Wild West shows, and were censured—by
critics as diverse as Pratt and, decades later, members of AIM—for having
been exploited in the bargain.

Like other scholars I am not entirely comfortable with the use of either
Indian or *Native American* to label diverse Native groups, whom even
some tribal names do not accurately represent. *AmerIndian*, another
possibility, could be taken as signifying the Indians of the Americas, not
just the United States. *U.S. Indian*, while indicating national boundaries,
may make Indians seem almost like U.S. property. Acknowledging some
of the naming problems I have outlined, Weaver opts to get on with his
work and use " 'Native American,' 'American Indian,' 'Indian,' and 'Native' more or less interchangeably."[64] In general this would be my tack.
For the purposes of clarifying my argument, however, I have elected to
step back somewhat in time, to the era of the founding of early Native
American studies programs, and use the term *Natives*, sometimes *Native
Americans*—not *Indians*—so that I may better make distinctions between
Natives and ideological processes of Indianizing (sometimes generated
by Whites, sometimes by Natives, sometimes by both groups working, or
ostensibly working, together). I will often use "Indian"—in quotation
marks—to signal its status in my argument as a construction of racial and
cultural identity and employ the term *Native* to designate those de-
scendents of the indigenous North American peoples who responded to
Indianizing in a plethora of ways. In doing so I am not advocating the use
of the terms *Native* and *Native American* in cultural and social relations.
I make this distinction to better achieve lucidity in the confines of this
project.

The noun *Indian* was turned into the verb *Indianize* and was understood to be a social process and cultural identity at least as early as
1692, when Cotton Mather expressed anxiety that Christian colonizers
were becoming "Indians": "We have too far degenerated into Indian
vices. . . . They are very lying wretches, and they are very lazy wretches;
and they are out of measure indulgent unto their children; there is no
family government among them. We have [become] shamefully Indianized in all those abominable things."[65] His *Magnalia Christi Americana* (1702) registers how much he despised and feared the "half Indianized French" as well as the "half Frenchified Indians." In 1782 Hector
St. John de Crèvecoeur observed that many colonists who were reunited

with their captured children "found them so perfectly Indianised, that many knew them no longer" (federal Indian schools would endeavor to "individualize" students, in what some parents and students considered institutionalized captivity, so that they too would no longer know their parents and no longer figuratively as well as literally speak their language).[66]

From the 1870s to the 1940s diverse Whites who were socialized to think of themselves as being "individuals" of a certain stamp were keen to Indianize themselves, in some cases to partly escape, or pretend to escape, from what they regarded as the master captivity narrative—America. Likewise, diverse Natives who were resocialized to envision themselves as "Indians" have been eager to "individualize" themselves. If some Whites responded to historical pressures by projecting some of their needs onto prevalent cultural constructions of "Indians," some Natives also reacted to historical conflict by projecting some of their needs onto dominant cultural constructions of "individuals." Some Natives and Whites tried in varying degrees to develop a critical distance from both categories and accepted neither the regnant cultural definitions of "individual" nor those of "Indian" as an inherent base of identity or as a cultural blueprint of their human possibility. There are "individuals" and "Indians" only if particular groups, institutions, and discourses succeed in convincing some humans that it makes sense to label and identify themselves as such and to accept certain self-conceptions that go with the label.

Part 1, chapters 1 and 2, examines the rhetoric and practices of the most famous Indian boarding school, the Carlisle Industrial School for Indians (1879–1918). From 1879 to 1904 Richard Henry Pratt, a U.S. army officer, served as the school's outspoken and controversial superintendent. The theoretical perspicuity with which he aired his views on "individuality" production reveals not only how definite many White reformers were about what they wanted to do for and to "Indians" but much about how U.S. culture at large shaped "individuality" as a comprehensive means of socializing citizen-workers. Pratt's concept of individuality was infused with the values of nineteenth-century producer and sentimental culture: built into it was a firm endorsement of character, the work ethic, the virtue of self-control, and the sentimental model of familial relations.

Notwithstanding Pratt's advocacy of his blueprint of individualism and his fulminations against Indianness, I will show that both Pratt and Carlisle were far more subtle and flexible in the exercise of power than some of the school's rhetoric suggests. The school's official line that the category of race is a detrimental social fiction because it is an impediment to individual advancement is only one of the many interesting ideas that writings published by students elaborate and sometimes contest. Chapter 2 reviews some Native notions of agency, choice, and selfhood that schools like Carlisle tried to supplant with their institutional brands of "individuality." In some instances, however, schools shrewdly tapped Native identity formation to try to individualize students according to their institutional schemes. My archival research has drawn on Carlisle's newspapers and pamphlets, Pratt's extensive correspondence with intellectuals and writers (W. E. B. Du Bois, Frederick Douglass, Charles Eastman, Gertrude Bonnin, Luther Standing Bear), influential administrators (Secretaries of the Interior, Bureau of Indian Affairs commissioners, congressmen), and Native leaders (Carlos Montezuma, Arthur Parker, Thomas Sloan), and Pratt's collection of Carlisle photographs. No other study has focused in such detail on the Carlisle publications, not just as repositories of information but as complex ideological texts—their language, narratives, style, visual images, tone, repetitions, contradictions, and significant changes from 1879 to 1918.

Pratt was forced to resign from Carlisle in 1904, and the school's existence from then until 1918, when its doors were shut, was under the sway of a somewhat different educational policy that reflected a shift in the U.S. government's conception and management of "Indians." The school retained its rhetoric of individualizing, character, the work ethic, self-control, and sentiment; however, it introduced a (problematic) cultural pluralism that loosened up some of the ideological rigidity of individualizing. As the school began to accept Indianness, especially through its encouragement of the study of Native arts and crafts, it also reconceived Indianness as a disqualification for intellectual achievement or ambition. If Pratt saw many of his students as being destined for skilled and semiskilled manual labor, the Carlisle that followed his reign was even more insistent on ensuring this class and workforce fate. Carlisle's new concerns with commodifying Indianness are signs of the school's participation in the shift from the nineteenth-century producer culture to the twentieth-century consumer culture.

Over the past decade or so some books and articles have discussed aspects of Carlisle's history and Pratt's career, and they have stimulated my thinking.[67] Yet Carlisle, especially its publications, merits more historical analysis than it has received. Its football and track teams and marching bands, as well as its educational experiments, gave the school both a national and international reputation. Its many before-and-after photographs of ostensibly Americanized—or individualized—"Indian" students were widely circulated (some can be purchased even today in the form of postcards).[68]

Part 2, chapters 3 and 4, explores how and why some of the early-twentieth-century Taos literati made "Indians" and White self-Indianizing psychologically fascinating, the key to their "lost" "individuality." Mabel Dodge Luhan achieved renown as the wealthy patron of bohemian Romantic Rebels in Greenwich Village and Florence before taking up that role in Taos. Luhan was more than an indefatigable Lady Bountiful, however—she was a prodigious autobiographer and a creative participant in as well as a keen critic of her intellectual and ideological milieu. It was Luhan who was responsible for drawing John Collier, D. H. Lawrence, and many others to the Taos artist colony to play roles in and help confer literary, bohemian, and sometimes glamorously political significance on the venture. Luhan, Lawrence, Collier, and to a lesser extent Mary Austin are at the center of my historical critique of the Taos–Santa Fe bohemians. My archival research on Collier, in particular, has opened new dimensions of my investigation.

These four, like many other White Taos–Santa Fe colonizers, were heavily influenced by psychoanalysis, especially its repression model. Lawrence, Luhan, and Austin could be sharply critical of psychoanalysis, and Collier's work was always socially directed. But all four, I suggest, at times contributed to the cultural encoding of Natives as a kind of primitive solution to not only the repression within Euramerican "individuals" but the repression that America represented for them. The repression model, self-engaging as it may be for many, is a problematic framework within which to perceive the contradictions that gripped Natives and America. This style of thinking was part of corporate-consumer-therapeutic culture and was one trend in the making of "psychological" identities for what some historians label the professional-managerial class.[69] As I hinted above, what one finds with the emergence of "therapeutic" "Indians" in Taos is a curious reversal of ideological polarity: if Carlisle sought to transform Natives into American "individuals," many Taos colonizers searched for their "lost" "individuality" (an "individuality" that had communal, spiritual, sexual, and rhythmic characteristics) among the Taos "Indians." Many of the White Taos colonizers read "Indians" as the spiritual and psychocultural repository of a "primitive" "individuality" that a "puritanical" America had all but repressed out of existence. My research on Taos put me in touch with patterns I had become familiar with in some of my previous work—notably the professional-managerial-class tendency to "rebel" against aspects of possessive individualism by putting "psychological" "individuality" in its place.

I often put two cultural categories, besides "individuality" and "Indian," in quotation marks to help readers (and myself) establish some critical distance from them: "psychological" and "modern." Chapters 3 and 4 will clarify why "psychological" is a (too) commonsensical word worth flagging as ideologically inflected. The Taos and Indian New Deal chapters will suggest that "modern" "psychological" discourses breathed new ideological life into the categories of "the individual," "the Indian," "the modern," and "the primitive," as well as into the American corporate-liberal machine—a machine that would endeavor to use its mainstream and bohemian productions of "psychological" and multicultural "individuality" as a lubricant to enable its subjectivity production, incentive production, and worker production to run more smoothly.

"Modern"—like "prehistory," "preindustrial," and "civilization"—is packed with ideological premises. It is too frequently used to represent certain dominant lifeways and values as distinctively "modern" and others—such as equally contemporary Native lifeways and values, sometimes termed "traditional"—as "primitive" or "savage." The gist is: if one is not "modern," in certain ways, then one must modernize, or be modernized. It is crucial to realize that there are vastly different cultural ways—"modern" ways—of organizing and living in the present. Those who invoke the category of "the modern," moreover, frequently associate it with ideologies of (seemingly inevitable) progress to re-encode—to mystify—capitalist development, expansion, and power relations as human, cultural, socioeconomic, and technological evolution.

Chapters 3 and 4 introduce the idea of the *multicultural modern*. I use this term to signify two trends. First, I will trace how emerging ideologies directed at Natives deployed protomulticultural values and practices to try more effectively to draw them into what was termed the "modern" world. I nominate this process *multicultural modernizing.* Here I am chiefly concerned with investigating how forms of protomulticulturalism—in place of or in addition to earlier individualizing ideologies—were employed to attempt to give Natives the incentive to be "modern" workers. My research suggests that individualizing and then early protomulticultural policies were instituted by power structures (bureaucracies, schools) in part to produce willing workforces (in the afterword I trace this theme in pluralist and protomulticultural theory contributed by Randolph Bourne, Alain Locke, Horace Kallen, Louis Adamic, Carey McWilliams, and Collier). Second, I will clarify links among the Taos–Santa Fe modernists' modernisms, Southwestern corporations and businesses (intent on developing tourism and Native arts and crafts), Collier's Indian New Deal, and the formation of protomulticultural values and practices. Modernist multiculturalism—that is, protomulticultural aesthetic work (literature, art, material culture) produced or supported by Taos–Santa Fe modernists—sometimes contributed to and at other times resisted aspects of multicultural modernizing.

I have several reasons for using the word *multicultural* to characterize the early-twentieth-century critical and ideological developments I begin to examine in chapters 1 and 2, and focus on in chapters 3 and 4, and link with postmodern America's elaboration of diversity management in the afterword. *Multicultural* has been popularized only since the 1970s. But this term—like *ethnic* and *diversity*—had been coined and used at least three decades before this period.[70] David Hollinger posits distinctions between *pluralism*, which, in opposition to the aggressive nativist anxieties about immigrants and dual loyalties fueled by World War I, was a term that intellectuals developed to highlight and celebrate the heterogeneity of the United States (racially, ethnically, culturally) and *multiculturalism*, which, born of the 1960s social movements, migrations, and immigrations, led to significant institutional changes in the production and dissemination of knowledge and culture. Pluralism, he suggests, did not take the organized critical and institutional form of multiculturalism—it did not become a "positive program" and gain prominence as a social initiative that called into question economic as well as cultural inequalities.[71] But the Indian New Deal pluralism—or protomulticulturalism—did just that, as evidence in chapter 4 makes plain. (Indeed, Native-White history demonstrates that from the Carlisle era to the Indian New Deal and beyond the U.S. government has established institutions dedicated to the reproduction of notions of ethnoracial difference and tried to shape subjectivities based on these changing notions.)[72] The ideological, cultural, educational, and economic transformations I discuss might be described as bicultural (Native-White). However, as I have noted, "Indians" were made up of many distinct cultures—"Indians" is itself a multicultural category.

Moreover, it is striking to see how much the reforms in attitude, knowledge production, and critical awareness I analyze in the last two chapters resonate with what scholars now think of as multicultural critique. Central to my books' argument, in fact, is the contention that forms of protomulticulturalism, without being called such, emerged several decades before the 1960s and 1970s social struggles, migrations, and immigrations made their multicultural presence felt in legislation, judicial decisions, the media, universities, schools, and hegemonic common sense. Parts of chapters 3 and 4 and the afterword chronicle early-twentieth-century contributions to the theoretical foundations of what is now nominated *ethnic studies.*

In sum, I agree with Dos Passos that America does not crudely reproduce itself, its workforce, or its incentives by trying to produce robots. America makes "individuals." We differ about what this cultural formation of subjectivity means, why it emerged, how it has changed.

My study of Native-White history suggests that the institutionalized "individuality" so many Natives negotiated must be reconsidered as conspicuously blueprinted, very basic forms of American *incorporated individuality.* In elaborating Antonio Gramsci's theory of hegemony, Raymond Williams developed the concept of "incorporation" to better chart how complexly dynamic hegemonic orders often try to incorporate, control, or transform "alternative or directly oppositional politics and culture"—ostensible free play, free thinking, free speech—frequently by attempting to produce "forms of counter-culture," channel its critiques, or commodify (subsidize) its "rebellions." Through "incorporation," power structures may seem democratically responsive, or pluralistic, rather than uncompromisingly repressive.[73]

Williams's concept, like Monty Python's send-up of mass-hypnotic individuality, provokes many questions for students of American culture. To what degree can the "individuality" that Dos Passos propagandized—with its ideological accent on being nonconformist, different, original, unique—be evaluated as a subtle, albeit sometimes risky, hegemonic form of incorporated subjectivity and agency? Has this formation of subjectivity proven indispensable to U.S. hegemonies as a tactic of incorporation partly because it contributes to the individualizing of reasons to resist and of forms of resistance (for example, making resistance a matter of "individual" "expression" more than collective reorganization and action)? Is "individuality" management one of the fundamental ways in which America developed the incentive that—usually, if not always—powers the system? Yet have compensatory forms of "individuality," even when tied to the hegemonic, challenged the hegemony and provoked collective resistance, reform, and rebellion? Is incorporated individuality merely a fabrication of *pseudoindividuality* that disguises or confuses our understanding of *real individuality*—our All-American hero misrepresented by bad press? Given the complicated history of definitions of and uses of "individuality," is it viable to try to define "real individuality"? Is "individuality" too tainted a word to signify whatever this is, if one thinks it exists? Have Natives chosen to develop concepts other than "individuality" that reconceive this concern? *Individuality Incorporated* explores Native-White histories that help us better formulate and address such questions—questions that call for a sufficiently complex history of the cultural formations of subjectivities.

PART ONE

Categorizing and Institutionalizing

Indians and Individuals

1

Carlisle as Individualizing Factory:

Making Indians, Individuals, Workers

[White invaders] were only men who could be killed with their own weapons.
—James Welch (Blackfeet and Gros Ventre), *Fools Crow*, 1986

Word by word these men were disposing of him in language, their language.
—N. Scott Momaday (Kiowa and Cherokee), *House Made of Dawn*, 1968

Every time I work my way up—say I'm next in line for promotion
—they shaft me. . . . Stuck down at the bottom with the minnows. . . .
the big fish eats the little fish and the little fish eats the littler
fish. The one with the biggest mouth eats any damn old fish he wants.
—Louise Erdrich (Chippewa), *Love Medicine*, 1984[1]

Recently I had a casual conversation with a historian about Carlisle. If there is a common view of Carlisle, this historian probably expressed it in something like these censorious words: "It was a prison camp. Pratt's first experiments in Indian education took place in an actual prison camp at Fort Marion, St. Augustine, Florida. Carlisle was no different, except that the prisoners were children." I am sympathetic to this view.[2] Linda Hogan's (Chickasaw) novel *Mean Spirit* (1990) features one character who had escaped from a Carlisle fully capable of breaking bones in its efforts to break and remake spirits: "At school, Calvin had been hung by his thumbs as punishment for 'insolence.' The result was that his skin and nerve had torn away from the bone. He lost the use of his thumbs."[3] Not only did Native "emotions [run] so high" in the Carlisle era, as Berenice Levchuk (Navajo) observed in 1997, they frequently still do when Natives reflect on the scholastic imperialism that too often prevailed during that "phase of our Native American holocaust."[4] From 1876 to 1878 Captain Richard Henry Pratt supervised the Fort Marion prison camp and it was indeed the testing ground for what many students called Carlisle Barracks.[5]

Yet the camp quickly evolved into what was known as a "prison *school*" for the inmates.[6] Pratt's "Florida boys" also became an attraction in Florida's burgeoning tourism and leisure industry—the prisoner-students often had the run of the town, gave boat rides to tourists, and made and sold paintings as well as bows and arrows and polished sea beans (shells).[7] Robert Perkinson observes that two kinds of "Indian" performances drew tourists, visitors, and reformers to Fort Marion: wild "Indians" reenacting war dances, battles, and buffalo hunts (the *before* being "civilized" phase) as well as stagings of the "Indian" undergoing schooling, Christianizing, and army routinization (the *after* phase). These seemingly contradictory performances, Perkinson suggests, "relied on each other for their cultural and ideological meaning." Pratt, not unlike Buffalo Bill, made himself the focus of attention as the star of the show (wild Indian tamer). Thus even Fort Marion was more multi-faceted—as an experiment in institutional domination, a school, a theater, a tourist site, a boot camp, a factory—than what can easily be classified as a prison camp.[8]

Carlisle too was more complex and polyvalent than the historian's impression of it, which was based in part, this scholar acknowledged, on a PBS television documentary, *In The White Man's Image* (1993). There is much evidence that supports critiques of Carlisle's campaign to remake students in "the white man's image." Yet a good deal of evidence I will present suggests the limitations of such critiques.

Two images, worth keeping in mind as I range over the Carlisle material, exhibit aspects of this complexity. These images begin to demonstrate, as others will below, that the student experience of Pratt's Carlisle was multidimensional not only because of the backgrounds the students brought to the school, but because of the institution's own design. The first image is Mr. See All (figure 1), who appeared in the first issue of Carlisle's publication *The Indian Boys' and Girls' Friend* on July 31, 1885. Beneath the drawing is a description of him: "Mr. See All is old and not pretty, but when he looks through that glass, Oh! My! He can even look into the minds of people and tell what they are thinking about!" The drawing shows a tiny man, with furrowed brow, smiling, who replicates the stereotype of the Victorian schoolmaster. He is eagerly looking through a spyglass and standing on binoculars facing down. Another pair of binoculars, resembling cannons, is to his right.

1. Carlisle's Mr. See All, in *The Indian Boys' and Girls' Friend* 1 (July 31, 1885), Yale Collection of Western Americana, Beinecke Rare Book and Manuscript Library

This image can be read as confirming the historian's Carlisle stereotype—Mr. See All's mind-seeing abilities, ascribed to him in the description, make him seem downright nefarious. Was he concocted to frighten students and keep them in line? Yet Mr. See All has a toylike quality. His smile and the hyperbolic "Oh! My!" in the description convey an element of self-parody, a gamelike tone. The title of the publication, *The Indian Boys' and Girls' Friend*, printed directly above his image, may be taken as a caption that guides readers how to read Mr. See All: as minuscule, as somewhat ridiculous, maybe even as a friend. Mr. See All might in fact have provoked more student laughter than student anxiety about invigilation. In doing so Mr. See All may have drawn notice to the limits of the school's ability to survey its students' minds and hearts.[9] Could this cartoon figure have been invented for this purpose? It is telling that he is a White man—made diminutive, odd, funny. Students who were being recast into "the white man's image" would have had to think about this playful White man's image and wonder whether White self-surveillance "individuality" always took itself *so* seriously.

My second image, from Pratt's collection, stages Indianness as a theatrical performance. The photograph shows two Native girls, probably Carlisle students, standing, attired not in Carlisle uniforms but in "Indian" costumes, waiting to be photographed (figure 2). They are smiling, especially the girl on the right, perhaps ironically, and are holding

2. Two Native American girls photographed while waiting to pose, Yale Collection of Western Americana, Beinecke Rare Book and Manuscript Library

hands, presumably waiting for the photographer to place them in their pose. The photograph is self-reflexive—the "Indian" props are exposed as props, along with other props including a classical bust. Both girls are obviously modeling. In this instance the photographer chose not simply to photograph their marketable Indianness but rather to shoot their Indianness in the process of its being posed, staged, and framed as a commodity for consumers.

If Mr. See All may prompt one to reflect on how Carlisle produced "individuality," via instructors who knew that they never really saw it all, the photograph of the girls moves one to contemplate how Carlisle's occasional self-conscious staging of Indianness may have influenced students. Some students who were expected to enact an Indianness that helped Carlisle advertise its ostensibly transformative powers—especially in before-and-after photographs—may have responded by smiling ironically or even tolerantly between scenes. Both images suggest that some of the experiences, authorities, costumes, poses, and roles students encountered at Carlisle and its environs made them aware of and in some cases probably critical of the ways in which they were directed to perform "individual" and "Indian."

The writings produced by and linked to the Carlisle Industrial School for Indians (1879–1918) are of broad historical interest partly because they foreground key assumptions built into the ideological making of late-nineteenth- and early-twentieth-century Americans: the social production and organization of their emotions, incentives, fears, sense of purpose, and identity. Some Gilded Age Americans praised Americanization as a form of selfhood manufacturing. As one prominent theologian put it in the 1890s, American culture at large could be viewed as an innovative and praiseworthy experiment in the "manufacture of men and women."[10] Others criticized this manufacture. Mark Twain, for example, satirized it in his dystopian novel *A Connecticut Yankee in King Arthur's Court* (1889). Twain's cocksure yet earthy and often humorous Yankee, Hank Morgan, is a Hartford arms factory superintendent who, when knocked unconscious by a refractory worker, wakes up in King Arthur's Camelot. Morgan's mechanical know-how and Barnumesque flair for self-promotion get him appointed The Boss, the King's right-hand man. He soon defines his managerial goal as the Americanization of "savage" Britain—comparing the knights to Comanches. To pull this off, he establishes covert "civilisation factories" to teach boys technological skills, the work ethic, and the idea that the industrial and commercial transformation of everyday life into capitalism constitutes democratic progress and individual freedom.[11]

Carlisle, in some ways a subtle, in other respects a crude institutional microcosm of the American experiment in manufacturing citizenworkers' self-perceptions, was characterized by its founder as a "civilization mill." As I indicated above, this mill branded the U.S. product it tried to manufacture—from the material of Native youth—*individuals.* The school's pedagogical rhetoric transformed nouns into verbs to explain its mission: to civilize, Americanize, citizenize, and *individualize* Indians. Carlisle's "individuals" were educated—and proletarianized— as skilled or semiskilled manual workers if they were male and skilled domestic laborers and future homemakers if they were female. As my analysis and narrative take shape, I will argue that the students' "manufacture," and their recorded resistance to and reencoding of this enterprise, makes visible an attempted cultural and governmental structuring of selfhood deemed essential to the production of a compliantly aspiring American working class. At the same time I will also suggest that the manufacturer or mill metaphor does not quite capture either what the students experienced with one another at Carlisle or what the school itself taught the students.

I will be drawing mainly on the many Carlisle school publications—newspapers, magazines, pamphlets—for my analysis. In Pratt's era (1879–1904) the school newspapers I have read are *School News, Eadle Keatah Toh* (which became *The Morning Star*), *The Indian Boys' and Girls' Friend, The Indian Helper, The Red Man* (the latter two merged as *The Red Man and Helper*). After Pratt was fired (1904–1918), the school's newspaper was *The Arrow* (retitled *The Carlisle Arrow* in 1908) and its more elaborately produced paperbound magazine was *The Indian Craftsman* (which soon readopted the older title, *The Red Man*). The two publications united in 1918 as *The Carlisle Arrow and Red Man*.

Sometimes it seems clear that the writing published was principally collected and edited by students. In the inaugural issue of *School News*, the first Carlisle newspaper, one finds the notice "Samuel Townsend, Editor. A Pawnee Indian boy." His initial editorial asserts: "We put everything in this paper that the Indian boys write for us. Not any white man's writing but the Indian boy's [*sic*] writing." Issues of *The Morning Star* also list student editorial boards. Many articles were written by students. Other publications do not list student editors, and many pieces—some indicate the author, some do not—are patently by either Pratt or his staff. Mr. See All edits *The Indian Boys' and Girls' Friend*. Often Carlisle newspapers reprinted articles from newspapers and magazines around the country or addresses made by congressmen or bureaucrats thought relevant to Carlisle or its ideologies. In the post-Pratt era every page of *The Red Man* magazine boasted that its articles were "by Red Men." This elaborately decorated magazine featured the writing of Native luminaries. But many were not by Red Men (for example, pieces by Bureau of Indian Affairs commissioners) and most were not written by students. The students, however, probably played a major role in creating the decorative artwork for the magazine's design. School publications—presumably considered evidence of Carlisle's success in Americanizing, individualizing, and citizenizing—were often distributed to Friends of Carlisle sympathizers, fund-raisers, and powerful authorities in the state and private sectors as well as to students and former students.

As I noted in the introduction, my work on Carlisle differs from that of other scholars in part because of the literary-critical attention I place on these publications as multifaceted ideological representations whose language, narratives, style, images, repetitions, tone, contradictions, and changes from 1879 to 1918 exhibit much about the school's aims and about the students' discursive agency. Most of the work published by students about Carlisle and related matters appears not in former students' autobiographies—which Michael Coleman, in particular, has shown to be immensely important—but in the voluminous school publications.[12] Material that the staff published and articles that were reprinted also provide significant evidence of the strategic flexibility of Carlisle's attempts to establish control. Overall, these publications suggest aspects of the multiple histories that made up "Carlisle."

Richard Henry Pratt (1840–1924) came from humble pull-yourself-up-by-your-own-bootstraps beginnings. He was born in New York's Genesee Valley but at age six moved to Logansport, Indiana (Potawatomi country, before the tribe was exiled to Kansas a few years prior to Pratt's arrival).[13] His formal schooling concluded when he was thirteen. Pratt's father, on the verge of striking it rich, was murdered in the California gold rush. Committed to helping support his newly widowed mother and three brothers, Pratt spent most of his teens as a printer's devil and then apprenticed as a tinsmith. Thus he had approximately the level of education that Carlisle made available to students who matriculated for about eight years and graduated.

When the Civil War erupted he enlisted in the Union army and was promoted to sergeant. Pratt realized that his best opportunity for career advancement was with the army (his retirement in 1903 entailed his automatic promotion from colonel to brigadier general). When that war ended, many more troops, including Pratt, were redeployed to serve in the intensifying Indian wars in the West. The military land-clearing forces spearheaded the gold rushes and land rushes of the 1860s and 1870s. In 1867 Pratt was commissioned second lieutenant in the Tenth Cavalry, a Black regiment comprised primarily of ex-slaves. Having demonstrated expertise in leading Native scouts often used in battles against Native resistance in the West, Pratt was promoted to first lieutenant. In 1875 he was given command of allegedly hostile Kiowa, Comanche, Cheyenne, and Arapahoe prisoners, who were transported by train from Oklahoma to Florida. Then for three years at Fort Marion Pratt experimented with how to "civilize" and "Americanize" his prisoners and, of crucial importance, how best to make them their own jailors.[14]

The inmates not only took classes in subjects such as English, impressing the likes of Harriet Beecher Stowe, they created and sold "Indian" art and crafts, helped put out a fire in St. Augustine, and cleared fields for agriculture. They were so productive and cheap to hire that a U.S. senator from Florida attempted to introduce a bill in Congress that would limit their work for pay.[15] One prisoner, uninterested in such new opportunities, was chained in solitary confinement for most of the time before he died. Several Kiowas tried to escape in 1876.[16] Pratt made his apparent successes in Native education, self-incarceration, and worker training known to his supervisors. His dramatic move from control-through-coercion to administration-through-hegemony earned him a transfer to Hampton Normal and Industrial Institute, which, under the direction of General Samuel Chapman Armstrong, prepared Black students for "civilization." To whet Armstrong's appetite, Pratt informed him that his prisoner-students, some of whom were superb artists, had netted $5,000 from their art sales.[17]

Armstrong, Booker T. Washington—Hampton's most famous alumnus and founder of Tuskegee Institute in 1881—and Pratt agreed on much. All three were committed to training students to *want* to perform semi-skilled and skilled manual labor. Washington testified: "At Hampton I not only learned that it was not a disgrace to labour, but learned to love labour, not alone for its financial value, but for labour's own sake and for the independence and self-reliance which the ability to do something which the world wants done brings." He tactically condemned slavery as a "degradation" of the character-building work ethic—an arrangement, he suggested, that degraded slaveowners perhaps even more than slaves. Both Pratt and Washington subscribed to the idea that (in the words of the latter) "no white American ever thinks that any other race is wholly civilized until he wears the white man's clothes, eats the white man's food, speaks the white man's language, and professes the white man's religion."[18] Hampton and Carlisle both sponsored an individualism that encoded the dispensing of government money, goods, or treaty reparations to Natives as unearned advantages that could retard their moral development as producers.[19]

Yet Pratt differed from Armstrong and Washington in numerous ways. Pratt felt that African Americans may need race leaders and a racial identity—which Hampton and Tuskegee tried to develop in their fashion—to enable them to survive the intransigence of prejudice and exploitation, but that Natives—who, he argued, suffered less discrimination—did not. Thus Natives needed to be integrated fully within, not segregated from, White culture and should be taught to look out for themselves as "individuals," not as members of a group.[20] He thought that the "Indian" "plane of life had always been above that of the African in his native state."[21] Strategically, he did not want the racial predicament or image of Natives to be equated with—tainted by—that of African Americans. Despite Armstrong's belief that "inherited traits and ideas rather than mere ignorance is the difficulty with low and savage races," the Hampton curriculum included some study of Native culture, and Armstrong criticized Pratt's hard line against this. It was Hampton, not Carlisle, that experimented, as had earlier missionary schools, with the usefulness of nascent protomulticulturalism as a means of producing incentive for workers. (Hampton, however, encouraged Native students to identify more with individuality and race than with their tribes.) "The Indian," Armstrong held, "will not respect our civilization the more for being taught to despise his own."[22] Pratt, by contrast, had no interest in promoting the category of race, not grasping White "individuality" or Americanness as race-based ideologies. But Pratt's individualism and Americanism had a combustible quality. Pratt, more than Armstrong, was a rousing agitator whose students saw him issue relentless public criticisms of the Bureau of Indian Affairs (BIA), the Bureau of Ethnology, and the government in his efforts to fight for what he took to be their individual rights as Americans.

When Armstrong in 1878 asked Pratt to oversee the education of Natives at Hampton, he allowed him to bring fifteen of his prisoner-students.[23] Pratt helped supervise them for about a year. Part of his responsibility was to go West to recruit Native children for Hampton. The government liked the idea of obtaining voluntary, and often involuntary, young hostages whose instruction in the East might facilitate Native pacification and colonization in the West.[24] But Pratt, who believed that the two races should be educated separately because of their different problems and characteristics, requested that he be authorized to establish an institution for the industrial training of "Indians" only, so that he could more thoroughly test his ideas. Congress and the BIA gave him his chance.[25]

Pratt and some of his supporters, including Etahdleuh (Kiowa), a former Fort Marion prisoner-student, again went West to persuade Native parents to let him transport their children to Carlisle for a minimum three-year stay. (Pratt would often have Natives, such as Dr. Charles Eastman [Santee Sioux], Gertrude Bonnin [Yankton Sioux], and Luther Standing Bear [Brule Sioux], recruit for him out West.) Sometimes Carlisle representatives were able to force youth who had run afoul of the government to attend.[26] Some boarding school "recruitments"

3. Carlisle promotional photographs, photographed by John Nicholas Choate, Yale Collection of Western Americana, Beinecke Rare Book and Manuscript Library

amounted to kidnappings. In 1879 Pratt brought his first group of 136 Native boys and girls to the army barracks at Carlisle, Pennsylvania (figure 3). No one in this original group, however, remained to graduate.[27] The school enrolled 1,218 students from 76 tribes in 1900.[28]

Pratt would have concurred with Twain's Hank Morgan (and Pudd'n-head Wilson), whose dictum, much like the efficiency expert Frederick Winslow Taylor's, was "Training—training is everything: training is all there is to a person." (Significantly, Taylor's early-twentieth-century "scientific management" tried to coerce and bribe workers to think of themselves as competing against rather than cooperating with one another in quest of higher wages, a tactic he labeled "individualizing.")[29] Pratt, Twain, and Taylor understood selfhood and incentive as products of organized cultural labor. "The Indian," Pratt insisted in 1904, is "raw material in the forest, mountains and plain to be brought and put through the proper refining influences of our civilization mills of today, and wrought into shape and then sent to work on the great oceans of our industry and thrift."[30] This manufacturing metaphor appeared in Carlisle's student publications for decades. The anonymous author of "A Boy Like a Piece of Iron" (1886) asked students whether they preferred to be molded into horseshoes or "converted into [more valuable] delicate watch-springs."[31] In 1892 Pratt published in Carlisle's *Indian Helper* a letter from an executive of a large Bessemer steel mill who voiced approval of Carlisle because its smelting of "Indians" was so similar to the transformation of "red ore" into commodifiable steel: "Our method of treatment is one agains [*sic*] which it constantly rebels, notwithstanding every process adds more value to it, and gives it greater power and possibilities; and we have to bring most powerful forces to bear on it to bring it into submission."[32] John Bakeless, director of Carlisle's education department, imagined students as raw material moving through the school on an assembly line: "bringing the crude Indian in at one end and sending him out the other, a man and a woman and a citizen."[33] Pratt reiterated popularizations of John Locke's philosophy of the culturally inscribed self: "It is a great mistake to think that the Indian is born an inevitable savage," Pratt held. "He is born a blank slate like the rest of us."[34]

Several dominant ideologies of the individual—the self-made "individual," the possessive "individual," the sentimental "individual," the appropriately gendered and sexed "individual"—provided Pratt with the cultural armory he used in his ideological maneuvers. Pratt learned much from his culture's worship of "the individual"—a potentially productive formation of self—as well as from the army's systematic regimentation of bodies and minds. He recognized that the means by which American culture had achieved a certain channeling of behavior, effort, aspiration, need, and desire was through its (class) molding of "individuals." Pratt knew that the very word uttered most frequently to oppose conformity—the "individual"—was in many if not all of its uses the most ingenious, though never wholly predictable, American formula to attain a basic range of conformity. With that uniformity in mind he dedicated Carlisle to the manufacture of Native youth as "individuals"—a manufacture that was in its operation more culturally multidimensional and in some ways more self-contradictory, even strategically so, than it sounds.

Digesting "Indians": Assimilation as Individualizing

Carlisle's popular before-and-after diptych photographs that typically exhibit a student in "Indian" garb and in the adjoining photograph show the newly "civilized" version propagandized the *now you see it, now you don't* disappearing act that the school officially hoped to accomplish in mind as well as body.[35] Before being individualized by Carlisle, the long-haired, befeathered, noble-looking Timber Yellow Robe (Yankton Sioux) is posed—that is, Indianized—so that he looks isolated, wary, out of place on the patterned carpet wrapped in blankets (figure 4). Here

4. Timber Yellow Robe before being Americanized and individualized, photographed by John Nicholas Choate, Yale Collection of Western Americana, Beinecke Rare Book and Manuscript Library

5. Chauncey Yellow Robe after being Americanized and individualized, photographed by John Nicholas Choate, Yale Collection of Western Americana, Beinecke Rare Book and Manuscript Library

he does not stand on his own two feet; by implication, he is not yet self-reliant and does not quite know how to act in what the photographer stages as a domestic space. This photographic stereotype of the lone "Indian" attempts to make its subject seem insufficiently "individual." However, the photograph, included in Pratt's collection, has been crudely cropped—what has been excised is the group of new "Indians" who stand and sit at Yellow Robe's side.[36] In his "after" photograph, the Carlisle individualizing program has reoutfitted the renamed Chauncey Yellow Robe in a double-breasted suit and collar, regroomed him with a haircut, and transformed him not only into a proud and smiling businesslike adult who can stand erect with confidence on his own two feet, but a handsome suitor. Suitable "individuals" who adopt the proper posture, perhaps strategic imposture, get the girl (figure 5).

Carlisle's publications frequently represented this reconfiguration of subjectivity and body as redemptive death (Pratt's "Kill the Indian in him, and save the man").[37] The school enlisted students to supply testimonies to attest to the inevitability and desirability of this racial suicide. Thus in 1891 a Carlisle girl (Seneca) forecast sweetly that soon Whites and "Indians" would step into the future hand in hand. Their unity was predicated on the premise that the erasure of Indianness was ineluctable. She hoped that the "Indian" would be: "Not murdered, but 'killed' from Indian to white man, and be made to march along in life with the superior race till even the thought of Indian language will be no more. Then the Indian will be independent."[38] The Indian's "independence" would be in his or her apotheosis as an *individual*. (How many students were "redeemed" by this figurative death is up for debate, but in the early years literal death claimed many young lives. "The change in clothing, housing, food, and confinement combined with lonesomeness was too much," wrote Luther Standing Bear, a member of the first class, "and in three years nearly one half of the children from the Plains were dead and through with all earthly schools.")[39]

Articles and testimonies repeated this assassination metaphor with evangelical and jingoistic zeal. Mr. Man-on-the-band-stand, a White character invented by the Carlisle newspapers who, like Mr. See All, claimed to monitor unseen every student, exhorted his readers, parroting Pratt, to "lose" the Indian in them to "save" their lives: "Eugene Tahkapuer, who was once a Comanche Indian, but is now a voting citizen of Massachusetts, has killed his Indian." The students themselves, like Pratt's Native scouts in the Tenth Cavalry, were conscripted as Indian fighters. The "Indian's" glorious rebirth, Mr. Man-on-the-band-stand stressed imperatively, in the manner of "Simon says," would be as a nonconformist "FREE individual."[40] This ideological violence was packaged as regeneration through individuality.

The school encouraged students to see themselves as diseased. Indianism, the dreaded pathology, necessitated Carlisle's cure. Howard Gansworth, a Carlisle alumnus who went on to study at the Conway Hall preparatory school of Dickinson College, and who was in 1899 a sophomore at Princeton, participated in Carlisle's twentieth-anniversary exercise. He hailed Pratt as "one of the greatest medicine men living." After the laughter died down, Gansworth bestowed his Princeton endorsement: "He gives doses which if all the Indians would take would cure them of all their Indianism and forever make them white men and white women [Applause]." The cured "Indian" would be a self-reliant "individual" schooled in White ambition, empowered and motivated to "fight" his "own battle." For Gansworth the best place to achieve "individuality" and remedy his malady was what in the 1930s would come to be known as the Ivy League: "I wanted," he stressed, "to become an individual, if I could, and see how the medicine tasted. . . . I made up my mind that I was going [to a university] and that the choice lay between Harvard, Yale, and Princeton."[41] Jason Betzinez (Apache), in his autobiographical accounts of his Carlisle years, similarly regarded his education as something like a reform school "rehabilitation" of his "primitiveness."[42] If Native students could be convinced that they should want to reinvent themselves as "modern" White "individuals," then White people would no longer have to feel too uneasy about the theft of Native land that had undergirded Native-White relations for hundreds of years—for "Indians," like an evolutionary setback that had been rectified, would no longer exist culturally or politically.

In addition to metaphors of killing (suicide) and disease, Carlisle's newspapers frequently featured the metaphor of hegemonic digestion. In order to be Whitened and made "individual," the "Indian" had to be— had to want to be—eaten and digested by the capacious stomach of White culture. For BIA Commissioner Thomas Jefferson Morgan, who seems not to have foreseen the need twentieth-century Western tourism would have for "authentic"-looking "Indians," reservation "Indians" constituted an inedible crop: "The growing of savages as a National Industry is neither honorable nor profitable."[43] Carlisle's *Red Man* often reprinted a statement made by the minister Henry Ward Beecher about public schools and immigrants. Beecher sanctified the survival-of-the-fittest rhetoric of national power and assimilation with the religious halo of the parable: "When a lion eats an ox, the lion does not become an ox but the ox becomes a lion. So the emigrants of all races and nations become Americans, and it is a disgrace to our institutions and a shame to our policy to drive them away."[44] The process of becoming a lion in no way impinged on the individuality of the ox, of course, because the lion, not the ox, was defined from the start as the creature who possessed individuality, along with greater strength. Senator Henry Dawes held that by treating the "Indian" "as an individual," not an "insoluble substance" (the tribe), he or she would be much easier for the nation to "digest."[45]

Pratt's appreciation of the digestive power of daily life is apparent in his much touted educational innovation at Carlisle—the "outing." Each summer, and sometimes during part of the school year, students would be placed in the homes of Whites both to earn money (farmwork, domestic labor) and to be "absorbed" in the stomach of White culture.[46] Not all students thought of this indentured labor as educational.[47] Pratt actually wanted his students to go on one or two year outings, but was able to arrange this for relatively few students.[48] The interracial contact intrinsic to the slave system inspired Pratt to create the outing.[49] Pratt realized that Carlisle was only useful as an interim phase until the students could attend public school, where they could be more thoroughly digested by American culture. When he referred to "civilization mills" in 1904, Pratt was partly thinking of Carlisle but more of public schools and of the home: the aim was not to feed "our civilization to the Indians," he stressed, but to feed "the Indians to our civilization."[50] He knew that American culture was not a neutral system that simply permitted one to "discover" one's individuality; more subtly, it was a great manufacturing system that—through ideology, structures of sentiment, and labor—influenced one to "express" specific conventions of "individuality."

For this reason Pratt wanted students to attend Carlisle for only five years and then transfer to public school, a next step that rarely occurred. He tried to place many students in public schools while they were enrolled at Carlisle. When it was suggested that Carlisle might expand as a college, Pratt rejected this idea precisely because he had no wish to segregate his students from the more pervasive "civilization mills" in American culture at large, which were less visible as mills and thus potentially more effective. Related metaphors that appeared in Carlisle publications had baptismal as well as more fatal connotations—to "soak" and "immerse" (to drown) the "Indian" in U.S. culture and individualism.[51]

Native schooling in what I shall call *inevitability discourse*—the idea that White American conquest was inexorable—dates back to the seventeenth and eighteenth centuries, not only because some missionaries and other Whites disseminated forms of this discourse but because the indigenous people found themselves becoming materially dependent on trading within the emerging colonial marketplace.[52] Natives needed not only guns but a steady supply of ammunition to contend with White invaders and warring bands and tribes that had secured firearms through trade and political alliances.[53] "While the Indian eagerly sought guns and gunpowder, knives and whiskey, a few articles of dress, and, later, horses," Charles Eastman acknowledged in 1915, "he did not of himself desire the white man's food, his houses, his books, his government, or his religion." Over time those who propagated the inevitability theme no longer required overtly coercive Winchesters, howitzers, or blankets that carried smallpox to drive their point home. Cultural and bureaucratic weaponry took over.

Pratt's tactical confidence in the digestive capacity of American society was evident in his practice to have students travel by railroads through America and later write home about the scale of what they saw. What students were schooled to see was that they were outnumbered, that American cities were towering and permanent (they saw the first American skyscrapers), and that "progress"—meaning the extinction of the "Indian" as anything but a usable American "individual"—was futile to resist. In this era and that which followed, such architecture cast its imperial shadows over Native students, Blacks migrating North, new immigrants, and rural folk. Theodore Dreiser's *Sister Carrie* (1900) portrays its power: "[Chicago's] entire metropolitan center possessed a high and mighty air calculated to make the gulf between poverty and success seem both wide and deep. . . . [Carrie] sank in spirit inwardly and fluttered feebly at the heart as she thought of entering any one of these mighty concerns and asking for something to do—something that she could do—anything."[54]

The earliest Carlisle publications printed students' frightened testimonies and letters. Some exhorted their parents, still on the reservations, to surrender militarily, economically, culturally, and emotionally. Of course, some parents had sent their offspring to Carlisle because they had already reached this conclusion. Luther Standing Bear had been skeptical of Carlisle until his father visited him after the completion of his first year there and reflected on his journey to the school: " 'They greatly outnumber us and are here to stay,' he said, and advised me 'Son, learn all you can of the white man's ways and try to be like him.' " Luther clarified what he took to be his father's meaning: "He did not say that he thought the white man's ways better than our own; neither did he say that I could be like a white man. He said, 'Son, try to be like a white man.'

So, in two more years I had been 'made over.' "[55] Even the valorous Chief Sitting Bull (Hunkpapa Sioux), after he, his starving warriors, and their families were compelled to return to the United States from Canada in 1877, could in a moment of despondency tell a reporter, "I am nothing . . . neither a chief nor a soldier."[56]

In 1880 Harry Raven (Arapahoe) proved how well he had learned to read the industrialized East: the "savages" had not dug up the coal, lead, iron, and copper just waiting to be made profitable; rather, they were "lazy." His reaction to the pollution of Pittsburgh and Allegheny was one of wonder, not repulsion. Raven mimicked the interrogatory style of a teacher: "Those cities were full of smoke why was that boys? . . . The smoke comes from fires which keep big manufacturing place [*sic*] running."[57] "Indians" never built iron mills, paper mills, bridges, or steamboats; they wasted the continent. Articles compared the Native population, estimated at 250,000 or 260,000, to that of U.S. cities with a larger population—about ten cities in 1888.[58] Some students seemed to identify with the scale and power of the cities: "The United States," one Apache boy bragged, "can whip any nation in the world because it has New York to back it."[59] Students were instructed to see that the raising of the Carlisle smokestack in 1887 was symbolic of Yankee ingenuity and superiority: "To lift a hollow piece of iron eighty-five feet long, and weighing 3½ tons, up to a perpendicular position then onto a base ten feet high, would to the average reservation Indian seem like a task too prodigious to attempt, but a few of our boys, with ropes and pulleys, and a man with KNOW-HOW in his head, to direct, put the monster into the desired position in 30 minutes."[60]

For one female student the forced displacement of the Native pastoral with towering cities signified White salvation: "[Indians] roamed the beautiful forest, not dreaming that the day was approaching when instead of forest, large cities and manufacturing places would exist and the coming generations were to be lifted out of ignorance by the builders of these large cities."[61] Some students encoded schoolroom knowledge as a sign of White racial predominance. "How wonderful the White people are," one girl wrote her uncle: "The white people know how to makes [*sic*] anything."[62] The staff wanted letters like the girl's, and that of the boy who informed his father, "I don't like your Indian ways," to blackmail parents emotionally into adopting the White American way.[63]

This instruction in cultural and familial repudiation led some student individuals-in-training both to recount White oppression and to sanctify it as divine destiny. After Nellie Cary (Apache) described how soldiers hunted and killed many members of her tribe—including her mother—in her presence, she concluded fearfully and piously, "Some day there will be no Indians if they give up the Indian ways and confess themselves to GOD, and walk in the right path. They will have cities, and farms, and raise cattle. If they do not do it the white people will have all their lands, and they will be driven away or killed."[64] Cities, farms, and cattle had come to signify taking the "right" path: being Christian, American, individual. Another student in 1886 lamented the absence of unity among tribes in the early White occupation of what became New England. However, the lesson he apparently gleaned was one that pertained not to continued collective resistance to White imperialism—a seeming impossibility—but to the self-control requisite for *individuals* who wish to conquer rather than be conquered: "It is true of the Indian, as it is true of the white man, each of them must control himself if he does not want to be controlled by others. Captain Pratt must have had thoughts of this kind, when eighteen years ago, he determined to teach the Indian how to control, and how to help himself."[65] The "Indian," students were taught, sacrificed the continent due to inadequate individual self-control—as well as laziness and no Yankee KNOW-HOW. Indianness was represented as an anachronistic invention of self that had stalled both White and Native development: "We shall all be glad when we get into the civilized way of living," Sam Townsend editorialized apologetically in *School News* in 1881, "then the Indian will not make so much trouble for the American people."[66]

Possessive and Domestic Individualizing:
Treason to the Tribe

The Friends of the Indian, a group of mainly White Protestant middle- and upper-class reformers, contended that "Indians" had caused so much trouble for Whites and for themselves because they lacked the emotional dispositions associated with being acceptably and productively "individual." Elaine Goodale Eastman, a White reformer who wed Sioux author Dr. Charles Eastman and who wrote a laudatory biography of Carlisle's controversial superintendent, *Pratt: The Red Man's Moses* (1935), echoed the prevailing opinion in 1901 when she wrote in Carlisle's *Red Man and Helper* that "primitive," uncivilized "Indians" had neither "complicated emotions nor conflicting ideas of duty."[67] The more complicated emotions that many Friends of the Indian wanted to see take root in "Indians" were those that would produce *possessive individuals* who saw their main duty as owed to themselves and to the nation, not to the tribe.

Merrill E. Gates, a member of the Board of Indian Commissioners who had served as president of Rutgers University and later as president of Amherst College, explained what needed to be changed in order to inculcate a "stronger personality" in the "Indian." The "Indian" must be taught to feel "wants," to be "discontented" with his or her lot, to be "intelligently selfish," and have a grasping "desire for property": he must be dressed in "trousers—and trousers with a pocket in them, and with a pocket that aches to be filled with a few dollars."[68] Too many "Indians" lived according to the ethos of communal giving and welfare, an interpretation of collective responsibility insufficiently cognizant of the virtues of self-making and self-interest. "The last and best agency of civilization," Senator Dawes emphasized in 1883, "is to teach a grown up Indian to *keep*." Keeping fueled the incentive to own land, his "exclusively to enjoy." Land ownership fosters the separation of "the individual" from "the mass" (the tribe), and this breeds usable money-generating citizens and workers.[69]

Individualizing provided the ideological impetus for the Dawes Severalty Act of 1887. Indian schools celebrated the day of its enactment as Franchise Day. This audacious legislation was the culmination of previous schemes to "individualize" or allot—carve up—reservation lands: heads of families would receive 160 acres and others would get less acreage, presumably for the purpose of farming. Dawes Act supporters used the Bible and Lewis Henry Morgan's theory of evolutionary progress to bestow ideological benedictions on agriculture as culturally redemptive and overlooked the long history of Native agriculture, developed by many, though not all, tribes.[70] However, complications with the "individualizing" of reservation land were manifold.

Not all of the land allotted was arable and not every Native desired to be a farmer. White reformers knew that the shift to "modern," "civilized" agriculture would wreck the economic self-sufficiency that many Natives attempted to perpetuate through hunting—a labor they did not classify as work.[71] Carl Schurz, German immigrant and Secretary of the Interior, advised in 1881: "It is difficult to make them work as long as they can live upon hunting. . . . Even those of them who have so far been in a great measure living upon the chase, are becoming aware that the game is fast disappearing. . . . In a few years the buffalo will be exterminated."[72] Apparently BIA Commissioner Morgan saw some sense in the statement he made in 1889: "A wild Indian requires a thousand acres to roam over, while an intelligent man will find a comfortable support for his family on a very small tract."[73]

As one Carlisle student noted dutifully in 1887, ownership of land stimulates the "ambition" to labor and improve oneself and one's property.[74] *The Red Man* reprinted an article by General Lewis Merrill in which he restated the anthropologically based premise that owning property is "at the very root of civilization" and that it intensifies the desire for "permanent rewards" and surplus accumulation.[75] Natives, perforce, had to be educated in the more "civilized" capitalist satisfactions of piling up property and profits.[76]

Carlisle publications, the Friends of the Indian, and other commentators had no hesitancy about acknowledging that White possessive individualism had been unrestrainably rapacious when it came to confiscating and acquiring Native real estate. Although this admission had a certain critical element—censorious of a capitalism that will suffer no one to constrict its expansion—and an element of shame—popularly exemplified by Helen Hunt Jackson's *Century of Dishonor* (1881)—land-grabbing was represented as a fact of "life," as an inevitability that the government itself could do little or nothing to alter. Native students were taught that their only recourse against an insatiable and unstoppable White possessive individualism was to become possessive individuals themselves and join the fray.

Pratt opined that "Indians" must not block "the way of civilization and commerce any longer. . . . the Indian [must be] made an individual and worked upon as such with a view of incorporating him on our side."[77] In 1885 Carlisle students perused an article by Hampton's General Armstrong in which he admitted that "Indians" "have been brought to bay on lands they cannot long hold in a tribal way—for the reservation must go—pressed on all sides by our strong, selfish civilization."[78] Carlisle newspapers reprinted articles such as one from the *St. Louis Globe Democrat* arguing that "Indians" did not know how to use land properly, except for looking at it, riding over it, and "chasing . . . jack-rabbits," and that they must therefore "yield" it "to the uses and necessities of civilization."[79] In several ways "rugged individualism"—imperial individualism—proved to be an effective land-clearance and Indian-removal invention. For hundreds of years the theft of Native land functioned as a safety valve for tensions among Whites stemming from class and economic inequality: disparate Euramerican groups, from indentured servants to entrepreneurial aristocrats, from new immigrants to business leaders, could imagine "Indians" as their common enemy and the absorption of "unused" Native land as their legitimate objective.[80]

Ezra A. Hayt, Commissioner of Indian Affairs, recommended land-in-severalty legislation in the late 1870s on the grounds that the government was unable to protect "the Indians against the encroachments of the whites upon their reservations, or from the acts of the government itself whenever an active demand [by "white settlement" or business interests] is made that the treaty stipulations . . . should be abrogated." Charles C. Painter, the Washington agent of the Indian Rights Association from the mid-1880s to mid-1890s, considered treaties as pragmatic business and military deceptions: "not made to be kept, but to serve a present purpose, to settle a present difficulty in the easiest manner possible, to acquire a desired good with the least possible compensation, and then to be disregarded as soon as this purpose was gained and we were strong enough to enforce a new and more profitable arrangement."[81] In fact, Congress outlawed the signing of treaties in 1871.[82]

Two concepts associated with American "individualizing" were put under strain by such acknowledgments about the onward progress of land theft: citizenizing and civilizing. If Natives became American citizens, how could citizens hold treaties with their own government? American citizens do not belong to "independent nation[s] in the heart of *our* nation."[83] Citizens' "rights" did not encompass the "right" to hold lands collectively that had been granted to them by "alleged treaties."[84] The lobby to citizenize Natives, by implication, provided the government with a pretext to reconsider whether treaties were still applicable. In 1889 Carlisle students read a reprint of a bold article from the *St. Louis Republic* in which the author professed that tribal lands were being stolen under the cover of the word *civilization*: "No Indian tribe will twenty years from now be left in possession of land that is worth cultivating. . . . The best that can be done now is to tell the truth and to avoid the shameful cant which seeks to cloak Punic faith under the 'interests of civilization.' "[85]

Students often encountered the argument that many immigrants were quickly citizenized and civilized once they were individualized. "Under dispersing individualizing systems," one author wrote proudly in 1885, immigrants, unlike "Indians," "have become English speaking and American, adding to the wealth and prosperity of the country."[86] As another observer framed it the year before, training immigrants as "individuals" was the means by which "America has been so successful in Americanizing foreigners; she has brought all the force of free institutions to bear upon them naturally and individually."[87] Obdurate efforts to misrepresent Natives as immigrants elided not only the historical fact that they occupied the continent long before White immigrants to their land "discovered" and conquered or in some eyes stole it,

but that Natives had not emigrated to America to become Americans—
they had their own tribal traditions and values and sometimes wished
mainly to perpetuate them in the face of the U.S. occupation that labeled
itself progress.

White reformers who promoted Americanizing and individualizing frequently vilified the Native ethos of communal giving and welfare as a
communistic or socialistic production of self, emotions, and values.
Pratt tried to redefine possessiveness rather than communal concern as
the greatest social and racial good for "Indians": "If [the Indian] gets his
living by the sweat of his brow and demonstrated to the nation that he is
a man, he does more good for his race than hundreds of his fellows can
who cling to their tribal, communistic surroundings."[88] Commissioner
Morgan urged that Native "socialism [be] destroyed" because its communal protection inhibited the development of familial economic dependencies and responsibilities that place pressure on men to become
competitve "individuals." One *New York Tribune* attack on a Jesuit,
Dr. Edward McGlynn (a supporter of Henry George, the noted progressive advocate of land reform), reprinted in Carlisle's *Morning Star* in
1887, accused the priest of being a socialist for contending that "land is
rightfully the property of the people in common." McGlynn's critic
made the "Indian" connection to further discredit the priest's position:
"What is [socialism] but the practice of our wild Indians? They hold
their lands in common." He added sarcastically: "The wild Indian is the
type you should imitate!"[89]

Individualizing not only involved producing an "Indian" workforce
of propertyholding citizens, discarding treaties, and making tribal land
more available for *legitimate* use—the use of government, business, real
estate interests—it gave the government a reason to deny responsibility
for providing Natives with financial support. Necessity would be the
magical mother of self-reliance, Pratt predicted: "I would blow the reservation to pieces. I would not give the Indian an acre of land. When he
strikes bottom he will get up."[90] The Carlisle student Charles Kihega
(Iowa) apparently felt much the same in 1883 when he defended "standing alone": "If the Government will stop feeding them and help those
who want to help themselves, Indians will soon know what to do."[91]
One *Indian Helper* piece in 1885 listed numerous names of Carlisle's
first students to assert, "Every ONE [has been] able to get along without
Government help."[92] An article reprinted from the *Sioux City Journal*
had Carlisle students consider the claim not simply that the "Indian"
did not deserve government annuities and reparations (the "Indian"

must "go to work and earn his living or starve") but that the "Indian" "has not more or better right to this land than he had to the land from which he has been driven by whites."[93] Such fulminations gave vent to White resentment: "Indians," unlike Whites, had not "earned" the land they held—in 1600 or 1900—and government support unfairly protected them from a sink-or-swim marketplace in which White "individuals" sometimes drowned.

The school inundated students with the doctrine of individualism-as-self-interest. "The Indian as an individual separated from the tribe is all right, for then he truly learns to look out for number one, which after all is the real basis of individual progress."[94] Kihega, editor of *School News*, felt that desiring to "save every penny we earn" was as important to "Indian" education as "learn[ing] how to speak the English language . . . of our country."[95] The willingness to "STICK TO [work]" would gauge one's growth as an "individual."[96]

Carlisle's publications printed anecdotes of "self-made" men to inspire students to adopt possessive individualism as a value. Stories of success chronicled and ennobled dogged self-denial, self-interest, and saving. Students read that Benjamin Franklin "began in a printing office. Did he get pay for his work? Not a cent. He spent several years working for nothing, but he was getting knowledge all of the time, which was of more use to him than money."[97] Franklin's Poor Richard maxims, such as "Without industry and frugality nothing will do, and with them everything," were published to excite students about perseverence.[98] Carlisle's *Morning Star* gave Franklin's "GOD HELPS THOSE WHO HELP THEMSELVES" the place of honor as the motto beneath its masthead. Railroad magnate and Yale graduate Chauncey Depew's story was instructive in its symbolism: his rich Dutch father reputedly developed his son's character by refusing to give him so much as a dollar. In the same way Natives should refuse and be refused help from their "great father" in Washington. Cornelius Vanderbilt, who "saved his pennies" until he "was worth $95,000,000," was lionized as a hero—not haughty Geronimo, who dissimulated to generals and thus deserved to "be hung." Real warriors worked tirelessly, saved time and money ("He who will steal time cannot be trusted very far with money"), and made their killings in the marketplace.[99]

Carlisle celebrated Natives who excelled as ambitious "individuals" in "civilization" as examples of what could be accomplished with persistence. Susan La Flesche (Ponca and Omaha), who ranked first in her class at Hampton and was soon to attend Women's Medical College of Pennsylvania in Philadelphia in 1886, where she would also graduate at the top of her class, was applauded by Mr. Man-on-the-band-stand; he hoped "that some Carlisle Indian girl would push ahead in her studies and prepare to go to a college for doctors, too. Why not?"[100] A 1901 issue of *Red Man and Helper* proudly announced that "George W. Ferris, 1901, intends entering Stanford University before long."[101] One year later the new scholarship founded by the South African Cecil Rhodes was described as being available "for American boys, without distinction of race or color. . . . [for] the right kind of Indian student, Oxford opens up her doors without cost."[102] Such articles were overinflated with optimism about "individual" opportunity for the "Indians" who truly sought it.

But Carlisle's rhetoric of ambition and self-denial also took another slant: it prepared young students to be exploited and rejected as workers and, true to the ideology of individualism, to blame only themselves, not their exploiters, if they did not prosper. This was a momentous accomplishment to turn the gaze of students away from anything resembling a structural critique of American society and to fault themselves instead. "Take the very first work you can get," students who returned to the reservation were advised in 1885, "even if you receive little pay. . . . do not blame the Agent. Look at yourself and see if you are doing the best you can."[103] Another article that year announced, "The agent MAY be a bad man. The man over you MAY be cheating you, but ten chances to one it is all YOUR fault."[104] It was the Indian agent who had all the agency, whereas Natives in quest of work were systematically forced into dependency. Extending this ideology, Booker T. Washington went so far as to contend that racist exploitation worked to the advantage of Tuskegee's students because it made them work harder. "Intrinsic individual merit," not a racist unequal distribution of opportunity, was for Washington—and Pratt—the issue worth pondering. Yet Washington, unlike Pratt, upheld the idea of working and partly assimilating not just for oneself, or for America, but to "lift up" one's race.[105]

Some of Carlisle's success stories seemed designed to obfuscate the reality of racial prejudice in their comparison of ostensibly "self-made" Whites and Natives. Students were told in 1890, for example, that Commissioner Morgan, the man who controlled their destinies, "was not too proud to do any kind of work [on school vacations]. . . . And he saved his money."[106] The implication was that Morgan had contended with the same obstacles that they would meet after leaving Carlisle (that is, during his school vacations). When success anecdotes registered racial discrimination as a concern, it was often framed merely as a productive test of one's "individual" willpower and character. A story about the triumphant self-reliance of a young man named James suggested that this Native lad's initial failure to find work was due to racism. But James did not succumb to the "temptation" to relent and return to the "dirt" of the reservation and accept money from the government—he was too "MANLY." James found a job, "save[d] every penny" he could, and in five years had accumulated $600 to buy a farm.[107] Codes of deferential speech and polite bodily deportment were adumbrated in numerous pieces on how to find employment, any employment for any pay. Making "Indians" embrace "individuality" often meant making them accept life as a manual laborer or subsistence-level farmer, rancher, shepherd, or fisherman.[108]

Sometimes former Carlisle students wrote letters to Pratt that, laced with a certain sadness, testified to the difficulties of work even when they secured it. Rosa La Flesche (Chippewa) not only studied at Carlisle but later worked as a matron and manager of the outing system there. In 1921 she was employed at Fort Mason in San Francisco. Despite her managerial experience, she was hired as a typist. La Flesche, whose fellow workers were White, was resigned to the idea that she had to "take a back seat when I am alone among white people as I am at Ft. Mason." The nervous strain that may well have resulted from the mix of her Carlisle training and her typing job was one that she read as racially biological rather than social in genesis: "The Caucasian race has that everlastingly-hang-on disposition which the Indian race has not. . . . I can see how easy it is for [Indians] to give up. We don't have the same dispositions that you people have."[109] If Carlisle tried to school its students to be uncomplaining—hence more easily exploited—at work and to fault themselves—never the social system—for their failure to "rise," the institution also, though not always successfully, even with its most dedicated pupils such as La Flesche, encouraged students not to credit prevalent stereotypes of inherent racial dispositions.

Pratt sought relentlessly to plant in his wards "treason to the tribe." Students were instructed that tribal reservations were in conflict with (what Charles Painter called) the operations of the American "civilizing machine" and trod on Natives' individual "rights."[110] Pratt wanted his students to subvert the authority of the tribe from within. His young charges, like Twain's Connecticut Yankee's "civilisation factory" boys, were trained to reject their indigenous culture as just so much dirt and savagery—the shameful antithesis of individuality, civilization, and progress.

An article titled "The Farewell Meeting" (1890) endowed the strife between heroic Carlisle students and their oppressive parents with biblical significance: "David needed no greater courage to attack the giant Goliath than do these boys and girls need to fight the giants that will come their way." Howard Logan (Winnebago), distressed at having to leave Carlisle ("civilization and culture") for his tribe, echoed some of the Puritans' fears when they landed in what they labeled New England: "We are going where the Devil reigns. Are we able to withstand the temptations we shall meet?" Pratt urged his graduating students to "Flee away from that which drags you down. Go where . . . you can rise and become INDIVIDUALS."[111] Another piece in 1880 asked Carlisle: "Will you not build up a separating wall of new tastes and sympathies between [the student] and his people?" The (apparently personified) institution's reply was a resounding yes: "We desire to so thoroughly unfit these children for the conditions now existing in their homes that they will find it absolutely necessary to create new conditions. We hope to build the separating wall of a better nature and build it up so high that it will be absolutely impossible for them ever to get over it and sink down to the level of their old life."[112] In some cases Carlisle succeeded so well in unsuiting students for reservation life that on their return home they could not find any jobs in which they could use their "civilized" and "industrial" skills (tinsmithing, shoemaking, dressmaking). In addition, some students could not stomach the tribal life and rituals they were taught to abhor as unclean, unchristian, uncivilized, un-American, unpragmatic, unprofitable, and communistic.[113]

Students' articles served as rehearsals for the tests of "individuality" and "character" that awaited them. "I think the Indian language is one that few person [*sic*] who wish to live as human beings can use," Dennison Wheelock (Oneida) concluded in 1887. "It is a language that is of no use in the world, and should not be kept any longer."[114] Wheelock's larger implied point was that the tribes themselves were of no "use." For some students, speaking and writing in English seems to have signified their erasure of tribal origins—or limitations. "Dear Uncle," wrote one Carlisle girl in a perfunctory tone, "I have not talked Indian since January, and I am glad. I hope sometime I will forget all my Indian language." Carlisle forbade students to talk in their tribal language. Another student began proselytizing on behalf of White "civilization" while she was still at Carlisle: "I want you to stop wear Indian clothes," she wrote her father. "Now I want you give up Indian way." But such letters sometimes betrayed the students' ambivalence about their education in tribal repudiation and indicated a deeper loyalty to and need for their parents. She continued: "Dear Father, you must tell my mother if she glad to hear from me when I write to you. I never write to her, because I forget her name." Worried that her parents might be confused by the American name she was assigned at Carlisle, she added a poignant postscript: "That's me, White Horse. I sent [*sic*] love to you all. Write to me as soon you get this letter. You must not wait."[115]

Twain's Connecticut Yankee's struggles with Merlin the magician for cultural authority in King Arthur's court had its counterpart in Carlisle's strenuous efforts to discredit medicine men—figures who stood for tribal cohesion, tradition, and power. The school's papers printed pieces with titles like "How to Break Up the Medicine Dance" (1886) and "The Indians Are Beginning to Lose Faith in the Medicine Dance" (1886). One fictional dialogue between a student and her teacher highlights the girl's newly learned feelings of shame about the medicine dance: "they try to do the same as animals,—buffaloes, horses, deer or bears." Another critique of the medicine men proclaimed, "Every medicine-man is a hinderance to the progress of the tribe."[116] Carlisle decreed that the greatest progress a tribe could make would be to disband itself; its best medicine was American "individuality."

Individualizing was associated with cleanliness—the opposite of the "physical and moral filth" that supposedly characterized tribal ways.[117] Carlisle secularized what one mid-nineteenth-century missionary-educator called the "gospel of soap," a term that sanitized lessons in bodily shame (lessons paid for mainly by Native treaty money).[118] A didactic reminiscence of the first batch of Carlisle students harped on their disorderly bodies: "long [uncombed] hair," "dirty faces and hands," and "dirty clothes."[119] Dirt, signified as shameful, was frequently linked to the Natives' refusal to labor in White ways. The tale of young James—who abandoned the "dirt" of his reservation, was employed for five years, saved his (small) earnings, and bought his own farm—closed with a strong monitory moral and economic note: "He is not one of those lazy Indians on the plains at whom everybody looks with disgust, and says in his breast, 'Keep out of my way, you filthy thing. Stay on your own ground, and I will stay in mine." Indianness here is portrayed as not only dirty but akin to physical, moral, and economic leprosy.[120]

In 1888 Joshua Given (Kiowa) wrote Pratt a letter that praised his Carlisle schooling as a process of inner cleansing. He applauded Carlisle as "the Soap of the U.S. Government. . . . *It* not only washes away the dirt and habits of an Indian—but washes away and out of him the *ignorance* and *superstitious rites*. . . . [and] *indolence*." Judging from his letter, Given had been trained to imagine himself as being engaged in nothing less than an ideological contest to cleanse his "Indian" subjectivity: "I have been fighting—using the war-weapons given me at Carlisle Barracks."[121] Thus energized he went out into the world, yanked his well-shined bootstraps, and became president of the Citizens Bank of Ponca City (Oklahoma), until it went bust in 1904.[122]

Middle-class sentimental and domestic ideologies were deployed to make Carlisle students perceive the tribal organization of family life as dirty and savage. The dearth of Native habitations that resembled White middle-class sentimental homes permitted land-hungry Whites to argue that tribal lands were not really occupied or being used. Many Native residences had little spatial provision for privacy, and by the late nineteenth century this too could seem—to Whites and to Carlisle students—to disqualify "Indian" homes as homes.[123]

Carlisle's publications often featured sentimental poems such as Ione L. Jones's "Home" (1892), whose rhymes informed students that men can build mansions, but only women can make "that precious thing called home."[124] Reformers envisioned "home" as a stage set for the performance of productive individuality and sentiment. Senator Dawes, explaining his severalty legislation in *The Indian Helper*, listed the cast of actors necessary to perform on this set: "He will have a home and a wife and children just as white men do, and the cattle and ponies and everything else belonging to him will be kept for him by this law, just as they are kept for the white man now."[125] Carlisle students, especially the girls, were inculcated to express distaste when the proper backdrops and props were missing. Thus Carlisle's *Eadle Keatah Toh* reported beamingly in 1880 that while on a summer camping trip "some of the girls manifested disgust, quite in civilized, school-girl fashion. They evidently agree with one of the Florida boys, who wrote that he would never walk in the Indian road any more, but would 'live in houses forever.' Camp to them means not only freedom but filth, and the absence of all the comforts and conveniences which they have learned to prize."[126] Houses, not "tents," were essential for heartfelt sentimental American family life.[127]

Earlier in the century missionaries had noted the strong affective bonds between Native parents and children, but some were disturbed because these bonds were not bonding families to the network of socioeconomic dependencies and desires that provided a social foundation for a Christian and "civilized" regimen. For them "Indians" exercised an annoying amount of choice in maintaining or dissolving the conjugal bond, moving their residences seasonally or on whim, and working, not regularly, but when they thought it requisite.[128] The perceived material and ideological relationships among getting Natives to farm, stimulating them to want to own land, persuading them to adopt regular work habits, and programmatically creating "civilized" desires and dependencies are overt in one Episcopalian missionary's blueprint for change: "[Stop] *wandering* tribes. . . . Induce them to become fixed and permanent, and more than all, let them be *dependent on the produce of the ground* for subsistence; then they are within our reach, and from that moment they have a special interest in the country in which they live. Industry then becomes *necessary* to prolong life, and *private property* is invested with an interest which the hunter knows nothing of."[129]

Although Lewis Henry Morgan's influential *Ancient Society, or Researches in the Lines of Human Progress from Savagery Through Barbarism to Civilization* (1877) mystified conflicts between "civilized" Whites and "barbaric" "Indians" as evolutionary rather than political struggle, some of his arguments have a materialist base.[130] One of the keywords he employs is *produce*, and what he writes most interestingly about is the evolutionary importance of "the production of property" (549), especially the evolutionary "dominance" of the "passion over all other passions" (6) to *possess* "individual property in houses and lands" (32).[131] The turn toward agriculture as a "basis of subsistence" (19), in place of fishing and hunting (24), was a crucial development, Morgan argues, because it led to "struggle[s] for possession" (550), to the organization and regularization of labor, to the "possessory right" of the "individual" and not just of the "tribe" (540) to own land ("allotment," 551), and at long last to the growth of larger trading populations that became (warring) nations (550). The "individualize[d]" (553) *monogamian family* (based on monogamous marital relations), he believed, was established to institutionalize the incentive to accumulate wealth and property; new traditions (finally laws) of inheritance passed this wealth and property on to the children of the familial unit. Property fostered the invention of subjective styles that dominant groups employed to assert and legitimate their rule—ancient aristocrats envisioned themselves not only as more cultivated but more "individual" than members of subordinate social groups (560).

Morgan's conclusion put this property-loving "civilization" and its "individualized" values in evolutionary perspective: "The outgrowth of property has been so immense, its forms so developed, its uses so expanding and its management so intelligent in the interests of its owners, that it has become . . . an unmanageable power. . . . A mere property career is not the final destiny of mankind. . . . The time which has passed away since civilization began is but a fragment of the past duration of man's existence; and but a fragment of the ages yet to come" (561). His vision of a postcivilization future, though vague, is almost socialist in its support for the making of a society whose interests "are paramount to individual interests" and its prediction that possessive society "contains the elements of its self-destruction" (561).

Friends of the Indian, more attuned to Morgan's thoughts on family life and property passion than on capitalist self-destruction, were zealous to have dominant middle-class domestic "sentiments" reshape Natives' cultural values and emotional needs. The weight they placed on "the cultivation of home virtues" reveals much about the role played by family ideology—principally the middle-class model of the sentimental family—in the late nineteenth century's dominant White culture.[132] They realized that the sentimental idea of home and the economic and emotional commitments it demanded was significant in promoting the privatization of desires and the drive to own property. If the sentimental domestication of Natives worked effectively it could redirect their sense of responsibility for the overall welfare of the tribe.

Carl Schurz, Secretary of the Interior, supported the sentimental and feminine elevation of "Indian" women in tribes, not merely for the sake of the women but so that men, under the sway of sentimental femininity, would become more attached to the idea of building and buying "permanent homes." Schurz's sketchy but fascinating real estate logic implied that the proper domestic education of women would result in more sentimentalized marriages and would therefore spark the desire to acquire homes.[133] This investment would be predicated on the willingness of Native men to labor, buy, and sell in ways that Whites preferred (for the sake of wife and home). Domestic and feminine ideology could thus help stimulate Indian possessiveness. The cultivation of certain kinds of feminine women, then, could assist in providing men with the *incentive* to assimilate.

Merrill Gates was more explicit about the ideological usefulness of the home as an individualizing factory set up to produce the preferred "Indian" incentives and loyalties. Gates believed that the sentimental family had the ideological capacity to sanctify possessive individualism as productive of private good: "The tribal system paralyzes at once the desire for property and the family life that ennobles that desire. . . . There is no way of reaching the Indian so good as to show him that he is working for a home." In Gates's blueprint, home, sentiment, and feminity were seen as effective means of drawing "Indians" into the cultural and economic system: sentimental emotions would bribe the male to work steadily and his dependency (as well as his dependent's dependency) on his regular income would keep him in line. Whether or not the worker enjoys or approves of the labor he performs becomes, within the context of such domestic dependencies and emotional needs, not the main consideration. "The steadying, educating effect of property will take hold upon these improvident children of the West, who have for too long lived as if the injunction, 'Take no thought for the morrow,' in its literal sense, were the only law."[134] Commissioner Morgan advocated substituting "the family and the autonomy of the individual" for tribal "socialism."[135]

Reformers identified gender ideology as central to their project. Gates gendered acquisitive individualism and the privatization of interest as manly: "The tribal organization, with its tenure of land in common, with its constant divisions of goods and rations per capita without regard to service rendered, cut the nerve of all that manful effort which political economy teaches us proceeds from the desire for wealth."[136] Carlisle hammered this home: "Which do you prefer, sir," *The Indian Helper* asked rhetorically, "to stay with your tribe and be a child, or leave your tribe and become a Man?"[137] As cited above, male students learned from Pratt that one of Carlisle's goals was to "Kill the Indian in him, and save the man."[138] Manliness was scripted in exclusively *capitalist* terms: competing in the marketplace, laboring in prescribed fashion at particular occupations, and supporting oneself independent of the government. No other cultural invention of manhood was credited.[139]

Carlisle had its female students scrutinize themselves and their costumes exhaustively in their portrayals of well-mannered femininity. Feminine "individuality" was secured through the girls' meticulous observance of prohibitions. "A girl that is not neatly dressed is called a slattern, and no one likes to look at her. Her face may be pretty, and her eyes bright, but if there is a speck of dirt on her cheek, and her fingers' ends are black with ink, and her shoes are not laced or buttoned up, and her apron is dirty . . . she cannot be liked."[140]

Mr. See All and Mr. Man-on-the-band-stand encouraged, yet partly parodied, self-surveillance: "From his stand [Mr. Man-on-the-band-stand] could see everything," one notice cautioned students, "If you wish ever to have another sociable, you must behave gentlemanly and ladylike ALL THE TIME—at work, at play, in the school-room, in the chapel, or any where else."[141] Boys were expected to react accordingly to the correct rendition of approved femininity. When two boys rose from the steps of a building to make way for two ladies, Mr. Man-on-the-band-stand "held his head high": "They know that ladies don't like to crowd past gentlemen on steps or in door-ways."[142] Carlisle's exercises in gendered self-surveillance were intended to remain in force, especially when students returned to the reservation and again encountered older, more familiar social productions of selfhood, culture, and manners. If all went according to plan, their tribal culture would appear to them as it did to some Whites—dirty, insufficiently domestic, unsuitable for "individuals."

The most popular assimilation novel that exemplifies Carlisle's battle with the tribe for the hearts, minds, and labor of Native girls and boys was serialized in *The Indian Helper* in 1887 and republished with some modifications (the heroine's name was changed from Mollie to Stiya) as *Stiya, A Carlisle Indian Girl At Home* (1891). The author was simply named Embe, a pseudonym for the longtime Carlisle teacher Marianna Burgess (whose initials are MB).[143] One grossly exaggerated testimony in praise of *Stiya* likened its power to Harriet Beecher Stowe's sentimental anti-slavery epic, *Uncle Tom's Cabin* (1852). In the novel, slavery means having to return to one's tribe and family ("home slavery") after having been individualized and civilized at Carlisle.[144] (The Pueblo heroine's experiences were based on some student accounts of their homecomings.)[145]

Predictably, Stiya, the Carlisle student, is mortified by her Pueblo parents' "grimy" appearance and is almost unwilling to accompany them to their reservation home when she arrives at the train station. But she responds obediently to her teacher's dictate—"Be a woman"—which resounds in her mind.[146] Stiya's parents do not speak English, while she barely recalls her Native language, having been away for five years. The usual parent-child relationship is reversed; the daughter is the one who must rely on her Carlisle maturity to uplift her primitive parents. Stiya is repulsed by their "dirty" domestic habits and space. True to her Carlisle training in White femininity, she is devoted to domestic orderliness and thus spends the $47 she earned at Carlisle on furniture and utensils for their home. The plot comes to a head when Stiya refuses to dress as a Pueblo and attend the sundance, ashamed to take part in such cultural filth. At first her parents remonstrate with her. But when the imperious Pueblo governor commands her to join the dance and threatens to punish her, Stiya's father defends his daughter and compels his nerve-wracked wife to do so as well. All three are publicly stripped and whipped: the father and daughter are stoical and courageous martyrs (these are encoded as Carlisle virtues, not as Pueblo traits), while the lugubrious mother, a poor candidate for White femininity, is overwhelmed with self-pity.

This fiction is a novella of ventriloquism—Stiya mechanically enunciates versions of Carlisle's "WHERE THERE IS A WILL THERE IS A WAY" maxims.[147] Other Carlisle students may succumb to resignation and temptation, but Stiya will not. Carlisle has programmed her to be *individual*: "I am proud to have a mind of my own," she declares, convinced of her nonconformity.[148] Stiya's feminine civilizing power is also exhibited by her ability to help individualize men. Her father, impressed by his daughter's mettle, converts to "the white man's way." They move outside the Pueblo and he lands a job shoveling coal at the railroad station ten miles away for a dollar a day (no job is too lowly or can seem too exploitative for an "Indian" who has been sentimentally individualized). His "coal-blacked" face is not really dirty; it is a propitious sign of one who will soon be civilized, individualized, and domesticated.[149] Stiya takes over the management of their new home-sweet-home from her mother and presumably they live tidily ever after. Stiya's treason to the tribe is triumphant on several counts; Carlisle authorities, we learn, used their influence in Washington to imprison the villainous Pueblo governor.

Frances Sparhawk's *A Chronicle of Conquest* (1890) is another sentimental Carlisle assimilation novel, though more artful and conceptually subtle than *Stiya*.[150] Sparhawk paid long visits to Carlisle and, inspired by what she saw, dedicated much of her reform energy to writing and publishing novels, the royalties from which she used to help establish libraries at Carlisle and other Indian schools. Sparhawk retained her friendship with Pratt over many years and in 1920 wrote to him, "We were always of one mind on the Indian question." In that letter she conferred on him the same sacred halo that graces "the Captain" (whose last name is never mentioned) at Carlisle in her novel. She adored Pratt as the Indian Emancipator.[151]

A Chronicle of Conquest is about how best to conquer "Indians"—by getting them, as the Carlisle Captain had done, to (seemingly) conquer themselves. The fascinated witness of this institutionalized "Indian" self-conquest is Polly Blatchley, who, as it happens, writes novels in her spare time so that books can be purchased for Carlisle's library. Poor Polly is ailing from upper-middle-class neurasthenia, having worked so diligently in her studies at Vassar. Rather than going West for a rest, she beseeches her parents to let her visit her friend Lance, a young woman who teaches at Carlisle. They indulge her curiously obdurate preference for "studying the Indian to amusing herself with her companions" (6).

Polly's friend has an appropriately symbolic name for a dedicated Carlisle instructor: a lance is a weapon. In addition, a surgeon uses a sharp lancet to lance (to pierce and get under) a patient's skin. Polly is enchanted by the history of Carlisle, especially the story about how the Captain, in Florida, tamed his wild Native prisoners by removing their chains. She comes to realize that the Native "needs no other whip than duty" (197). Sparhawk suggests that civilized, sentimentalized femininity is fundamental to this psychological conquest. Hence the Captain understands that he must "capture" the Native girls and prevent them from "mocking" and ridiculing" (124) Carlisle, if he is effectively to get to the boys. The "human nature" of the "Indian" students is applauded by the two girls when it mimics White middle-class "human nature" and gender roles: "Indians," Lance avers, "when they are well dressed and well trained, come to be like white people" (30)—or as Polly herself puts it, "like other human beings" (26).

The novel hints that Carlisle is significant not only because it demonstrates civilization's ability to "individualize" (21) and pacify "Indians" but also because it stands as a testimony to White Americans' capacity to control themselves: "We Anglo-Saxons," Lance explains, "have been a thousand years getting the savage out of us, and there are occasions now when it doesn't seem as if we succeeded well" (57). Her phrasing resonates with Polly's desire to "get the Indian out of them" (197). Clearly, the Captain's Evolution Factory is renowned because it "puts its savages, its American Indians, into the mill, and grinds out the American, and leaves the Indian by the way" (212). Perhaps Carlisle's most reassuring aspect—to Polly, Lance, and others—is that, if only by implication, the Carlisle Evolution Factory reaffirms the presumed evolutionary status of Whites.

The "race battle" that Carlisle resolves, by ostensibly expunging Indianness, is thus associated with White middle-class anxieties about the success of the White evolutionary campaign to "get the [White] savage out of us." Insofar as Carlisle is sometimes intriguingly represented by Sparhawk as "one of the theatres of a new war" (36), this "battle" is seen as a *performance*: Carlisle's "Indians" and Whites are geared to self-consciously rehearse, stage, and applaud what is scripted as individualized self-control and civilized behavior. Yet this "new war," a subjectivity war, was not always victorious onstage or off. Carlisle students who returned to the reservation and embraced "Indian" rituals and lifeways threatened to expose the instability of controlled evolutionary Whiteness as just one cultural performance of being human among others, an anxiety that *A Chronicle of Conquest*, like *Stiya*, registers in several tales that recognize the endurance of Natives' "reservations."

Notwithstanding Carlisle's policy of "treason to the tribe," there is evidence in the Carlisle publications to suggest that some students perceived tribal traditions and issues of Native identity in complex, sometimes conflicting ways. On the one hand, Carlisle's radicalism was in its insistence that racial stereotypes and economic disadvantages should in no way impede individual development and success. The stress on education as that which makes the man or the woman functioned as a theory of social construction—education, not Whiteness, was represented as what gives people "the light of knowledge."[152] It is not hard to see why Carlisle's concept of the individual may have been appealing to some students, for it reencoded systemic institutional, racial, class, and economic barriers to advancement as primarily *individual challenges*. In 1899 Carlisle alumnus Howard Gansworth, whose stock sentiments were still going strong in Dos Passos's 1958 paean to American individualism, likened the individualistic spirit he found at Princeton to "that spirit of democracy which does not know any person; no matter who he is; does not recognize any sect or any class of persons, but it simply looks at the man, appreciates what sort of stuff he is made of and honors him."[153] If individualism-through-education was a form of social construction theory, the ideology of the individual also, as Gansworth's remarks show, posited inner stuff—stuff underlying social constructs that America's cultural, political, and economic system would allow an individual to express.

Carlisle promoted the idea that "Indian nature is human nature bound in red" and published articles like "Individuality Not Color" to help students adopt a concept of individual self that would strengthen their self-confidence.[154] America, within this framework, was principally a test of character. Carlisle's authorities were strategically aware that fabricating the idea of the (somewhat) autonomous "individual" could bring about a denial of race on the basis that race skews the perception of "individuals." As one article reprinted in *The Red Man* argued, "The word 'Indian,' to be sure, is an accident and a misnomer—but why try to dispense with a name altogether? We are not on exhibition and do not require a label."[155] Yet, at Carlisle, to express human nature meant acting White.

On the other hand, the school sometimes introduced students to a more systemic understanding of individuality and self-making. Frederick Douglass visited Carlisle in early April 1893 to deliver a lecture on "Self Made Men."[156] Douglass discarded stereotypical individualistic assumptions when conceptualizing self-making and replaced them with a more encompassing social and institutional view of the cultural production of self. Three years later, in a debate on the question "Do External Influences Make the Man?" parts of which were printed in *The Red Man*, Gansworth quoted Douglass as contending that "there are in the world no such men as self made men. . . . We shall have all either begged, borrowed, or stolen." Gansworth added: " 'Poets are born not made?' We say No. No man ever became a poet without being influenced." True to his Carlisle "self-making," Gansworth used this social insight as an argument for placing Natives "in the midst of civilization."[157]

In 1889 BIA Commissioner Morgan, discussing Indian school curricula, underscored that courses should steer clear of the U.S. "wrongs" and "injustice" imposed on Natives.[158] Yet the Carlisle publications sometimes acknowledged systemic racial oppression and kept students abreast of atrocities committed against the Chinese, of the lynchings of Blacks in the South, and of England's colonization of Ireland.[159] This occasional willingness to confront the reality of widespread racial violence introduced Carlisle students to critical perspectives on America.

Thus in 1885 *The Morning Star* printed "Indians Versus Civilization." After commenting on the recent "cold-blooded massacre of Chinese laborers," the author fumed that if the newspapers had substituted " 'whites' " for " 'Chinamen,' and Indians for whites, a howl of 'Exterminate the savages'! would have sounded through the length and breadth of the land; and yet the brutal ruffians who used knives and hatchets and applied fire brands in this second Wyoming massacre, claim to be civilized Americans!" A follow-up essay on this slaughter bears the title "Were They Civilized?" (1885). The angry conclusion is no. In "Where Are the Savages of the Nineteenth Century?" (1891) the author described phases of a forty-minute lynching that a Black man endured in Louisiana, then added: "If history can show up anything more horrible in the tortures inflicted by the Indians on their captives, we would like to know where to find it." Another piece on a Georgia lynching, "Not All Savages Are Red" (1899), queries: "Who ever heard of Indians cutting off the fingers, toes and ears of a victim and passing the same around as trophies, before striking the slow fire by which he was to be burned?"[160] Expressions of racial solidarity encouraged Carlisle students to think critically of race as a social system that necessarily affected them, no matter how much they wanted to believe that success depended solely on one's individual "stuff." In questioning whether America had earned the descriptor by which it represented itself—"civilization"—such articles raised doubts about America's moral worthiness when compared to tribal ethics and culture.

Numerous pieces in praise of Native traditions, skills, and powers appeared in Carlisle publications (which were, nevertheless, largely consecrated to advertising so-called civilization and individualizing). The skill of Native archers and horsemen was lauded by army officers as being greater than that of White soldiers. Articles reminded students and any Whites who read the Carlisle publications that many of the names of states—such as Connecticut and Massachusetts—are Native words.[161] Tales of Native courage and skill must have excited and inspired students. "The Exploits of Spotted Horse" (1891) was a particularly adventurous series. In order to steal horses from and then evade the Cheyenne, Spotted Horse had to draw on his extensive knowledge of the animals of the plains and of his "charm medicine" (the expertise of the same medicine men whom Carlisle sought to debunk). Spotted Horse's intrepid exploits demonstrated an almost superhuman self-reliance inseparable from his allegiance to his tribe. The series opened by telling of Spotted Horse's "tragic end a few years since at the hands of a United States Marshal": "although by many considered the terror of the South West, [he] was one of the bravest Indians that ever lived."[162]

The Red Man even printed a report about the Apache Kid, who, the piece claimed, had been a Carlisle student. After being exhibited at many society gatherings in the East, the story went, the young Apache reverted to savagery. Once out West the Kid abruptly abandoned his job as a teacher, led the Native resistance, and foiled all efforts to capture him—achieving invisibility through his knowledge of languages, acting skills, and cunning. Pratt asserted that the Apache Kid never attended Carlisle. Nonetheless the Apache Kid offered his students a model of someone who used Carlisle for the purpose of tribal defense.[163] What Pratt probably knew, and neglected to acknowledge, was that there was a Carlisle Kid, named Nah-deiz-az, who had achieved notoriety for his violent refusal to submit to White authority in some real estate conflicts.[164]

As Pratt's own writings make clear, Carlisle's great selling point to parents who considered entrusting their children to the school was that their education would aid them in protecting the tribe from White bamboozlers and from the government's deceptions. One father wrote to his child in 1882, "I want you to stay [at Carlisle], so that you may be well educated and fit for any position your tribe may call you."[165] Not all students felt that this was Carlisle's prime purpose; some expressed their discontent with Carlisle in published letters and asked or implied that they would like to go home.[166]

Many students, in their published Carlisle writings, used their insights into rhetoric, their grasp of sarcasm and irony, and their knowledge of history for the defense of Natives. At the core of the "Indian problem," as several students saw it, was an unscrupulous White civilization bewitched by possessive individualism. After recounting the wars and enslavement imported by the early Spanish imperialists, and the nineteenth century's confinement of tribes on reservations, Ellis B. Childers (Creek) explained that the Indians were not savage, they were just logical in "showing cruelty and revenge for these wrongs." In answering why Whites hated "Indians," Henry Kendall's (Pueblo) response was concise and historical: they "want to get every portion of the land that is owned by the Indians." The anonymous "A Bit of History" (1891) imagined Benjamin Franklin not as a worker and self-made individualist but a strategist of "Indian" clearance: Franklin, the author claimed, was the first White man (nine years before William Penn's grandson) to introduce a bounty for Native scalps. A piece by a White author on the rhetoric of the "Indian problem" added its sarcasm to these historical critiques: "We rob [the Indians], we shoot them, we drive them from their home, . . . we starve them; we murder their women and children; and then we talk about 'the Indian Problem.' Let us cease robbing and murdering; and perhaps we may discover that there is no problem about it." In what could be taken both as a parody of Carlisle's didactic teacher-students dialogues and as a criticism of bureaucrats' dismissals of treaties as legal fictions, *The Red Man* reprinted a fictional conversation between two boys who decided to play "Indian" in 1891, the year following the Wounded Knee massacre of several hundred unarmed Sioux. The boy who plays "pale face" to his companion's "Indian" spells out the rules: "I'll make a new treaty with you that I'll eat your apple. . . . If you don't do the way I say you'll be a hostile . . . and I'll blow you full o' holes."[167]

The theme that America was a rigged game in which Natives got less than fair play surfaced occasionally in Carlisle's newspapers. "How is an Indian to become a civilized individual man if he has no individual civilized chances?," one author wondered. An account of the newspaper coverage of two Yale men who encountered one another in an Omaha jail and gave "the old time Yale yells" commented, "Had these been graduates of Carlisle or any other prominent Indian school a double headed column would hardly have been sufficient to inform the public of the fact." Sometimes authors perceived the forces Natives were up against not only in racial but in class and economic terms: "The words LABOR and CAPITAL are seen together in the newspapers almost every day," one article observed in 1886. "CAPITAL means RICH MEN who employ the working men. . . . Labor wants more money and fewer hours work. Capital refuses to give either."[168]

The irony and sarcasm in some of the pieces students wrote for Carlisle's publications also may have been present in the school's many debates, where the speaker's tone and nuance would have been crucial in producing meaning. In 1886, for example, Carlisle staged a debate among its own students on the subject "Resolved, That the Indian Should Be Exterminated." If at first some of the arguments in favor of extermination only sound like Carlisle's ventriloquism at work, a more careful reading reveals a surfeit of hyperbole—hyperbole suggesting the possibility that students may have been *performing*, parodying not parroting, the Carlisle line. "The red man is not to remain an Indian because he is born an Indian: no more so, than a man who is born in *sin*, should remain a sinner," Chester Cornelious (Oneida) pleaded, with the ostensible zeal of the converted. "I have so strong a conviction that the '*Indian*' must be exterminated in order that we might be successful in civilizing him, that I am even in favor of exterminating the thoughts that prefer to preserve the Indian." Stacy Matlack (Pawnee) introduced the technology-as-progress argument to maintain that Indians should be eliminated because they have accomplished nothing "that will be useful to the white race." Joel Tyndall (Omaha), repeating Pratt's ruthless sink-or-swim position (perhaps with a twist of satire), insisted: "If he can't make his living, let him starve. . . . We cannot afford to raise any more wild Indians."[169] Taken at face value some of these positions may have flattered some Whites who heard or read them. Yet it must be remembered that many students were committed to developing skills, such as taking a variety of positions in a debate, that they knew they would use later on behalf of their tribes.[170]

The debaters' arguments against extermination brought one particularly salient historical point to the foreground, an issue that Carlisle's students knew well was a serious one for Whites: the sacredness of property and possession. "Mr. President," said Kish Hawkins (Cheyenne), with evident sarcasm, "is it possible, that you are to exterminate the race whose property is making you above the other nations?" Henry Kendall contested the technology-as-progress argument for extermination by noting that not all Whites were inventors and inquired whether they merited extermination. Kendall, like Hawkins, played the property angle: "I for one would not at any rate use my means to destroy a race, and the race that own [*sic*] the soil where this prosperous Government stands."[171] The legalized theft of Native property, in other words, did not mean that Natives in their own eyes no longer owned the land that had been taken from them.

The debates hint at one of the most strategic lessons students may have absorbed at Carlisle: *performance*. Students learned to play two key roles: how to act the White imagination of "Indian" and the role of White "individual." Some articles discuss performance skills. *The Red Man* reprinted an interview with a half-Creek, Miss Severs, who was studying at the New England Conservatory of Music. The interviewer notes that only her square jaw might distinguish her from a dark-complexioned White. Severs was not only an accomplished musician, she was expert at negotiating and, for her amusement, performing White stereotypes of Indianness: "Come confess that you expected to find a Reservation Indian in a blanket! . . . Sometimes, I can't resist the temptation to 'bluff' people and answer their questions in the way they evidently expect to be answered." She adds, mischievously and sarcastically, "It seems a shame to shatter their cherished illusions about us."[172]

Carlisle's Indianizing of its students is manifest in two photographs from Pratt's collection. The first is of a young "Indian" posing on a horse in full headdress with one of the Carlisle buildings as a backdrop (figure 6). The occasion on which this undated photograph was taken is unclear, perhaps some special celebration at Carlisle. Nevertheless, the fact that such a pose and costume would even be allowed or encouraged may complicate one's notion of life and education at Carlisle. The photograph evokes an actor in a Wild West show.

What makes this photograph so curious is that Pratt continually reviled Buffalo Bill's "show business" use—or exploitation—of Natives. In 1886 *The Indian Helper* contrasted playing "savage" in the theater with the real work that builds character and individuality: "We are sorry to hear that some of the Pawnees have joined Buffalo Bill's Show, as in such an exhibition the Indians are made to show their worst savage characters. . . . Mr. Man-on-the-band-stand wants the Indians to make friends for themselves, and let people see what Indians can do in the way of *work*, and in things higher than shooting and riding swift horses and scalping people, and killing buffalo." Buffalo Bill nostalgically romanticized "Indian" resistance to "civilization" that is martial and inevitably ineffective. Whereas Pratt advocated American resistance to the tribe that takes the form of labor, "individuality," and conformity to "civilization." A couple of years later *The Red Man* intoned: "Buffalo Bill, by running a show of one hundred Indians dressed in paint and

feathers, has taken more gate money in London, England, *within the
year*, than the total sum allowed *this year* by the Government, combined
with all missionary and charitable societies and individuals, for the
education of all the Indian youth in the United States."[173] Yet Pratt, who
staged war dances, buffalo hunts, and battles for the crowds at Fort
Marion, boasted, "Had I been so minded I could have handled the Indians more wisely and out 'Buffalo Billed' Mr. Cody in his line."[174]

Notwithstanding such criticisms, the multidimensional Pratt invited
Buffalo Bill Cody and his Wild West Show to perform at Carlisle in 1898.
The anonymous *Red Man* report of the event noted condescendingly
that students "were privileged to witness the best exhibition in existence of some of the ruder manners and customs of the people of the
western frontier in the fifties and sixties." Still, with a fussy businesslike
superiority, the reporter acknowledged that "we are yet able to recognize
and credit success and good management in whatever direction" and
complimented "the admirable discipline of Col. Cody's army of per-
formers and employees, and especially of the Indians." Romanticizing
the ever-handy discourse of inevitability, the author continued: "Although [Cody's] duties as a scout had made it necessary to lead troops
against the Indians he never did it without regret, knowing that the
Indian was always in the right." Despite their contrary training of "Indians," Captain Pratt and Colonel Cody, who "have known each other
for many years," "remain friends agreeing to differ on the one point of
the effect of the show upon the growing Indian and the public."[175]

The other photograph from Pratt's collection that merits examination
is of the student cast of Seymour S. Tibbals's and Harry C. Eldridge's
comic operetta, *The Captain at Plymouth* (1908–1909), which was performed for three evenings to a sold-out audience of a thousand during
Carlisle's 1909 graduation (figure 7). Based in part on Henry Wadsworth
Longfellow's poem "The Courtship of Miles Standish" (1856), this odd
and campy musical "history" of New England colonization is laced with
seemingly satirical throwaway lines that reference the rise of corporate
and consumer America. Standish, an imperialist buffoon, voices the
prescient notion that the Pilgrims are conquering America to prepare the
way for John D. Rockefeller's Standard Oil and looks forward to having
his name adorn cigars.[176] Students are costumed not only as Pilgrims
and soldiers but as "Indians," complete with paints, beads, buckskins,
and headdresses. The painted warrior-in-headdress sitting cross-legged
in the front row on the right seems distinctly unhappy about his "Indian" performance in a play that appears to mock founding American
myths—without seriously challenging them—for the purposes of enter-

6. "Indian" student in headdress on horse at Carlisle, photographed by John Nicholas Choate, Yale Collection of Western Americana, Beinecke Rare Book and Manuscript Library

7. Cast of *The Captain at Plymouth,* 1909 graduation performance, Yale Collection of Western Americana, Beinecke Rare Book and Manuscript Library

tainment. One of the many intriguing points to be made about this photograph is that it makes obvious Carlisle's schooling of students in role playing, the enactment of White "individuals" and of White images of "Indians." Five years after Pratt left Carlisle, Indianizing and individualizing are exhibited as theatrical undertakings not to everyone's liking. One wonders how Pratt read the photograph and if some of the students, such as the glum headdressed brave, read it the same way.

Students did not need exposure to Buffalo Bill or to Carlisle's theatricals and pageants to be aware that White fabrications of Indianness were used in a variety of bizarre ways to sell products, including literature. In 1901 one *Red Man and Helper* critic lamented the "Indian" stereotypes that cluttered Charles Eugene Banks's novel *A Child of the Sun* (1900): "The high-flown language is that of the Indian warrior of fiction." And in 1904 that same publication reprinted a piece from the *Arizona Republican* that takes to task the commercial interchangeability of "Indians." The object of critique is a photograph of "a beautiful Apache maiden . . . on one of the opening pages of the 'Home of the Original Beadworker' " in a Bentham Indian Trading Company book on Apache beadwork. The photograph already had a commercial past: "the first wide circulation of the 'Home of the Beadworker' was in a similar publication called 'The Papoose,' written by Tom Barnes . . . where the same picture did duty as the 'Pima Maker at Home.' The Apache maid on the cover is in reality a Canadian Indian girl and in the picture she wears a Sioux apron and Cheyenne moccasins, while at her right stands a Zulu shield and at her left a Pima basket."[177]

Some Carlisle students may have been quite cognizant that conventions of Indianness and Whiteness could be performed for purposes other than the ones that those who commanded the performance had in mind. "If the Indians wish to get up equal with the white man they must become as strong and wise as the white man," one writer advised in *The Indian Helper.* "The only way the Indian can do this is to live with the white people and try to find out their secrets of success."[178] Success could mean—learn their game, beat them, *outperform* them.

This was exactly what Carlisle students did on the football field beginning in the mid-1890s. Carlisle's football team, drawn from relatively few potential players (about 250), rose to national prominence in its first well-publicized full season, 1896.[179] It was essentially a traveling team, often drawing crowds of 15,000 (and thus lacked the vital presence of student-body support).[180] One of its most celebrated contests, in which Carlisle won extraordinary sympathy and praise, was its controversial loss to Yale (which in this era generally fielded the best team in the country). The game was lost (12–6) on what almost every newspaper and observer viewed as an egregiously incorrect call by a referee. The *Yale Daily News* complimented Carlisle's "hard tackling" and "strong interference," glossed over the disputed touchdown, and eschewed any melodramatic reference to the Carlisle players as "Indians."[181]

Professional reporters, however, played up the symbolic historical and ideological significance of what was being dramatized on the field. "Decidedly, the red-skinned young gentlemen from Carlisle had the better of the contest," the *New York Sun* affirmed. "But in the end the struggle was only a reduplication of all the contests between white men and Indians that have gone before it. For at the last the white man stole from the Indian. . . . As the Indians have always done, they protested against the injustice of the whites, vigorously at first, but with decreasing energy and vehemence. And at last, as all their race have done, they patiently submitted to the outrage." This reading, suffused with inevitability discourse and racial stereotypes, was further dramatized in the coverage of Carlisle's loss to Harvard shortly after: "How old Geronimo would have enjoyed it!," the *New York Journal* reporter fantasized: "The point of view of the warriors was terse but plain: 'They had stolen a continent from us, a wide, wide continent which was ours, and lately they have stolen various touchdowns that were also ours. . . . Let us, then, brothers, be revenged.'"[182] Even Stephen Crane's piece on the Carlisle-Harvard game evoked the "gallant" but failed red retribution and featured five drawings of "Carlisle players, three in loincloths, two completely naked."[183] Football, when Carlisle competed, was seen as being about real estate and revenge—a Wild East show in which the "Indians," if they could transcend their evolutionary limitations, might reverse history and conquer.

The racial warfare theme had several dimensions and sold big. The *Boston Globe* effused that Harvard's last stand was more successful than Custer's. It allegorized that match as one between "500 years of education" and "centuries of fire and sun worship." The *Boston Herald*, as so many other papers would in the early years, conceded the physical prowess of the "Indians" but questioned their capacity to grasp the "scientific" fine points of the game: "[The Indians] were far and away the superiors of Harvard in strength and endurance; they knew the game fairly well, but were lacking in its scientific development. If they but knew how to use their natural strength to best advantage, no team in the country could hold them." Another newspaper asked, "Was it the degeneracy of their race and the enervating influence of civilization that handicapped them, or was it simply the superior skill of their adversaries? Probably the latter."[184] What might Carlisle students have learned from reading many of these reports, which were reprinted in the school's newspapers? Would they have felt overwhelmed? Or would they have responded with a sharpened irony and sarcasm?

Football became critical to Pratt: he wanted to show the White world that his "Indians" could be well managed and keen to compete within the bounds of American rules. The Carlisle players earned high marks for this from the press. One review of the Yale game was typical of many commentaries: it marveled at both the players' ability to tackle and at their demeanor ("like men of breeding") and "politeness." But the Natives' manners and self-control, their traditional stoicism, was also branded as their drawback: they were too slow to be "roused"; they did not "dissemble" their intentions well enough; they were too gentlemanly.[185]

Carlisle's "Indians" may have dissembled, more than reporters or spectators ever suspected, on and off the field. The 1902 Carlisle football banquet assumed a patently theatrical "Indian" style to acclaim the team's major victories: "Attached to two pillars were effigies, made of tackling dummies with football heads and nose protectors for probasses. On the sweater of one was a big 'C' and Cornell colors, on the other the Pennsylvania colors. Around their feet were placed fagots ready for the match. On the opposite pillars were their scalps which had been taken by the Carlisle team, and considered the greatest trophies of the year."[186] Cornell and Penn were the students' imaginary prisoners of war. Carlisle's team, which may have had more "Indian" stereotypes thrown at them than tackles, turned the "Indian" warfare theme to its ideological advantage: in the school's sportive revels the students staged tribalism not individualism, resistance not assimilation.

One thing that football provided for the players was the opportunity to establish their status in something fairly close to traditional ways— through warfare. As the nineteenth century progressed and warfare became more frequent for many tribes, the men who became leaders within their tribes, particularly in the West and on the Plains, were usually those who demonstrated skill and bravery in warfare, often in conflict with Whites and with other tribes. Eventually, as the U.S. invasion took hold, generational tension resulted when the male youth were counseled by their elders to adapt to new circumstances and restrain themselves from trying to establish social and spiritual distinction through the traditional way—fighting.[187] To some extent, Carlisle football restored warfare as a path to social prestige. Where Pratt saw future clerks and industrial workers running on the football field like well-managed gentlemen not too distinguishable from White college students, the students themselves, as the Cornell-Penn war celebrations suggest, may have seen young warriors. Pratt's overbearing emphasis on inculcating a military style of "individuality"—complete with uniform, and, for some, a football uniform—may have without his knowledge undergone student translation into traditional endeavors to establish tribal-based distinction. Three years after Pratt stepped down, Carlisle's newspaper rejoiced: "Indians Scalp Harvard—The 'Big Four' now the 'Big Five.'" Many Whites also perceived Native athletes not simply as competitors but as "Indian" players on a mission—and in part this was their draw.[188]

In 1898 Dennison Wheelock, the school's celebrated Oneida bandleader, gave a compelling speech in which he explained why football should not be abolished at Carlisle, despite the risk of injury. Years before, as a young Carlisle student, Wheelock had published a piece (quoted above) on the futility of speaking "Indian" languages. But in 1898 he ruminated critically on the bloody history of Native-White encounters: "Long ago, it was said that what the Indian could not understand was the greed, the grasping selfishness of the white man in this country, and when the Indian learned that his habitation and the hills he so dearly loved were being invaded, he justly cried, 'There is eternal war between me and thee.' And when he resisted, who will say that he did not do right? Who will say that he would not have done the same?" It is within this context of imperialism and capitalist possessiveness that football took on symbolic significance for Wheelock, the team, and the school. Indeed, the playing of football was synonymous with how at least some of the students read their mission at Carlisle: "Today the Indian is beyond the Mississippi. The only way I see how he may reoccupy the lands that once were his, is through football, and as football takes brains, takes energy, proves whether civilization can be understood by the Indian or not, we are willing to perpetuate it."[189] Wheelock invoked "civilization," but mainly to suggest that football—"civilized" competition—was a metaphor for learning how to beat—to outclass—the Whites at their own game of possession.

For Wheelock, and no doubt for others at Carlisle, football and Carlisle were about learning how to reclaim yardage—symbolically, their land.[190] Moreover, Carlisle football was about working together, not just individually, so as to avoid being overrun by Whites. If a specific model of individuality was imposed on Natives at Carlisle, particular images of Indianness were thrown at them by the culture. The challenge they faced was to try to turn both of these largely White abstractions, individuality and Indianness, to their advantage.

Michael Oriard, a perceptive historian of American sports, quotes from one contemporary magazine's account of a dramatic scene in which a lone Harvard player had to prevent a Carlisle running back from making a crucial touchdown in 1906. After the "famous [Harvard] sprinter" succeeded in making this tackle ("the stands rocked with relief"), "the fair-haired representative of New England, while still clasping the dark-skinned descendant of American savagery, felt something fumbling, and presently became aware, at the bottom of the heap there, that his right hand was being shaken. 'Good tackle,' muttered the Indian." In the reporter's narrative, Oriard observes, "the Carlisle ballcarrier represented his race as a model sportsman, but more: an honorable, uncomplaining, and wholly reconciled loser in a fair fight, the overt stake a football game, but the implicit one a continent."[191]

What falls outside the scope of Oriard's astute analysis is the complexity of Carlisle: the players did not behave at the Cornell-Penn war banquet as gentlemanly losers who accepted the apparent inevitability of being tackled by so-called civilization, grinning obsequiously at "the bottom of the heap." The students were more strategic; their response to football was more artful; and what actually went on in the day-to-day learning and life at Carlisle was more multidimensional. As Wheelock's battle speech suggests, these students wanted to win big and fully appreciated the social symbolism and publicity of winning, as players on and off the theatrical field of the gridiron. The Cornell-Penn evening demonstrates that they were quite eager in their official school celebrations to *Indianize* and *tribalize* these victories (scalps and all), and that they could adapt the props of the Wild West show to their own ends. Pratt, well aware of the Indianized theatricality of their victory celebrations, wanted them to win too and on a stage where Americans could see what they and he had done.

Pratt's Carlisle (1879–1904): Class, Race, Warfare

In 1904 the army and the Interior Department forced Pratt to step down because of his splenetic attacks on the BIA. The Pratt who charged in 1892 that "Indians" "occupy so much more space than they are entitled to either by numbers or worth" had a few years before unsuccessfully headed a government commission established to persuade the Sioux to "individualize" their lands: enraged at their persistent resistance, he proposed that allotment be forced on them.[192] He succeeded in getting permission to administer corporal punishment even when it was officially (though not in practice) prohibited in other boarding schools.[193] Yet evidence suggests that many of Carlisle's students valued this same unbending soldier. Although Pratt merits a complex analysis, I can only broach a few significant historical perspectives here. I will begin by raising the issue: *why* was Pratt the stalwart *Indian exterminator* so respected by numerous Carlisle students for a quarter of a century and by former students long after he retired?

Clues to Pratt's popularity with some may be found in his speech after the football victory over Cornell in 1902. He hailed Carlisle's win as a "demonstration of equality": "If in addition to strength we exhibit equal skill and equal knowledge in even such a thing as football, which is supposed to be for universities especially; if we show we have the skill that can meet and overcome a university like Cornell, then we have additional ground for claiming equality." Pratt, with his characteristic lack of humility, or insufficiency of middle-class mock humility, was claiming superiority for *his* institution. His pronouns—*we, our*—suggest that he identified with the "Indians." At the same time Pratt took advantage of his audience's elation to hammer home his extermination propaganda and to homogenize their putative "Indian" identity: "WE DON'T want to hold onto anything INDIAN."

On some level both Pratt and his staff must have known that this ethnoracial, cultural, familial, and historical erasure was impossible and that the students derived fighting strength from playing "Indian" in their own ways. Pratt genuinely wanted to, and wanted his "Indians" to, pommel what became the Ivy League. He promised his students that if they would "thrash the biggest team in the country" he would hire "the best coach"—he did, Glenn "Pop" Warner—"no matter what it costs."[194] Pratt consistently presented himself as a fighter and pledged that he was fighting for them.[195] As Lance, the penetrating Carlisle teacher in Sparhawk's *Chronicle of Conquest*, observes, "Carlisle is, in a way, the army too, and doesn't believe in putting down fighting qualities" (189).

Throughout his life Pratt received letters from some of his former students and Carlisle's Native teachers and employees that testified to his pugilistic charisma. Some of them endearingly called him "father" or "school-father," one signed off "school-daughter."[196] Others acknowledged how much they identified not just with "civilization" or individualism but with him. Wheelock, who had become an attorney and was gathering support to make a (futile) political bid to become BIA commissioner in 1920, wondered "whether [Pratt's] teaching has so permeated [him] that if appointed Commissioner the administration of that office

will be as if Gen. Pratt was Commissioner."[197] Gansworth, who worked
for a time under Pratt as a Carlisle assistant disciplinarian and procurer
of students in the West, thanked Pratt for systematically energizing and
agitating the students, for shaping pupils who were "not content with
anything and everything."[198] Charles Eastman called his tenure a "wonderful success." In 1935, during John Collier's Indian New Deal, Gertrude Bonnin cast Pratt as the Natives' Moses who opposed the BIA:
"General Pratt would have led [the Indians] out of the desert!"[199]

Occasionally former students or their Native associates sought Pratt's
practical assistance in finding them employment, in wielding his political influence on their behalf, in providing publicity for their cause with
his writing or public presence, or in smoothing the way for their efforts
to win backing from wealthy men like John Wanamaker. Some of these
letters were adorned with flattery.[200] But when Natives wrote these sorts
of letters it was because they knew that Pratt had long distinguished
himself as someone who in his own intractable ideological way had
actively tried to help "Indians" and cared about their future. Whether or
not all of these former students or their associates agreed with everything Pratt did or said, they did see themselves as being engaged in
ongoing political, economic, and cultural struggles, and he was, in their
minds, a powerful general.

Paradoxically, Pratt may have been more effective at extending the
government's influence over Native self-image, value, and incentive
because he punctured some of the government's flagrant hypocrisies.
Pratt's skirmishes with the government, often reported in the school
newspapers, repeatedly confirmed for himself and his students that Carlisle was a training ground for battle. When the first students arrived at
Carlisle, Pratt found that his charges were handicapped with a shock-
ingly meagre food allowance and shoddy clothing. He wrote directly to
the Secretary of the Interior to shame those responsible for the mess and
to rectify matters. When the BIA gave him only two-thirds of the funds he
needed to build a hospital for the students, Pratt secured the rest of the
money through private contributions. Since he wanted to make Indians
competitive in the marketplace, he had no hesitation about telling his
superiors that three years of schooling was woefully inadequate, as it
would be for White children. Indeed, many of Carlisle's students could
not speak English on their arrival.[201] In 1892 Commissioner Morgan
acknowledged to Pratt that he had negotiated "adverse influences at
every step of the way."[202] For many years Pratt pounded out the message
that Natives were "reservated and Bureauized."[203]

As hegemonic as Pratt was in his insistence on assimilation, he also assailed the hegemony that supported the BIA, reservation internment camps, and, for that matter, segregated Indian schools.[204] He saw himself not as a radical advocate of integration but as a loyal American. Early in his army career he found himself commanding, and objecting to the formation of, army companies "composed entirely by colored men, officered by white officers." Such organizations were a "violation" of "the Constitution" and provided "warrant for all the 'Jim Crow' car and other harsh enactments of States and communities in denial of equal rights to the colored race." He realized that the government was not ready to commit to a color-blind and race-blind digestion of all racial and ethnic groups. Pratt favored neither a multiracial nor multicultural concept of America. True Americans, he believed, were nonracial and proindividual. Thus he opposed economic, social, political, and bureaucratic forces that gained in power, wealth, or prestige by producing hierarchical and often exploitative forms of racialized difference.

Of course, he did subscribe to the production, or what he would consider the cultural "expression," of gender difference, but he supported the idea that women could gain higher education and enter the professions. Pratt also composed many anti-Catholic statements brimming with invective (he particularly despised Catholic missionaries who countenanced the perpetuation of Native cultures and languages).[205] While he espoused the U.S. digestion of African Americans as well as Natives, he sometimes considered the former group less "noble" and evolved.[206] Yet in general Pratt paraded himself as a diversity abolitionist: "Why compel [Natives] to carry two loads, to become civilized and at the same time to remain uncivilized? I inherit the blood of several races, but the only thing of real value to me is my Americanism." He defended an incorporation management that did not utilize diversity management. "Indians" should be incorporated as "individuals," he pressed, "incorporated in the nation."[207]

What may have accounted for some students' identification with Pratt in part was Pratt's partial class identification with them.[208] No West Pointer either in educational pedigree or gentlemanly polish, Pratt adumbrated four goals for Carlisle, listed "in their order of value": to teach "usable" English; to instruct students in "civilized" industry; to incite treason to the tribe and foster Natives' eagerness to enter civilization; and last on his list was what he himself had relatively scarce acquaintance with, to disseminate "knowledge of books, or education so-called."[209] He may well have enjoyed the tendency of sports reporters to misrepresent Carlisle as the great Indian college; he made sure that his well-groomed and orderly players looked the part. As mentioned, when officials hinted that Carlisle might be expanded as a college Pratt rejected the idea because he thought "Indians" should not be segregated from civilized Whites. But Pratt also may have paused to consider the improbability of his being allowed to remain as a grammar school-educated head of a college. Notwithstanding his rhetoric about equality, Pratt knew well that Yale and Harvard were educational institutions that by and large preserved, shaped, and legitimated class hierarchy in America's democracy. He took pride when his dispossessed "Indians" took possession of the ball and the field.[210]

Pratt exulted in lobbying in Washington, arguing with congressmen and bureaucrats, and being perceived as a man of inflexible integrity who would not flinch at calling foul play no matter who was implicated. Several of his letters to high-level bureaucrats, such as BIA Commissioner Hayt and Secretary of the Interior Schurz, were imperious. "Let us have no division!" Merrill Gates, the reformer, beseeched Pratt. "We love you too well, and the work is too important."[211] Commissioner Morgan hinted that Pratt had let his uncompromising ego become too self-important: "I have thought you might do the cause of Indian education some harm . . . by condemning so utterly other methods than those which you recommend."[212]

Still, Pratt was more ideologically complex than some of his rhetoric suggests. In 1891 that curious propagandist for Americanism, possessive individualism, and ownership, bragged, "I never owned an acre of land, and I never expect to own one."[213] He saw himself as serving causes, not lining his wallet or his ego. However, Pratt's autobiography and correspondence also show that, like Booker T. Washington, he relished the prestige of getting money, attention, and favors from rich men like John Wanamaker or Russell Sage—on behalf of Carlisle.[214]

While Pratt did his best to compel students to "individualize" themselves through military uniformity, he made it (loud and) clear to the BIA that *he* was not uniform—*he* was too individualistic to be their run-of-the-mill team player. Pratt had his supporters, much to one commentator's regret: "Every Commissioner and Secretary has been terrorized by Pratt on the theory that to dismiss him would be to call down upon the administration a storm of abuse from well-meaning but misguided champions of Carlisle."[215] But the principled and truculent superintendent made at least as many enemies. His students saw him take risks in his denunciations of Congress for not spending the money on Indian education that treaties had allocated and his relentless condemnations of the BIA, which sponsored tribalism, he claimed, solely to perpetuate the bureau's political existence. Shortly before his dismissal in 1904,

The Red Man and Helper reprinted a piece from the *New York Sun* reporting that the BIA had lost "patience" and wanted "to secure Col. Pratt's scalp."[216] This risk taking seemed to incite rather than deter him. To a degree Pratt encouraged his students to envision the state as their collective main problem while viewing capitalism, which supposedly rewarded a self-help work ethic, as their individual solution.

Some of Pratt's reckless haughtiness in the political arena may have been a histrionic effort on his part to assert what he tried to inculcate in the Carlisle boys—"manliness." He had to suffer military gossip that he remained in his Carlisle post to evade active military service. A photograph of an overweight Pratt sitting almost grumpily on his horse Kiowa in 1898 seems to convey the school superintendent's wish to take hold of the military reins (figure 8). When the Spanish-American war broke out he offered to command Native troops against the Spanish.[217] Pratt's angry, defensive, and agonizing correspondence with General H. C. Corbin and others in 1903 not only records his threat to resign as superintendent if he was not promoted, it exhibits his boast that Carlisle is really a "semi-military" organization and that he is better qualified than anyone to do what he most desires—lead a company of between 200 and 250 Carlisle students and 1,000 former students and graduates.[218] "If the government seemed to me to intend to give the Indian a fair chance I should be willing to make sacrifices to stay and help," Pratt wrote BIA Commissioner William A. Jones in 1903. "As the contrary is the case I shall not regret a change."[219]

Pratt's naiveté about American equality and his underestimation of deep-seated White racism may have misled some of his students who came to believe that, as Pratt assured them, "Equal ability can always take care of equal rights."[220] He was too hopeful that if he could make his students perform like "individuals," their identification with individualism and Americanism would be embraced by Americans as a sign of equality—that "individuality" and nationality would overshadow the categories of race and class. But numerous Carlisle students, equipped with three-year educations that commenced with instruction in the English language, remained economically and socially unaccepted, at least as equals, by dominant White American culture.[221] Pratt had many indications that the government had no intention of investing in educational schemes designed to make large numbers of "Indians" truly competitive with Whites.

W. E. B. Du Bois sought to puncture some of this stubborn naïveté when he responded to a letter Pratt wrote him in 1916: "I fail to see why we could assume on the part of the Republican candidate any greater

8. Pratt in military regalia on horse, Yale Collection of Western Americana, Beinecke Rare Book and Manuscript Library

honesty than on the part of the Democratic candidate. Mr. Wilson promised justice to the colored people and broke his word; Mr. Hughes has not even promised this, except in very vague and general statements." Du Bois went on to explain that the production of racial differences was a structural feature of the U.S. system and that this could not be glossed over with rhetoric of democracy, equality, and citizenship: "It is not true that the colored people must simply demand the same protection that other citizens have. They have got to demand greater protection, and very positive action on the part of the executive government because their rights have so long been denied."[222] He rejected an Americanization that asked Americans of color to deny systemic racial exploitation and oppression.

Yet Pratt's naiveté could itself be a form of strategic role playing. He knew, for example, that racial prejudice was far too pervasive for "Indians" to be enlisted in outing programs out West. The school father, like Twain's Connecticut Yankee, could be something of a con man. His con was most manifest, perhaps, when he was recruiting students for Carlisle and reassured Native parents that educated children would better help the tribe and its tricky dealings with businesses and Washington.[223] This crafty would-be Pygmalion of "Indians" neglected to say that his school was founded not just to make students literate but to make them "individuals" who would cast themselves as Davids fighting the Goliaths of their tribe. Pratt often made radical acknowledgments of the injustices done to Indians: "The Indians were simply put in our way, to be ejected whenever our covetous people wanted the land which was the Indian's home." However, he would typically conclude that the "Indians" had no other recourse than to "bow to the inevitable."[224] The fact that land theft, massacres, and systematic starvation seemed inevitable to Pratt and others did not make these injustices less unjust, but it may have made them somewhat less worrisome because the inevitable demands adaptation (agreement to be digested and resurrected).

Pratt never let up. His dream for Natives was almost a parody of the idea of self-possession, a self-possession possessed by allegiance to national identity, capitalist forms of labor, sentimentalized gender roles, middle-class domestic values, dominant ideologies of progress and of what counts as history: "The thing for you to think about all the time is to be a complete individual. Don't lean on anybody else! . . . [I am] hoping that before I pass away it will come about that there are no Indian schools in this country—that every Indian is his own man and her own woman." Pratt came of age in the era of military Indian removal. On one level, Carlisle was his cultural and industrial version of governmental Indian removal. Yet on another level, the school itself signified, and thus perpetuated, the category "Indian"—a "school for Indians." On his deathbed he wept because "still there did not seem to be any hope for the red man." His daughter suggested that perhaps "God has another and a better plan" for these "red men." Pratt retorted, before expiring, "There is no better plan."[225]

Carlisle, Consumer Culture, and Loaded
Cultural Relativism (1904–1918)

Captain W. A. Mercer assumed his post as Carlisle's superintendent in July 1904 and served until January 1908. He was succeeded by Moses Friedman, an educator who specialized in industrial arts. Under their administrations the school went through some major ideological changes. In 1913 student complaints brought about a Department of the Interior investigation and shortly after a congressional committee investigation. Friedman's references to the students as "savages," his apparent allowance of brutal corporal punishment, his approval of a poor diet for the students, and his preferential treatment of athletes, who it was said received gifts and better food as well as insults and kicks from Coach Warner, led to his dismissal. He was replaced by Oscar Lipps, who presided over the school until 1916. John Francis Jr. ran the school until 1918, when it closed its doors forever, ostensibly because the army needed to use it as a hospital.[226]

In the new Carlisle, *The Indian Helper*, which Pratt had merged with *The Red Man*, was replaced by *The Arrow*. And the post-Pratt version of *The Red Man*, at first retitled *The Indian Craftsman*, was published in a magazine of essay format for supporters of Carlisle as well as for the students themselves. While the Carlisle publications in the Pratt era featured Pratt's writings, his annual reports, and accounts of his activities, comparatively little was written about the superintendents who succeeded Pratt. There was still a great emphasis on character building, individualizing, self-support independent of government support, and domestic femininity, but often the tone was less insistent, the didacticism was not so thumpingly repetitious, the criticism of the government and Congress (which threatened to terminate Carlisle in 1908) was judicious, and the advice about control and success was more general.[227] In some respects *The Arrow* was more "assimilated" than the earlier Pratt-sponsored publications that preached assimilation.

If the messages sent by Carlisle's publications in the Pratt era were not monolithic, as I have argued, those sent in the phase that followed were even less so. For all its emphasis on industrious individualism, *The Arrow* could reprint an article from *Success* magazine that was critical of American "success at a pace that kills"—it induces a "strain that ruins thinking faculties" and a frenzy "which crushes out all the finer and nobler instincts." The author came out on behalf of genuine "self-culture," maintaining that "repose, harmony and leisure are necessary for real growth, for higher attainment."[228] Such advice to Native youth would only have ignited Pratt's wrath.

For Pratt was an orthodox product of the nineteenth century's producer culture values: the work ethos, character, frugality, self-denial. But the new Carlisle, beginning with the regime of 1904, showed signs of having entered the twentieth century's consumer culture—where appearance, style, image, subjectivity (increasingly called personality), and consumption-oriented leisure (higher attainment defined as the purchase of commodities) were becoming overt as American values (more on this transition in chapter 3). In its earliest issues *The Arrow* included advertisements for photography supplies in the town of Carlisle and for photographs of Carlisle. By the second decade of the new century, *The Red Man* featured ads for the school's own products sold by its "Indian" souvenir shop: its Leupp Art Studio carried Navajo blankets (authentic, not machine-made), pottery, beadwork, basketwork, silverwork, reed work, weaving, and of course photographs of Carlisle, and published a catalogue for twenty-five cents. In 1914 Carlisle's alumni organization advertised "a splendid assortment of beautiful Carlisle pennants, pillow tops, etc., of felt, in exclusive design, executed in the school colors of red and gold; also assorted pins, watch fobs, cuff links, hat pins, etc. designed especially for the Carlisle Indian School."[229]

The stress was on redesigning, aestheticizing, and commodifying Indianness—something Pratt usually frowned on in his official kill-the-Indian statements. This "Indian" design business was in sync with the new Carlisle's qualified support for Native culture, identity, and individuality. Articles like "Native Art of the North American Indian" (1904) in *The Arrow* celebrated the artistry of traditional embroidery, beadwork, basketwork, carving, and blankets.[230] A 1916 *Red Man* piece, which disclosed a certain admiration for Native obliviousness to White culture, noted that Natives had by and large shunned White dances, whereas their "desire to shake [their] feet," to dance in their own tribal ways, remained strong. Many student drawings, designs, and borders encasing photographs of the school in the new Carlisle publications depicted the Native capacity to be independent of or resist Whites. Thus an *Arrow* photograph of retiring Superintendent Mercer was graced with borders of Native designs.[231] And in *The Red Man* of 1913 there is a large silhouette of a brave on his horse shooting two cowboys with his rifle: it provides a visual climax for an article in which the lawyer Robert Yellowtail (Crow) argues that Natives should become physicians and attorneys to better defend their tribe, not just themselves.[232] A *Red Man* piece in 1910 regretted that Native students had been trained to "exterminate" their cultural traditions and "imitate" Whiteness (another dig at Pratt). Skill in Native arts opened the door to "decorative" work for the "Indian," who is naturally "an artist-artisan and not a mechanic, a farmer, or a trader." Yet in that same essay the author, a White expert on industrial arts, did not assign the "Indians"—whom he viewed as still "primitive," preindustrial, and culturally static—the artistic capacity to create what he deemed "higher" art.[233]

The new governmental move toward cultural relativism, at times a stilted and even insidious cultural relativism, often entailed greater respect for Native "individuality." Consequently the BIA's Emily S. Cook wrote in defense of the retention of Native names (something Pratt opposed) in *The Arrow* in 1904: "Why should Imogen be preferred to the Kiowa name Imuguna, or Jack to Zapko? . . . Let the Indian keep both his personal and his race identity. Individuality is as highly prized by him as by us. . . . We want to EDUCATE the Indian—lead him on, not stamp him out."[234] Such statements seemed to grant students some choice as humans in determining the mix of their cultural identity and implied that Pratt had "individualized" his charges in the cultural mold that he preferred.

The spirited artist Angel DeCora (Winnebago)—who studied at Hampton, Smith College, Drexel Institute, and the Boston Museum of Fine Arts and taught art at Carlisle for nine years—instilled racial pride in her students.[235] "[White] educators made every effort to convince the Indian that any custom or habit that was not familiar to the white man showed savagery and degradation," she wrote. "In looking over my pupils' native design work, I cannot help calling to mind the Indian women, untaught and unhampered by the white man's ideas of art, making beautiful and intricate designs on her pottery, baskets and beaded articles, which show inborn talent. . . . The best designs were made by my artist pupils away from my supervision." DeCora went so far as to claim that her students often exhibited more "pictorial talent," endowed as they were with "accurate eye[s] and skillful hand[s]," than White children. She ascribed to "Indians" a creative and subjective potency based on the blend of their race and traditional tribal practices.[236] DeCora viewed her students not as what Pratt thought of as raw material to be manufactured in "civilization mills," or as former "blank slates" available to be reinscribed with capitalist "individuality," but as active and creative forces in their own right.

One can understand how Pratt's conceptualization of individualizing as treason to the tribe could prompt countervailing Native responses such as DeCora's that Natives as a group possessed some racial instincts superior to those of Whites. But the invocation of these "natural [Indian] instincts" (discourses of instincts would become increasingly common in twentieth-century consumer culture) would also be deployed against Natives—as was the changing ideology of cultural evolution.[237] Howard Fremont Stratton of the Philadelphia School of Industrial Art of the Pennsylvania Museum, for instance, was the "expert" I quoted who saw in "Indians" only primitive "decorative" instincts incapable of developing, without extensive remedial White training, "higher types" of art.[238]

Acknowledgments of (what was taken to be) the Natives' culturally specific "individuality" could work to their disadvantage. In *The Arrow* of 1905, BIA Commissioner Francis E. Leupp—an inveterate opponent of Pratt and a member of President Theodore Roosevelt's unofficial "Cowboy Cabinet" (with Hamlin Garland, Frederick Remington, Owen Wister, George Bird Grinnell, and Charles Lummis)—railed against the Pratt "assumption that [the Indian] is simply a white man with a red skin. . . .

The truth is that the Indian has as distinct an individuality as any type of man who ever lived." He also rejected the idea that the "Indian" possessed definable "racial" instincts. Nonetheless, he went on to spell out the implications of what he considered to be the "Indian's" "individuality": "He will never be judged aright till we learn to measure him by his own standards, as we whites would wish to be measured if some powerful race were to usurp dominion over us."[239] By "his own standards" Leupp had in mind lower standards.[240] What hampers the "Indians," he believed, are "primitive instinct[s] common to all mankind in the lower stages of social development."[241] Therefore the "Indians," still evolutionary infants, were too primitive to be entrusted with so much land and government funds.[242]

What the "Indian" required most from education, Leupp—himself a graduate of Williams College and Columbia Law School—determined, was "the development of character. Learning is a secondary consideration." Why bother teaching the "Indian" how to "extract the cube root of 123456789" when educators need only be concerned that their student "can read the simple English of the local newspaper, can write a short letter, intelligible though maybe mispelled, and knows enough of figures to discover whether the storekeeper's cheating him." "Indian" "individuals," he overgeneralized, would probably work on ranches and would thus benefit most from "learning how to repair a broken harness, how to straighten a sprung tire on his wagon wheel, how to do the hundred other bits of handy tinkering which are so necessary to the farmer who lives thirty miles from a town." While Leupp acknowledged that some "Indians" possess an "individuality" that suits them for college, these "talented" students will be a small minority, as in the case of Whites. One must remember too, Leupp observed, confidently wielding the category of "Indian," that "unlike the average Caucasian, the average Indian hates new things on the mere ground of their novelty." "Indians," by his definition, can be expected to "enter the general labor market as lumbermen, ditchers, miners, railroad hands, or what not."

Leupp underscored that these considerations must be placed in the context of the ongoing un-American real estate dilemma: the "absurdity of keeping one class of people in a condition of so many undivided portions of a common lump. Each Indian must be recognized as an individual and so treated, as the white man is."[243] The "Indians'" "common lump" of real estate was just too big and too tempting to ignore. And how would uneducated and unambitious "Indians" know what to do with such lumps anyway? Hence both land and tribal funds must be "individualized."

Leupp used his grand idea of "Indian" "individuality" not only to justify putting a ceiling on the level of education offered to most students but to suggest that they be given certain kinds of training—not educations that would equip them for intellectual and political leadership. "Individualize and specialize," he advised in 1910. "What [the Indian] needs is practical not showy instruction. . . . Wherever we find the Indian idle, we find him a pauper and unruly; wherever we find him busy, we find him comfortable and docile."[244] Too many "Indians" who were educated as professionals—lawyers, doctors, businessmen—might disrupt the real estate goals of "individualizing" if they remained loyal to the tribe, as Yellowtail advocated. Farmers and ranchers who knew mainly how to fix wagon wheels might incite less effective and less publicized resistance to bureaucracies and laws. Such "Indians" would do best with schooling in "character," a development of self that would guide them to conform dutifully as laboring "individuals."

Leupp's ideas were not entirely foreign to those of Pratt, who was rigid about dividing the Carlisle school day into half education and half labor training. Nevertheless, Pratt, at least in his rhetoric and tone, tried to excite student ambition, to help his charges see the cultivation of character as a requisite step to social advancement, to believe in an "individuality" that would open possibilities if one only worked hard enough (and *denied* a great deal). Pratt, like many of the reformers of the 1880s and 1890s, believed in the possibility that all humans, properly guided, could progress, and therefore he was committed to laying what he thought was a strong foundation for the "Indians'" future as citizens, "individuals," and workers. By the time Leupp became BIA commissioner (1905–1909), evolutionary ideologies of inherent racial differences in intellectual ability were taking hold and the growing acceptance of "Indian" cultures was concommitantly an ideological assertion that these cultures, however picturesque, were backward and redeemable only to a degree.

Furthermore, changing early-twentieth-century concepts of the evolutionary ideology of progress, of the novelty of "primitive" "Indian" cultures, and of the limits of "Indian" potential were accompanied by a shift in political power from the East to the West and the South—as far as western matters were concerned. Several territories had been admitted to statehood and expanding business interests were more efficiently lining up congressional support.[245] Even many easterners who were engrossed by Indianness, like Theodore Roosevelt and his Cowboy Cabinet, subscribed to the assumption about "Indian" ability voiced by one of Hamlin Garland's White characters: "Fifty thousand years of life proceeding in a certain way results in a certain arrangement of brain cells which can't be changed in a day, even in a generation."[246]

Pratt would have objected to this appraisal. "Indians" were being inscribed by the ideology of distinct racial individuality rather than by the early optimistic (and, I would add, self-servingly naive) assimilationist reform ideology of individuality based on American "equality." If both ideologies to some extent sanctioned the economic exploitation of "Indians" as manual workers and the "legal" appropriation of their land through allotment, the ideology of Pratt's reform era was geared rhetorically to giving them a fair shot at opportunity in America (the limited educational programs of this era, of course, did not begin to come close to actually doing this). Whereas the ideology growing stronger in Leupp's era not only endeavored to consolidate the notion of "Indians" as a "race," an inferior group with inherently restricted capacities, but more brashly announced its intent to transform this "race" into a usable working class, for the most part a working class only.

Robert G. Valentine, after serving as Leupp's protegé, succeeded him as Commissioner of Indian Affairs in 1909. Valentine appeared to entertain unusually decent ideas in a piece published in *The Red Man*. In 1912 he argued that a dimension of the "Indian problem" was the counterproductive look-out-for-number-one "individuality"—by implication, the ideology Pratt's Carlisle sought to cultivate. Valentine, instead, counseled loyalty to the tribe: "Leave behind the somewhat over-individualism, which it is perhaps partly your inheritance to possess, and partly our training to make adhere to you." He pleaded for "a more social view, a more altruistic view." Valentine redefined self-reliance and persistence as goals best tempered by an ethos of collective responsibility and welfare. He admitted that there existed "great hostile forces which seek the injury, the despoiling of the Indians" and urged students to "get together for the upbuilding of your own peoples." His seemingly candid self-critical message was for the Carlisle "individual" who would sustain his or her allegiance to the tribe: "Nothing that we can do will stop you, not the most evil forces can stop you, if you won't stop."[247]

Alas, history suggests that Valentine, like his mentor Leupp, earned his place in the category he labeled "hostile forces." Valentine's rhetoric of collective incentive and cultural acceptance belied some of his other statements about "Indians" and his actions as commissioner. In the Congressional Record this Harvard graduate, former English instructor at the Massachusetts Institute of Technology, former banker, railroad manager, and settlement house worker, expressed views on "Indian" potential that would have made Pratt erupt: "Our error has been attempting to do something that was impossible in all our history, and that is make a white man out of an Indian; to so educate him . . . that he could compete in the business or professional enterprises of the world with white civilization." During his administration Valentine aided the White appropriation and use of "Indian" land and facilitated the issuing of fee patents so that "individualized" land could be sold (usually to Whites). There was no doubt in his mind about the sort of "individual" he was helping produce when in 1909 he wrote a White farmer, "If you were hiring white labor to do this work, in all probability you would have to pay them more wages than you do the Indians."[248]

The Red Man, however, did publish several pieces by Natives who had established places for themselves in the emerging professional-managerial class. Arthur C. Parker (Seneca), a prominent ethnographer, was quoted extensively on the Iroquois ethos of hospitality, welfare, and giving. Parker's historical perspectives on the Iroquois "law of common hospitality" that sprang from the "law of communism" contextualized the collective altruism and solidarity that Valentine appeared to esteem as a long-standing Native tradition: "There was never any need for any one to go hungry or destitute, the unfortunate and the lazy could avail themselves of the stores of the more fortunate and the more energetic. Neither begging nor laziness were encouraged, however, and the slightest indication of an imposition was rebuked in a stern manner."[249] He made it clear that you are not giving "yours" if "yours" is from the outset conceived as belonging to "everyone." Parker himself was a complex, ambitious figure. Yet he may be viewed as an example of a Native intellectual whose learning helped him think critically about American individualism and the value of Native collectivity.

Thomas Sloan (Omaha), a graduate of Hampton and a self-taught lawyer, published an article in 1912 in *The Red Man* that, like Valentine's piece, exhorted Carlisle students to think collectively rather than just individually. His analysis of the "Indian problem" moved away from the label of "civilization" and closer to capitalism: "Every Congress has before it legislation detrimental to the Indian. In nine cases out of ten the legislation is promoted by capitalists, speculators and railroad men who are more able than the Indian Office and the Department of the Interior." Sloan held that education was the best Native defense against governmental graft and the campaign to designate tribal property "surplus lands"; but Native students had to learn more than how to fix wagon wheels and mend dresses. Sloan, like Yellowtail, wanted more Natives to be educated as professionals who could go onto the new battlefields—courts, Congress, bureaucracies—where the economic and real estate war on Natives was being waged. Far more so than Pratt, and unlike Leupp, Sloan envisioned education in political terms, not as individual aggrandizement: "Education, courage and integrity are the weapons with which the Indian may hope to struggle successfully for the well-being of his people."[250] Nevertheless, both Parker and Sloan belonged to the proassimilationist Society of American Indians, which contributed to class stratification among Natives and in the process attempted to resignify what the category of "Indian" meant.

The new Carlisle, notwithstanding the low ceiling it placed on education, sometimes sponsored a cultural relativism capable of acknowledging the worth of Native cultures, artistry, and traditional welfare practices. It sometimes recognized that education was necessarily an empowerment connected to tribal self-defense, and sometimes even made available to students the notion that White culture, in trying to reconstruct the "Indian" as "individual," was obscuring *Native individualities* that were both creative and intelligently resistant to American colonization. Leupp even established a vocational center for training in Native art at Carlisle (and had it bear his name).

Yet these governmental gestures toward cultural pluralism and relativism were conjoined with a smug rejection of Native intellectual possibilities. Before the government terminated Carlisle, its central role as a cultural factory for the production of workers was made all too patent. When Cato Sells took office as BIA commissioner under Woodrow Wilson, his aim was to eliminate work training connected with farming on Native lands and to abolish instruction in domestic science, and instead get to the point: educate "Indians" to work on Ford assembly lines.[251]

Education for What?

What Carlisle needed all along, among many other things, was a combination of the Pratt school-father let's-tackle-them optimism and the post-Pratt cultural relativism and "Indian" self-affirmation. Taken together these features still would not have addressed the needs of Native youth in this period. But the synthesis would have been an improvement over the "education" that either phase of Carlisle offered students. Both phases may make one wonder: *education for what?*

The title of David Wallace Adams's overview of late-nineteenth- and early-twentieth-century Indian schools provides a short answer: *Education for Extinction* (1995). The book's research on the history of reformers, students, tribal identity, school administrations, educational philosophies, and the BIA complicates its title. In the early twenti-

eth century there was indeed an ideological emphasis on "Americanizing," "civilizing," "individualizing," and "citizenizing." Nevertheless,
as Frederick Hoxie, Adams, and others note, there were emerging cultural pluralisms that had various origins, manifestations, and effects:
the "extinction" of Indianness does not seem to have been Carlisle's all-
encompassing goal. Even in the Pratt period, as my readings of the
school newspapers and photographs show, the school never tried to
make Native culture wholly extinct. When Carlisle's publications mentioned the name of a student, they typically indicated the student's
tribal membership. During Pratt's reign the occasional official recognition of Indianness not only gained publicity for the school and the-
atrically dramatized its before-and-after claims (recorded by commercial souvenir photographs), the acknowledgment of Indianness also
probably functioned for the students and the administration as an ideological lubricant that helped keep the individualizing machinery running more smoothly. Education for extinction does not appear to convey
comprehensively what Carlisle was set up to do either during or after
Pratt's rule.

It is perhaps closer to the truth, yet still a partial perspective, to say
that Carlisle in both its phases, more openly stated in the latter phase,
sponsored *industrial education for exploitation.* Francis Paul Prucha's,
Hoxie's, Adams's, Coleman's, and my research all underscore that Carlisle and other schools were dedicated to producing *usable* "Indians": if
students could not employ their skills on returning to the reservation,
then even that difficulty, administrators hoped, would provide incentive for them to leave the reservation and find appropriate work in the
larger world (as noted, usually more easily said than done, especially in
the West).[252] Carlisle's Americanizing and individualizing processes
were in many, not all, respects ideological dimensions of another process that might be called the *workerizing* of "Indians." Here I build on
Karl Marx's term *proletarianizing.* I label the Carlisle process *workerizing* because of its ideological reliance on the work ethic. The American
discourse of inevitability had to represent class-divided, often routinized versions of work as beyond question, as "making a living," indeed, as simply "living." The many school newspaper photographs of
students laboring at Carlisle's machines and in the shops were meant to
show students as well as outsiders that this was their inevitable position
in the "modern" era.[253] Pratt was delighted when Henry Ford hired sixty
Carlisle students to labor in the Hog Island Shipyards during World
War I. Part of his dream had come true.[254]

The Carlisle material is of great historical significance partly because it exhibits so clearly the ideal subjective blueprint to which dominant groups wanted workers to conform—well-mannered workers who would comply with regularized labor, blame themselves not their bosses for their exploitation and difficulty in rising, and maintain a sense of compensatory subjective value by labeling themselves and their culturally shaped motivations and fates "individual."[255] Yet the people involved—students, their parents, school staff—were not blueprints. In the next chapter I will contend that the category of assimilation insufficiently references the range of motivations, thoughts, and feelings that Natives brought to their struggles, successes, and hardships within the marketplace. In addition I will suggest that a more radical side of Carlisle, which may have been partly unintended, partly intended by the school, shows students getting or getting for themselves an *education in performance*—strategic experience in the cultural work of performing "Indian" and "individual."[256]

2

The School of Savagery:

"Indian" Formations of Subjectivity

and Carlisle

Back in time immemorial, things were different, the animals
could talk to human beings and many magical things still happened.
—Leslie Marmon Silko (Laguna), *Ceremony*, 1977

To some extent we have tried to live in both worlds.
An Indian knew he could be faithful to his native creed and still
pray every day to the God of the whites.
—Christine Quintasket (Okanagan and Colville), *Mourning Dove*, c. 1920s

[One of the] most terrible aspects of our situation today is that none of us feels that we are authentic. . . . We . . . expect ourselves (or each other, I should say) to be "pure" and untouched by the larger society which so constantly beats against the sides of our heads; and we accuse each other of not being true to our traditions. That phenomenon is part of the romantic exploitation.

—Jimmie Durham (Cherokee), *Columbus Day*, 1983[1]

It would be illuminating to profile the sorts of Native subjectivities that students imported to Carlisle, in an attempt to better grasp the effect of the school's stamp of individualizing on them. But trying to do so would entail the difficulties Prucha outlined when he reflected on how one might study Native responses to the reform programs sponsored by the Friends of the Indian: "I am not sure that it is possible, except in a very general way, to describe Indian reaction as though it were uniform throughout the great diversity of groups to whom it was applied." Even if one divided the diverse Native tribes into the usual three groupings— plains, woodlands, desert—there would be some differences in tribal socialization in each grouping. One would have to contend with many other tangled classification problems as well. How might one categorize offspring of intertribal or interracial marriages; how should one examine the individualities nurtured by Natives who were assimilated or in large part assimilated; what might one make of the effects of intertribal migration? "Each Indian tribe," Prucha emphasizes, "—in many cases each individual Indian—received the program in a particular way, and the story of each calls for separate telling."[2] Practically speaking, this vast multiple storytelling cannot be done.

Krupat, weighing the diversity of Native cultures and traditional Native tendencies to eschew the use of highly abstract cultural categories, underscores that there is no Native "literature," "philosophy," or "religion" by Native reckoning—these are all "Western" categories Euramericans have imposed on Native cultural production.[3] By the same token, there is no Native cultural subjectivity that one can abstract. Yet, as Brian Swann and Krupat have pointed out, while "there are no inevitably inherent Indian subjects" in Native autobiography, "certain themes and images come up again and again."[4] In concurrence with this perception, what I offer here is provisional, a modest sketch of a few important themes that surface mainly in several Sioux autobiographical writings, some of which comment on Carlisle directly and generalize about Native cultural formations of subjectivity.[5] As Coleman suggests, Native cultures socialize their youth in ways that help account both for students' resistance to some aspects of their boarding school training and for their receptiveness to other aspects of their education. Students' tribally based responses could fuse resistance and receptiveness or fluctuate between the two responses at different times.[6] What follows is an effort to shed more light on this complexity.

Literary Indianizing: Discourses of Native Cultural Subjectivity

Dr. Charles Eastman (whose Santee Sioux name was Ohiyesa, meaning "victor") (1858–1939) wrote several studies of what he called "Indian" subjectivity. He served as a Carlisle outing and recruiting agent from November 1899 to September 1900. The school newspaper made much of the fact that he had earned his medical degree, but he does not seem to have been employed specifically as school physician. Eastman was a friend of and correspondent with Pratt until the latter's death.[7] I will draw on most of Eastman's many volumes, including *Indian Boyhood* (1902), *The Soul of the Indian: An Interpretation* (1911), and *From Deep Woods to Civilization: Chapters in the Autobiography of an Indian*

(1916). Gertrude Simmons Bonnin (1876–1938), who first published her stories under her Yankton Sioux name Zitkala-Ša (Simmons married Raymond T. Bonnin [Dakota Sioux]), eventually became a friend of and lifelong correspondent with Pratt, and a powerful political force as a Washington lobbyist and as secretary-treasurer of the Society of American Indians. But her initial frustrating encounter with Pratt occurred when she taught at Carlisle (1898–99). Bonnin included not-so-veiled criticisms of Carlisle and Pratt in her turn-of-the-century autobiographical fiction, much of which appeared in the *Atlantic Monthly* (collected as *American Indian Stories* in 1921). Her mother was a full-blood Sioux; her father was White. Luther Standing Bear (his Brule Sioux name was Plenty Kill) (c. 1860s–1939), as noted, was in the first group of students to attend Carlisle and remained, as one of Pratt's favorites, till the mid-1880s.[8] His autobiographies, *My People the Sioux* (1928) and *Land of the Spotted Eagle* (1933), contain subtle and ironic reflections on Carlisle and Pratt.

Another figure I will occasionally refer to is Black Elk (c. 1863–1950), an Oglala Sioux medicine man and seer who related parts of his life story to the poet John G. Neihardt in 1931. Neihardt's highly edited rendition of these interviews was published as *Black Elk Speaks* (1932), a book that scholars now think of as being more accurately described as a literary narrative that has for its protagonist a fictional character named Black Elk who resembles the historical Black Elk and sometimes speaks his thoughts.[9] Even Black Elk's ostensibly traditional tribal life was touched by the presence of Carlisle inasmuch as he chose to send his son, Ben Black Elk, to study there. Ben corresponded with Neihardt about coming to interview Black Elk and assisted as his father's interpreter during the sessions.

As Swann and Krupat observe, the word *autobiography*—which largely replaced the terms *memoirs* and *confessions* around 1827—was coined in 1809. The first American book with *autobiography* in its title was published in 1832. Ideas of egocentric individualism, romantic originality (as in the artist-as-genius), and the hero-as-solitary that were connected with the rise of autobiography in Europe and America, Krupat attests, had "no prior model in the collective practices of tribal cultures."[10] Niehardt's Black Elk opens the narrative: "If it were only the story of my life I think I could not tell it; for what is one man that he should make much of his winters?"[11]

When Swann and Krupat assembled a volume of Native autobiographical writings in 1987, they discovered that it was still typical that "the notion of telling the whole of one individual's life or taking merely personal experience as of particular significance was, in the most literal way, foreign to [Natives], if not also repugnant." One vexed contributor complained about the difficulty she experienced "blithering on about your own life and thoughts" and added that "Indian critics" of poetry recommend "that it is best if there are no 'I's' in it."[12] Nevertheless, it must be remembered that late-nineteenth- and early-twentieth-century Native groups had developed diverse oral cultures, could excel in the aesthetic production of narratives in their storytelling, and were complex—not uniform—in the variety of their responses to European, American, and African American cultures and historical change. Thus H. David Brumble's reminder that some tribes, like the Winnebagos, adopted "Western" autobiographical forms rapidly and creatively is useful: Natives, as Brumble and others demonstrate, did promote multiple, historically mutable notions of the self that were of course distinguishable from what some might (mis)construe as collective "Indian" or even tribal identity.[13]

The rise of the autobiographical genre in America during the antebellum era was coextensive with the mass-cultural popularization of domestic-sentimental writings that enshrined privatized middle-class personal life (fiction and advice books) and with the ascendancy of Manifest Destiny imperialism (the Trail of Tears and the Mexican-American War).[14] Krupat and others have noted that Manifest Destiny's discourse of inevitability—"Indians" must vanish from preferred real estate—and romanticism—the Vanishing Noble Savage's spirit must be preserved in literature and art—operated in league with one another. The Native "I," in place of tribal land, was romanticized as that which must be saved (in print for the consumption of White culture) and appreciated (as a not wholly feasible alternative American self). At times Eastman, a graduate of Dartmouth College and of Boston University's medical school, seems to have participated in this romantic ideology: "I feel that I was a pioneer in this new line of defence of the native American," he wrote in 1911, "not so much of his rights in the land as of his character and religion."[15] The ideological challenge for Eastman and other Native autobiographers was both to redefine the representation of "Indian" individualities in ways that would have clear political implications and to recast what America called its history. "[My writing] is just a message to the white race," Standing Bear explained, "to know the truth about the first Americans and their relations with the United States."[16]

To appreciate the historical significance of these autobiographical reminiscences, however, it is critical to grasp that they were written and published as "Indian" commodities in a particular ideological and marketing context. Even Eastman, whose fame was international, felt constrained by the well-established "Indian" genre in which he intervened.[17] Some of his letters to Pratt suggest the dilemma of the Native autobiographer or writer of fiction whose ability to sell his or her product was conditioned in part by reigning Euramerican ideologies of what constitutes marketable Indianness, a concoction of imperial and racist romanticism.[18]

In 1911 Eastman wrote Pratt for advice about how best to approach the department store magnate John Wanamaker. Eastman, who had already published several books, wanted to write a history of the Sioux but was afraid that it would not be the kind of "Indian" book that was commercially profitable. "I have gratifying recognition for my work but am very short of cash. People do not care so much to hear the truth; the general public likes something sensational, some 'Indian faking.'" Bonnin, as mentioned, published her stories in the *Atlantic Monthly* under her Sioux name, Zitkala-Ša, a name that would have sounded "Indian" and perhaps exotic to White readers. She used this name again in 1921 when she collected her tales, titled not "Sioux Stories," or "American Sioux Stories," but *American Indian Stories*. Whether Bonnin or her publisher chose this title is uncertain, however the use of the word *Indian*, as Eastman's letter testifies, had market potential. In 1921 Bonnin's work as secretary-treasurer for the Society of American Indians signaled her dedication to making tactical cultural and political use of the category *American Indian*. Standing Bear, in his title, chose to call his people the Sioux, not the Indians or the American Indians. Elsewhere he drew attention to the distinction between Lakota and "Indian": "Lakota love songs are sung, or what the white man had chosen to call the love songs of the Indian."[19]

Eastman's letter maintained that he could "do much more valuable work" than what he had published, but he also recognized that "no poor man can do research work or serious writing unless he has some other means of support." Eastman noted that Edward S. Curtis's photographs of vanishing Indians were made possible by the patronage of J. P. Morgan and that he too needed a suitable "rich man" to sponsor him "in order that this work of preserving and presenting the truth about my people might be done in time."[20] In another letter written a few days later, Eastman asked Pratt's advice for how specifically to beseech Wanamaker for funds that would enable him to "devote a few years to setting the Indian right with the people, without seeing my family suffer."[21] What Eastman had intended to write is not completely clear from these letters, but what is obvious is that a history of the Sioux was not as sellable as another romantic and exotic book about "Indian" boyhood or "Indian" "souls."

Dr. Carlos Montezuma (Apache), a well-known and impassioned Native spokesman for the sort of reforms Pratt advocated, had no reservations about commercial Indianization. A few months after Eastman sent his appeals for assistance, the Apache wrote Pratt, "The reality of the new life confronts nature's child. He must resign to the inevitable." But with just a hint of romantic wistfulness he continued: "Indian life is beautiful and ideal. I enjoyed the Doctor's 'The Soul of the Indian.'" For Montezuma, Eastman's romantic representation of "Indian" souls did not launch any serious critique of White American culture; rather it made the case that the "Indian" possesses the inner "stuff . . . to become a good citizen." Perhaps thinking of Eastman as well as "Indians" in general, Montezuma concluded, "Commercialism he must recognize."

What authors who were classified as "Indian" had to negotiate, even Eastman, was a readership that would allow a measure of social critique and a measure of actual history as long as it was placed in the service of fostering the White romance with "Indian" souls, "Indian" nobility, "Indian" indignation (tempered by the acknowledgment that their defeat and assimilation were as inevitable as the march of civilization and human evolution). Eastman's *Indian Scout Talk: A Guide for Boy Scouts and Camp Fire Girls* (1920), like other Eastman texts, demonstrates how certain romantic renditions of "Indians" had become important elements in the early-twentieth-century formations of Euramerican leisure activities and hobbies for youth. His ironic term for his literary production, one he places in quotation marks, is the "'School of Savagery.'" Eastman's school trains readers to appreciate Native "individuality and initiative" and to consider the possibility that "the other man" should be "regarded more than self."[22] Although he was relatively powerless in his efforts as a lobbyist to modify the U.S. political structure on behalf of Natives, Eastman used the "out-of-doors," ecological, spiritual, self-sufficient (in "nature") "Indian" who could make fires without matches, cook without pots, and track without a compass as a nostalgic model. His hope was that this model would be ideologically fascinating enough to reform Euramerican "character" and "common sense"—to make them more "wholesome."[23]

Hence the autobiographical texts I discuss *do not* provide an unmediated window on "Indian" subjectivity—again, Native cultures were too diverse and enmeshed in historical change to be described by the ideological abstraction "Indian." More complexly, writers like Eastman, Bonnin, and Standing Bear exhibit strategic attempts to repackage aspects of Native subjectivities amid a welter of marketplace restrictions and incentives to engage in "Indian faking" (as Eastman phrased it). Still, much that they write about "Indian" or Sioux cultural subjectivity formation takes on critical force when reread in part as ideological rejoinders to the U.S. government's educational, economic, and political efforts to "individualize" Natives and their land. Their rejoinders also contested dominant cultural and governmental misrepresentations of Indianness as primitive, barbaric, wasteful, irresponsible, impractical, and defeated.

The characteristics "Indians" prized as ideals, Eastman wrote, included self-control, poise, decorum, silence, patience, gentleness and soft-spoken habits of address (especially in warriors), stoicism, respect for one's elders, hospitality, generosity, service to the tribe, humility about spiritual matters, temperance in sexual expression and in eating, and well-exercised bodies with highly developed senses. Eastman often accompanied his rosy descriptions of these characteristics with criticisms of White culture. For instance, the "Indian's" religion, unlike White Christianity, "forbade the accumulation of wealth and the enjoyment of luxury. . . . The love of possessions . . . appeared a snare, and the burdens of a complex society, a source of needless peril and temptation." "Indians" had established no cities because they considered a great "concentration of population" inhumane.[24] Distrustful of some Euramerican stereotypes of "Indians," Standing Bear inserted his own generalizations in their place: "He has been adjudged dumb, stupid, indifferent, and unfeeling. As a matter of truth, he was the most sympathetic of men, but his emotions of depth and sincerity were tempered with control."[25]

In Sioux cultures, as in many other tribal cultures, it was not a nuclear family but rather an extended family, based on extensive kinship within the clan, that instilled some of the values that Eastman and Standing Bear sketch. Parents, grandparents, relatives, and older members of the tribe, as Eastman noted, were the chief nonbureaucratic educators of the young.[26] A keyword that captures intimate relations among Eastman's Sioux is *choice*: sons and daughters had not only a biological father and mother but kinship systems within the clan that provided them with many "fathers" and "mothers"; the adoption of dependents or semidependents or persons one liked (captives, orphans, nieces, nephews, the elderly) was uncomplicated and common; marriages were easily dissolved; in some tribes men could take on women's roles and women could engage in warfare.[27] Even when there were divorces and plural marriages, young people could benefit from this domestic, affective, and sexual flexibility, as Standing Bear's remarks about his upbringing testify. After his father and mother divorced, his father married two sisters: "We all lived in the *same* tipi, and they were both very good to me. . . . There were more relations to look after me."[28]

Eastman, describing "Indian" manners, remarked on how appropriate the custom of the "soft, low, voice," for women and men alike, was to "the enforced intimacy of tent life." Tent togetherness "would soon become intolerable were it not for these instinctive reserves and delicacies, this unfailing respect for the established place and possessions of every other member of the family circle, this habitual quiet, order, and decorum."[29] Ella Cara Deloria (Yankton Dakota Sioux) emphasized the importance of nonchalance and civility in the Dakota formation of character.[30] Of course, domestic harmony did not always reign when one family member fought with another (as seems to have been the habit with Sitting Bull's two wives), or when adultery was discovered or admitted, or when generational squabbles took place between parents and children.[31] Nevertheless, the elastic clan, kinship, and extended family system that ventilated life in close quarters—one could always stay with other loved ones—did not breed the White middle-class sentimental hothouse family with concentrated psychological dependencies, tensions, and possessiveness.[32]

It is evident why Carlisle's treason to the tribe propaganda harped on treason to parents, for Native parents often nurtured in their children the seeds of resistance to White colonization. In Bonnin's tale "Indian Childhood" a mother wonders if the river from which they get their water will still be theirs in the near future and defines "paleface" for her daughter (the narrator): "'He is a sham, . . . The bronzed Dakota is the only real man.' Stamping my foot on the earth I cried aloud, 'I hate the paleface that makes my mother cry.'"[33] Although Pratt understood the significance of fomenting treason to the parents and to the tribe in general, he may not have grasped fully the affective power of the clan and kinship network to rekindle the love and loyalty of returning students.[34]

Instruction in sacred beliefs as well as widespread kinship affiliations strengthened Natives' sense of tribal connectedness and responsibility. The teaching of possessive individualism may have been a more difficult lesson to ingrain in students than some of Carlisle's teachers were aware, for Native religious training, Eastman states, devalued "the accumulation of wealth and enjoyment of luxury."[35] The ethos of hospitality and giving often encouraged not the development of capitalist emotions but keeping one's "spirit free of the clog of pride, cupidity, or envy. . . . [Possessiveness] appeal[ed] . . . to the material part, and if allowed its way it will in time disturb the spiritual balance of man."[36] The "Indian," he counseled Boy Scouts and Camp Fire Girls, "develops a wholesome, vigorous body and mind, to which all exertion seems play, rather than painful toil for possession's sake. . . . Let us have more of this spirit of the American Indian, the Boy Scout's prototype, to leaven the brilliant selfishness of our modern civilization!"[37]

Eastman, seeming to forget the prestige of excelling in warfare (an honor he himself yearned for in his youth), portrayed "Indians" as recognizing that virtues "are more readily cultivated where the 'struggle for existence' is merely a struggle with the forces of nature, and not one's fellow man."[38] His pop-Darwinian representation of the Native relationship with "nature" as "struggle" may be a sign of his own changing preconceptions within White culture. Standing Bear's descriptions of the Sioux buffalo hunts—how many buffalo would be killed, how they were used—conveyed the traditional ideal of *sufficiency*.[39] Yet this ideal changed as Natives on the plains needed to kill more buffalo to acquire guns, blankets, horses, and tools in trade to survive. Excess could be good, particularly if one was sharing the goods.

When Standing Bear was made a chief of the Lakota Sioux, he—in spite of his Carlisle indoctrination in the "manly" virtues of ownership—unhesitatingly put into practice the Sioux belief that it is better to give than to receive and garnered even greater tribal status by giving away a wagon, horses, beadwork, blankets, and other goods.[40] Native dances often functioned as public "giveaways," celebratory occasions on which the wealth of the tribe was redistributed to the needy and fame was secured by the great givers.[41] Kinship networks animated the spirit of giving.[42] Eastman's Sioux "hero," Crazy Horse, exemplified "bigheartedness, generosity, courage, and self-denial." The very virtues that qualified him to be a Sioux public servant would be regarded as "weakness[es]" by those who live "a life founded upon commerce and gain."[43] Ideally, the Sioux, like Crazy Horse, practiced self-denial not for self-advancement but for the general good. The Sioux's prereservation social prestige system, according to Robert Utley, was one in which "people counted, not property."[44] But the word Eastman's White education taught him to use to describe this cultural production of self, value, and status, the word he eventually accepted as accurate, was *improvident*.[45] The more contemptuous word Commissioner Leupp employed to reprove the "Indian" generosity he regarded as a manifestation of unthrifty evolutionary infantalism was *squander*.[46]

No wonder that Pratt and other reformers censured the Natives' traditional care for the needy as communistic and socialistic. "Our poor lost nothing of their self-respect and dignity," Eastman wrote. "We could not conceive of the extremes of luxury and misery existing thus side by side."[47] The Sioux ethos of giving was a *redistribution ethos.* Standing Bear emphasized, "There must be no hungry individuals; so long as one had food, all would have food."[48] Eastman did not use the word *socialism,* nor did he invoke the words *capitalism* and *imperialism,* but his critique of American "civilization" must have then as now brought such categories to mind: "When I reduce civilization to its lowest terms, it becomes a system of life based on trade. The dollar is the measure of value, and *might* still spells *right*; otherwise, why war?"[49] In 1911, the year before the socialist Eugene V. Debs ran for president and received almost one million votes, Eastman observed: White Americans "bought and sold everything: time, labor, personal independence, the love of woman, and even the ministrations of their holy faith! The lust for money, power, and conquest so characteristic of the Anglo-Saxon race did not escape moral condemnation at the hands of his untutored judge."[50] Eastman quoted Sitting Bull's class critique of White democracy: " 'The love of possessions is a disease in them. These people have made many rules that the rich may break, but the poor may not! . . . They even take tithes of the poor and weak to support the rich and those who rule.' "[51] As Bonnin put it, in the America of possessive individualism the "Indian" has for several hundred years been "somebody's loot."[52]

Her *Old Indian Legends* (1901)—written for Whites as well as Natives, as the preface indicates—was comprised of animal fables. Employing kinship logic, the Winnebago artist Angel DeCora provocatively humanized Bonnin's animals as Natives in her illustrations for the book. In repeatedly counseling young readers not to be selfish, the morals of these Native legends grated against the Euramerican premise that one must want to stuff one's pockets with money to achieve "individuality" and intelligent selfishness.[53]

Standing Bear praised the Lakota for being "industrious; his whole life's necessity tending to make him so." He suggested that the Euramerican ideological category "lazy" mystifies the Native social organization of life, choice, and value. He generalized that the "Indian . . . has never been able to adopt the course of economic action which the white man chooses to call 'enterprise.' " For a Native to be viewed as "enterprising" by Whites, he or she had to alter his or her "whole idea of human evaluation." He contrasted the Lakotas' efforts to "preserve the identity of the tribe" with "the European concept of . . . 'every man for himself.' " Crucially, Standing Bear linked the Lakota commitment to the humane distribution of resources with "human rights" (his term) and the absence of hardened social classes.[54]

The historical appreciation of the ethical centrality of generosity, gift giving, and social welfare in Native cultures is seminal, but it must not be overly romanticized, or viewed ahistorically, to the point where it obscures other historical trends in Native social behavior and permits an absolute "Indian" exceptionalism regarding the issue of the desirability of possessions within capitalist conditions. Many Natives adapted with alacrity to the opportunities of the colonial marketplace and were interested in trading, in accumulating possessions, and sometimes in acquiring "loot" by less than virtuous means. Competition, as Eastman, Standing Bear, and many other commentators have underscored, was an essential part of the training most Native boys underwent. Keen competition—in sports, hunting, warlike valor, wooing—encouraged ambition and the willingness to take risks (though a sense of tribal interdependence mitigated extreme rivalry).[55] Especially as the nineteenth century progressed, highly desirable possessions included guns, horses, clothes, alcohol. Social prestige could be achieved not only by public giving but also by distinguishing oneself in battles, stealing horses from an enemy tribe, marrying several wives, and developing spiritual powers.[56]

Successful efforts to make a name for oneself literally could win one a new name. Because Natives did not conceptualize individual worth as static, Native names were descriptive, often singular, and not necessarily fixed. Sitting Bull (c. 1831–1890) began life as Jumping Badger and then received the name Hunkesni (Slow) because of his carefully considered actions. At the tender age of fourteen Slow killed his first Crow warrior and his proud father, Sitting Bull, gave his son his own valiant name and himself took the name Jumping Bull.[57] This legendary warrior also witnessed in his life, as did many of his people, Sioux who could be just as possessive, opportunistic, and unscrupulously individualistic as any Gilded Age robber baron. It would be fanciful to think that Carlisle enrolled Native students whose historically developing cultures only geared them to give away wealth and spurn possessiveness. Making a name for oneself took on different aspects in American capitalist culture, and some Natives adapted, in their own selective, diverse ways, to this new prestige system with skill and eagerness.

Being renamed at school was not necessarily as oppressive as it sounds, especially if one's tribal notion of what naming signified differed from notions of naming prevalent in the culture that did the naming. Standing Bear's responses to his renaming were multiple. In one book he complained that Carlisle did not simply translate pupils' names into English.[58] In another book he viewed school renaming as supplementary—not the extinction of his Sioux "individuality" but the opening of a new world of power and possibility through different forms of code-reading: "I was one of the 'bright fellows' to learn my name quickly. How proud I was to answer when the teacher called the roll!"[59]

Traditional forms of Native tribal "individuality" may have been less visible to Whites—when it did not take the form of capitalist possessive individualism—because Whites were often blind to some of the ways their own social organizations did not cultivate or countenance individual behavior. "The American Indian was an individualist in religion as in war," Eastman asserted. "He had neither a national army nor an organized church."[60] And Standing Bear observed: "The whole system of [U.S.] army deportment seemed to deprive a man of individuality in the eyes of Lakota warriors with whom fighting was not a salaried business but a chosen calling, usually from sentiment or from love of sheer excitement."[61]

Keywords in understanding this warrior individualism, exhibited in Standing Bear's upbringing, are *choice* and *independence*. Standing Bear used the word *individualize* to describe Lakota socialization, agency, and value: "Though each person became individualized . . . could even go to battle upon his own initiative, he could not consider himself as separate from the band or nation. Tribal consciousness was the sole guide and dictator, there being no human agency to compel the individual to accept guidance or obey dictates, yet for one to cut himself off from the whole meant to lose identity or to die."[62] Similarly, Eastman claimed: "With us the individual was supreme; all combination was voluntary in its nature; there was no commerce worthy the name, no national wealth, no taxation for the support of government, and the chiefs were merely natural leaders with much influence but little authority."[63]

The influence of the warrior ethos and of the value placed on independence can be detected in an array of student efforts to resist authority and routines at Carlisle and other "Indian" schools. Adams has surveyed the broad variety of resistance that students tried out: escape from the school (in 1901, 45 of the 114 boys expelled from Carlisle were punished for attempted escape); arson (in 1897 two Carlisle girls were sentenced to eighteen months in the penitentiary for trying twice within one hour to burn down the girls' dormitory); the clandestine performance of sacred ceremonies; punching, kicking, and biting school officials; work or classroom slowdown (controlling and retarding the pace of lessons during classtime); total noncooperation (work strikes, school strikes, hunger strikes); death (from extreme despondency, illness, escape attempts, suicide). "Much of this resistance," Coleman writes, "was a form of escape without escaping." Institutions could try to absorb, if not officially sanction, he adds, some naughtiness, transgression, even defiance as a hegemonic safety valve—a way of "making the school more bearable." Schools often branded warrior-students who actually escaped "deserters."[64]

What the works of Eastman, Standing Bear, and Bonnin, as well as the scholarship of historians, suggest is that in some ways many Natives—who relished choice in family relations, sexual relations, military affairs, political arrangements—were much more concerned about collectively creating and preserving individual agency than may have been possible in U.S. capitalism. In sundry respects Carlisle's militarized "individualizing" was much less individual than many tribal patterns of "individualizing." One Indian school official observed, "A school uniform is a great cross to Indian pupils. One Indian never likes to appear like any other."[65] Their Native "individuality," however, ensured that their responses even to the wearing of uniforms would be heterogeneous.[66]

By eroding the subjective value Euramericans ascribed to their construction of individualism, and by stressing the flexibility of Sioux lifeways, Sioux authors sought to weaken the authority of Euramerican capitalist "civilization." There was nothing savage about not building fixed, permanent homes that would prevent individual, familial, or tribal movement. "We were at liberty to move any time we chose," Standing Bear recalls. "We stopped when we wanted and stayed as long as we pleased. There was no great rush."[67] In *Mourning Dove*, her early-twentieth-century Salishan autobiography, Christine Quintasket (Mourning Dove) emphasizes how much she "loved the free life of moving from one camping place to another all summer long."[68] Although Standing Bear doubtless received his share of Carlisle instruction that permanent "homes" were more civilized than dirty "tents," in his autobiography he made a point of discussing the marvelous advantages of the tipi, as did Bonnin in her fiction, especially in summer when the bottom could be raised to let prairie breezes waft through.[69] For Sitting Bull, domestic and geographical mobility, rather than a White preoccupation with economic "upward" mobility, was at the heart of the Sioux freedom to choose: "[Whites] are prisoners in town or farms."[70]

Both Standing Bear and Bonnin drove home the point that the Sioux were eminently capable of feeling culturally superior to Whites.[71] Standing Bear reiterated a nineteenth-century belief that even in 1928, the year he published his reminiscences, may have held cultural currency for many Sioux: "Killing a pale-face was not looked upon as a brave act. We were taught that the white man was much weaker than ourselves."[72] Bonnin's fiction exposed readers to the idea that students were in no way raw material to be molded—they entered White schools already the social products and producers of Native educations and etiquette, and they could feel, within their tactical and censorious silence, profound resentment when mishandled. Natives judged Whites on the basis of their own cultural codes.

To illustrate this, Bonnin relates her young heroine's harsh sensory response to her first moments in a White boarding school for "Indians" in the Midwest. She was repelled by the alien thud of hard shoes on bare wooden floors, the glare of gaslights, and the enclosed look of towering walls. Her dignity was compromised by being "tossed in the air like a wooden puppet."[73] Natives, even frightened young ones, were in no way decorative playthings for Whites—they were thinking subjects who remembered all that was done to them. Bonnin also made it evident that White education in "individuality" was often regimentation within a "civilizing machine," an "iron routine" of school bells and religious proselytizing. "Within a week" of seeing her schoolmate die from inadequate medical treatment (clutching her Bible while expiring), Bonnin's heroine reasserted her resistance: "I was again testing the chains which tightly bound my individuality like a mummy for burial."[74]

Bonnin's fiction celebrates a notably unregimented Sioux female individuality. Her autobiographical and nonautobiographical tales suggest that Sioux women could be independent (uninterested in taking the name of a husband), daring (one rescues her beloved from an enemy tribe), resentful of White oppression, and fully able, if "literate" in White ways, to publish their anger in the *Atlantic Monthly*. A review of her stories in Carlisle's *Red Man* attempted to put her back in line. It concludes superciliously that the former Carlisle teacher's fiction exhibits her as imaginative but, alas, unfeminine: "a person of infinite conceit. . . . [an] enraged spirit . . . unthankful for all that has been done for her by the pale faces, which in her case is considerable." The author's self-portrait, the reviewer claimed, was unlike "the true picture of all Indian girls"; by implication it was too individual in its nonconformity.[75]

The issue of women's status in Native cultures is enormous and difficult to address because of the differences in cultures on this matter.[76] In some cultures female adultery could be punished with mutilation, such as amputation of the nose, and the adultery itself could be the consequence of an arranged marriage or of the sale of a wife or daughter. On the other hand, certain cultures permitted or encouraged women to hold great religious or political authority. In some groups women wielded significant matrilineal and matrilocal economic and affective power: "Far from being a mere drudge," notes one historian, "the Lakota mother . . . dominated tipi affairs. She, not the husband, owned the lodge and all the family belongings. She exerted the paramount authority over the children—daughters until wed and sons until their voices began to change."[77] Standing Bear profiled the Lakota "woman of the household" as "the 'lord and master' when it came to deciding where she and her children were to live."[78]

Sioux girls, wrote Eastman, were trained not only as domestic helpers but as athletes.[79] Quintasket discussed at length the training females received to become Salishan medicine women.[80] Standing Bear also expressed awe before the power of Lakota holy women.[81] Sioux women helped stimulate incentive in male warriors and hunters, often through their affection and their capacity to shame men.[82]

Ella Deloria's novel *Waterlily* (written in the 1940s, published in 1988) offers extensive fictional ethnographic-style representations of nineteenth-century Dakota gender and domestic roles. Dakota women had to show that they were independent even while pregnant and not expect special consideration from their husband or family. Yet this independence was part of her demonstration that she did not consider herself to be unique. Deloria, like others, valued a kinship system that put no economic pressure on women to remain in a bad marriage.[83] White reformers often claimed to wish to release "Indian" women from "unfeminine" drudgery and disrespect. Yet, as suggested in chapter 1, many of the reformers' statements, including Pratt's, imply that they were keen to have young women sentimentalized and feminized—affectively reoriented according to Euramerican patterns—so as to redeploy their existing social and familial power on behalf of the assimilation and allotment campaigns.[84]

Native sacred "vision quests"—the accessing of spiritual powers— were at once revered as a singular experience and as a benefit to the tribe.[85] A male youth would often go alone to a deserted place and remain for several hours or days until he received a vision, which was often of an animal, a totem who would impart to him sacred knowledge. His vision did not have to conform to a religious orthodoxy, for none existed. Because Native social relations rather than "religion" structured morality, schools like Carlisle had to teach what it meant to be "sinful" as an effective way of structuring consciences, guilt, and self-monitoring along Christian lines. One Carlisle student caught writing "vile thoughts" had a "vision" of a punitive Pratt-like divinity: "I cry inside of my heart . . . Oh I am very sorry, but Captain I only believe that God has the power to take away our sins. . . . pray for me."[86]

This anecdote conforms to what Calvin Luther Martin calls "the micro-surgery of separating self from nonself." The vision quest, by contrast, "envision[s] all as self"; it consolidates one's kinship and communications not just with other humans but with animals and plantlife (a "thought-world" common in paleolithic times). In Christian ideology, "Even our God is a man." This anthropomorphism effaces older Native cultural and epistemological achievements—understandings of hyphenated relationships such as fox-human, crow-human, frog-human, wind-human, tree-human.[87] Many Native cultures viewed bears, eagles, and beavers as relatives, persons, advisors, and empowerers. The medicine man's power to heal, see the future, influence the weather, and locate missing horses was grounded in multispecies kinship knowledge.[88]

Prompting these different understandings is what Martin terms the "shift from forager to producer mentality," a material transformation that promoted an "I-Thou" view of the earth as "dangerous, a place removed from human beings." By contrast, "plenipotential" identifications could include the idea that one can shape-change into animals and they can shape-change into humans.[89] Hunters saw animals as the other-than-humans whose nourishment insured human survival and whose body was transformed into humanity. This *kinship epistemology*, ethos, and spiritual practice constituted the larger traditional Native concept of "citizenship."[90] Native multispeciesism counters Euramerican self-possession; it is the effort "to be possessed by the place" and the awareness that "oneself [is possessed] by the wholeself"—something "larger than ourselves."[91] The early colonial clash occurred between "barn-yard" Europeans with reductive concepts of individualistic egos and Natives "who were not afraid to assume the shape and mind of the soil and stone and waters and creatures."[92]

Standing Bear and Eastman both affirmed communications between humans and animals. Frequently animals rescue humans in their narratives.[93] Eastman's *Old Indian Days* (1907) relates the story of the marriage of a Sioux and a Ree who, in flight from the conflict between their tribes, are adopted by their new animal neighbors.[94] Such tales represent kinship relations as offering humans not simply culturally relative but *biologically* relative perspectives that expand human knowledge and sympathy. In Eastman's *Red Hunters and the Animal People* (1905) Natives debate the analytical, linguistic, parental, and pedagogical abilities of animals: "They think, and think well, too." Wolves, an Eastman tale suggests, tolerate Natives but hate Whites.[95] Standing Bear also praised the cultural importance of *kinship literacy*.[96] The Indian, Eastman stressed, traditionally "considered it a sacrilege to learn the secrets of an animal and then use this knowledge against him" and killed animals "only as necessity and the exigencies of life demand[ed]." In one of Standing Bear's tales an old woman "had been with the wolves so long that she had lost the odor of her people and now was able to see that, while man often considers the animal offensive, so do animals find man offensive."[97] Eastman too presented the animals' point of view as hunter and hunted, as mate and as parent. His and Elaine Goodale Eastman's *Wigwam Evenings* (1925) collects Sioux animal legends that encourage readers' humility, industry (like the beaver), and respect for difference. It even tells of a young man who marries a bear and sires a son who is half-human and half-bear.[98]

The use of the ideologically tainted word *individual* to describe the value many Natives ascribed to choice and agency may not be apposite, since this cultural "individuality" derived much of its power from not being understood as solely "individual." The Sioux imagined inner power in primarily spiritual and collective terms, not within the discourse of egocentric individualism. "Of course it was not I who cured," Neihardt's Black Elk acknowledged with humility. "If I thought that I was doing it myself, the hole would close up and no power could come through."[99] Crazy Horse, the nearly invulnerable Sioux warrior who was stabbed in the back by Native U.S. soldiers while under truce, would fit the White romantic and individualistic stereotype of the solitary, brooding leader, except for the fact that, as Neihardt's Black Elk made plain, Crazy Horse attributed his power not to his inner "individual" genius but to his connection with spiritual powers greater than himself. The concept that there are powers far greater than and beyond the self—the spirits, nonhumans (Euramerican "nature")—seemed foreign to many Whites driven by possessive individualism to steal land. In 1932 Neihardt's Black Elk, not unlike a socialist, charged: "There were some who had more of everything than they could use, while crowds of people had nothing at all and maybe were starving."[100] Native self-reliance was typically synonymous with the establishment of *tribal-reliance*.[101]

For Eastman the land was central to what made Native childhood, bodies, and lives, prior to the White conquest, truly great—a greatness that he felt Natives and Whites alike had lost: "The Indian boy enjoyed such a life as almost all boys dream of and would choose for themselves if they were permitted to do so."[102] Eastman's repeated use of the word *choose* is fundamental to his larger point about what U.S. capitalism has lost.[103] He rhapsodized over the economics of this perpetual campout: "Food is free—lodging free—everything free! All were alike poor in the winter and early spring."[104]

The Sioux social invention of time, Standing Bear explained, was not for the purpose of regimentation (the function of Bonnin's insistent school bells), "only the month and year were observed."[105] Time was not money, as Franklin averred, nor was it used to standardize labor. "Our own life, I will admit, is the best in a world of our own such as we have enjoyed for ages," said the newly Christianized Many Lightnings to his son, the son who would adopt the name Charles Eastman. "But here is a race which has learned to weigh and measure everything, time and labor and the results of labor, and has learned to accumulate and preserve . . . wealth."[106] Capitulation to the pace of this Christian race seemed inevitable to Eastman's father, even beneficial under the circumstances—but not to Eastman's grandmother, who objected to his White schooling.[107] The Sioux sense of time was more spiritual than possessive (the White capitalist focus on saving, losing, wasting, spending, making time). Past, present, and future, many tribes believed, were integrated with one another by supernatural powers greater than humankind. Many White reformers who assumed that "Indians" did not know the value of time and work may not have understood that it was because Natives *did* value their time that they often considered repetitious and degrading forms of labor in the U.S. capitalist marketplace a preposterous misuse of time.[108]

If Christianity added ideological freight to the idea that the conquest and "civilization" of the Indian was inevitable and providential (Divine Manifest Destiny), and if it functioned effectively to obfuscate (rechristen) capitalism as Christian "civilization," it also gave Natives a legitimate opening to criticize America's spiritual and moral hypocrisy. When Eastman worked as a representative of the Young Men's Christian Association (YMCA) among western tribes, he found himself asking "how it was that [Natives'] simple lives were so imbued with the spirit of worship, while much church-going among whites and nominally Christian Natives led to such very small results." His answer: it "was machine-made religion . . . supported by money." He happened to notice that Whites "are anxious to pass their religion to all races of men, but keep very little of it themselves. I have not yet seen the meek inherit the earth, or the peacemakers receive high honor."[109]

Eastman had grown accustomed to hearing even more radical sentiments than these from the Natives he conferred with on his YMCA proselytizing tours. His skeptical auditors were interested in descriptions of "primitive" Christianity and suspected that God was neither a capitalist nor amenable to bribery: "We have followed the law you speak of for untold ages! We owned nothing, because every thing is from Him. Food was free, land free as sunshine and rain. Who has changed all this? The white man; and yet he says he is a believer in God!" Another listener inferred that Christ must have been a Native because He was not possessive, did not value real estate imperialism, and put no price on love. Standing Bear's own evaluation of Christianity led him to conclude: "We were then true Christians." Eastman came to believe that "there is no such thing as 'Christian civilization.' . . . Christianity and modern civilization are opposed and irreconcilable."[110] He saw the United States, as did many socialists, as motivated not by what he considered individualism but by crass materialism: "The day of individualism and equity between man and man must yield to the terrific forces of civilization, the mass play of materialism, the cupidity of commerce with its twin brother politics."[111] Native youth, sometimes trained by parents, relatives, tribal leaders, and medicine men to think in such critical ways about American hypocrisy, were the "raw material" Carlisle attempted to remold as "individuals."

Bonnin, Eastman, and Standing Bear realized that the "untutored judges" sent to be tutored at Carlisle and other White schools for "Indians" were often shaped in multiple ways by late-nineteenth-century U.S. government and culture well before the educators tried to teach them their lessons. According to Eastman, both reservation and boarding school Natives were different productions of self—"remnants"— from the Sioux he knew as a boy. Too many of the former, he believed, had lost their "manliness," "independence," and "self-respect," and along with the latter had been engulfed in "the warfare of civilized life," a process that had begun about a hundred years before the nineteenth-century establishment of reservations. Standing Bear, Bonnin, Eastman, and Black Elk all discuss the phenomenon of Natives betraying and robbing their people for the sake of possession. As noted in chapter 1, the "civilizing machine" was in many ways a marketplace machine that forced Natives to be dependent both on the government and on business for food, shelter, and defense. By 1916 Eastman was aware of only three tribes in America that could "still sustain themselves after the old fashion by hunting, fishing and the gathering of wild rice and berries."[112] Bonnin's fiction shows poignantly that, as self-interest held sway, self-sufficiency was too often replaced by starvation and graft. Daily survival on reservations, not just instruction at Carlisle, gave Natives advanced lessons in the values attached to property owning, property selling, exploitation, graft, and bribery.[113] The reservation Sioux, Neihardt's Black Elk lamented, "were traveling the black road, everybody for himself. . . . I was in despair, I even thought that if the Wasichus had a better way, then maybe my people should live that way." It may have been because of this despair that Black Elk sent his son to Carlisle. He added ruefully: "I know now that [the black road] was foolish."[114]

Eastman's fifteen essay-length biographies, collected in *Indian Heroes and Great Chieftains* (1918), offer accounts of lives to emulate, but also cautionary tales of talented men who succumbed to self-interest in swiftly changing power structures. He celebrated the tactical brilliance of Gall, Crazy Horse, Chief Joseph, and Sitting Bull in battle but recorded the strategic betrayals of those who were convinced that resistance was impossible and who sold out their people for money, government prestige, and homes. Three of the first four biographical chapters are of Sioux collaborators: Spotted Tail, Little Crow, Tamahay. Despite his admission that "we have too many weak and unprincipled men among us," Eastman often pulled back from excoriating them, as if on some level they remained tragically and even understandably fallen heroes and chieftains. Little Crow and Hole-in-the-Day (Ojibway), we learn, made efforts to return to the fold and oppose the government. American Horse (Sioux) was "influential and energetic in the cause of the government. . . . yet he could say very sharp things of the duplicity of whites." Eastman's photograph was reproduced along with those of several of the "heroes and chieftains" he wrote about (he bears a striking resemblance to the Sioux hero Red Cloud, "an ardent lover of his country," whose photograph appears beside his). It may be that he saw in himself—as an unofficial cultural, intellectual, and literary chief not only of the Sioux but of all "Indians"—the tribally ambitious resistance and loyalty, yet also the self-ambitious resignation and doubt, that his biographies adumbrate. It is tempting to imagine Eastman thinking of some tendencies in himself as he wrote of Hole-in-the-Day: "like Spotted Tail and Little Crow, he adopted too willingly the white man's politics. . . . Like other able Indians who foresaw the inevitable downfall of their race, he favored a gradual change of customs leading to complete adoption of the white man's ways."[115]

Eastman, like other Sioux, experienced a conversion-and-deconversion tension in his thoughts and feelings about "civilization." He oscillated between gratitude for the "civilized" kindnesses shown him by Whites and his critical perceptions of "civilization" as organized savagery. Like many of the students at Carlisle he was sometimes overwhelmed by the inevitability discourse and, echoing his father, was convinced that "there is no chance for our former simple life, any more." Standing Bear and Bonnin too went through phases of learning and unlearning. Pratt expected tribal cultures to challenge his students' faith in "civilization," but he may have underestimated the role "civilization" itself played in shattering students' confidence in the U.S. version of "civilization" they were taught. Writing about White visitors to schools like Carlisle, Bonnin asserted, "Few have paused to question whether real life or lasting death lies beneath the semblance of civilization."[116]

While Eastman was on his way to Dartmouth to begin his preparatory studies, his train pulled into Chicago, which he had never seen. His response to the size of the buildings, the city, and the population provoked the same "realization" it did in some of the Carlisle-bound students: "the Indian had passed forever." But his resignation was conjoined with critique, as it may have been for some of the not-yet-"individualized" Carlisle students: "I saw a perfect stream of humanity rushing madly along, and noticed with some surprise that the faces of the people were not happy at all." While at Dartmouth and later at Boston University's medical school he found himself impressed by Boston's landscaped parks, flower gardens, and the Arboretum—all symbolic of controlled, assimilated growth—"a school in itself." But here too he witnessed "people [who] hurried along with the gray wolf on their trail."[117]

Natives may have been in awe of the scale of cities and the velocity of railroads, but this did not mean that they automatically and wholeheartedly surrendered their tribal ways of seeing, systems of valuing, and sense of self. The fright experienced by Standing Bear and his fellow students on their first train ride to Carlisle evoked distrust as well as fear. Bonnin's young heroine looked forward to traveling by train to her first school in the Midwest but was hurt and angered by the Whites whose "rude curiosity" and gazes kept her "on the verge of tears."[118]

Both Standing Bear and Eastman either explicitly or implicitly transformed the word *primitive*—used by Carlisle and other institutions to debase Native cultures—from a condescendingly evaluative word to a descriptive word. Standing Bear elucidates, for example, why his grandfather cut a piece of the lining of the stomach of a newly killed buffalo, washed it in blood, and gave it to him to eat: "The Sioux in those days learned to eat raw meat, so when we were in the enemy's country and did not dare light a fire, we could still get along. . . . We did not know, in those days, what it meant to be anaemic." Such "primitivism" was skillful and intelligent. By contrast, his first impression of Whites—buffalo hunters who piled up skins for market—was that they were like what Whites term primitive: "dirty," hairy, "repulsive," wasteful, and subhuman, "living in dugouts . . . like wild bears." Eastman cleverly linked the word *primitive* to Christianity when describing what it was about Christ—his "hard sayings to the rich"—that appealed to the Natives he met on his YMCA sojourns. Notwithstanding his use of notions of "complex society" (White "civilization") and "simple society" ("Indian" cultures), Eastman had abundant praise for the emotions, virtues, morality, and manners often promoted by the latter.[119]

Pratt's tirades against the BIA would have appealed to students who in all likelihood heard their parents say similar things. Both Eastman, who served as the physician at Pine Ridge, and Standing Bear left their Sioux reservations because the autocracy of the agent, the graft (sometimes pertaining to the awarding of allotments), the organized production of Native helplessness (often termed "pauperizing"), and the spoilation of the loveliness each of them once knew convinced them that they could be of greater help to their people in "civilization." Pratt's speeches about citizenizing also must have kindled the hopes of students whose experience of the reservation rackets made them sick of being, in Bonnin's words of denunciation, "legal victims," "wards" (economic, military, juridical captives) of the state's representatives. Within these new wartime conditions the dollar became one of the weapons Natives wielded to proclaim their "rights." "The properties and funds of the Indians today are estimated at not less than one thousand million dollars," Bonnin wrote. "The government itself owes many millions of dollars for Indian moneys which it has converted to its own use."[120]

Hence some Natives—Eastman, Bonnin, and Standing Bear among them—considered the selective "assimilation" of—not necessarily assimilation to—White culture to be a smart defensive and offensive measure. Judging from the autobiographical texts of these three authors, Natives often mixed assimilation with a degree of disassimilation. Assimilation/disassimilation was frequently critical as well as improvisatory. Originating sometimes, perhaps, in a sense of resignation, selective "assimilation" need not have been passive. If Eastman seems to wind up as a partial advocate of "civilization," along the way he exposes self-critically his dangerous naiveté about "civilization" and the government. "I had overmuch faith in the civilized ideal," he confessed, about his stint as a lobbyist for Natives, "and I was again disappointed."[121]

The word *assimilation*—like the words *American, individual* and *Indian*—is a problematic ideological abstraction. "Rather than simply 'assimilating,'" Philip Deloria (Dakota Sioux) writes of Vine Deloria Sr.'s (Yankton Dakota Sioux) activities in high school and college, "my grandfather helped to create a new, cross-cultural world for himself and his companions."[122] The binary opposition—resistance to assimilation (being true to one's cultural identity) versus submission to assimilation (betraying one's cultural identity)—does not capture the complexity, multiplicity, or intercultural fluidity of the range of Native responses to White American capitalist power. There is no single authentic way of being "Indian" or Sioux. Perhaps "Indian" better describes a relationship and an understanding of relationship than an identity. In fact, "Sioux" was never a fixed or static cultural identity. *Sioux*, a Chippewa word, means "enemy." In the nineteenth century the Sioux consisted of several semiautonomous groups, which included the Dakotas (eastern), Lakotas (western), Santees, Tetons (which divided into the Oglala, Brule, Miniconjou, Two Kettles, Sans Arc, Hunkpapa, Sihasapa). Eastern Sioux groups, tribes, and bands came to call themselves Dakota—meaning "ally"—a word that western Sioux altered into Lakota. At the outset of the twentieth century "Sioux" was even less uniform as a cohesive identity. Eastman, Bonnin, and Standing Bear recognized this and in their own ways fought to give new meanings and possibilities to abstractions like Sioux, Indian, and, for that matter, American. Their ostensible "assimilation" was informed by a political knowledge of the construction and uses of categories of identity.

Bonnin's Sioux heroine who attends a White school remains a warrior and learns the voices, language, and acting necessary to win an oratory contest. Her spirit comes to defy the restrictions of her "Indian" culture (she eventually and symbolically rejects the roots her medicine man gave her when she returns to school) and aspects of her Americanized, regimented "individualizing." The heroine's ongoing organization of self is manifested in the choices she makes in adopting the costumes and language of both cultures: "I had no hat, no ribbons, and no close-fitting apron," the narrator of one of her stories complains, envious of the other girls on the reservation who had adopted "civilized" dress.[123] But wearing that costume does not disable her years later, as a teacher, from responding critically to her interview with the superintendent—who resembles Pratt—of an eastern Indian school very like Carlisle: "I am going to turn you loose to pasture!" says the superintendent. She reflects bitterly: "He was sending me West to gather Indian pupils for the school, and this was his way of expressing it."[124] And so the heroine learns how to negotiate the dangers and possibilities of two cultures in flux, two power structures in flux, and in doing so bears some resemblance to her author, who earned distinction as Zitkala-Ša *and* Gertrude Bonnin.

Here I will elaborate what I have already hinted: the challenge of imagining the sort of Native cultural subjectivities that students brought to Carlisle is made even more complex when one entertains the possibility, the likelihood, that students playfully, ironically, and strategically performed the roles of "individual" and "Indian." What Eastman called "faking Indian" may also have been, at Carlisle, *faking individuality*—the Carlisle definition of "individuality."

Standing Bear, with no little irony and sarcasm, often suggests that what Carlisle sponsored was on some levels "Indian" enactments, almost burlesques, of individualizing and Americanizing. Even if Pratt and his teachers occasionally fancied themselves as Mr. See All or Mr. Man-on-the-band-stand, they never quite saw all that was happening behind the scenes, the smiles, the silences. Although students were forbidden to speak their own language, so that they could better learn English, some could communicate silently through Native sign language. Standing Bear was critical of Carlisle's language training—which compelled students to speak English "like a bunch of parrots"—but he may have learned more than he was supposed to about caricature and performance from this "parroting." Thus when he and his friends soiled the two collars they were issued, they playfully tried their "best to wear the ties without the collars, but I guess we must have looked funny."[125] This theme of playfully enacting an ill-fitting Whiteness is a persistent one in Standing Bear's tales of Carlisle and beyond.

He first saw a model of this playfulness at home, when his father, a chief, returned from a trip to Washington attired in a shirt, coat, and top hat. "When it came time to go to bed, Father kept on his stiff-bosomed shirt. He felt too dressed up to remove it. . . . The next evening he dressed up to go to council . . . [and] stuck an eagle feather in the left side of his silk hat."[126] The scene resembles George Catlin's well-known before-and-after diptych, *Wi-Jun-Jon, The Pigeon's Egg Head (The Light), Going to and Returning from Washington* (1832): the left panel represents the traditionally dressed "Indian" in generic headdress and leather jerkin holding a peace pipe, with what may be the White House in the far background; the right shows him resuited in ceremonial top hat (with feather) and military uniform holding an umbrella and a fan, seeming excited about his new costume, with tipis in the not-so-distant background. One reading is that Wi-Jun-Jon has gullibly and childishly accepted the bribe of new American military clothes to yield to "civilization." In his insightful interpretation Clive Bush detects "two tell-tale gin bottles . . . visible in his back pocket" and argues that Catlin intended to depict a Hogarthian tale of "inevitable decline" that indicts "civilization." At the same time Wi-Jun-Jon's still-conspicuous long hair, red-feathered top hat, and body position—which Catlin chose to turn away from the viewer and painter and toward the tipis—suggest that this uniform may not have had the uniform meaning for him that it did for Whites and that he may have worn it to signify different things and a different status *within* his homeland than Washington officials may have expected. It may be that Catlin wished to complicate Euramerican readings of his subject.[127]

The polysemous uniform reappears in Linda Hogan's *Mean Spirit*, which portrays the legalized oppression of Natives in early-twentieth-century Oklahoma. In this novel native women get married dressed in elaborate army coats with gold braids and epaulets, a tradition that began in the previous century when "an Osage elder had visited the White House" and "admired the coat of a dignitary and received it as a gift from the president." In Standing Bear's anecdote about his father, perhaps in Catlin's painting, and in Hogan's novel, Natives take—and take to—"civilization" as a theatrical game, complete with props and costumes.[128]

Standing Bear certainly relished making a scene. At Carlisle he was issued "too large" boots that were " 'screechy' or squeaky. . . . I liked the noise they made when I walked, and the other boys were likewise pleased." When he went to his Lakota reservation, after leaving Carlisle, costumed in a vaudevillian cutaway, a derby, and cuffs that were too long, he was delighted by an appearance that some may have misread as an ill-suited Whiteness: "All I lacked to resemble Charlie Chaplin was a cane." Even during his tour as keeper of the "Indians" with Buffalo Bill's Wild West Show he learned the lessons of performance: when attendance was not great, "I might take the part of a cowboy if I chose. This was a change for me and I enjoyed it very much."[129] Buffalo Bill's cowboys ("Indians" as well as Whites could play Indian fighters) and "Indians" (chiefs could perform "chiefs") were both fictional—shot through with stereotypes.[130]

Standing Bear achieved some distance from certain styles of individualizing, Americanizing, and Indianizing by consciously and playfully parodying, caricaturing, parroting, and marketing these styles. Indeed, he reveled in, though sometimes severely criticized, their ill-fitting patterns.[131] If only implicitly he tried to tell Pratt that this was the strategy he had learned at Carlisle, when in 1920 he sent the general greetings for his eightieth birthday. Standing Bear *typed* his good wishes to the old soldier below a letterhead that depicted him dressed in his chief's outfit, a suitable image for one who owned an "Indian" archery range in Venice, California. His letterhead advertisement read: "Chief Standing Bear, Sioux South Dakota, True Authority on All Questions Concerning the Sioux Nation" (figure 9). To the left of this headline is a photograph of him standing in a blanket and headdress, and to the right is another photograph of him shirtless and in headdress pointing to the sky with one hand while the other holds a bow and arrow (as if mockingly quoting Longfellow's hackneyed line, "I shot an arrow into the air,/It fell to earth, I knew not where").[132]

Standing Bear, Sitting Bull, and many other Natives realized that Natives increasingly would have to wrestle with pressures and opportunities to perform themselves, or White images of themselves, in strategic ways. "I felt that I was no more Indian, but would be an imitation of a white man," Standing Bear wrote. "And we are still imitations of white men, and the white men are imitations of the Americans."[133] Even Dennison Wheelock, one of Pratt's most devoted proteges, recognized how Carlisle performances of "individuality" were symbiotically linked to performing "Indian." After finishing at Carlisle, Wheelock stayed on as bandleader, and in this role he brought the school and the band much fame. But Wheelock reached a stage when he found it necessary to appeal to Pratt's ethos of competition and success and explained that he had to leave Carlisle to move on to conduct a professional Indian band. Wheelock's American Indian Concert Band would convey the idea that "Indians can now be competitors with the greatest."[134] Yet his letterhead, like Standing Bear's, made commercial use of the stereotype of the "wild" pre-"civilized" "Indian"—with feathers on either side of his shaved head, like demonic horns—to captivate the Euramerican commercial public (figure 10).

Sometimes this playfulness—"faking Indian"—reproduced baneful stereotypes. Hence Standing Bear was frustrated in his work as an actor in Hollywood. Although "Indians" were visible as characters in Westerns, Standing Bear contended with directors, playwrights, and screenwriters who ignored his efforts to tell them about Native ways. Actors who played "Indians" but were not Native—examples of Whites imitating (first) Americans—rose through the ranks, while the Native thespians languished in obscurity. (Jim Thorpe [Sac and Fox, Potawatomi], Carlisle athletic star and Olympic gold medalist, aspired to star in a movie about himself, but eventually Burt Lancaster won the part.)[135] Standing Bear discovered that the "civilization" consecrated to making "individuals" was hooked, especially in its twentieth-century consumer

9. Chief Standing Bear's Archery Range letterhead, 1920, Yale Collection of Western Americana, Beinecke Rare Book and Manuscript Library

10. Dennison Wheelock's "American Indian Concert Band" letterhead, Yale Collection of Western Americana, Beinecke Rare Book and Manuscript Library

culture guise, on distorted performances of racial and ethnic identity. American individualism itself was not the expression of the core of the self, or the revelation of one's uniqueness; it consisted, Standing Bear realized, of marketable routines, props, stages, and roles that contributed to the ideological assumption that the conquest of "Indians" was as inevitable and progressive as the human evolution of "civilization." Chief Standing Bear had migrated from Carlisle's individualizing factory to Hollywood's individualizing movie set and was chagrined, yet oddly fascinated, by both.

Eastman's portrait of Spotted Tail—the Washington, D.C.-recognized chief who made a habit of signing away Sioux land to the government and of aiding in the capture of "hostiles" in return for money, a fine home, and preferential treatment—highlights the dangers of overeager performance. Spotted Tail, wrote Eastman, was "apt at mimicry and impersonations" as a boy. "He had come into contact with white people at the various trading posts, and according to his own story had made a careful study of the white man's habits and modes of thought, especially his peculiar trait of economy and intense desire to accumulate property." Deciding that White rule was inevitable, "he copied the white politician too closely after he entered the reservation. He became a good manipulator, and was made conceited and overbearing by the attention of the military and of the general public."[136] Spotted Tail sent his children to Carlisle and then retrieved them. Finally he was assassinated by Crow Dog for betraying and humiliating his people.

Many Natives who had been associated with Carlisle endeavored to use—or exploit—the appearance of American capitalist "individuality" and of Indianness in tactical ways. Carlos Montezuma, who served as Carlisle's school physician for a time in the 1890s, was one of the most strident advocates of assimilation and launched a belligerent publicity campaign that called for the abolition of the BIA. Writing to Pratt in 1892, the "individualized" Apache physician's pronouns—"we," "our"—reflect the distance he saw between himself and tribalized "Indians" (perhaps exemplified by the Shoshones he treated on their Nevada reservation): "We have enslaved the Indians in ignorance and superstition long enough and have fed and clothed them without any recompense. . . . They are expensive failures."[137] Yet when Pratt was fired from his post at Carlisle, Montezuma was so aggrieved that, to use Eastman's term again, he resorted to flowery "Indian faking" in his complaint to President Theodore Roosevelt: "In silence I have looked upon you as a great father at Washington to my people. . . . There is not a wigwam throught [sic] the country that can smoke the pipe of peace with you for such an act of injustice to our veteran leader."[138]

In one of his missives to Pratt, Arthur Parker remarked wryly that the magazine Montezuma published to denounce the BIA (whose cover depicted Montezuma in a suit charging the door of the BIA with a battering ram) was titled with Montezuma's Apache name, *Wassaja*—"he has been so against everything aboriginal."[139] Parker, who was becoming successful as a New York State anthropologist, was fed up with the way White culture forced the category of "Indian" on Natives, especially successful ones. In 1914 Edward Dixon, author of the nostalgic *The Vanishing Race: The Last Great Indian Council* (1913)—featuring Rodman Wanamaker's highly romanticized sepia photographs of elaborately staged and stereotypical vanishing "Indian" chiefs—masterminded a highly publicized celebration of the evolution of Manhattan. Dixon had no qualms about using any "Indians" in the publicity: "Our New York Senecas," Parker objected, "were advertised as 'lineal descendants of the first occupants of the Island' which is a lie and an imposition."[140] Continuing his critique Parker (mistakenly) assumed that his preferred category of "man" stood outside the networks of social scripting that in his eyes forced Natives to perform "Indian": "The idea that because an Indian is an Indian he must be more or less of a show clings everywhere; the idea that the Indian is a man and may develop in progressive lines is only slowly penetrating."[141]

Yet Pratt, as I have suggested, was himself a clever showman who knew how to take theatrical advantage of a specifically "Indian" individualizing to promote Carlisle. Writing to Pratt in 1923 on the historical significance of Carlisle, Sparhawk underlined "the vast importance of educating the Indians at the East where the country could see their possibilities and accomplishments."[142] When Carlisle was founded, the East harbored less prejudice than the West against Native students, but it also made them stand out more as distinctly "Indian" individuals-in-training. Pratt's before-and-after photographs of students were ideal for gaining the attention and support of sympathetic and wealthy easterners. Uniformed Indianness (the before) as much as uniformed individuality (the after) was essential to the theatrical and photographic illusion of Carlisle as an Evolution Factory.

Pratt's stagy Indianizing of "Indians" never restrained him from righteously condemning reservations as sites that "Indianize the Indian," or from insisting that in order for "the Indian" to be "a man" and "a citizen" he had "to quit his Indianism."[143] What riled Pratt most of all were "Indians" who had evolved beyond being "Indians" (as he thought he understood them) into "individuals," but who then continued to Indianize themselves. This sort of impenitent Indianism disrupted commonly held evolutionary assumptions that being "individual" was more progressive than being "Indian"—something Standing Bear probably had in mind when he wrote Pratt on his Chief Standing Bear stationery. In 1887 Pratt lamented that the "greatest chief of the Osages" who had just died was a tragic product of Catholicism's tolerance of Native ways. The chief, "educated by the Romish church in their Osage mission and in their great school at St. Louis," was obdurately "Indian": "He was said to be proficient in Latin. He spoke the English language; but when he returned to his people he donned the blanket, and never made any attempt to use his education when meeting in council with the whites, but always talked to the whites through an interpreter, and demanded to be talked to through the same channel." Pratt saw the chief's behavior as his rejection of "education" rather than a practice shaped by what he learned from his Osage and Catholic educations.

Worst of all, for Pratt, were Carlisle students who went back to "the blanket" and publicly performed their allegiance to their culture. In 1903 Pratt painfully recalled observing a "smoke dance" near Fort Sill, Oklahoma, in which Wichitas danced for Comanches. One of the first two dancers was John Tatum, a former Carlisle student, who was "entirely nude except for a breech cloth" and "hideous" body paint. Some of the Wichita scouts who had served with him in the cavalry were also participants. The main feature turned out to be the eminent Comanche Chief Quanah Parker, a "half-breed." Parker's father had been a war chief. His mother, captured by Comanches, was "from one of the most prominent white families of Parker Co., Central Texas." Pratt had enrolled "four of Quanah's children at Carlisle." Two of Parker's daughters, one an assistant matron at a local Indian school and the other an assistant clerk, attended the ceremony "dressed as refined and educated young women" and watched their father attack the "effigy of a white man": "He dashed forward with his gun toward the effigy, sometimes circling and retreating several times until finally he demonstrated how he gave the successful shot. Having killed his man, he dashed up and struck the effigy with his bow or gun, thereby claiming that scalp. He then went forward in front of the dancers and musicians and told with a loud voice when, where and how he had overcome that particular enemy."[144] Pratt's disgust with the episode did not wholly mask his respect for this martial and cultural warrior.

Parker is an excellent example of someone who self-consciously meshed cultures and formations of subjectivity in ways that Pratt could not countenance or even begin to grasp as intelligent. He adored his mother, who was recaptured by Whites with her young daughter and died not long after her daughter died. The Comanche chief gained great repute as a fighter, and when he was forced to surrender became a prosperous farmer and rancher whose house contained "a separate room (with sewing machines) for each of his seven wives." One of his sons who had attended Carlisle became a Methodist minister. Parker, who spoke English well, lobbied vigorously in Washington and hunted with President Theodore Roosevelt, his friend, in Indian country. He opposed the ghost dance, advocated the peyote religion, disdained the drinking of alcohol, and was treated by a White physician and a peyotist before dying in 1911.[145]

This elastic integration of cultural identities was not unusual. Several of Carlisle's former students, like Albert Hensley (Winnebago) and Arthur Bonnicastle (Osage), not only dressed in suits and had short hair, belonged to the Society of American Indians, and converted to Christianity, they practiced and Christianized the peyote faith and fought to keep it legal. Numerous Carlisle students were just as flexible culturally and emotionally during and after their training at Carlisle.

Recent work on Black Elk has sought to account for the fact that the man whom Neihardt portrayed as extremely traditional in his religious and cultural ways and as living spiritually and nostalgically in the Sioux past converted to Catholicism in 1904 and soon after worked as a catechist. Clyde Holler outlines several considerations that may also be related to understanding how some Native students may have responded to Carlisle. Holler emphasizes that Black Elk, like other Sioux and Sioux holy men, was not just a victim of social changes but a creative agent who adapted to change in ways useful for the Sioux and for himself. As a holy man Black Elk was particularly committed to living in the present, not the past, and to helping resolve his people's pressing difficulties. The Lakota holy man acted as a mediator between himself and the supernatural to gain access to *power* to ensure the survival and well-being of his people. Lakotas could be far more flexible, elastic, and pragmatic in what they believed than White missionaries or scholars ever guessed. Here again Sioux constructions of what is termed individuality must be reckoned with: "Lakota religion exhibited considerable individualism in both belief and ritual expression. There was no credo, no catechism, no prayer book, and no hell to threaten those who failed to believe." Indeed, as noted above, there was no word for "religion" in the Lakota language. Holler concludes: "If Black Elk believed what the Catholic Church taught was to a certain extent true and that it was to a certain extent doing good, he could have served it in good conscience."[146] The Sioux were open to a *simultaneity of beliefs* in what Whites considered to be competing and contradictory ideas.[147]

To the degree that Carlisle students also came from cultures that taught them the importance of gaining access to power and, as part of this objective, of maintaining an elasticity of belief, then they may well have learned performance skills at school. For some of them these performance skills added up to a strategically flexible empowerment, which might be shared with the tribe at home, rather than a standardized assimilation to a fairly fixed, rigid, orthodox concept of U.S. capitalist "individuality." I will rework Holler's formulation: if some Carlisle students believed what Carlisle taught was to a certain extent true and useful for tribal and individual survival and well-being, they could have learned and performed what they were being taught in good conscience.

Note two before-and-after drawings in an "Autographs" sketchbook dated 1880 with the signed name Charles Ohetoint (spelled Ohettoint elsewhere, on the allotment rolls Oheltoint, on the police payroll O'Hetowit), from Pratt's collection (figures 11 and 12). Ohetoint (Kiowa), also called Charley Buffalo and Padai (meaning "twin"), was one of Pratt's Fort Marion prisoners. He went on to Hampton and then Carlisle (at the age of twenty-seven). Shortly before going to Hampton, where he was baptized, he wrote: "When I go home . . . I can reach all the Indians and try to do good. . . . I am white men now." Interviewed with six other prisoners by President Rutherford B. Hayes, he recounted: "Pratt told us each what to say to the President—that we wanted a school for just Indians. And we said it." He left Carlisle in June 1880 and served on his reservation as a teacher, policeman, farmer, carpenter, stock raiser, and recruiter for Carlisle. After some successes and setbacks in his employment, this man of many names resumed his stock raising in traditional Native garb, lived in a tipi (in 1908 he moved into a house), married a couple of wives (this cost him his police job), and befriended the ethnologist James Mooney (whom Pratt reviled). Prior to his arrest he had distinguished himself as a warrior. His renditions of the before-and-after process show a marked change in costume—from fringed buckskin and flowing headdress to uniform and cap. But Ohetoint's-Ohettoint's-Oheltoint's-Charley Buffalo's-Padai's reclothed person remains the same, with identical posture, smiling throughout.[148] The image supports Francis La Flesche's belief, based on his own experience, that "the school uniform did not change those who wore it."[149]

Pratt learned much from serving with Native scouts and from his prisoners at Fort Marion. His sales pitch, as I have stressed, tapped Native audiences' interest in regaining *power*: have your children learn how to read and speak English at Carlisle, he advised, so that you can read the writing on the wall and on the page and will not be cheated. But what Pratt may not have taken into account or fathomed was the flexible subjectivities students from diverse tribes brought to Carlisle in their pursuit of power. Carlisle helped equip Natives with the skills to negotiate Euramerican power in ways that the school could not regulate once students left it. As Hoxie points out, Carlisle's former students, including Reginald Oshkosh (Menominee), Patrick Miguel (Quechan), Delos Lone Wolf (Kiowa), and William Paul Jr. (Tlingit), used their English and knowledge of White values, such as the sacredness of property rights and individual rights, to help them guide tribal councils, advocate for their tribes in courts, appropriate the rhetoric of "civilization" and Americanness, and circulate petitions and lobby in legislatures and Congress on behalf of Native causes. This access to power frequently required some self-transformation and "countless choices, poses, and trade-offs" as they defended and in some cases modified "ancient traditions."[150] Former students were able to fight the dominant hegemony in ways called "modern"—within Euramerican hegemony's own terms and structures.

The effects of Carlisle's individualizing programs were no doubt complex. Carlisle's ideological radicalism, during Pratt's reign, was that it taught students that no matter what religious authorities, evolution theorists, authors, government bureaucrats, politicians, newspaper reporters, cattlemen, farmers, or any White persons wrote or said about "Indians," there were no inherently determinative racial qualities. By focusing on the individual and not the race, Pratt's Carlisle could try to look beyond ideologies of evolution and teach students that they were capable of anything, not as "Indians," but as "individuals."

But if Carlisle's critical strength, during Pratt's reign, was its putative refusal to accept the notion of racial essence, its schooling framed a host of ideologically and historically shaped categories—such as individuality, manhood, and femininity—as incontestably fixed, desirable, and good. Being a uniform Carlisle "individual," a uniform Carlisle "man," a uniform Carlisle "woman" in certain ways carried with it as much cultural self-hatred as any evolutionary ideology that proclaimed the existence of unalterably inferior racial essences. Pratt promoted Carlisle's brand of individuality as signifying independence, but it aimed to make "Indian" students more economically and emotionally reliant on White culture than ever before. Some boarding school students complained that on leaving the school it was difficult to structure daily experience without bells, whistles, commands, and collective regimentation.[151] The "individualizing" of "Indian" students was the culmination of a Euramerican-Native history whose defining trend was legal, educational, religious, and bureaucratic campaigns to make "Indians" *dependent on* dominant Euramerican culture. In one of Pratt's candid statements published in *The Red Man*, he acknowledged that "the order and system so necessary in an institution retards rather than develops habits of self-reliance and forethought; individuality is lost. They grow into mechanical routine."[152]

Students came from diverse tribal and sometimes multitribal cultures, family backgrounds (cross-blood, full-blood), religious instructions, and social experiences with White Americans, African Americans, Asian Americans, and European immigrants. Their multifaceted and labile responses to boarding school and *to one another* ranged across the spectrum from mutual aid to competitive individualism and from solidarity to gang-organized bullying.[153] Some students located

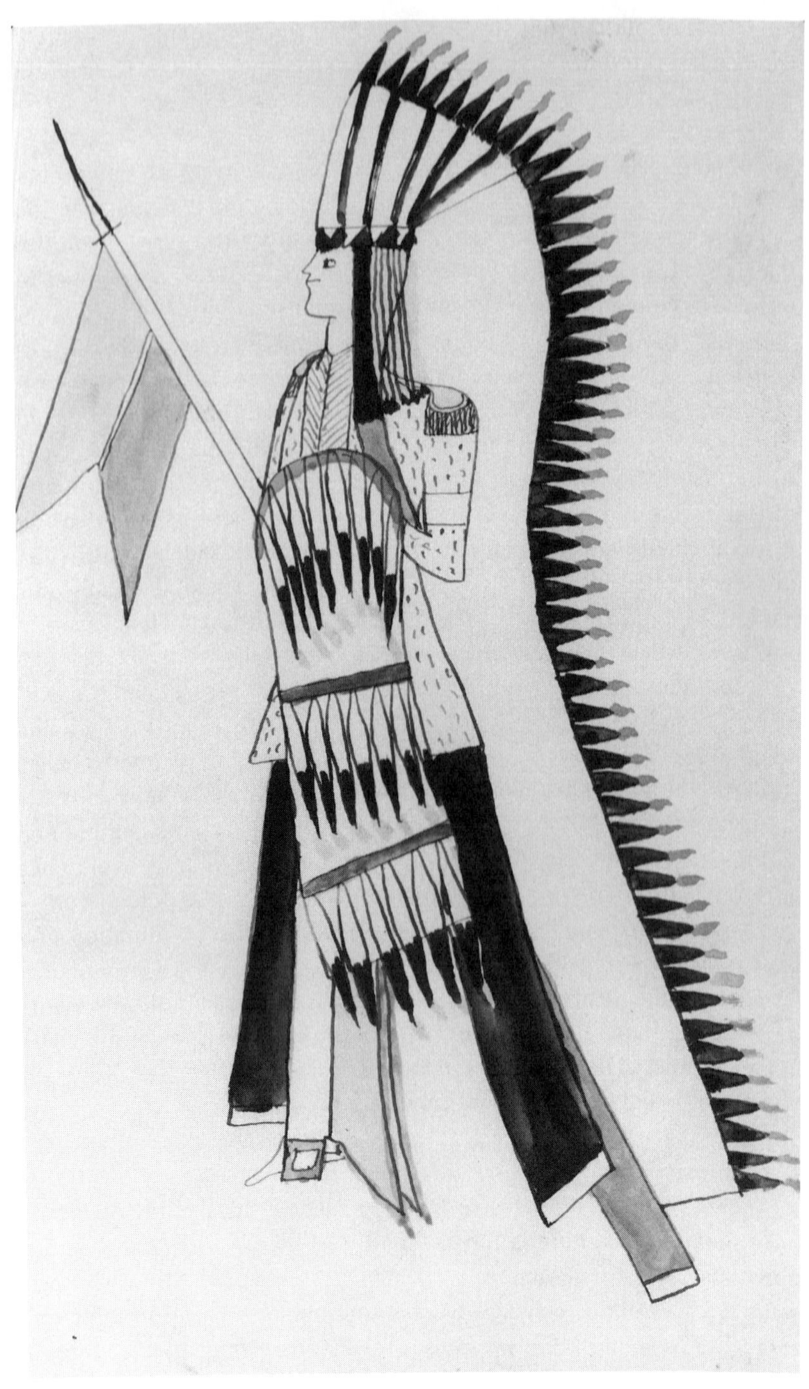

11. Charles Ohetoint's Carlisle drawing of boy in "Indian" garb, Yale Collection of Western Americana, Beinecke Rare Book and Manuscript Library

12. Charles Ohetoint's Carlisle drawing of the same boy in school military uniform, Yale Collection of Western Americana, Beinecke Rare Book and Manuscript Library

Carlisle's power in performance and exulted in their self-conscious enactment of an ill-fitting and parodic off-White "individuality" that may never have been anywhere near as uniform as it seemed to Pratt. It may be that these students, like Standing Bear, came to regard American "individuality" not as superior but as just one among many possible forms of the cultural organization of life, labor, affection, and value. Other students, overwhelmed by what Carlisle wanted them to believe about themselves, their families, their cultures, and America, rejected Carlisle's uniforms of individuality altogether and escaped or served their sentence or died from the shock of it all. Still others—whether or not they were displeased with life and definitions of life, and opportunities and definitions of opportunities on the reservations—may have studied to "improve" themselves and emulated the brand of individual Pratt exhorted them to become. Of course, students may have experienced various mixes of the intercultural responses described above and in fact may have responded in ways that neither I nor other scholars have yet begun to imagine.

What Carlisle also began to expose students to, sometimes intentionally, was the idea that youth from tribes throughout the continent shared political, economic, cultural, and emotional concerns that united them as "Indians"—something that, as Gerald Vizenor (Anishinaabe) notes, the learning of English in schools facilitated.[154] Once they perceived some possibility of unity, they could begin to take steps to redefine the word *Indian* and start tactically to *Indianize themselves*.[155] (Some students learned not only better English but their own tribal languages from other students at boarding school.)[156] The first pan-Indian congresses in the United States were those held informally and without design at nonreservation Indian schools. One reason some former Carlisle students sent their children to Carlisle may have been that they knew their offspring would meet children from other tribes and contemplate what it would mean to identify themselves as "Indian"—*and* as "individual" or *not* as "individual"—in swiftly changing social conditions. At times all Carlisle students must have in sundry ways reflected on how they were being taught, and how they were actively and creatively teaching one another, to read the emerging category of Indian as well as the categories of individual and American, and must have contemplated their own and their tribe's future possibilities living with, against, and in such potentially malleable categories.[157]

PART TWO

Multicultural Modernity

Incorporated

3

Modernist Multiculturalism:

Lawrence, Luhan, and the White Therapeutic Indianizing

of "Lost" White Individuality

[The Zuni] sink individuality in them. . . . The Pueblos are not a neurotic people.
—Ruth Benedict, *Patterns of Culture*, 1934

We watched karate movies
at the East Sprague Drive-In
and I didn't mind the dubbed dialogue
It would be years before my voice was lost the same way.
—Sherman Alexie (Spokane and Coeur d'Alene), "Spokane, 1976," 1993

Every neurosis, every abnormal manifestation, every affective erethism in an Antillean is the product of his cultural situation. . . . There is a constellation of postulates, a series of propositions that slowly and subtly—with the help of books, newspapers, schools and their texts, advertisements, films, radio—work their way into one's mind and shape one's view of the group to which one belongs.
—Frantz Fanon, *Black Skin, White Masks*, 1952[1]

The thought that famous educated Whites might actually identify with "Indians" and believe that non-neurotic "Indians" nurtured something life-giving beyond economic prosperity that the overcivilized—overneuroticized—White world had *lost* would no doubt have seemed ludicrous to Pratt and most of the middle- and upper-class Anglo-Saxon Protestant Friends of the Indian. But this did indeed take shape as an ideological—and commercial—trend, even as Indian schools busily stamped "individuals." Carlisle's truculent superintendent was a staunch ideological product and agent of the nineteenth century's industrial-producer-sentimental culture, whereas notions of psychologically redemptive "Indians" tend to be ideological expressions of the twentieth century's corporate-consumer-therapeutic culture. The complex and contradictory transition to liberal corporate capitalism—which Pratt witnessed, having lived until 1924—is important to reflect on because it encompasses a shift in the production of *subjective styles* that affected the encodings, uses, agency, and organization of "Indians."

In this chapter and the next I mount a historical critique of two related developments: the ideological resignification of "Indians" as therapeutic in the early twentieth century and the governmental reorganizing of Natives as subjects of protomulticultural administration in the 1930s and 1940s. This entails, first, analyzing the roles that one largely White group of modernists in the Southwest—featuring Mabel Dodge Luhan, D. H. Lawrence, and Mary Austin—played in the psychological, aesthetic, and commercial rewriting of Indianness, and, second, the interactions between John Collier's protomulticultural Indian New Deal and Natives. To place these connected formations in context I must trace briefly some of what I see at stake in this modern shift in subjective styles. Below I sketch a few aspects of the shift—involving discourses of character, of personality, of depth, of puritanism versus paganism, of the modernisms—to introduce the more substantive investigations that follow.

Jackson Lears and other historians have pointed out that there was in early-twentieth-century class-stratified corporate America a weakening of confidence in Franklinesque self-making—the premise, espoused by Carlisle's teachers and publications, that hard work and perseverance will eventually enable one to master one's social and economic challenges. In response, "modern" subjective styles emerged that can be comprehended partly as compensations for worries about the greater difficulty of "making" the "self" in a liberal corporate order reliant on mass-cultural standardization. One mass-cultural style was "personality." Warren Susman has studied a shift from a nineteenth-century producer and entrepreneurial "character" model (a cultural form of self that values morality, self-denial, self-sacrifice, the work ethic, respectability) to a modern corporate and consumer culture of "personality" model (a cultural form of self that promotes self-gratification, sex appeal, consumption, popularity). "Personality" not only provided uneasy worker-consumers with a compensatory sense of attractive or even glamorous "individuality," but modern advice book authors also hawked the cultivation of personality as essential for success in the business and sexual marketplaces (impression management).[2]

Another crucial subjective style that appears is one I have written about at length elsewhere—"depth."[3] The early twentieth century is not only the age in which there is a heightened consciousness of the corporate, industrial, and mass-cultural standardization of self, it is also the era in which mass culture circulates ideologies about instincts as hot commodities and "psychological" common sense. If this same period can be seen as one in which management tactics become more sophisticated in their methods of controlling "personnel" (often "psychological" in orientation), it is also a period in which consumers are persuaded that self-realization is contingent not on *controlling* the self but on the "psychological" *release* of repressed desires and "individuality." While Benjamin Franklin understood secular sin as failing to work hard and falling into debt, and secular salvation as succeeding economically as a worker-citizen, growing numbers of modern corporate workers in therapeutic culture were more likely, at least according to what the critic Joseph Freeman wrote in 1936, to imagine sin as "suffer[ing] from suppressed desires" and salvation as living unrepressed.[4]

Increasingly, modern consumers keen to shore up their shaken sense of individuality in liberal corporate America bought and bought into discourses of personality *and* of depth. Personality glamorizes the idea that one must scrutinize surfaces and consciously manipulate one's appearance based on a knowledge of behavioral patterns. Whereas depth glamorizes the idea that one possesses an essential, instinctual, unconscious core of self that drives one regardless of one's conscious motivations and denials. Therapeutic depth discourses in both pop psychology books and more orthodox psychological publications offered consumers a new "psychological" sense of "individual" significance and a scientific permission to fascinate themselves with themselves as complicated, sexy texts and subtexts—akin to the textual multidimensionality of some modernist literature and art. By focusing their attention on much-publicized rosters of individualized and familialized "psychological" problems and narratives, psychologized consuming "individuals" could feel that the corporate world could never quite grasp—in both senses of the word—their "inner self."

A related aspect of consumer-therapeutic culture subjectivity formation is the re-representation of the family, the body, and femininity as psychologically primitive. The nineteenth-century bourgeoisie usually used the category of the "primitive" as a means of degrading subordinated groups such as "primitive" workers, "primitive" racialized others, or biologically "primitive" women. By the second decade of the twentieth century, writers writing for the professional-managerial class, often influenced by psychoanalysis and sometimes by ethnography, redefined "primitivism" as the "psychological" core of "deep" "individuality" that had to be acknowledged and within limits released from repression. By imagining their bodies as harboring a psychologically primitive essence, members of the professional-managerial class, with invaluable assistance from this social group's own dissenting countercultures, hatched a new ideological strategy tending toward self-mystification and self-affirmation. The ideological attraction of this psychological-primitive union was so strong that even the nineteenth-century middle-class sentimental "angel in the house" got to go "primitive" in her "modern" makeover.[5] Pop psychology books, such as Dr. Louis Bisch's *Be Glad You're Neurotic* (1936) and William J. Fielding's *The Caveman Within Us: His Peculiarities and Power; How We Can Enlist his Aid for Health and Efficiency* (1922), tried to appeal to consumers not only within but beyond the professional-managerial class in their mass-cultural mission to disseminate and mesh simplified ideologies of personality, depth, and the primitive as keys to the self requisite for "modern" success.

Many who rebelled on behalf of their *primitive individuality within* gradually came to see this psychological insurgency in terms of national culture—as a distinctly American rebellion against American "puritanism." Romantic Rebels often nominated themselves not primitives but "pagans." The most popular (re)definition of puritans is one that H. L. Mencken crafted in 1920: "The haunting fear that someone, somewhere, may be happy."[6] Four years earlier Randolph Bourne offered a critique of "puritans" that may never have achieved the popularity of Mencken's quip but was a far more penetrating analysis of twentieth-century cultural constructions of subjective potency and styles. Bourne associated "modern" "puritan" incentive with the "cult of efficiency," the "cult of making good"—values promoted by the nineteenth-century discourse of character—and opposition to the "new paganism." The key to his analysis was that puritans do much more than abase, control, or deny themselves, actions that in and of themselves do not generate potency; rather they take enormous satisfaction and pride out of doing so. They invest abasement not just with self-regard but with moral, spiritual, and cultural prestige. This is how they feel powerful and how capitalism uses forms of subjectivity vigorously to reproduce itself.[7] His analysis derives from the psychoanalytic repression model: repressed drives achieve egoistic satisfaction in substitutive form (puritan efficiency and money-making). If one applies Bourne's definition, Pratt endeavored to transform "Indians" into "puritans." He tried to produce a form of this subjective potency for his charges through Carlisle's individualizing and character-manufacturing programs—ego-building via self-abasement.

Bourne turned the psychological analysis of substitutive satisfactions into a social indictment of American producers, competitors, success fanatics: "The primitive currents of life are not blocked and turned back on their sources, but turned into powerful and usually devastating channels."[8] He represents repression as a form of colonization, or *assimilation* (of "primitive currents"). As I ponder this, especially the multivalence of his language, what comes to mind is not just uniformed Carlisle "primitives" photographed while working industriously at machines, but also the 1909 photograph of the Carlisle cast of *The Captain at Plymouth*, in which "primitives" have been costumed as Pilgrims. Interestingly, Bourne published both "The Puritan's Will to Power" and "Trans-national America" in 1916. In the latter piece he repudiated "melting pot" assimilation as a form of "Anglo-Saxonizing" with the same zeal that energized his attack on "puritan" repression as a mechanism of capitalist organization. Considered in tandem, these two essays allied psychological antipuritanism's war against repression with pluralist anti–Anglo-Saxonism's protest against assimilation. The pairing makes sense, for some of the Euramerican bohemians, artists, and intellectuals who helped reinvent "puritans" as distinctly American psychological types would increasingly side with "Indians" (as will become clear) as focal points for their revolts against repression and assimilation. The battles against repression and against assimilation, on behalf of one's *Indian within* and one's suppressed "primitive" "rhythms," were complementary tendencies within emerging therapeutic modernisms.

Quite quickly consumer culture proved adept at incorporating psychological and pluralist antipuritanism into its reproductive strategies and weakened its links with economic critiques of capitalism. Generally, it was to the capitalist hegemony's advantage to allow itself to be cast as a "puritanical" more than as an economically oppressive system (a development that very likely would have disappointed Bourne had he lived to perceive it clearly). Stated oversimply, if critics perceived capitalism as posing a problem principally because it prevented one from expressing one's "self," why then capitalism would have to provide commodities, therapies, and rebel ideologies that would profitably address that agitated need for self-expression.

This antipuritanical and antiassimilationist "individuality" rebellion and other related rebellions were informed by and contributed to the development of American modernism, or, using Ann Douglas's adjective, the "mongrel" modernisms.[9] The modernisms never coalesced to form a dogmatic aesthetic or cultural movement partly because cultural producers' views of and hopes for "the modern" were so multiplicitous. Modernism, like multiculturalism, is, above all, as Carla Kaplan put it, messy.[10] Daniel Singal admits that "we currently have almost no agreement on how to define it."[11]

Some scholars conceive of modernism narrowly as a literary, artistic, architectural, or musical movement or tendency; other scholars, as Kaplan notes, imagine it more expansively as a cultural period during which many, often conflicting modernist forms, preoccupations, perspectives, ways of life, and institutions were established.[12] Scholars have long recognized that two of the hallmarks of the modernisms, paradoxically, are the antimodernisms and primitivisms.[13] Of particular interest to me in this chapter are aspects of the confluence of the modernisms and cultural relativism. In 1903, only three years after Sigmund Freud published *The Interpretation of Dreams*, a magisterial volume that contributed much to professional-managerial class ideologies of psychological interiority and the unconscious, W. E. B. Du Bois published *The Souls of Black Folk*, also a groundbreaking book that examines how American racism socially produces a "double consciousness," a "twoness," a "second sight" in "Negroes" that compels them to view themselves through the White racist gaze. Freud focuses on what he considers to be the bedrock of "human nature," while Du Bois concentrates on how social categories of racial difference produce what comes to be experienced as "human nature." Many modernists embraced therapeutic ideologies of individualized "psychological" "depth." At the same time, many modernists, including some "psychological" modernists, became interested in how constructions of race structure subjectivities.[14] Both Freud and Du Bois helped put in motion intellectual approaches, concerns, and problems that would preoccupy—or haunt—intellectuals and artists throughout the twentieth century.

Hence the *therapeutic modernist* campaigns against "psychological" repression (Bourne's antipuritanism) were accompanied by *ethnomodernist* campaigns against "melting" minority groups in the assimilation pot (Bourne's anti–Anglo-Saxonism).[15] The modernist recovery of "psychological" "depth," which revitalized "individuality" (and sometimes self-absorption), and ethnomodernist cultural pluralism, which reinvigorated cosmopolitanism (and sometimes exoticism), were often integrated projects in artist colonies like Greenwich Village, Taos, and Santa Fe. Both campaigns frequently entertained a too narrow notion of the social power against which they rebelled, a power they imagined as modern standardization. And both camps valued *difference*: the modernist "psychological" "individual" would prize his or her difference from everyone else, while the ethnomodernist pluralist would appreciate differences among ethnoracial cultures. Just as the modernist "psychological" "individual" endeavored to be nonjudgmental about (especially sexual) behavior, the ethnomodernist pluralist often attempted to be open-minded about the customs of other races and cultures. The unrepressed individual would try to recognize his or her unconscious drives and accept his or her sexuality, while the pluralist citizen would attempt to value the presence of immigrants and ethnoracial "others" (sometimes encoded as excessively sexual). Bohemian therapeutic and modernist self-discovery, then, could take the form both of engaging in sexually and psychologically liberating behavior *and* of rubbing elbows with immigrants and ethnoracial "others." In these ways the psychological modernist repression model and the cultural relativist modernist assimilation model, and their sometimes limited conceptualizations of power (understood too reductively as repression or homogenization), were intertwined.[16]

Chapters 3 and 4 clarify the historical significance of the *modernist protomulticulturalisms*—promoted by artists, novelists, intellectuals, bohemians, community activists, tourism companies, museums, schools, the Indian New Deal's BIA. Discourses of "depth," the "primitive within," antipuritanism, cultural relativism, and in some cases socialism contributed to and were in turn shaped by the ideological formation of these modernist protomulticulturalisms. Some of what modernist protomulticulturalists stood for may seem unambiguously liberatory; but liberatory in what ways and for whom? As Native scholars in particular warn, critiques of internal colonization too often turn out to be new forms of that colonization.

As I indicated in my introduction, I have elected to employ the word *multicultural* (made popular since the early 1970s) rather than *pluralist* (the word first used to label this kind of thinking beginning in the early decades of the twentieth century) for two reasons. First, it has been argued that one great difference between early-twentieth-century pluralism and the multiculturalism of the 1960s and beyond is that the former did not take institutional forms and initiatives. Pluralism, however, was more than an intellectual argument in this period. In the 1930s and early 1940s "Indian" pluralism took numerous institutional forms—museums, publishing houses, tourism companies, and the Indian New Deal's bureaucracy. Second, this chapter and the next will show that many of the views held by modernist protomulticulturalists and more

contemporary multiculturalists are strikingly similar.[17] A better knowledge of the ideological crosscurrents that informed the earlier phase
may reveal something about the political implications of the latter.

*Toward Therapeutic Imperialism: Garland and the
Modernizing of Digestion Management*

Hamlin Garland prepared to write his "Indian" novel of 1901, *The Captain of the Gray-Horse Troop,* by living among numerous Native tribes in
the mid-1890s.[18] This tour produced quasi-ethnographic pieces on the
Utes, Navajos, Moki, Zuni, Jicarilla Apaches, Cheyenne, and Creek. He
often vented his anger about the Natives' predicament. In "The Red Man
as Material" (1903) he criticized American fiction for ideologically abetting the military and cultural colonization of Natives. His most radical
published essay from this period was "The Red Man's Present Needs"
(1902). In this critique he relabeled reservations "'corrals,' or open-air
prisons, into which the original owners of the continent have been im-
pounded by the white race." He attacked allotment as a futile "attempt to
make the Sioux a greedy land-owner." Garland dismissed off-reservation
boarding schools, specifically naming Carlisle, and much of the work of
missionaries as "inelastic" and unchristian.

Yet many of his forward-looking critiques and suggestions were inflected by the belief that Whites must serve faithfully as the custodians,
or managers, of "Stone Age" men and women who were still "children"
on the evolutionary scale: "We are answerable for them, just as we are
answerable for the black man's future. As the dominant race, we have
dispossessed them."[19] This evolutionary hierarchy legitimized the existing racial hierarchy. The keyword here, notwithstanding Garland's
enlightened intentions, is *dominant.*

Many of Garland's ideas in these pieces reappear as characters' didactic speeches in *Captain of the Gray-Horse Troop.* The novel is in illuminating ways awkwardly poised between producer-culture perceptions of "Indians" and some other ideological views of "Indians" that
would grow more powerful and defined in the emerging corporate-
consumer-therapeutic culture. Captain Curtis, assigned to oversee Fort
Smith and its artist colony in Indian country, is eager to experiment with
new ways of managing the Tetons. Curtis's managerial premises blend
producer- and therapeutic-culture notions of "Indians." Osborne Lawson, an ethnographer, holds equally mixed views. The most obvious
representative of producer culture aggression against "Indians" is Senator Andrew Brisbane, who has numerous clashes with Curtis. He iterates

the producer thesis that the Indians should not "be allowed to camp on land which they can't use" (126). His daughter Elsie, an aspiring artist, undergoes a conversion from her father's genocidal racism to a position closer to that of Curtis's more therapeutic imperialism (she eventually marries him).

Even Curtis's sympathy for "Indians" is structured by dominant producer culture assumptions about racial hierarchy. "It's a little difficult to eliminate violence from an inferior race when such cruelty is manifested in those we call their teachers" (385). The social foundation of the captain's ostensibly well-meaning racism, uncriticized by Garland, is his upbringing in the Potomac Valley, where "it was pleasant to meet the darkies swarming, chirping like crickets, around the train" (88). He dutifully subscribes to the inevitability-of-progress thesis, using nature metaphors such as "the old man never grows young, the tree that falls does not rise up again" (414). Curtis supports Native dancing, though not if it distracts them from "their work" (406). Lawson the ethnographer believes that the Tetons' position on the evolutionary ladder—not their cultural preferences and sense of what is worth learning—circumscribes their educational and occupational capacities (56). The novel climaxes with a tribal parade in which Curtis and Elsie dress up as "Indian" rulers of the Tetons (he dubs himself their "resident duke" [410]). During the procession Elsie praises not the Tetons' cultural difference but their steady climb up the ladder of evolution, "from hunting to harvesting, from primitive indolence to ordered thrift" (413). Garland's Indian West has a barren beauty, but it is not encoded as therapeutic—it will be in later fiction. The traces of early multiculturalism here are tainted with racist and assimilationist values evident in producer culture hegemony.

But just as Elsie articulates a neurasthenic gospel of release—"The strung bow needs relaxation" (40)—some of these uptight attitudes about "Indians" undergo an ideological relaxation. Curtis insists that Elsie's opinions of the Tetons are neither feminine nor sentimental enough (119). Eventually "Elsie's blood" is "thrilled with excitement . . . to be in the presence of primeval man" (253), but, unlike later heroines I discuss below, she does not equate knowing "Indian" "primitiveness" with getting in touch with her "primitive within." Curtis succeeds not only in teaching her that Tetons have "hearts" but that the best way of governing them is through their "hearts—their inner thoughts," something he learns as their "interpreter" (153). He challenges her artistic sensibility in his efforts to demonstrate the existence of Teton primitive subjective multidimensionality. Curtis notes that her painting of a Teton beggar praying is "picturesque," but it fails to probe the man's bewilderment with his people's suffering and the "soul of the redman" (101). Elsie sees this "redman" subjectivity later in Grayman's oratory, which "thrilled every soul in the room" (255). She moves toward a new understanding of the American artist as she or he who respects and represents cultural difference.

Perhaps Curtis's most extreme statement on behalf of this perspective is one that implicitly contests assumptions basic to Pratt's Carlisle and the White middle-class Indian reform movement. "The older I grow the less certain I am that any race or people has a monopoly of the virtues," Curtis lectures Elsie. "I do not care to see the 'little peoples' of the world civilized in the sense in which the word is commonly used. It will be a sorrowful time to me when all the tribes of the earth shall have cottonade trousers and derby hats" (81). Here Curtis equates an embryonic multicultural tolerance with a live-and-let-live cultural individualism. Those who would dress the peoples of the world in the same uniform are cultural conformists. He advocates a more relaxed, more colorful, more "modern" management style: "If I could, I would civilize only to the extent of making life easier and happier—the religious beliefs, the songs, the native dress—all these things I would retain. What is life for, if not for this?" (81). In effect, he proposes a flexible protomulticultural model in place of a rigid assimilationist model of the hegemonic digestion of "others."

Lawson echoes this managerial remodeling in his debate with Parker, a sculptor: "Why submerge [Natives]? Is the Anglo-Saxon type so adorable in the sight of God that He desires all the races of the earth to be like unto it?" This standardization, he continues, would be a "beautiful scheme for tailors, shoemakers, and preachers, but depressing to artists" (297). By implication, new artist colonies must be founded on such multicultural insights—artistic individuality rides in tandem with artistic multiculturalism. Artists should now revalue primitivism: "My conviction," Lawson adds, taking a view that White intellectuals from John Collier to Calvin Luther Martin would modify and promote in later decades, "is that savagery held more of true happiness than we have yet realized; and civilization, as you begin to see, does not, by any construction, advance the sum of human happiness as it should do" (298).

Thus Garland's novel moves toward "modern" ideological and critical trends that will conjoin artistic individualism and a fascination with "primitives" and cultural pluralism. His novel sometimes seems to recycle conventional notions of the categories of civilization and savage, while at other times it questions the ideological meanings assigned to such categories ("What is a savage?" [297], Lawson asks Parker). Its sometimes spasmodic gestures toward these "modern" positions may be personified by Elsie, who in the end, despite her love for Curtis and her cultural respect for *his* Tetons (whom Curtis often proprietorily terms "my people"), is eager to leave with him for Europe for a six-month honeymoon and is not at all sure that she can stand to spend more than one year on the Teton reservation after they return (415). The most intriguing historical aspect of the novel is its recognition that these shifts in ideological orientation—toward the therapeutic multicultural—are all part of Captain Curtis's "field of experiment" (12) in "Indian" digestion management. Convinced that he really knows "Indians" and respects the value of their culture, Curtis can play their "despotic monarch" (407) with greater confidence, comfort, and righteousness.

White Therapeutic Primitivism and the Indian Business:
Environmental, Soulful, and Literary "Indians"

In the early twentieth century, White intellectuals, artists, critics, reformers, bohemians, and businesspeople increasingly turned their attentions to "Indians" as objects of desire. At least as early as 1904, Carlisle's *The Red Man and Helper*, still under Pratt's supervision, linked "Indians" with a lost ecology and health. The anonymous, presumably White author of "It Is the White Man Who Is the Savage" acknowledges ironically that "we are the savages" and laments: "The Indian breathed pure air, lived without diseases, had the best of food and enjoyed the beautiful scenery." Prior to their contact with Whites, "Indians" lived long, thrived as athletes and inventors of games, and had good physiques. "All this was not savagery," the author concludes. "Savagery exists only among the white races."[20] Similar "Indian" ecology sentiments were expressed in magazines like George Bird Grinnell's *Forest and Stream* (1873–1937), Charles Lummis's *Land of Sunshine* (1894–1901), and its successor *Out West* (1902–14).[21]

Over the next decade or so Carlisle's publications added another dimension to this: "Indians" possess a spiritual—or therapeutic—ecology and health. Rev. Dr. George P. Donehoo's "The Soul of the Red Man—A Study" (1911) contrasts White America's "practical" and "humdrum grind of life" with the "Red Man's" unpractical yet leisurely pastoral world of "beauty," "grandeur," and "mystery." The "Indian's" success, he suggests, is now judged by his "poetic soul" rather than his economic accomplishments. Because the "Indian" has been endowed with an ecological innerness, it was predictable that this "depth" would rebuke

White (polluted) progress: "When civilization, with all of its materialism, came into the world of Nature in which the Red Man had been living
for countless generations, his soul shrank from it, and he retreated into
the brooding silence of the forests." Although the "Indians" lost many of
their lands, they retained their ecological spirituality in their "brooding"
silences and survived as primitive reminders of a natural body, spirit,
and individuality that Whites have lost: "We dwellers in cities and
towns have many things to teach the Red Man, but when we are in danger
of becoming swamped in the mire of materialism; when we find that our
artificial living is blinding our natural senses; when we cannot hear the
voices which speak to us in the silence of the starlit sky—then the Red
Man can teach us many things."[22] As Helen Hunt Jackson formulated it
in her bestselling novel *Ramona: A Story* (1884), when she compares her
Native hero Alessandro to his beloved Ramona, niece of a wealthy and
haughty Spanish landowner in California: "Alessandro was undeniably
Ramona's inferior in position, education, in all the external matters of
life; but in nature, in true nobility of soul, No!" (227).

Writers even began to reimagine "Indian" blood—a corporeal sign of
this lost body, spirituality, and ecological individuality—as a social asset
for aristocratic Americans. *The Red Man* reprinted a piece titled "Indian
Blood" (1916) in which the author points out that "many of our older
families are showing pride in having in their lineage some infusion of
Indian blood. Among them is Mrs. Galt, the President's fiancée." "Indians" were increasingly encoded with stylish racial, biological, and
subjective potency. The "Indian," in this author's view, is the aristocrat
of aborigines: "Most of the aboriginal strains are thick-witted, earth-born
creatures, slow of thought and dull of apprehension. The Indian was
quick, alert, nervous, lithe of motion, passionate. . . . He was the poet of
the stone age, a dreamer and a mystic." In a turn of interpretation that
would no doubt have mortified Pratt, the "Indian's" seemingly unambitious reserve and lack of interest in plodding industrial and agricultural labor were re-represented as indicative of his subjective nobility
and sensibility: "Other under-developed races have gradually adjusted
themselves to the white man's regimen of sober industry. The negro
never rebelled at being a hewer of wood and drawer of water. But for the
red man, tilling the ground has been but slavery to a proud spirit."
"Indians" are romanticized as self-sufficient owners of themselves; they
are not slave laborers: their bodies, spirits, and individualities are spontaneous, not regimented. Thus if one's blood combines the "Indian"
"qualities of endurance and imagination" *and* the White "yoke of industry," the admixture is "valuable."[23]

In a *Red Man* article published in 1916, the year Bourne published "Trans-national America," Tom Jones, a wealthy Bostonian suffering from ennui, undertakes a pilgrimage to Florida and the Seminoles in a therapeutic romance of primitive origins that involves stripping himself of his "thin veneer of civilization." The "Indian" is viewed as being in some ways more advanced than the rich, educated White man because "Indian" primitive and pastoral spirituality harbors the secrets of lost White "natural" individuality. Tom "was desirous of laying aside the veneer and taking on the full panoply of the primitive. He was eager to pierce the uncharted Everglades, eager to penetrate that unfinished part of the universe, where unremoved scaffolding yet betrayed the design of the builder." Tom searches for a Seminole who will serve as tour guide not just through the Everglades but through the unexplored and labyrinthine swampland of his primitive psychological self. The "modern" category of "the primitive" is thus what makes "Indians" appear therapeutically usable to Whites, for through it they seem to share an elemental human substance. This is the romance of primitivist pluralism.

What usually bothered wealthy Americans about "Indians"—their dearth of interest in alienating labor—is reinscribed in Floridian travel advertisement leisure-language as the Seminoles' "seductive," "sunbathed" "indolence." Tom (mis)reads the very silence that remains a racial barrier between him and his "primitive" guides as further evidence of the "Indians'" subjective aura—their status as mystical gatekeepers to the *deeper* mysteries of the alienated White individual.[24] "Indians" are signified as psychologically scenic as well as spiritually ecological. By implication, to "individualize" "Indians" entirely as semi-skilled working-class Whites—the conventional Carlisle program—would mean either making these sacred characteristics vanish or disrupting the White therapeutic fantasy that "Indians" are endowed with such adorably "primitive" "Indian" qualities.

Zane Grey's *Vanishing American* (1925) tells the tale of Nophaie, formerly star "Indian" athlete at a prestigious Eastern university; Marian, his White paramour who follows him out West; and the Nopahs, his tribe.[25] Grey's narrative connects the discourse of vanishing Indians with the discourse of a vanishing yet still reclaimable White "individuality." One of the ironies of American individualism is that American "progress" makes everyday self-sufficiency impossible—a vanishing self-sufficiency still upheld as an ideal by older Nopah Indians who, unlike Nophaie, cannot yet read the American writing on the wall. These older Nopahs wish that the "civilized" Nophaie "too could be as happy and self-sufficient as they" (113).

Grey suggests that "Indian" self-sufficiency is mainly that of the "soul." His Southwestern landscapes could be better termed soulscapes, depthscapes, selfscapes. He invests canyons and deserts with a subjective "glamour" (77) symbiotic with "the Indian's inner life" (150). Sympathetic Whites, like Marian, undergo Indianizing through landscape immersion: the Indianscape is where they repossess a long lost subjectivity and *primitive individuality*. Grey's "Indians" are in his own eyes less evolved culturally and intellectually than Whites (113), but they have excelled in a *soul evolution* to which knowing Whites aspire: "That some women and men did grow wonderful through a strange evolution wrought by desert life was proof of the divinity that was in them. These were closest to the Indian" (152). As Marian listens to a description of the Southwest landscape's power (on her way to visit Nophaie), she exclaims that it "express[es] something vague and deep within me—that wants to come out" (41–42). Marian experiences what might be nominated *White ethno-individualizing.*

Literature such as *The Vanishing American* suggests that an ideological territory has newly expanded meanings: the Indian West is now not simply "rugged," it is therapeutic, the Subjective West. Indian hating was often built into forms of nineteenth-century rugged individualism. But in the early twentieth century rugged individualism was supplemented by and in some instances superseded by therapeutic individualism as a cultural-subjective value. Indianscapes became the sites for the recovery of lost White "individuality"—as well as "souls" and "instincts." Grey profiles Nophaie, with his soul educated in the West and his mind in the East, as a figure akin to the moody Romantic Artist, the culturally alienated and angst-filled Literary Individual: he was "aloof and strange. . . . What he loved most was to be alone, out in the desert, listening to the real sounds of the open and to the silent whisperings of his soul" (6).[26] Once reunited with Nophaie and his soulscapes, Marian begins to recover her lost Indian within—a lost (White) "individuality" associated not only with the soul (an older religious discourse) but with the "primitive instincts" (a more modern pop psychological discourse). If White discourses often associated the "Indian soul" with Southwestern tribes like the Zuni and the Hopi and frequently assigned more volatile "primitive" "Indian" instincts to Southwestern tribes like the Apaches, Grey makes it evident that Marian, a White woman, is drawn to both as resources for the release of her repressed Indian within. As enchanted as Marian is with Nophaie's luminous and sometimes shadowy subjective depthscapes, she is equally seduced by his physical prowess (indeed, his athletic victories in the East are what first catch her eye).

One scene, for example, in which Nophaie kicks the White villains like footballs rather than killing them, is much like erotic and violent passages in which Edgar Rice Burroughs's Jane is palpably turned on by watching Tarzan defend and kill for her: "That liberated something deep in Marian's blood. It seemed to burst and shoot in fiery currents all over her. The Indian's actions fascinated her" (183). Her confession to Nophaie is revealingly sexual: "If you were an Indian, I was a *savage*. I just swelled and tingled and burned with fiendish glee every time you kicked one of the—footballs" (199). Here the White woman's devolution into Indianness is exciting rather than exalting, instinctually more than spiritually "deep": "the sheer backward step to the uttermost thrill of the senses—deep in the marrow of her bones" (279). Lost instinctual "individuality" often meshed with lost spiritual "individuality" in White ideologies of Indian subjectivity, but the latter—in Eastman's words, "the soul of the Indian"—was usually the Puebloesque "primitiveness" attached to Southwestern tourism, commodities, and "Indian" performances.

Two years after Grey published *The Vanishing American*, Burroughs, perhaps with Grey's novel in mind, published the first of his two Apache-as-Tarzan novels, *The War Chief* (1927).[27] This fiction, like Grey's, attempts to press even the aggressive "Indian" warrior, not just the peaceful Pueblo, into service within therapeutic culture. Burroughs contributes to making the moral critique of capitalist imperialism, however much he may see capitalism as inevitable, commonsensical within the new therapeutic culture. The narrator, criticizing the maxim "The only good Indian is a dead Indian," editorializes: "To have said, 'He is an Indian. He stands in the way of our acquisition of his valuable possessions. Therefore, having no power to enforce his rights and being in our way, we will destroy him,' would have been no more ruthless than the policy we adopted and cloaked with hypocrisy" (129–30). But the critical thrust of the narrative is not anticapitalist; it stresses protherapeutic primitivism. For "civilization" is linked even more with the imposition of "inhibitions" than with expanding marketplaces. "Ever in the seed of the savage is the germ of savagery that no veneer of civilization, no stultifying inhibitions seem able ever entirely to eradicate" (2). Noble savagism is here defined not as quasi-civilized nineteenth-century "Indian" sentiment but as twentieth-century "Indian" pop psychological instincts, adventurous instincts, typically "stifled" by "the repressive force of civilization" (5).

The War Chief supplies the background for the troubled interracial romance that occurs in the sequel, *Apache Devil* (1933).[28] The first novel recounts the Apache capture of the boy who will grow up, thinking he is an Apache, as Black Bear, the Apache Devil, Burroughs's "Indian" Tarzan figure. He becomes—reminiscent of the Apache Kid of legend as well as of Tarzan—the scourge of White oppressors. Black Bear's father is White and his mother is part Cherokee; both are killed by the Apaches. Only near the end of the novel will Geronimo disclose the Apache Devil's White parentage to him (which, unbeknowst to Geronimo, is in truth not wholly White). Black Bear falls in love with Wichita Billings, spunky daughter of a racist rancher. But the Tarzan and Jane jungle affair is more complicated in the Southwest. Notwithstanding Wichita's visceral attraction to and admiration for the Apache Devil (who rescues and helps her), and in spite of the fact that she herself is perceived by a friend as "a regular little Apache" (59), she confesses that the thought of loving him "revolted" her, "and that he must have seen it in my face [when he kissed her]. . . . No, I cannot love him! . . . I wish to God that he were white!" (60–61).

Burroughs narrates Wichita's gradual conversion to protomulticultural love grounded in the release of the instincts and the cultivation of racial tolerance. The spokesman for the novel's antiracist cultural relativism is Geronimo, as he tells the Apache Devil about his parentage. "You are as much an Apache as any of us in heart and spirit, but in your veins flows the blood of your white-eyed father. . . . It is not the color of our skin or blood that runs in our veins that makes us good men or bad men" (235). Cultural relativism—culture and character are thicker than blood or race—is thus coupled with the psychological appreciation of instinctual primitivism as the therapeutic attitude Whites should adopt in their management of protomulticultural America.

Related therapeutic ethnographic reencodings of the "Indian" were surfacing in 1882, the year the ethnographer Frank Cushing took six men from the Zuni pueblo in New Mexico on a much publicized pilgrimage to the Atlantic Ocean and Plymouth Rock (they later stopped at Carlisle). As historian Curtis M. Hinsley has noted in his analysis of the encounters between the Zuni and Boston's Brahmins, the press conferred on the Zuni magical powers usually assigned to artists—the capacity to make space sacred. This sacred power was heightened by magazine illustrators and writers who dramatized the dark, hidden, secret mysteries and practices of the kiva (into which Cushing had been initiated as an adopted member of the Zuni). Such representations manifest the Gilded Age need to romanticize "Indians" as antimodern possessors of a timeless and primitive spiritual group subjectivity. Cushing was celebrated as the explorer of primitive enchantments indigenous to a unified Native community life—a structure of life and meaningfulness that White culture had lost.

But the White preoccupation with sacred "Indians," which exhibited some White ambivalence about America's internal imperialism, was accompanied and supported by the recognition that a doom hung over the "Indians," a *romantic doom*. Reporters perceived this poignant doom in the Zuni visit to the Worcester, Massachusetts, factories, where these sacred people, like some of Carlisle's students, paid what was taken as endearingly childish homage to the seemingly more potent "sacredness" of American technological force. To the delight of Cushing and other White onlookers, the Zunis were particularly awestruck by the wire factory that, it so happens, was the major producer of the barbed wire used by Whites to fence in property (sometimes Native property) in the West.[29]

Despite their apparent barbed-wire doom, "Indians" were increasingly associated with a utopian psychological-spiritual renewal (White renewal). James Mooney, another influential ethnologist employed by the Bureau of Ethnology in this period, studied the power of Native rituals to buttress tribal identity in *The Ghost-Dance Religion and the Sioux Outbreak of 1890* (1896), a work Pratt despised. Mooney's first chapter, "Paradise Lost," glamorizes "Indian" cultures as being mythic in significance, infuses them with romantic Arcadian nostalgia, and infantalizes them as irresistibly emotional: "The lost paradise is the world's dreamland of youth."[30] On the one hand, in concluding his chapter Mooney recognizes that the Natives' political, economic, cultural, and spiritual "loss" was systematically and often ruthlessly exacted by White "civilization." On the other hand, in Mooney's work, as in Cushing's, there is present the growing ideological tendency partly to *identify* with the Indians so as to translate or transmute their "loss" into an emotional version of White loss—a longing for some imagined primordial essence buried by American social individuality.

Thomas Eakins's *Frank Hamilton Cushing*, painted in 1895, depicts the ethnologist costumed in what might be described as an Indianized Western outfit: wide circular earring, bow and a quiver of arrows slung around his shoulder, pipe with feathers in his hand, long hair with headband, what may be boots or moccasins topped by leather leggings, and shield, horns, and leather bag with fringe hanging behind him ("vanishing American" props). It is no wonder that Eakins endeavored to represent Cushing in his *theatrical* role as mediator between the "civilized" and the more "primitive" Southwestern Native culture—this translator image was the source of Cushing's fame.[31] What is fascinating about this dark, brooding painting is the downward turn of Cushing's head and his introspective here-but-not-here glassy-eyed gaze. Cushing exhibits what Eakins represents in so many of his late-nineteenth- and early-twentieth-century paintings and portraits of the professional-managerial class, what I have called a rhetoric of "depth" or what David Lubin more specifically focuses on as a "rhetoric of dejection."

Lubin advances the provocative argument that many members of the White professional-managerial class in this period were gradually becoming intrigued with visual representations of themselves, not as confident (also a trend in this period), but as subjectively "deep," alienated, conflicted, and suffering, and that, as Eakins's painting attests, there was an imperialist romanticism of defeated peoples' looks of "dejection."[32] The "rhetoric of dejection" that Eakins adopts to signify psychological "individuality" and angst in his painting of Cushing is that of the "dying Indian" (also present, as Lubin notes, in Edward S. Curtis's twenty-volume publication of photographs, *The North American Indian* [1907–30]). Eakins both participates in the development of this class-based "visual language of sensitive, suffering interiority" and frames it as a performance of "individuality"—pure theater.[33] Therapeutic discourses, including bohemian discourses, that rescripted the "modern" meanings of "Indian" helped reduce the meaning of capitalism to the problem of overcivilized repression. One of Cushing's most significant capitalist contributions, perhaps, was the early publicity he garnered for Southwestern *therapeutic tourism.*

Giving Them the Business: "Indians" in the
Therapeutic and Modernist Marketplace

In the early twentieth century, writings of various sorts were published that echoed elements of Cushing's and Mooney's fascination with "Indians" and their lifeways, especially with Southwestern tribes. Seemingly sympathetic White writers glamorized, spiritualized, psychologized, and aestheticized the ethnoracial sentiment expressed by the White settler Aunt Ri in Jackson's *Ramona*: " 'Pears like I'm gettin' heaps er new idears inter my head, these days. I'll turn Injun, mebbe, afore I git through!" (72). Anthropologists, authors, artists, intellectuals, bohemians, and countless tourists flocked to the Southwest's therapeutic "playground" of identity. The two strategic outposts of what Hinsley terms the "aesthetic claiming of the Southwest"—also the *therapeutic claiming,* I would add—were the artist colonies of Taos and Santa Fe.[34]

The young Francis Parkman's reconnaissance mission, *The Oregon Trail* (1849), begins in 1846 with him and his companion, fresh out of Harvard, boarding a Missouri River steamboat teeming with "Santa Fé traders, gamblers, speculators, and adventurers of various descriptions."[35] Through the late nineteenth century, Taos and Santa Fe (originally the Spanish capital of New Mexico) were regarded mainly as modest trading centers in the vast desert that separated commercial centers in the Mississippi Valley and the West coast. Santa Fe's population was about 6,000 in 1890.[36] Not until 1912 were the New Mexico and Arizona territories admitted to statehood. But Taos and Santa Fe had been gaining in reputation as artists' havens since the 1890s. The cost of living there was appealingly low.[37] Moreover, the efflorescence of early-twentieth-century literary and artistic regionalisms contributed to the Southwest's cultural appeal, a growing fascination supported by New Mexican magazines such as *Laughing Horse* (1921–39) and *Morada* (1929–1931), by local galleries, and by museums and publishers in the East.

It was Mabel Dodge Luhan (1879–1962), the wealthy impresario of bohemian artists and social critics, who did more than any one person to promote Taos (her "discovery" of Taos was a bit tardy—late 1910s).[38] Luhan helped put Taos on the cultural map as a mecca for the revitalization of subjectivity (in some ways a more ecological competitor of the bustling, colorful Greenwich Village she left) and as a region whose natural beauty, multiethnic mix, and indigenous, handcrafted art objects were distinctively American (in truth, as her own hacienda demonstrated, the aesthetic and cultural influences of Spanish colonization were long-standing).[39] The bohemian glamour of individualistic psychoanalysis and the glamour of the more bohemian individualistic versions of socialism assumed new ideological packaging as the glamour of therapeutic tribal Indianism (a Euramerican Indianism that frequently ignored the ways in which Natives themselves had formed nonmodernist—not premodernist—subjective values and styles antithetical to therapeutic confessionalism and intimacy).[40]

While Pratt's Carlisle Evolution Factory set out to individualize "Indians," Luhan's Taos tricultural colony—which attracted powerful modernists such as D. H. Lawrence, Mary Austin, and John Collier—made chic the game of Indianizing White individuals who figuratively and sometimes literally staged their "return" to the blanket (see figures 13 and 14). Luhan, who was born into a wealthy Buffalo banking family, could have been photographed more accurately as going back to the mink stole. This form of bourgeois ideological blanketing, a therapeu-

13. Mabel Dodge Luhan posing in "Indian" blanket, Yale Collection of American Literature Photographs, Beinecke Rare Book and Manuscript Library

14. Mabel Dodge Luhan posing with blanketed "Indian" women, Yale Collection of American Literature Photographs, Beinecke Rare Book and Manuscript Library

tic security blanketing of sorts, was something newly fashionable, a simultaneously modern and antimodern fabrication of class, cultural, and "psychological" status. As pointed out in chapter 1, the Carlisle teacher Lance, in Sparhawk's *Chronicle of Conquest* of 1890, gives voice to the conventional middle-class producer culture value, "We Anglo-Saxons . . . have been a thousand years getting the savage out of us" (57). By contrast, Luhan and many of her White artist confrères, as contributors to therapeutic culture and critics of the genteel middle class, romanticized cultural and psychological *disassimilation*: the idea that by seeming to rub up against "Indians," they could begin to put the "savage" back into themselves and thus evolve as artists, "individuals," and spiritually and psychologically indigenized Americans.

These artists formed a colony (resembling aspects of other colonies, at places such as Provincetown on Cape Cod, Massachusetts, and Carmel in northern California), not so much to engender group solidarity as to support their "individual" aesthetic development in an environment whose attractions were natural, not urban or mass cultural. The *Taos Valley News* reported in 1920 that "the group [of Taos Euramerican artists] is made up of strong individuality."[41] For many of these artist-individuals, the Natives and Hispanics who labored in the mines, on the railroads, in the large farms and irrigation projects, and as domestic servants (in the homes of artists, government officials, railroad personnel) may have been less visible as signs of capitalist management than skyscrapers, highways, and billboards. What some of these artists did notice about many of the ethnic locals was their apparent cultural acceptance of Euramerican artistic labor—Natives and Hispanics, unlike some of the region's merchants and members of the genteel middle class, did not fall within the category of philistine. "Thanks be to God," the composer Ernest Block, who lived in Santa Fe, rejoiced, "I have found a place in America where men can do nothing." If Block had looked more carefully, it would have been all too clear that not everyone in the area had the option that Robert Henri praised as being so precious for the nourishment of sensibility: "to work or not to work."[42]

For some artists the "Indians" of the Southwest represented an original American cultural identity, one that grew out of singularly American deserts, mesas, mountains, and canyons. This "natural," pre–Puritan-conquest Americanness, as they imagined it, contested the national identity formed around the capitalist ethos of worker production. Yet many of these same alienated artists not only consolidated but sought to expand their ties with Eastern art and literary establishments to obtain the money that would finance their maintenance of these views in scenic Taos and Santa Fe. In 1912 the Taos Society of Artists formed in order to better circulate the group's Southwestern and "Indian" images in national exhibitions. Taos and Santa Fe became rustic art capitals for modern artists with national and international reputations, among them Henri, George Bellows, John Marin, Marsden Hartley, Maurice Sterne, John Sloan, and later Georgia O'Keeffe. Many of them, along with corporations, pioneered in the development of Southwestern therapeutic protomulticultural modernism and modernizing.

Aspects of Luhan's reading of Taos as a therapeutic terrain capable of replenishing alienated Whites had long been systematically popularized by some of the business interests whose ethos and standardization the earliest art colonists originally sought to evade. It was in fact a railroad corporation that hired many artists to commercialize the Southwest as a subjectively appealing romantic alternative to America's mechanized society, conventionally symbolized in the nineteenth century by the railroad.[43] In the 1890s the Santa Fe Railway remedied its financial ills by pitching its appeal to tourists more than to potential settlers. It began to reconceive itself in part as a driving force in the flourishing leisure industry. The Santa Fe Railway forged an alliance with the Fred Harvey tourist, hotel, and restaurant services (famous for its Harvey Girls), and also with legions of ethnographers, artists, photographers, and authors. The goal of this business-artist-intellectual alliance was to present and commercialize the Southwest not as a potential modern business center but as a nostalgic, unalienated region of "the unique, the handmade, the rural, and the authentic."[44] Taking its cue from the region's increasing number of ethnographers, the Fred Harvey Company set up an "Indian department." Its "ethnographic" mission, which concentrated more on the production of revenue than of knowledge, was to better stage "Indians" as picturesque and the objects they made (blankets, baskets, pottery, silverwork, leather goods, moccasins, beadwork) as consumable. This shaping of images and values accelerated the development of a marketplace network comprised of artists, artisans, traders, dealers, and collectors.

The Santa Fe Railway and the Fred Harvey Company had been making ever greater profits for close to two decades before Luhan's arrival in New Mexico by sponsoring and distributing calendar art and posters that romanticized the "primitive" landscape and the brooding but peaceful Pueblos as scenic, colorful, therapeutic tourist sights available to be painted and photographed. Artists and photographers, sometimes commissioned and guided by the Santa Fe Railway and Fred Harvey organizations, created images for mass distribution that made the Pueblos seem as if they were living an idyllic almost timeless tradition-bound, artisanal, spiritually, culturally—not politically—collective existence. As Taos and Santa Fe artists became celebrities and as more famous artists migrated to the region, the Santa Fe Railway and the Fred Harvey Company even included artists' studios on their tours.

Corporations and artists banded together to fashion the sort of Indianness for Natives to enact and fabricate in material form that would appeal most to Euramerican tourists, collectors of arts and crafts, publishers, museums, and galleries. Thus "Indian" pottery and baskets were scaled down so that tourists could tote them as souvenirs. "Indian" blankets were redesigned (sometimes "Orientalized") in size and pattern so that they could be used not as clothing (their Native function) but as rugs and wall hangings. Corporate experts oversaw "Indian" silverworking—originally a Spanish craft—by distributing materials and designs to the artists and by lightening the weight of the silver jewelry so that it could more comfortably grace Euramerican bodies. The Santa Fe Railway and the Fred Harvey Company, along with many local artists, sought to prevent the BIA from outlawing the highly publicized Hopi snake dance (a religious ritual in which Hopis carry rattlesnakes in their mouths), at least in part because they saw it as such a spectacular moneymaker and publicity stunt—tourists and celebrities loved it, painters and authors

exoticized, dramatized, and, of course, sold their often modernist renditions of it. "Indian" decorations, produced by Natives and Euramericans
who mastered the "Indian" styles, adorned hotel rooms, railroad cars,
department store windows in major cities, advertisements, and middle-
and upper-class homes around the world.

Native artisans and artists were free to innovate in their artwork, but
only within certain parameters commercially recognizable as "Indian";
their objects had to "retain their 'Indianness' more than exhibit [the]
individuality [of the maker]." Indianizing—not individualizing—had
become a corporate investment indispensable for selling the Southwest.
The Fred Harvey Indian Detour exemplifies the extent to which the
"Southwest" and "Indians" underwent a corporate redaction as a commercial style. Harveycars would pick up tourists at railroad stations and
transport them directly to Pueblo sites, artisans, and rituals. The male
driver sported Tom Mix cowboy duds, while the female "courier," the
Harvey Girl-style guide, wore a Navajo dress. "Just a show!" D. H. Lawrence inveighed. "The Southwest is the great playground of the white
American."[45]

This corporate and artistic multiculturalism often centered on the "Indian" artisan as the nostalgic, get-back-to-the-land-and-the-hand preindustrial figure who, according to this logic, was inspired by "primitive" "tradition" more than artistic "individuality." This arts-and-crafts
image did not reference pervasive socioeconomic changes that had taken
place in the region. Even by the late nineteenth century the area had been
transformed into a cash economy that relied on the widespread proletarianization of labor. As Leah Dilworth has argued, the revival of the
"republican myth of artisanal labor" provided consumers, tourists, and
Euramerican Taos and Santa Fe residents with a reassuring image to put
in place of those that depicted urban industrial laborers (including immigrants), laborers who sometimes organized into collectives to defend
their interests against the capitalist class and economic system that some
of those White Taos and Santa Fe residents seemed to find so spiritually
and aesthetically unsatisfying. Such images also offered a pleasant alternative to perceptions of the Native and Hispanic laborers who mined the
silver that the silversmiths used, who as agricultural workers grew the
crops that the restaurants and hotels bought, and who as railroad workers built and maintained the tracks that the tourists rode over in quest of
exoticized leisure.[46] Some of these arts-and-crafts images of, to quote
Collier, the "indolently industrious" Pueblos who knew how to experience the "fullness of life through leisure" also seemed to frame them
as being so preoccupied with and so pacified by their seemingly time-

less handicrafts and rituals that they appeared not, in contrast to the Apaches, to be angry about the systematic Euramerican military and economic occupation of their country.[47]

A BIA "Report of the Committee on Indian Arts and Crafts" (1934), probably supervised by Collier, addressed the predicament of Native artists and craftspersons squeezed in the grip of the Southwestern marketplace. The authors noted the irony that Natives rarely used many of the Indian products they made, except for ceremonial purposes; many preferred mass-produced shoes to moccasins, mass-produced pails to pottery, and so on. Producing arts and crafts was for most Natives "a spare time operation" that paid poorly (usually about "ten cents per hour"), but it was a labor that helped them get cash, for they have "acquire[d] wants which only a cash income will supply." Dealers and traders often dictated what was commercially "Indian" or "Southwestern," "as when a trader sets a whole group in a Pueblo to turning out hundreds of small pottery sombreros for ash trays." The committee expressed concern that Indian products will be too Whitened and will blow their cover—this will "destroy the primitive, individualistic, noncommercial connotations which now lie back of so much travel and handcraft business." Yet they pointed out the limited stylistic appeal of Indian products: except as decorations in boys' rooms, dens, or country cottages, the Indian colors often clashed with those predominant in middle-class homes. Thus they proposed that Natives be taught to use and be helped to acquire technical equipment that would accelerate production and that they try to make more Indian-style goods "useful" for "American homes," such as salad bowls. The report articulated the goals of an emerging hegemony and market that were multiculturalizing; they promoted colorful ethnic goods and citizens but also intended to make them usable, that is, efficiently manageable and marketable.[48]

Slavoj Žižek generalizes that "the multiculturalist respect for the Other's specificity is the very form of asserting one's own superiority."[49] Writing about 1920s White modernist texts, Walter Benn Michaels observes that "the preservation" of Native "culture has emerged as an issue that must be understood as separable from the preservation of the people."[50] Dilworth, also skeptical of the politics of modernist multiculturalism, argues that dominant White culture made Natives "usable *only* as a past."[51] Charles Briggs and Richard Bauman have taken modernist anthropologists, notably Franz Boas, to task for succumbing to "modernist angst" in their ideological construction of a "social opposition between traditional and modern worlds" that legitimated the modern capitalist assumption (or hope, in some cases) that Natives and their culture were indeed disappearing. These ethnographic modernists, they maintain, concocted ostensibly scientific accounts of "the mind of the American native" that removed Natives from their social and historical situations, ignored their colonial context, and failed to advocate "specific strategies for resisting domination and marginalization."[52] These critical perspectives have merit. But it is equally important to recognize that some modernists launched campaigns and initiatives to identify Natives *as modern* and get an elite public concerned with Native arts as a means, in part, of raising consciousness about Native economic and political predicaments.

Fred Kabotie's autobiography moves, if not from rags to riches, then from a Hopi childhood affected by the military occupation of reservations, coerced schooling, and tribal factionalism (over the issue of assimilation) to an adulthood full of opportunities opened not only by Kabotie's remarkable artistic talent but by basic training in painting (in school) (27–28), artistic commissions from the Fred Harvey business (49, 80), and Indian Arts and Crafts Board support for an Indian silversmiths guild (82).[53] In 1940 the Museum of Modern Art commissioned his colossal reproductions of the ancient Hopi Awatobi murals and asked Kabotie to give Eleanor Roosevelt a much-publicized guided tour of them (69–70). Powerful professional-managerial class and ruling-class backers of Native arts who admired Kabotie's work saw it as influenced by tradition, yet also as experimentally *modernist* in its developments of form and color. They sponsored his successful (and late) application for a Guggenheim fellowship (73). Kabotie stresses that his friendships with elite Euramericans were two-way learning experiences. "He knew a lot about the Hopis," Kabotie wrote of the eminent archaeologist Frederick Webb Hodge, "and it was through him that I became interested in Southwest history" (47). In his preface, Bill Belknap, Kabotie's coauthor, emphasizes Kabotie's triple consciousness: a "modern" Hopi (invested in building the Hopi cultural center), a traditional Hopi (his final chapter is titled "The Hopi Way"), and a nationally renowned modernist artist.[54]

Modernist institutions and artists sponsored the Exposition of Indian Tribal Arts, which debuted in New York and toured the country in 1931. The radical artist John Sloan, director of the exposition, and novelist and anthropologist Oliver La Farge were the major coauthors of *Introduction to American Indian Art* (1931), written and compiled to publicize the exposition (images of much Native art were included).[55] In their long introductory essay, Sloan and La Farge, both residents of Santa Fe, debunk the view that "Indians" are lost in the past, vanishing, and intrinsically therapeutic: "The Indian artist deserves to be classed as a Modernist, his art is old, yet alive and dynamic; but his modernism is an expression of a continuing vigour seeking new outlets and not, like ours, a search for release from exhaustion" (15). Native art, they stress, is intellectual, subtle, sophisticated, versatile, "at once classic and modern" (15). Sloan and La Farge dispute the "ethnological" concept of Indians as "curio[s]" whose ways are frozen in time, for "they have always borrowed freely" (25). Sloan and La Farge point to Indians' "constant experimentation in design, treatment of surface, and methods of manufacture. The modern Pueblo potter has at her disposal one of the richest and most complete stores of design elements in the whole world. There is hardly anything from a Greek wave through a Norman dogtooth to a Modernist abstraction to a leaf that one cannot find" (35). Political, economic, and institutional efforts to preserve Native arts are not, as Pratt maintained, encouraging Natives to step (or stay) backward; rather, Sloan and La Farge believe, these efforts help give Natives the incentive to be "modern" in their distinctive ways. For there is not just one version of "modern," or one way to be "modern" or authentically Native.[56]

Not only do Sloan and La Farge see Native artists as "modern," they see them as having always been so. The book's authors underscore that Native artists have selectively and inventively assimilated Euramerican and diverse Native influences rather than having been passively or coercively digested by White culture. "For the art of weaving, use of wool and other materials, various weaves, dyes, patterns, they have drawn upon Hopis, Pueblos, Spaniards, North Americans, even England and Germany. Yet the product which results from this assemblage is not only Indian, but deeply expressive of Navajo character" (25). Natives have Indianized new colors, beads, silverwork, floral designs, painting. "There is no attempt to work in our manner: a new Indian form has been evolved as a result of contact with us" (55). For hundreds of years Native cultural sovereignty has been transnational, transcultural, and *modern* in content, material, and form.

Collective culture, even more than the "genius of individuals" (35)—which, however, Sloan and La Farge acknowledge—has contributed to this "modern" artistry because Native life is itself a "modern" aesthetic production. The tribe, not mainly possessive egoistic individualism, has provided the incentive. "Potter and artist draw their spiritual sustenance from their tribal life, and that life is all a design, a dance and a ceremonial. . . . It is a whole, individuals are part of a pattern" (41). Hence the Native organization of the "modern" differs from White modernist ideologies that frame individual depth as the fundamental source of creativity. "Art is not to them individualistic self-expression, not subjective, not précieux," Alice Corbin Henderson suggests, though possibly revealing more about her own peers' aesthetic ideologies than those of Natives. Then, presuming to know much more than she can about levels and types of Native self-consciousness, as if Native self-consciousness is somehow uniform, she overgeneralizes: "It is this complete freedom from self-consciousness that gives their work its feeling of fresh spontaneity" (101).

Sloan and La Farge, in particular, draw some attention to the economic and political—in effect, colonial—circumstances within which too much Native artistry has been confined. Capitalist art dealers have forced Natives to produce less labor-intensive, more profitable (for the dealers), often fake (swastikas, thunderbirds, ornamental rabbits feet) "Indian" commodities for the tourist trade. Natives, proletarianized as cultural day laborers, are often pressed by a "sweat shop system" (27) and sometimes "factory mass production" (59) to "meet their demand for little sweet grass baskets, absurd bows and arrows, teapots, candlesticks, and any number of wretched souvenirs which they never made until white men decided that these, and these only, were genuine Indian souvenirs" (13, 15). Sloan and La Farge hope not only that the exposition will aid in redistributing the assignment of cultural value so that Native art is recognized as art, but that this reassignment of value will contribute to some redistribution of economic resources, giving Natives more of the profits from labors that are "modern" and truly Native. "The Pueblo of San Ildefonso was until recently in a bad way, having lost much of its land and water rights. The people were depressed and discouraged, all were poverty stricken. They revived their almost forgotten pottery-making . . . and began to develop their water colour." Artistic and economic revival are enmeshed: "They were able to earn the additional money so that today the pueblo is advancing, and increasing in numbers" (61). Some of the coauthors were not uncritical of their overwhelming focus on Native arts. Henderson, for instance, with some uneasiness, quotes Oscar B. Jacobson's *Kiowa Indian Art* (1929): " 'The Anglo-Saxon smashes the culture of any primitive people that gets in his way, and then, with loving care, places the pieces in a museum' " (109).

When Sloan and La Farge assert that Native art must be "classed as modernist" (15), they mean *classed* in both senses of the word. What the book and the exposition endeavor to do is associate the acquisition of modern handmade, labor-intensive Native art with the conspicuous display of professional-managerial class and ruling-class taste and identity. Scientists and artists, Sloan and La Farge write, "realize that if the arts are to survive, they can do so only as other arts do, through the support of discriminating buyers anxious to possess the creations" (61). By re-reading Native art as modernist, yet distinctively Native, Sloan and La Farge try to endow Native art with a class aura (are you discerning enough, do you have enough class, to own *authentic* Native art?). This is a problem and a challenge because "as yet not enough Americans are looking for beautiful and valuable objects to keep good jewelers from being forced into factories" (69). Moreover, most art consumers of this social stature preferred to collect work by individual artists (Kabotie, Marie Martinez) whose marketed reputations functioned as brand names that enhanced the monetary value of the art object (art investment). Much of the art that Sloan and La Farge hoped would be valued was not produced by such "names"—a good many artists remained anonymous. The contributors to *Introduction to American Indian Art*, as well as the Native artists whose work is represented in it, therefore, had to try to establish a new kind of elite American consumer and collector of *modern* art who would see that Native art "enrich[es] our modern life"—and their class life (61).

This multicultural modernism, as the Henderson overgeneralization about the absence of any Native self-consciousness makes clear, is not without ideological slips. These may make one skeptical of some motives of some modernists. Sloan and La Farge seem to have no doubt about the power assymetry—note the repetition of "our"—built into dominant *versions* of "the modern" when they issue claims that Native artists will make "a valuable contribution to our modern scene" (61), will prove "worthy of our appreciation," and, as quoted above, "will enrich our modern life" (61).[57] Sometimes authors' condescending Indianism offsets their efforts to endorse the value of Native modernism. Herbert J. Spinden of the Brooklyn Museum found "our Indians" useful insofar as they embodied "a reality of Arcady that is not dead, a spirit that may be transformed into a potent leaven of our own times" (74).[58]

Overall, I view this influential exposition as an effort to use modernism's institutions to signify Native arts and cultures as modernist

and traditional. Also, it was a limited attempt to heighten White awareness of a rampant capitalist exploitation of Native artists and artisans
that could be resisted (the authors did not specify organizations that
could have intervened politically, but they did focus on consumer re-
education and by implication encouraged art-institutional interven-
tion).[59] Some ethnomodernists, notwithstanding ideological contradictions in their perceptions, saw *exploited* Natives, not vanishing Natives,
and tried to combat that exploitation.[60] They discerned linkages between the formation of Native cultural and political identities.

Taos and Santa Fe bohemian-Indianism, modernist-Indianism, and
corporate-Indianism flourished in the early 1900s while the Santa Fe
Indian School, located just two miles south of the plaza, attempted to
turn out "individuals" and workers based on the Carlisle mold. The
Santa Fe Board of Trade favored its founding in 1890 in the hope that
the school would bring more business to town. As at many Indian boarding schools, students commonly complained of hunger, sometimes suffered from contagious diseases (trachoma, which often led to blindness,
plagued the school), underwent excessive drilling in military uniforms,
were often conscripted by BIA authorities from parents (some cooperative, some not cooperative), ran away and were punished when caught
(one runaway froze to death and another lost his legs to frostbite in the
1920s), worked in the summer on the equivalent of the Carlisle outing
(for example, laying track for the Santa Fe Railway), and received, if they
stayed the course, no more than an eighth-grade education geared to
produce skilled and semi-skilled manual laborers (shoemakers, tailors,
wagon menders, blacksmiths, mechanics, servants).

The school, where Kabotie took his first art lessons in the 1910s, was
partly Indianized in the 1930s, especially under Collier's regime (in a
way that must have further benefited the tourist trade): the budget was
increased; the architecture was remodeled in Pueblo style; marching
was abolished; high school was established; Native culture, art (including crafts such as silverwork), and history were taught; and beginning
in 1932 the Studio School set up by Dorothy Dunn nurtured students
whose artistry won national and international fame. Yet, as one historian of the school observes, even in this more flexible protomulticultural
phase the "Indian self-government" encouraged in the school (which
had hired few Natives to fill academic posts) remained BIA-government
in actuality, and the institution continued to see its function as being a

provider of training for manual laborers (though greater numbers of students developed interests in applying to college).[61]

The Taos and Santa Fe campaign to commercially Indianize the Pueblos was in many ways the opposite of Carlisle's campaign to commercially individualize its students. Popular representations of both groups depicted Natives performing manual labor. But where many Taos and Santa Fe representations of Pueblos characterized them as artisans, Pratt's Carlisle framed its students as skilled and semi-skilled workers equipped with technical knowledge useful in overtly capitalist enterprise. The Indianized Pueblos were frequently imaged as contented members of the tribe who almost instinctually expressed Indianness through their "primitive" crafts and tradition-determined work rhythms. Whereas the individualized Carlisle students were staged as clock-driven, ambitious, competitive proletarians and culture-learners capable of "civilized" self-modification. Both social organizations produced workers, but Carlisle was more up front about its formative role in that process. Commercially Southwesternized "Indians" may have *seemed* as if they were performing unalienated labor intrinsic to just being themselves, while Carlisle students were trained to perform useful labor of any kind as a practice essential to forging "individuality" and "character."

Pueblo domesticity decked out in artists' soft Southwestern pastels seemed tranquil, whereas Carlisle publications such as the novel *Stiya* condemned that same Pueblo domesticity as filthy and subject to authoritarian tribal rule. Images of Pueblos decorated middle- and upper-class homes; indeed, they helped constitute White class "individuality" and status. Carlisle's female students were trained to serve as domestics in such homes, while the boys were schooled as carpenters capable of constructing these homes. These students were also encouraged to aspire to earn and save the money to own houses. If Pueblo images suggested incentive to White viewers, it would be the incentive to be Pueblo in all that one thought, felt, and made. By contrast, photographs and articles in the Carlisle publications sought to cultivate a work-ethic incentive that would make students discontented with tribal identities and the lack of "civilized" opportunities in the tribal organization of life.

As observed in chapter 1, the Southwesternized decorative "Indian" trend is evident in the post-Pratt Carlisle of the early 1900s that sold "authentic" Indian blankets, taught Indian crafts, and published drawings showing Indian warriors bordered by Indian designs. Nevertheless, even post-Pratt Carlisle maintained its institutional image as a center for industrial training that addressed the manual workforce needs of American "progress." The Taos and Santa Fe "authentic" representations edited out much evidence of the historical changes—the "progress"—that enveloped the Pueblos, Navajos, and Apaches. Some members of these Southwestern tribes had partly "assimilated," lived on allotted land, intermarried with Hispanics or Whites or were products of such unions, or had become nonartisanal proletarians. Yet certain romanticized artisanal images almost seemed to preclude the possibility that contented but "primitive" Pueblos, creatures living in the distant past, could actively, skillfully, and intellectually participate in capitalism. It is important to underscore that *both* Taos Indianizing and Carlisle individualizing were in large part driven by a variety of capitalist interests. But the Taos and Santa Fe Indian chic (Hispanics were mostly excluded from this rendition of chic) was a sign that therapeutic culture was endeavoring to put "Indians" to new ideological uses for corporate capitalism and for groups within the dominant classes.[62]

Rhythmic Ethnomodernism: Luhan, Lawrence, Austin, and the Fantasy of Individualized Liberation in Tribal Scenes

Luhan sought to give the Taos artist colony and its "Indians" an aura of bohemian glamour as well as class exclusivity by recruiting some of the most illustrious authors, artists, psychologists, and Romantic Rebels to Taos. Most of the literary luminaries migrated there in the 1920s. Luhan's greatest recruit was D. H. Lawrence (1885–1930). Writing to Lawrence, and sounding not unlike the Santa Fe Railway and Fred Harvey publicists, she advertised the Taos "Indians" as inhabitants of a forgotten paradise of precapitalist selfhood: "a lofty, pastoral land far from railroads, full of time and ease, where the high, clear air seemed full of an almost heard but not quite heard music, and where the plainest tasks took on a beauty and significance they had not in other places." The note of urgency in her picturesque entreaty was that the leisurely, almost musical Taos would not be lost to White civilization for long and, succumbing to the inevitable, might soon be less able to gratify Lawrence's artistic sensibility: "Good roads would let in the crowds." She wanted Lawrence to be moved by the intrinsic magic of the land, yet she also wanted him, like a holy man, to bring his cultural celebrity to the region and anoint it as enchantingly "literary": "I wanted Lawrence to understand things for me. To take my experience, my Taos and to formulate it all into a magnificent creation."[63]

Luhan's correspondence suggests that she "wanted" Lawrence for the way he performed the romantic role of the *artist-as-individual*. Lawrence, the son of an English miner, had refashioned himself as an aristocrat of individuality, a member of subjective royalty, a potentate of originality: "I want to live my life, and say my say, and the public can die its own death in its own way, just as it likes." Much of the freshness of his letters and criticism is in the hyperbolic arrogance of his tone and his combative assertion of ideas. He fascinated as well as outraged Luhan and other artistic colonists of Taos with his emotional unpredictability and magnetic capacity to make everything he discussed seem, in Luhan's words, "significant and symbolic." Lawrence's pose was that of an unfettered, uncensorable, psychological *superindividual*. "When a mood or an impulse is in him," Luhan gushed, "there is no such thing as repression."[64]

This seeming X-ray vision increased Lawrence's subjective stock as the consummately *deep* "individual." Joseph Foster, a struggling author who lived in Taos with his independently wealthy wife Margaret, praised Lawrence's "depths and depths" and admitted abjectly, "I was unequal to his depths. And he was sorry." Lawrence, never one to be encumbered by humility, acknowledged that he was "the superior of most men" he met, not because of his birth or bank account, "Just in myself."[65] His presence in Taos, Luhan hoped, would help consecrate it as a place to which aspiring professional-managerial-class nonconformists—artists, authors, intellectuals, bohemians—would make their pilgrimage to reindividualize themselves.

On one level Lawrence recognized that his embodiment of romantic literary individuality and "moody far-offness" was a performance, one that elicited useful responses for his thinking and writing. In an intriguing essay, Lawrence contended that "everything, even individuality itself, depends on relationship. . . . Let us swallow this important and prickly fact. Apart from our connections with other people, we are barely individuals, we amount, all of us, to next to nothing." Notwithstanding this social awareness, Lawrence's theoretical gaze typically turned inward when defining "individuality." Luhan repined, and boasted, that Lawrence "was so strongly individual . . . he couldn't mix with others."[66]

Luhan was also drawn to Lawrence's conflicted interest in psychoanalysis. She had been analyzed by two eminent psychoanalysts, Dr. Smith Ely Jelliffe and Dr. A. A. Brill, and had written a column on psychoanalysis for the Hearst newspaper chain in 1917 and 1918. Her playful fascination with psychoanalysis, however, arose not only because of its novel codes, categories, and interpretive narratives but because of her status as a self-conscious consumer of all of these. This consciousness gave her some critical distance from psychoanalysis as an ideological system that produced particular brands of individuality— a chic cultural and class game (that could grow wearisome) of seeing oneself and others in psychoanalytic "types," "cases," and "pigeon-holes."[67] Even when Luhan proved skeptical of her analysts, she was self-consciously drawn to the glamorous theatricality of psychoanalytic identity and its bestowal of a sense of taboo-breaking agency: stylish psychological discourses gave her permission to perform an exoticized "individuality," a pretext to *stage "depth"* (figure 15).

While many of Lawrence's premises are clearly reworkings of psycho-analytic assumptions, like Luhan he was profoundly suspicious that the psychoanalytic technology of individuality falsified rather than ex-posed *his* "individuality." Lawrence lectured Luhan: "You want to send Brill to hell, and all the analytic therapeutic lot. . . . No, *never* adapt yourself. Kick Brill in the guts if he tries to come it over you." In re-sponse to Luhan's growing interest in Jung's diagnostic language ("ex-trovert" and "introvert"), Lawrence admonished, "I can feel you going like terrible clockwork." Before coming to Taos, Lawrence was appre-hensive about encountering its literary and arty neurotics. "I rather hate therapy altogether—doctors, healers, and all the rest. I believe that a neurotic is a half devil, but a cured neurotic is a perfect devil. They assume a perfect conscious and automatic control when they're cured . . . [a] conscious-automatic control that I find loathsome."[68]

Nevertheless, as Luhan well knew, Lawrence, author of *Psychoanaly-sis of the Unconscious* (1921) and *Fantasia of the Unconscious* (1922), was indebted to the repression model of self that Freud and his fol-lowers employed to define modern psychological individuality and make it seem like an emotional given. Lawrence's own "blood" psychol-ogy held that true "individuality" is located not so much in conscious effort or in "psychological" categories as in the *blood*: "No classification whatever means much to me. . . . The life that rises from the blood itself is the only life that is worth living, while the life that rises from the nerves and the brain is the life that is death." Lawrence, already a victim of literary censorship and ostracism by the early 1920s, insisted that "the mind and the spiritual consciousness of man simply *hates* the dark potency of blood-acts: hates the genuine dark sensual orgasms, which do, for the time being, actually obliterate the mind as the spiritual con-sciousness, plunge them in a suffocating flood of darkness." What Law-rence called the "mass self" and "mass feelings"—products of mass-

15. Mabel Dodge [Luhan] posing "depth" in Italy in her pre-Taos phase, Yale Collection of American Literature Photographs, Beinecke Rare Book and Manuscript Library

cultural modernity—were in opposition to the deeper, autonomous, "real" *blood individual.*[69]

Lawrence contributed to the formulation of a modernist "individuality" that redefined how "individuality" is "individual." Keywords he used to describe this were *blood, multiple* (selves within the self), *dark* (dark forest of the self), *wild, dirty,* and "IT" (the unconscious IT). Such words challenged the cultural authority of the attributes Lawrence associated with "character"—self-consciousness, self-control, purity. In opposition to the popular ideology of self-making, which so influenced Pratt, Lawrence made an impassioned case for unmaking, unmanaging, uncontrolling, untabooing, unrepressing "the self."

Lawrence encoded "Indians" as exemplary blood individuals and situated them therapeutically within an enlarged repression model that he used to criticize America—a nation "tangled" up in the "barbed wire" and "machinery" of its imperious "shall-nots." But White Americans, he saw, had devised a bonus for themselves when ostensibly contending with their "shall-nots": naughty thrills were to be held by transgressing what their "shall-nots" classified as wrong. Of Dimmesdale's and Hester's adultery in Nathaniel Hawthorne's *The Scarlet Letter* (1850), Lawrence wrote perceptively, "It was this very doing of the thing that they themselves believed to be wrong, that constituted the chief charm of the act." He then psychologized and universalized rather than historicized his analysis: "Man invents sin, in order to enjoy the feeling of being naughty."[70]

Lawrence's insight into the modern making of naughtiness and transgressiveness as fashionably sexy and "individual" was, perhaps, what made him suspicious of the self-consciously naughty bohemian therapeutic "individuality" he expected to find flourishing at "a colony of rather dreadful sub-arty people." He voiced this concern (previously expressed by the cultural critic Waldo Frank) at the outset of his correspondence with Luhan: "I still of course mistrust Taos very much, chiefly on account of the artists." Lawrence feared that the White products of America's mass-cultural individuality industries who sought exilic respite from angst and alienation at Taos—who leapfrogged from modernist neurotic to modernist exotic "individuality"—might not have his wealth of subjective capital or his skeptical sense that it is dishonest to make "Indians" instinctually glamorous and use their scenery for playing "Indian."[71]

Initially Luhan hoped that Lawrence's writing would draw public attention to the religious mystery and cultural value of the Pueblos and perhaps also to their political and economic plight. Luhan wanted the Pueblos to be seen as (even) more than a tourist attraction for artists in search of therapeutic repose. Not long before she enticed Lawrence to journey to Taos, she and Tony Luhan—her Pueblo lover, soon to leave his wife and children to be her husband—had persuaded John Collier, the community reformer, to visit them. Collier, mesmerized by the land and the Pueblos' tribal life, rapidly became a convert to the "Indian" cause and dedicated his energies, starting in the early 1920s, to defending Native rights against the BIA, rapacious economic interests, and White squatters. Lawrence might serve as a literary Collier, Luhan thought. She romanticized Lawrence's literary shamanism and his nonpsychoanalytic reverence for spirituality: "I counted so much on . . . his understanding, his deep, deep understanding of the mystery and the otherworldliness, as he would call it, of Indian life." Her hopes for the "Indians," as she represented them to Lawrence, were dimmed, and perhaps made more intensely romantic, by two stereotypical, wrongheaded, and infantalizing assumptions: a belief in the "Indians' " inevitable doom ("[Taos] will die and become American like Buffalo") and the notion that the "Indians" themselves were mute ("I wanted [Lawrence] to . . . give a voice to this speechless land").[72]

In the correspondence that preceded his move to Taos, Lawrence shared Luhan's romantic-literary sense of the "Indians' " inevitable vanishing, but he also made it clear that their political and socioeconomic predicament—not as literary a concern for him, perhaps—was not really his problem. "Are your Indians dying out and is it rather sad?" he wondered, seemingly more appreciative of their tragedy than interested in the possibility that they might resist oppression. In several instances he insisted that Luhan *"leave 'em alone."* Lawrence, always attuned to the subtlety of power relations, confessed some anxiety about his role, an anxiety that he attributed to skin color—"race"—rather than imperialism. The much abused "Indians" might "jeer at one," he wrote Luhan, nervously. "I find all dark people have a fixed desire to jeer at us." He censured "all this poking and prying into the Indians" as "a form of indecency."[73]

Of course, this self-righteous disapproval did not inhibit the ever-curious Lawrence from doing some eager poking and prying himself. More than one correspondent has succeeded in encouraging Lawrence to expect that the "Indians" could offer him "something different" as subject matter for writing. Lawrence too entertained some of the romantic-therapeutic expectations he excoriated in other Taos colonists: "I also believe in the Indians. . . . I do hope I shall get from [them] something which this wearily external world cannot give." At first he thought, in line with Luhan's plan, that he might "write a novel from that [Indian] center." To Luhan's vexation, he never did. Lawrence did befriend the "Indians," however, and often worked with some of them on his rented ranch. They called him "Red Fox."[74]

Luhan was partly correct in thinking that Lawrence never wrote a novel about Taos because he wished to gain the upper hand in their battle with one another for subjective and emotional primacy, a battle melodramatically and at times comically documented in Luhan's *Lorenzo in Taos* (1933). Luhan was upset that Lorenzo instead had elected to write two novels about Mexico: *St. Mawr* (1925) and *The Plumed Serpent* (1926).[75] When Lawrence did publish three essays about "Indian" dancing in New Mexico, he included them in his collection titled *Mornings in Mexico* (1934). Lawrence taunted her about Mexico: "This is really a land of Indians: not merely a pueblo."[76] But Luhan underplayed the significance of Lawrence's essays on dancing (and their indebtedness to her; he dedicated his book to Luhan). She also seemed to have overlooked the importance the "Indians" played in Lawrence's formulation of "blood" psychology in his seminal work, *Studies in Classic American Literature* (1923), a book he had begun around 1915 but rewrote and elaborated in Taos.[77]

Luhan's own romanticization of Native bodies most likely inflected Lawrence's reading of the dances. She viewed dancing "Indians" as a therapeutic solution to her repressed upper-class "individuality." Luhan saw in "Indian" bodies a "flow," a "happy resilience," a "radiance," a "gleaming awareness as though their flesh is wholly awake," a corporeal eloquence: "Yes, they talk, those brown bodies, and laugh. And in sorrow and anger their very backs and bellies are more eloquent than the speech of our lips."

In many though not all of her descriptions of Natives, Luhan perceived not mainly sunburned laboring bodies, used for farming, craftwork, and sheepherding, but celebratory, ritualistic, unrepressed, sensual, rhythmic bodies of resurrection (for Whites): "a call to awake and come back to life." By contrast, using images foreshadowing Edward Hopper's paintings, she characterized White bodies as alienated and "deserted" shells: "We do not live in them and they are like abandoned houses." "Indian" dancing is a "communion," the very opposite of "the usual ball-room entertainment with a tired cynical orchestra in white shirt-fronts, and the stoical masks of the anaesthetized dancers dreary." "Indian" bodies do not touch one another as ballroom dancers do; but there is a connection among them absent from the "speechless" ballroom bodies that "betray involuntarily their plight and at the same time their inability to escape it." Lawrence, encountering "Indian" dancers in Luhan's hacienda, "flowed off into it," according to Luhan, "dancing . . . with a dark one on either side of him, round and round in a swinging circle for hours."[78]

Although he was self-reflexively suspicious of "trying, with fulsome sentimentalism, to render the Indian in our own terms" and had at first been put off by the fearful yet seductive tribal primitivism he thought he detected in "Indian" dancing, Lawrence was keen to write about the corn dance.[79] He was most intrigued by what he perceived as its curious "non-individual" character, "without melody," so unlike the ballads, lyrics, and tales of European peasants that had chronicled the lives of "individuals" and "personal experience." "Indian" singing was more visceral, "from the consciousness in the abdomen," and communicated the experience of "any man, all men," experience that "is generic, non-individual." They did not conceive of this as "entertainment" (a concept foreign to Pueblos), rather "there is no division between actor and audience." Lawrence broached what he saw as the difference between psychoanalytic and "Indian" notions of dreaming to try to explain his idea of the significance of "Indian" dancing: "We whites, creatures of spirit, look upon sleep and see only the dreams that lie as debris of the day, mere bits of wreckage from day-consciousness. We never realize the strange falling back of the dark blood into the dominant rhythm, the rhythm of pure forgetting and pure renewal."[80]

Perhaps the most fascinating and complex Taos-colonizer text on "Indian" dancing is Mary Austin's *The American Rhythm* (1923).[81] This popular, perspicacious, and conceited author had much of interest to say about work rhythms, aesthetic rhythms, and class rhythms, but it is her representation of "Indians" that merits critique. Austin made no bones about her literary indebtedness to (her reading of) the "Indians" around her. She acknowledged rhapsodically that when she first moved to the Southwest she "lapped up Indians" to discover new "concepts of life and society" (38) that could be funneled into her writing of novels. While admitting that she had "never been . . . an authority on things Amerindian," she nonetheless made the extraordinary claim that "at times, [I] have succeeded in being an Indian" (41). As I noted, Helen Hunt Jackson's homesteader-class American Aunt Ri in *Ramona* jests that she will "turn Injun, mebbe" because of her increasing affection and respect for Ramona and Alessandro. But Austin's professional-managerial-class fascination with self-Indianization was far more literary, psychological, therapeutic, exotic, and self-directed. She regarded her "Indians" as attractive because she thought that they taught her the self-regenerating mysteries of "rhythm."

The rhythms one ostensibly discovers in "Indian" dancing and poetry, Austin felt, make it possible to get "caught up in the collective mind, [and] carried with it toward states of super-consciousness" (41). This ritual reorganization of "subjectively coordinated" (5) rhythms can "raise" the "energetic plane of the organism" and produce a "maximum of well-being" (6) characterized by an "acute, happy awareness" (28). The retribalizing of the body and consciousness makes one cognizant of a more collective self repressed by the socially constructed individuality of the "I" and the "personal": "There are tribes that have no word for 'I' as distinguished from 'ourselves.' . . . Among Amerindian tribes, whose culture is for the most part of the type called neolithic, we find a highly developed use of poetry both to express and to evoke states of mind which are in their nature social" (20). "Indian" rhythms show the dancer or poet that he is "not himself only" (26). "Self-realization" (24) is concomitantly a "reconciliation with the Allness" (54).

The "psychological" idiom Austin invoked shows the influence of Freud on her theorizing: "inhibition," "repression," "subconscious," "depth." But Austin criticized and revised the Freudian model in several ways. For Austin, psychology was far too individualized and was therefore unable to begin to imagine, much less describe, the foundational "group-mindedness" (21) that "Indian" rhythms make manifest: "If we began by supposing that the part of the Amerind's mind from which his poetry comes from is identical to the limbo of maimed impressions which the Freudian psychologist finds below the threshold of his contemporaries, we should be far from understanding him" (28). Again, "Indian" rhythms release happy awareness and well-being, not "maimed impressions." She reversed the spatial orientation of psychoanalysis that discovers individual "depth" ("the Deep-self" [28]) in the "subconscious" (below); Indian rhythms, by contrast, she claimed, reveal "super-consciousness" (41), a term that connotes transcendence. Freud deems "civilization" significant because it represses and displaces or sublimates drives. Austin, however, used "Indians" to focus on the "life-sustaining" (18) potential of cultural expression, rather than civilized repression. She reconceived the absorbing business of the "Dawn Man" as "the realization of himself in relation to the Allness" (25), not merely the instinctual gratification of the "sex urge" and "hunger urge" (25). In a letter written at Taos in 1919, Austin offered another reason why she believed her psychology to be far in advance of Freud's: "He derives his knowledge of primitive life from books written very often by people who got them from other books. I had a long and intimate acquaintance with primitives."[82] Hence psychoanalysis, its variants, and primitivism sometimes combined to foster an ethnomodernist protomulticulturalism—which often retained some sense of ethnoracial hierarchies.

Austin's profile of "Indians" and their rhythms enables her to restore the concept of spirituality to (secularized) "psychological" concerns. Austin, like some other Taos residents, was a lively participant in the ideological battle over what "therapeutic" would mean in professional-managerial-class culture. The artist community's primary "psychological" focus, as Austin envisioned it, was as a sort of life-enhancing spa, whose rhythms would be conducive to happiness, well-being, and the recovery of a lost body that houses a lost Dawn Man "individuality" that long predates Euramerican social productions of "individuality." Luhan also captured this vision in her discovery of Natives' "tribal" (non-Freudian) versions of "instincts," "where virtue lay in wholeness instead of in dismemberment."[83]

It should not be overlooked that Austin, along with La Farge, Collier, Sloan, and Witter Bynner, became one of the most active artists and intellectuals involved in the political and economic defense of New Mexico's Natives in the 1920s and early 1930s. She and several others were committed to the civic welfare of the community and the maintenance of its traditional arts and architecture. Moreover, she joined the effort to open up educational and professional opportunities for the community's Native artists—the Indian Arts Fund inherited the bulk of her estate. In 1932 she attempted to bully Secretary of the Interior Ray Lyman Wilbur into establishing more Indian day schools in the Southwest: "It will be a great annoyance . . . if we have to make another appeal, and thus stir up public antagonism toward the department." Austin also spearheaded the artist colony's campaign to protest John D. Rockefeller's censorship of Diego Rivera's RCA building murals that showed a figure of Lenin uniting a soldier, a worker, and a Black. Earlier in her life she associated with the Fabians in England and befriended Sidney and Beatrice Webb. She sought ideas on how to conceptualize and organize social change in the Southwest from Mexican revolutionaries hiding in New Mexico and Arizona before World War I.[84]

Nonetheless, her social critique-as-rhythm awareness used "Indians" to recast the problem of American imperial "civilization" as a problem of the repression of rhythm ("civilized inhibitions" [31]). Viewing "Indians" as a therapeutic solution for White "individuality," Austin sometimes psychologized and individualized the larger socioeconomic and political problems posed by "what we call civilization" (28). Her use of "Indians" to reinfuse spirituality into White therapeutic discourse at times deflected attention from the larger (imperialist) sociality that shaped Natives' needs and spirituality.

While Austin's political engagements and those of other artist colonizers on behalf of Natives must not be forgotten, she and many other well-meaning Southwestern interpreters of therapeutic culture often waged campaigns that contributed to the reduction of utopian vision to the scope of the "individual" (activating the inner "tribal" self). Her White, temporarily Indianized rhythmic self, it might be argued, was not the appearance of the Dawn Man beneath the socialized Euramerican capitalist "I." Rather, her rhythmic self may have been an "I"—that ideologically resourceful American "individual"—who was once again using the "Indian" to fascinate itself with itself as psychologically individual, spiritually restless, and complexly primitive.

At least, this is what Langston Hughes might have concluded. His story "Rejuvenation Through Joy," included in *The Ways of White Folks* (1933), is a keen satire on the rise of therapeutic "joy" cults for the wealthy.[85] The Westchester joy spa that the con artists Lesche (the sexy front man) and Sol (who finances the scam) set up hooks rich people on the therapeutic idea that "primitive" (76) rhythm stimulated by a hot jazz band (here led by the aptly named Happy Lane) will restore their "life-center" and "balance-points" (71). Initially lecturing them in a posh Central Park hotel, Lesche, the evangelist of "sway" (71), inducts his wealthy, angst-filled auditors into the mysteries of the protomulticultural nonconformism of rhythm: "That is one of the great crimes of modern life, one of the murders of ourselves, we sit in chairs! . . . Primitive man never sits in chairs. Look at the Indians! Look at the Negroes!" (71–72). Life-centered Indians and Negroes "dance to their drum beats, their earth rhythms" (72). This joy business is aided by a "Yale man who hadn't graduated" (75). The Yalie, like an ad man, synthesizes appealing mumbo jumbo and ideas—drawn from cults, Freud, the sexologist Havelock Ellis, jazz—for Lesche's lectures. These con artists realize just how marketable "soul" restoration can be and how much more profitable therapeutic joy scams are—easier on the dupes—than "the self-denial cults" (88). Releasing "individuality" is more lucrative than controlling it. Alas, too many affluent matrons fall head over heels for Lesche during his private "rhythm" lessons, which conduce a surfeit of release, and the operation collapses in a pandemonium of jealousy.

What Hughes realizes in his scathing yet outrageously comical satire of this feel-good strain of therapeutic culture is that Lesche and Sol succeed for as long as they do not simply because they sell joy and rhythm with panache. Their sales campaign works because they sell individualized versions, seductively reduced versions, of "the problem" to the dominant class, so that anxious members of this class can busily absorb themselves with the rejuvenation of a (market-invented) lost "individuality" *as* their compelling "problem." By implication, because "primitive" "Indians" and "Negros" have "rhythm," these rhythmic races must feel so good that they transcend the unequal social, economic, and political conditions that systematically and legally oppress them.

Hughes understood that the multifaceted therapeutic colonization taking shape in the 1920s and 1930s tried to accomplish several things at once: it was not just that oppressed "primitive" races were being reencoded as "psychological" solutions to repressed White "individuality"; and not just that the groups that were systematically continuing to oppress these races were concocting ways of feeling good about themselves by magnanimously "revaluing" the aesthetic and ritual practices of oppressed cultures; it was that some members of these dominant groups sought to gain subjective potency by *identifying* with the oppressed as the "Indian" inside them, the tribe inside them, the "Negro" inside them, the primitive inside them. They took this partial identification as evidence of their "individual" nonconformity. Hughes knew that the ultimate colonization underway was that the dominant classes ideologically ("psychologically") ingested the "primitive" within them and were then joyous about their apparently unrepressed liberation, a bizarre cannibalistic incorporation that Luhan, Lawrence, and Austin may have lacked the requisite critical distance to appreciate fully.

"Indians" in the Bloodstream:
The Politics of Lawrence's Psychological Critique
of American Individualizing

During the Harlem Renaissance, Hughes entertained a historical notion of African American "racial individuality" that, in reference to the "Negro artist," he associated with a "heritage of rhythm and warmth" as well as an "incongruous humor that so often, as in the Blues, becomes ironic laughter mixed with tears." He saw "racial individuality," like "racial culture," as a social "heritage" that shaped subjective, emotional, aesthetic, and politically strategic styles. His fear was that "Negro artists" would succumb to White, ideologically slanted constructions of aesthetic value and thus "pour [their] racial individuality into the mold of American standardization."[86]

Lawrence also conferred a racial individuality of sorts on "Indians." But for him their distinctiveness seemed to be biologically interior, corpuscular, arterial—not the conscious, strategic, organized product of cultural heritage, artistry, or skill. Lawrence cast dancing "Indians" as "blood" people, "heart" people, rhythmic "naked blood-beings" who circulate both communal power and their singular "isolation" in the universe. "It is an experience of the human blood-stream, not of the mind or spirit. Hence the subtle, incessant, insistent rhythm of the drum, which is pulsated like the heart, and soulless, and inescapable." He interpreted "the strange blind unanimity of the Indian men's voices" as consummately "tribal," an "experience . . . of the blood-stream."[87]

That Lawrence geared his reading of them somewhat to his own (therapeutic) needs is suggested by his interest in the absence of an "Indian" God who judges one (like the psychoanalytic super-ego): "There is no judgment. . . . I can't be judged, because there is nothing outside it, to judge it." Rather, the dancing "Indians" envision themselves as flowing in an "untellable flood of creation, which, in a narrow sense, we call Nature."[88] Lawrence figured the "Indian" dances as instinctive culture or blood culture. He categorized the Hopi snake dance as a "primitive performance," not with the conventional idea that "civilized" is culturally superior to "primitive," but, on the contrary, to indicate that the primitive contains evidence of an intense, communal, forgotten, rhythmic individuality—a blood individuality—that Whites need to recover for therapeutic, artistic, and social purposes.

Lawrence's and Luhan's "Indians" are now useful not as workers (Pratt's producer-culture campaign) but as a blood transfusion of therapeutic vitality for bored, alienated, nervous White anaemics-in-need. Luhan hoped that her dancing "Indians" would crystallize for Lawrence "the truth about America: the false view, external America in the east, and the true, primordial, undiscovered America that was preserved, living, in the Indian blood-stream." "Indians" are psychological "disinfectant," she decided. Whereas in Buffalo, Luhan's hometown, wealthy families "were sinking down into a diseased and melancholy inanition, for lack of knowing what to do to rouse the flagging blood current."[89]

Lawrence expanded his notions of blood "Indians" and blood psychology into a critique of American individualizing. In *Studies in Classic American Literature* he racialized his perception of American nervousness and of the White psychological individual. "The mind is 'ashamed' of the blood" and American "whiteness" symbolizes the victory of the mind over the blood: "Hence pale-faces." Americans are driven by the mind and the nerves, he concluded, and "the blood is chemically reduced by the nerves, in American activity." Consequently, White Americans, similar to Carlisle's individualized students, "are always busy 'about' something. But truly *immersed* in *doing* something, with the deep blood-consciousness active, that they never are." This "blood" critique targets U.S. imperialism and the colonization of "Indians": because "brittle" Whites repress their blood, they have had to repress "Indians."[90] And if after this conquest "Indians" are recognized by some as the therapeutic solution to weary White blood and nervous White individualism, the fact that "Indians" have their own problems—land, labor, health, education—that require solutions may seem ancillary. Such formulations moved toward representing America's problem not fundamentally as capitalism or imperialism, but as puritanism—puritan repression.

Lawrence and others suggested that the "Indians," however they have been encoded ideologically, psychologically, and aesthetically, possess an enviable obliviousness and a silence that maintains a barrier between the races, a wall that prevents their complete U.S. colonization, assimilation, or individualizing. "They have the remoteness of their religion, their animistic vision, in their eyes, they can't see as we see," Lawrence inferred. "And they cannot accept us. They stare at us as the coyotes stare at us: the gulf of mutual negation between us." Joseph Foster saw in this stoical silence a strategic imperviousness: "they danced, danced their indifference to hunger, to their poverty." During their ghost dance, he averred, they danced "desperately—exhausting their energies, wiping out their last connection with this life until they became the ultimate living thing they all were in this rhythmic madness."[91]

Lawrence extrapolated his notion of the irreconcilable relationship between blood consciousness and mind consciousness into a romance of racial red revenge. He conceived of the revenge of "Indians" on Whites not as political, economic, or military, but as psychological. What he learned about "Indians" from Taos and from nineteenth-century American literature, he thought, was the very opposite of the Americanization, individualizing, and pacification that Carlisle schemed to achieve: "The Red Man died hating the white man. What remnant of him lives, lives hating the white man." The more Red Men are exterminated, the more "unappeased, aboriginal demons" infect the blood to haunt White neurotic consciousness.[92]

What Lawrence did was to take historical reality—hundreds of thousands of Natives died because of the European importation of diseases and germs of various kinds—and psychologically turn it on White Euramericans. Lawrence went so far as to hint that "Indian" Americanization was at bottom a Native battle tactic. "The moment the last nuclei of Red life break up in America, the white men will have to reckon with the full force of the demon of the continent. At the present the demon of the place and the unappeased ghosts of the dead Indians act within the unconscious or under-conscious soul of the white American, causing the great American grouch, the Orestes-like frenzy of restlessness in the Yankee soul, the inner malaise which amounts to madness, sometimes." Lawrence, like a Native performing the ghost dance, envisioned a time of spiritual and psychological reckoning: "Within the present generation the surviving Red Indians are due to merge in the great white swamp. Then the Daimon of America will work overtly, and we shall see real changes." The Daimon's "disintegrative influence on the white psyche" will force Whites, for the good of humankind, to "give up their absolute whiteness."[93]

Notwithstanding the ridiculousness of his own stereotyped evocation of "Indians" as "naked blood beings" and his psychogothic homogenization of them as the Daimon of America, the strength of Lawrence's criticism is in his awareness that "the Indian bunk is not the Indian's invention. It is ours." This perception fed his skepticism of the trendy White "highbrow" idealizing and romanticizing of "Indians" he found at Taos. He discerned two fundamental White views of "Indians." The first is blatant in the capitalist project to picture the "Indians" as worthy only of extinction, a justification to grab their real estate. But the second view, au courant at Taos, is a more subtle colonization—the rewriting of Indianness to satisfy White therapeutic needs. Intellectual White savages (like Luhan), Lawrence believed, wanted "Indians" to be their pets. "White Americans do try hard to intellectualize themselves," he scoffed. "Especially white women Americans. And the latest stunt is this 'savage' stunt."[94] *Studies in Classic American Literature* can be read both as Lawrence's effort to write an "Indian"-centered critique of America and more narrowly as his attempt to explain why he thought Taos did not work as a therapeutic, White colony in "rebellion" against Whiteness.

His story "The Woman Who Rode Away" (1924) emplots this argument. One day a bored White Californian—who lives in Mexico, is married to a formerly wealthy silver-mine owner, and has two children—finds herself enchanted with her husband's brief description of "Indians" who live in a distant valley and kill missionaries. Possessed by "sentimental romanticism," later that day she sets out alone on horseback in search of them. She wants to give herself to their gods. In time she encounters three "Indians" and states her exotic purpose. She soon finds that they fail to respond deferentially to her initially confident, even arrogant, imperial femininity: "As if, perhaps, her whiteness took away all her womanhood, and left her as some giant, female white ant." They hold her captive in their valley. Gradually she perceives their "strange malignancy" toward Whites. But she also recognizes that she cannot read or encode them; they are distant denizens of another cultural and conceptual universe. The one young man who speaks Spanish is destined to be their chief. Part of his training has been to travel to the United States, where he worked, reflected on how he was treated, and studied the Whites. "You shut the gate," he tells her in a rare moment of explanation, "and then laugh, think you have it all your own way." These "Indians" too, she learns, want her to give herself to their gods, for her appearance corresponds with their prophecy that if a White woman is delivered to their gods, her death will reunite the male sun and the female moon and restore the world to the Natives. So they sacrifice her on the winter solstice, thus making her tour even more exotic, albeit less therapeutic, than she had expected. After writing this at times mercilessly sarcastic tale in June 1924, Lawrence showed it to Mabel Luhan, who doubtless got the point.[95]

Lawrence's dire insistence in his criticism that the relations between the races are spiritually irreconcilable was allied to his advocacy of what appears to be antipolitical individualism, an advocacy that in practice was by no means always antipolitical. Lawrence frequently derided "saviourism," which he linked with socialism. "When you got these dark-faced people . . . away from contacts like agitators and socialism," he wrote of the Mexicans, "they made one feel that life was vast, if fearsome, and death was fathomless." Apparently, fearsome life and fathomless death, not capitalist exploitation or imperialism, were worth getting worked up about. Social conflict and exploitation, so the logic goes, are simply the way of the universe and exist to be written about as such. "The world ought not to be a harmonious place," Lawrence reassured readers. "It ought to be a place of fierce discord and intermittent harmonies."[96]

Lawrence sometimes represented political agitation and reform as filth. In these instances he seems to have favored an individualized, privatized, and apolitically pure "soul." "To force the body of your soul into contact with uncleanness is a great violation of your soul." For Lawrence the "Indians" were not foremost a socioeconomic or political group whose rights had been abused, they were rhythmic blood people who had the potential to restore the (White) soul. "Saviourism" is "a despicable thing," he protested, especially when it aimed to make one feel uneasy about not doing anything tangible to contest oppressive relations.[97]

Taos and Santa Fe artists did manifest some saviourist tendencies— which Lawrence sympathized with—in their battles against mission- aries and the BIA on behalf of Native cultural and economic survival. As indicated, some formed societies to preserve Native art in museums and galleries, to promote interest in its excellence nationally and interna- tionally, and to prevent Native artists from being exploited by tourists. Luhan, notwithstanding her bouts of self-absorption, donated money to help establish a hospital in the area and involved herself in several political matters.[98]

But Lawrence was riled by one "saviourist" in particular: Collier. On his arrival in Taos, Lawrence was barraged with information about the Bursum Bill, proposed congressional legislation that attempted to legal- ize Euramerican land theft from the Pueblos. The Lawrences lived next to the Colliers at Los Gallos, Luhan's hacienda, for the first two months of their stay, so Lorenzo got an earful of Bursum, and undoubtedly of Collier, at the evening gatherings around the Luhan fireplace and proba- bly at other times too.[99] Collier, one of Luhan's recent Taos recruits, and Tony Luhan, Mabel's Pueblo lover, spearheaded the local resistance to the legislation and the former soon made it his full-time (salaried) work. In warning Mabel Luhan that crusades to "save" the "Indians" would be transformed by the "lust for power" and would only "destroy" them, Lawrence's complaint became more specific: "It is [Collier's] saviour's will to set the claws of his own white egoistic benevolent volition into them. Somewhere, the Indians know that you and Collier would, with your salvationist but poisonous white consciousness, destroy them."[100]

Lawrence satirized the pumped-up White reformist evangelism in a brief piece for the *New York Times*, which helped publicize what he saw as the full extent of the Pueblo crisis: "[The] Bursum Bill . . . affects the Pueblo Indians. I wouldn't know a thing about it if I needn't. . . . Oh Joy. No Joy, once Joy, now Woe! Woe! Whoa! Whoa Bursum! Whoa Bill, Whoa-a-a!" Dilettantish sentiments such as those Luhan expressed— that she was not sufficiently "thrilled" with the Taos trend to "amelio- rate and reform . . . though [it] seemed necessary"—probably only sharp- ened the edge of Lawrence's skepticism about the colonizers' motives.[101]

He ruthlessly psychologized the zealots' impulses: renegade "reform-ers" are "death-birds, life-haters." The true lover of life, by implication, is the *individual* who thinks principally, perhaps, of saving himself or herself and about the therapeutic cultural blood transfusions requisite to do so. Yet Lawrence agreed to have his name published in a nationally circulated emergency broadside, "The Protest of Artists and Writers Against the Bursum Indian Bill" (October 1922), along with the names of forty-seven others, including Collier, Mabel Sterne (later Luhan), Aus-tin, and Zane Grey.[102] In some respects Taos can be interpreted as a stage for the performance of competing radicalisms—perhaps not all of which, the next chapter suggests, were nearly radical enough.

4

Indians Inc.:

Collier's New Deal Diversity

Management

The Tribal Council decided it's a white man's disease in their blood.
It's a wristwatch that has fallen between their ribs, slowing, stopping.
—Sherman Alexie, *The Lone Ranger and Tonto Fistfight in Heaven*, 1993

[The Noble Savage] stereotype works within us even if we condemn
it and recognize it as racist and false. . . . The majority of the people of the
U.S. will remain blind or racistly romantic about us.
—Jimmie Durham, *Columbus Day*, 1983[1]

Even the upbringing of John Collier (1884–1968) was "saviourist" in orientation. His father, a mayor of Atlanta, Georgia, supported public ownership of power, light, and transportation, and his mother inspired him to love literature and battle injustice. He recalled an incident when he was only ten: an African American friend "went away for a year and when he came back he had learned the meaning of being a Negro in the United States. He was dumbly aggressive, and the pain in him could have no end, and he rejected our friendship." The young Atlantan's trauma over this "dumbly aggressive" deportment, however, transformed into an epiphany. "The interrelations and fusions of what are called 'races' were and are," he realized, "the positive, creative dynamic of history, past and future, and the makers of the human soul." Thus at age ten he grasped race not narrowly as "a troubling problem" but as "the seed-bed of the spirit of man."[2]

Inspirited by his protomulticultural soul, Collier studied at Columbia University and then less formally at the Collège de France and developed an extraordinarily interdisciplinary range of interests. He stands out as a protomulticultural modernist. As a young man he had expansive intellectual and political concerns encompassing cooperative developments, syndicalism, labor and community organization, William Morris's work, progressive educational philosophy, Friedrich Nietzsche's writings, anarchism, and psychology (Jean Baptiste Charcot, Pierre Janet, William James, William McDougall, Havelock Ellis, Sigmund Freud, A. A. Brill). While working for The People's Institute, a community reform organization at Cooper Union in New York City, Collier coauthored, with Edward M. Barrows, *The City Where Crime Is Play* (1914). This brief study investigated how the city's environment nurtured juvenile delinquency. Noting that "forty-percent of New York's population are foreign-born immigrants," Collier argued that immigrant citizenizing could be best effected by flexibly preserving rather than expunging immigrant cultures ("immigrant social wealth") and by utilizing public schools as neighborhood social centers that would make community cultural events more attractive than gang crime.[3] His work with a variety of ethnic community groups made him doubt the wisdom of more extreme efforts to Americanize immigrants, whose cultural traditions, he felt, greatly enriched American life. In 1914 he organized a Pageant and Festival of Nations that featured immigrant groups parading through Manhattan in their native garb.[4] During this phase he also founded the New York Training School for Community Workers. Funding for his projects grew scarce with the onset of World War I. Thus in 1919 Collier moved to California to oversee the state's adult education programs.

His experiences in the West confronted him with a variety of circumstances in which he expanded his ideas about how one might employ social policy to nurture a creative "individuality" and "personality" rooted in the commitment to a community. Collier, whose California lectures celebrated community life and examined the Russian experiment as relevant to community development, resigned his adult education appointment under budget-slashing threats and pressure from the Department of Justice during the Red Scare.[5] The following year he began an extended camping sabbatical with his family and accepted Mabel Luhan's invitation to visit Taos. He immediately fell in love with Taos and the Pueblos and remained, on this first visit, until the summer of 1921. Collier returned to California to assume an academic post for a year, but then, funded by Stella Atwood and the General Federation of Women's Clubs as their Indian research agent, rejoined the Pueblos in Taos to help them fight the Bursum Bill.[6] He sold his house in New York and used the seven thousand dollars he received to support the anti–

Bursum Bill campaign.[7] By 1923 Collier had formed an activist organization, the American Indian Defense Association.

Collier also published five volumes of poetry. His final book, *The Entry to the Desert* (1922), the only one he completed after deciding to take up the cause of the Pueblos, is suffused with modernist angst and alienation as well as conventionally poetic stagings of "deep" interiority (figure 16). He encoded Taos as a therapeutic depthscape.[8] In "Beyond Taos: An April Day," for instance, he exulted: "All day long on the mesas the changing color crowds, / All day long; / And duskily imaging worlds like these, the soul of man abides" (12). Other poems feature "the trench warfare of the modern soul" (45) and the poet's quest (jumping from the desert to the works of William and Henry James) for "the inner thrill" (42). Although the poet is entranced by the "ritual drama" (54) of the Pueblos' winter dance of the Red Deer, "Under the Sacred Mountain: Taos Pueblo" concludes that "the Red Indian [is] doomed to die" (58). The poet appears to assume that because the "Red Man strange" (57) is "starving" (54), the scene is imbued with heightened elegiac romance. Yet while he was rendering these death sentences poetic, Collier became determined to do all he could to help prevent the "Red Man strange" from being famished or doomed.

From his correspondence with Mabel Luhan (then Sterne) in this period, it seems patent that Collier had tricky negotiations with her, his exuberant, rich, and influential ally, as well as with White politicians and factions within the Pueblos. She offered to transform her home into "a kind of headquarters" or "plant" for "Indian" reform, citing Tony Luhan as a "symbol of my having gone over into 'otherness,' as Lawrence would say. When I left the white world I really left it—it was no mental attitude or superficial sensational gesture." (Her earlier idea was to turn her capacious residence into a "nut's home," packed with "neurotics and defectives" in repair.) She volunteered to take a contingent of Pueblos for a publicity tour in the East during the Bursum campaign and showed how much she had learned from the Santa Fe Railway and Fred Harvey stagings of Indianness: "[The Pueblos] always note that their smart short haired americanised ones shall go: just the wrong ones. . . . Can get theatre free [in New York City] if indians will dance and sing." Collier welcomed her fund-raising theatrics but cautiously told her to steer clear of "Washington during the time of the hearings." In a letter to Stella Atwood, she wrote movingly of Pueblos who were being turned into "slave labor" and were "losing their grip upon their own agricultural system." But she also repeatedly referred to the Pueblos as her pet "experiment" and commanded Atwood: "Don't send Collier to find out about

16. John Collier as a young man, northern Ireland, 1907, John Collier Papers, Manuscripts and Archives, Yale University Library

navahoes [*sic*] and apaches and others—any more. Free him loose among the Pueblos." She could be even more imperious in her tone with Collier. But he too could be forceful in his relentless ambition to achieve national, not just local, power: "We shall have to establish our right to dictate Indian policy," he wrote her as early as 1922, "and build up a truly national movement, and get ourselves strongly 'on top' politically."[9]

Collier's Saviourism: Radical Polemicist
against Individualizing

Much of Collier's writing on behalf of Natives is incisive materialist critique. One key theme that connects his polemics is his critique of imperialist individualizing as a systemic process that has made Natives legally, economically, and medically dependent rather than independent: "The 'individualization' process toward the Indians has been one century-long futile process of torture." In opposition to this reductive process, he believed that "how to enlarge the individual remains the central problem of the modern world."[10] It will become apparent that the enlargement he had in mind, to a degree, was a government-sponsored multiculturalization of individuality.

Collier indicted the BIA's undemocratic system of dependency production: "[It] has described itself as being a government within a government. . . . It makes accounting to no agency, juristic, legislative or administrative. . . . It enforces an unpublished penal code, arrests at will, tries without record or protection of counsel to the defendant, fines and imprisons without court review." The BIA is tantamount to a legal "monopoly" whose concerns are financial: "It is guardian over the Indian property valued at $1,650,000,000, the Indian income totalling more than $60,000,000 a year [1929]."[11] It dictates the development or sale of Native land, a substantial portion of which has rich resources that "could make the whole race of Indians far more than self-supporting."[12] Instead of this, he concluded somberly in 1927, "Reservation Indians are slaves."[13]

His articles of the 1920s and 1930s frequently went into detail about the ways in which allotment's individualizing of land not only failed automatically to individualize Natives but made them prone to BIA manipulation, exploitation, and demoralization. Under allotment, for instance, the BIA "determines the mental competency of the Indians— i.e., whether the Indian property and person shall or shall not be under its own control. Having determined 225,000 Indians incompetent,

Indians Inc.   189

thereupon." The individualized Native has been robbed of economic incentive: "The allotted Indian may not sell his land without the Bureau's consent; or lease it without that consent; or will it or inherit it without that consent; or even use it without that consent. The exclusion of court review is complete."[14] Moreover, the BIA specializes in "disinheritance": "The deceased allottee's heirs hardly ever can inherit the land or purchase it. Hence all Indian allotted land is destined for white possession by the second or, at the utmost, the third generation." Allottment has attacked "family unity" because "parcels of land went to individual Indians only, never to families." The allotted Native cannot get credit—vital for commercial farmers—because he or she "is prohibited by law from making contracts, unless the Secretary of the Interior assumes the responsibility, in each particular case." Surplus lands "so called," he stressed, "are bought from the tribe by the government, or sold by the government to whites, usually at a very low price fixed by law."[15] Collier consistently read individualizing as a mechanism and alibi for the "legal" Euramerican theft of Native real estate. His interest was in profiting from Native cultures, not their land.

"In practice," Collier wrote in 1929, even before the stock market crash, "all save a few thousand of the Indians—96 per cent of them all— are at or below the poverty line, and thousands, including whole groups of tribes, are destitute." Rampant poverty helps produce conditions conducive to illness. He noted that the BIA "concedes an Indian death-rate about 95 per cent higher than the general death-rate including that of the Negroes."[16] The "seventy-five institutions, called boarding schools" designed to "individualize" students have exacerbated Native economic and health crises. Collier relabeled them BIA "school prisons" operating outside the jurisdiction of child labor laws. These cheap labor camps "more than any other single factor" have caused "the excessive morbidity and mortality among Indians," for too many of these schools have been plagued by infectious diseases that students import to the reservation. He advocated culturally and physically healthy schools that cherish "diversity" rather than "uniformity."[17]

In "Hammering at the Prison Door" (1928) Collier expressed qualified admiration for the Brookings Institution's influential Meriam Report, *The Problem of Indian Administration* (1928), an 872-page catalyst for the major governmental reorganization of Indian Affairs in the 1930s. Though the report recommended numerous reforms of the government's policies, Collier was acutely critical of it as a liberal rather than radical analysis of the systemic problem. The report, he complained, fostered the impression that the BIA was inefficient because of "an innocent chaos of administration, a bureaucratic intelligence, and a shortage of appropriations." But Collier contended that the BIA was quite efficient in abetting "the theft of Indian water-power sites" and "trust deeds." He charged that "never has the material exploitation of Indians been so organized."[18]

Collier's frame of reference was hemispheric. He often countered dismal statistics of "vanishing" Natives (which Carlisle drummed into its students) with other statistics that resituated them in the context of the huge population of indigenous peoples in the hemisphere. "Our country's Red Indians number 400,000," he wrote. "They total 0.3 per cent of our people. From the Rio Grande to Cape Horn, the Indians are 28.2 per cent of the whole population. In eight countries they are more than 50 per cent of the population, and in three countries over 80 per cent."[19] And in 1939 he characterized them as "thirty million Indians. . . . marching toward power." His accent on hemispheric "power," including occasional references to ways in which Mexico and Canada had made great advances in their Indian policy, issued a warning to the United States: "What we are doing . . . to meet our Indian minority problem has a deep significance to these 30,000,000 other Indians, and to all the countries where they are located."[20]

The "radical cure" for this poor record, as he saw it in 1930, three years before his appointment as BIA commissioner, would be "a program incorporating the Indian tribes and groups." He envisioned this incorporation as a "type of federal guardianship," but one that would empower "the Indians" to "operate and develop tribal estates and recapture whatever valuable part remains of the allotted lands."[21] This was the germ of the tribal "self-government" program he attempted to implement as the Wheeler-Howard Indian Reorganization Act of 1934.

Collier recognized that conditions had grown more propitious for political reform because of foundational cultural changes that had occurred since the early 1900s. Native dancers and singers had appeared in theaters, Native authors had published more literature, Native athletes had excelled in much-publicized events such as marathon running, and "scores of thousands of tourists" had flocked to the Southwest. He could have added that increasing numbers of Euramerican consumers in the Southwest and elsewhere had purchased "Indian" arts and crafts.[22] All this had helped redirect sentiment away from the Pratt individualizing model toward support for the survival of Native cultures and political groups. Thus Collier strategically grasped the connection between the two fronts—political and cultural—in the campaign that the new style of reformer had to wage.

17. John Collier, Indian Commissioner, January, 1940, on top of a car stuck in the Big Cypress swampland on the Seminole Reservation, Florida, John Collier Papers, Manuscripts and Archives, Yale University Library

At its best, Collier's nascent protomulticulturalism went beyond a liberal emphasis on the therapeutic cultural acceptance of "others" to an activism that championed a broadly conceived multicultural democracy dedicated to the elimination of exploitative economic and racial stratifications. Collier's vitriolic assaults on Whiteness exemplified the expansive critical concerns he brought to his involvement with "Indians." In 1934, during the fracas over his Indian Reorganization Act, he let loose: "There is nothing in the world changing and going to pieces quite as fast just at the present time as the white race, as our own dominant civilizing." A few years later he elaborated on why he believed White values had crumbled: "Mechanical science swept the field. . . . It transposed the principle of sheer power into the heart of human social life. . . . We really came to that time in our world when the only seriously believed-in motivation was egocentric, status-seeking, wealth-seeking and pleasure-seeking" (figure 17).[23]

Anti-Imperial Romanticism: Collier as Social Theorist of "Indians"

Collier brought to Taos and his work with Natives not only a highly developed intellectual and spiritual commitment to social reform but also a fascination with concepts of psychological "depth." On the one hand, he valued Peter Kropotkin's anarchist tract *Mutual Aid* (1902) and contended that Kropotkin imagined "a human consciousness wider and deeper than Sigmund Freud was dreaming of." Kropotkin conceptualized consciousness as socially relational and morally responsible. On the other hand, Collier was intrigued by notions of the hidden self and its healing powers. The psychology that Charcot and Janet expounded captured his imagination because it demonstrated that "in hysteria, the daylight parts of consciousness have a way of dropping below the 'threshold,' and the twilight or hidden regions of consciousness have a way of erupting above the threshold."[24] Collier's friends were not only trade unionists and reformers but men like the psychoanalyst A. A. Brill. He corresponded with the celebrated psychiatrist Karl Menninger in the early 1930s about the "psychiatric and mental health aspects of the boarding school system." And in the 1940s he supported a psychological study that administered "tests of the depth-psychological type" on the Hopi.[25] In general he was keen on experimenting with "psychosocial science."[26]

This interest in theories of community development *and* of psychological "depth" help account for why Collier was particularly drawn to cultures, especially Native cultures, that he perceived as valuing the idea of inner power and why he sought actively to nourish what he thought of as inner power through social organization. He did not conceptualize inner power as a private or wholly individual force, rather he saw it as a holistic cultural achievement. Long before psychologists like Carl Rogers popularized the term, Collier thought about "societies as evokers of the depth of *human potential*" (my emphasis).[27]

Collier's understanding of the Pueblos' "depth" had a material foundation—the land. He often viewed the Pueblos not so much psychologically as having individual atomized psyches but ecologically as embodiments of the land. In his sometimes controversial work as BIA commissioner he sought to be a conservationist of both "Indians" and their soil. The "Indians" "appear as if to have sunken" into their landscape "with a deepening glow. . . . The land is theirs and they are the land." Here Collier echoes some Native beliefs. "It is the American Indian who contributes to this country its true folk-dancing," Standing Bear wrote, "growing, as we did, out of the soil. . . . [The dances] are heart-beats, and once all men danced to its rhythm."[28] In the 1920s the Museum of New Mexico set up an "Indian alcove" that exhibited, as the museum put it, "new art indigenous to the soil."[29] Those who live in "ecological balance" with the land, Collier theorized, develop values that create "depth" and identity. More specifically, the Pueblo social ecology made it possible for soil to become soul.

Collier embraced Native notions of time, concepts radically different from the American clockwork organization of time that regiments possessive individuals. The Natives' communal—not simply individual—past remained actively alive and was connected to the future through the present, and this experience of time, Collier opined, is "happier" than the "time" that Whites have devised for themselves. Native understandings of "past and future," he generalized, "are not only that which in linear time-sequence has been or is yet to be, but are propulsive, efficient, living reality here and now."[30]

Collier admired the ways in which Native therapeutics fortified the development of selfhood. The Navajo religion, for instance, serves "as the healer of sick bodies and souls, and sick communities—a function where the two ancient principles of mutual aid and of unanimity are paramount." Navajo physical, emotional, and spiritual healing is communal rather than individualized in its orientation; indeed, in Navajo singing rituals (the "sing"), "the community, led by the medicine man, cures the sick individual, reclaims the alienated sick soul of its own deeper psychological-spiritual strengths."[31] For Collier, the Native social body was not simply organizational; it had learned how to invest itself with the cultural and spiritual power to heal the individual body and mind.

Collier, like Mabel Luhan, Lawrence, Austin, and many other Taos colonizers, considered the "Indians," who "live their lives within the rhythms of this cosmical land," as being "so magnetic, so exciting, so healing and regenerating to starved [White] human nature." Therapeutic "Indians," Collier boasted, drew Carl Jung to Taos pueblo. If for Lawrence "Indians" supply the blood that culturally anaemic Whites need, for Collier "Indians" offer a notion of "depth" that has both pop psychological and pop anthropological characteristics: "Indians" bring Whites back to "the age of the dawn of man. . . . [where] the child is joined with the man." Therapeutic "Indians" exhibit a communal child-adult "individuality" that Whites have lost: "home of my own soul, as my own race possessed it long ago, and then possessed it no more. This is my recovered eternity." Collier sometimes homogenized "Indians" as changeless and wanted to preserve them as such for the sake of his idea of his race's "recovered eternity" (figure 18).[32]

Psychoanalytic notions of "depth" focus on the individual's repressed instincts and unconscious desires, whereas Collier sees "Indian" *communal depth* as more spiritual in nature, constituted by "the forces of

18. John Collier, Indian Commissioner, posing with Native family around cooking pot with suited men, probably BIA employees, in background, John Collier Papers, Manuscripts and Archives, Yale University Library

the wild and of the universe." "Indian" inwardness is neither individualized nor privatized in the Euramerican sense: "such deepening, such liberation, cannot be had by detaching the individual from his sources."[33] Unlike many Whites, Collier was in favor of the controversial sun dance as a ritual essential to the formation of Native communal "personality." Euramericans cultivate the ideology of the romantic individual genius (where power emanates from one's unique and unfathomable individuality), while Natives revere a communal genius that generates a different form of power available to humans. Collier argued on behalf of the sophistication of Native communal accomplishments by underscoring that it is the group that creates the "individual" and ideas of the "individual": "Many-sidedness within a group whose genius is cooperative and democratic means individual sophistication. . . . I have not known anywhere, and do not hope to know, individuals more richly sophisticated than a great many I have known among the Southwestern Indian tribes."[34]

Collier's boldest claim was that "Indians" manifest humanity better than Whites, and that Euramerican capitalism and democracy could learn much from their achievements in community and personality building. "They had what the world lost," he pleaded repeatedly. "Indians" learned the art of *therapeutic democracy*: "Our democracies are largely political. The Indian democracy was—and is—political, economic, social, and cultural. It was—and is—rich, colorful, emotionally satisfying beyond anything dreamed of by our materialistic—and hence soul starving—modern machine culture."[35] His romanticism went beyond arguing for the preservation of traditional Native cultures to advocating for the Indianizing of White Americans. Collier suggested, as did Lawrence, that the White Americans who colonized "Indians" colonized themselves in the bargain. "They speak to us from out of our long foregone home, and what hears them is the changeless eternal part of us, imprisoned and immured by our social epoch even as the Indian societies were imprisoned and immured by us in the century behind."[36] By implication, the eternal "Indian" within us makes us all "Indians."

But Collier differed from Lawrence in his idea of what therapeutic "Indians" could teach Whites. Lawrence instinctualized the "Indian" strength as blood. Collier employed the term *personality*—not the popular nineteenth-century word *character*, used by Pratt and the influential Friends of the Indian—to describe "Indian" accomplishments. For Collier "Indians" are deeper than Whites because they "are even today the keepers of a great age of man-with-nature-integrated, and inward seeking, which in behalf of our Race are warders even of the 'abysmal deeps of personality.'" In its essence what "Indian" culture holds out to the larger culture ("our Race") is social therapy; their personality is social personality: "keepers" of a "conception of public good . . . and of public good as being no solely material thing, but the affirmation of the Spirit of man." Collier contrasted the social "creation" of "Indian personality" with the nurturance of White possessive personality—the former adheres "to the concept of shared social good."[37] His work with the "Indians" inspired him to ask the crucial question that Pratt also posed: what kind of "individuals" do Americans want to have their culture *design*?

White modernists like Collier, Luhan, and Lawrence, who were so influenced by psychoanalysis, usually imagined community as the producer of taboos, repression, and conformist restrictions on "individuality." This model helps make ideological dichotomies like "individual" versus "society" seem commonsensical. But what Collier both brought to and learned from his therapeutic "Indians" was the idea that *community* is the creative source that shapes and enlivens individuals. This imagination of community challenges dichotomies like "self" versus "world." Hence Collier valued the "primitive" "Indians" as progressive rather than retrograde and in need of civilizing, individualizing, and Americanizing. In marshaling such arguments he tried to reverse the ideological polarity institutionalized by the government, the media, the arts, and institutions like Carlisle: "Indians" are not America's "problem," their "social genius" is America's *solution*.[38]

"Indians" are the solution in part because of their strategic inventions of cultures. The Pueblos, with their multiple religions (traditional and Catholic) and languages (Native, Spanish, English), are "laboratories of race-adjustment." They exhibit the "statesmanship and pedagogy [that] our present world needs to learn."[39] Lawrence's restless query was: How does culture *repress* individuals? Collier's theoretical investigation was: How can culture help us *live together* and *enhance* us? When Collier asserts that "Indians are most thoroughly poetic," his ethnoromanticism is conjoined with sociological considerations.[40] For him the study of "Indian" cultures broaches significant questions about what culture is capable of making. "How shall man influence and empower the spirit?" How might a culture achieve a "translation" of "man into more than man"? How might a deprivatized, unindividualized "communal passion" facilitate this translation? "Utility is subordinate to beauty in [Indian] life as in no other."[41] Euramerican cultures, by contrast, tend to generate other formulations of value and purpose: "Our White Man's civilization is uniquely concerned with the means toward life rather than life itself." Collier rhapsodized over "the multi-personal and multiracial, isolated and blending and recombining" at Taos, a multicultural creation of possibilities threatened by the "white race," which he allegorizes as "the Antichrist." His therapeutic protomulticulturalism was often a spur to, rather than a deflection from, thinking critically about the economic, legal, political, and ideological positionings of Natives within what he terms the "white invasion."[42]

Still, the question remains whether what Collier deemed America's solution was the Natives' solution or just another imperialist ideology of subjectivity thrust on them. Sometimes Collier expressed skepticism of Euramerican efforts to translate "Indians" into White terms. "We cannot, individually, become a part of them," he admitted, "for we are men of our own time, not of theirs; yet we may be helped through knowing them." This caveat, however, did not stop him occasionally from effacing the cultural specificity of "Indians" and decoding their "deeper" significance as universal and "psychological." "A living contact with Indian symbolism and Indian culture is not mere contact with Indians," he lectured Camp Fire Girls in 1934. "It is a contact with universal life—with life at its fountain source of world-old, world-wide and world-foreseeing adolescent consciousness."[43]

Collier's portraits of himself as a St. John the Divine come to redeem the "Indians" whose "adolescent" spirituality has redeemed him did not always square with Natives' views of him, his assumptions, his style, and his policies. Disquieting aspects of Collier's Indianist romantic modernism can be seen in his and other Taos colonizers' conceptions of the ritually oblivious "Indian." What astonished Collier about dancing "Indians" was also what amazed Lawrence, Luhan, Foster, and Austin: "How in many Pueblo sacred dances the oblivion of self and the corresponding inrush of power becomes almost terrifying, is known to all who frequent the dances." Collier, like others, was susceptible to romanticizing this apparent social inwardness and transcendence in ways that could permit Whites to ignore the oppressive forces that the Pueblos and many other tribes actively, even desperately, resisted. In reference to the Navajos, Collier wrote, "Feeling of poverty there is none; squalor, graspingness, apology for obvious poverty, none." Yet when Collier attempted to reduce severely the number of Navajo sheep and goats to institute a program that would combat soil erosion (a serious problem due to overgrazing) early in his reign as BIA commissioner, these same, picturesque Navajos were anything but oblivious to their economic subsistence—many fought Collier in a bitter struggle. "The Indian made it his business to have fulness of life within material meagreness, and within a deep insecurity which his wisdom did not even want to see terminated," Collier believed. "He made, through his social institution and social art, this *external insecurity* into the condition of *inward security*—individually inward and group inward."[44] While Pratt accommodated himself to the reality of Native poverty by considering it an impetus for character and incentive development, at times Collier accommodated himself by supposing that Natives' poverty aids the development of their spiritual innerness.

One astute commentator on Collier's powerful critical vision has suggested that his enthusiastic cultural relativism and celebration of cultural differences could at times obfuscate "the immense imbalance in the power relations between the two societies."[45] And as Lois Palken Rudnick, a cultural historian of Taos, has (self-reflexively) recognized: it has been all too easy, from the early 1900s to the present, for even the well-meaning White middle- and upper-class "cultural imperialist[s]" who settle in, tour through, or study Taos and Santa Fe to really notice and think about the role they have played in "the acts of violence that

[have] punctuated this seeming rural paradise and . . . about the poverty and despair that [have been] a part of daily life in what is billed as one of the most idyllic communities in the United States."[46]

Imperial Self-Government: Reorganizing "Indians"

As BIA commissioner, Collier was well aware, to use Rudnick's words, of the "daily social and economic realities of Hispanics and Native Americans" in the Southwest, of the "interethnic, racial, and class strife that has been a persistent reality of the region," and, more generally, of the socioeconomic, political, ecological, and health conditions with which Natives contended across the country.[47] He had every intention of reversing the government's individualizing strategies when he became Franklin Delano Roosevelt's BIA commissioner in 1933 and helped draft the Indian Reorganization Act of 1934. Collier encountered effective congressional and bureaucratic opposition to the bill's more radical measures. This legislation sought to restore governing autonomy to the tribes, recover "surplus land" that had been sold, "re-assign allotments to their tribes," abrogate "governmental oppressions of Indian ceremony and ritual," and rescind "the Indian Bureau's power to suppress or interfere with Indian freedom of religion, speech, and association." The act also did much to encourage the production of Native arts and crafts. Civil service requirements were reformed so that many more Natives than ever before joined the BIA and assumed posts as superintendents of reservations and Indian boarding schools. Seeing himself, perhaps, as a sort of Abraham Lincoln for "Indians," Collier hoped that the repeal of the Dawes Act on June 18, 1934, would be considered Indian Independence Day.[48]

Many of Collier's views, some of which he put into practice in the Indian Reorganization Act, can be read as his repudiation of Pratt's Carlisle and of the premises that interpret Americanization as capitalist individualizing. His commitment to have the government sponsor and preserve Native arts and crafts, and the great value he placed on Native therapeutics and religion, countered Pratt's devaluation of tribal cultures. Collier's theme was "Assimilation, not into our culture but into modern life"—an American "modern life" that would embrace cultural pluralism.[49] Rather than classifying "Indian" cultures as unproductive and backward, Collier maintained that they exemplified spiritual productivity. It was against Native "social individuality," group inwardness, and spiritual productivity that Pratt's Carlisle waged war; but, Collier generalized, with homogenizing, ethnoromantic bravado, the

Indians Inc.   199

"Indian" "was never inwardly defeated."[50] Pratt tried to engineer the remaking of the "Indian" self, while Collier attempted, with mixed results, to engineer the fabrication of "Indian" self-government.

Collier's admiration for Native communality and social ethics had not just a saviourist but a socialist accent. When he worked for the Indian Rights Association and edited the association's journal *American Indian Life* in the 1920s, Collier and his Pueblo compatriots were accused of being "agents of Moscow," "anti-American," and "subsidized by Soviet money." BIA critics and other opponents of Collier claimed that the Council of All New Mexico Pueblos, which Collier helped reestablish in 1922 to combat the Bursum Bill, was "financed by Moscow."[51] Collier liked to cite these charges to demonstrate the lengths to which his adversaries would go to discredit him. In 1935 he issued a press release criticizing opponents of his Indian New Deal's development of "cooperative enterprises" who "say that it is communistic, anarchist and atheistic, that it derives from Turkey, Russia and Mexico and is in some way involved with China."[52] Shortly before he resigned as commissioner in 1945, "Indian witnesses were brought in to testify about the . . . communistic tendencies of Collier and his colleagues."[53] While he only advocated cooperative, municipal ownership, and labor movements, not socialism, what Collier venerated about Natives did evoke socialist as well as therapeutic values.[54] Their cultural presence enabled him to assert a hemispheric exceptionalism that much resembled socialism.

Thus he praised Peru's Natives' establishment of the "communidad," which appropriated "any unused portion of land." Alaska's Metlakatlans, Collier beamed, have produced for themselves an "all embracing co-operative commonwealth." The Hopi had evolved "a democratic cooperative social structure which tolerated no waste of human energy and individual self-seeking" and excelled in the cooperative "art of self-making." Red Lake Chippewas—a self-sustaining tribe and thus a twentieth-century rarity to be treasured—"fished from the lake, and they packed, refrigerated, and mechanized their fish through a co-operative organization which was all Indian." And 718 Mescalero Apaches, aided by the Indian Reorganization Act, decreed in their "charter that no per capita payments should ever be made out of corporate profits, but that all income should be used for such purposes as the construction of public works, the needs of charity, and the establishment of a loan fund for members of the tribe." Indianism clearly appealed to Collier as an indigenous form of aspects of socialism and could therefore, not being termed socialism, be put forward as a solution to an unsatisfactory capitalist production of "individuals." The ecological and spiritual "deep community" of Taos, not by implication the economic experiment underway in Russia, offered a homegrown model—*socialism as multiethnicism*—for an improved United States.[55]

Collier's various attacks on American individualizing resonate with numerous aspects of socialist critiques (see appendix). He bemoaned the fact that the "best minds of the Occident" have long theorized the "fundamental isolation of the individual" as an existential given and have paid little attention to relational values propagated by the labor, cooperative, and folk movements. Collier expressed outrage at Adam Smith's popularly disseminated premise that "hedonistic human nature will pursue the greatest individual satisfaction through the least effort." As for America's rampant possessive individualism, Collier mused: "Can we subordinate individual aggrandizement to social value as the end to be served by human effort?" In opposition to this cultural and economic invention of "individuals," he applauded the Sioux creation of a "prestige" system that values "giving, not getting . . . dispersing wealth, not accumulating it."[56]

Collier's historical criticism of capitalist imperialism and its strategies was explicit and scathing. He wrote about the imperialist strategies of the Portuguese, Spanish, Dutch, French, English, and nineteenth-century Americans—for whom "the cost [of Indian genocide] was in excess of one million dollars for each Indian killed." He had a lucid understanding of how, since the conclusion of the Indian wars in 1892, land-grabbing and colonization had been accomplished by judicial, bureaucratic, educational, and cultural means: "Indian landholdings were cut down from 139 million acres in 1887 to 47 million acres in 1930" and "one hundred thousand Indians were landless." Collier grasped that ideologies that encode "Indians" with characteristics such as "sloth," "benightedness," and sheer "racial impracticability" were disseminated with the backing of Euramerican business interests.[57] One who had such knowledge and sympathies would appear to be a worthy ally of Natives, and in manifold ways he was.

Some letters in Collier's archives, however, suggest the double-edged character of his treatment of Natives. In 1932 Robert Yellowtail (Crow) praised Collier's policies but later headed opposition to the Indian Reorganization Act. A year later George H. Roberts (Pawnee) congratulated Collier on his appointment as commissioner and concurred with his approach. In 1935 Chief Big Brave (Blackfeet) informed him that he had thrown his support behind the Indian New Deal, but insisted: "These are big words to fill, so work hard," and help "the Indians in the U.S. to REOWN their land again." Tony Luhan wrote him twice in 1927 about

Pueblo factionalism, portraying himself as Collier's inside man (he had helped gain Pueblo backing of the Indian Defense Association in the early 1920s).[58]

Of particular interest is the correspondence between Collier and Antonio Mirabel (Pueblo). In April 1936 Mirabel, leader of the Taos Pueblo Council, voiced his group's criticisms of the BIA superintendent Dr. Sophie Aberle (who, one Native observed, was Collier's adulterous "sweetheart") in the All Pueblos Council. She was slated to oversee three previously separate jurisdictions, which had political differences with one another, in order to better coordinate Pueblo economic activity. In addition, Mirabel, who also served as a BIA deputy special officer for law enforcement, arrested members of the peyote church and confiscated land belonging to a few of them on the grounds that some peyote users were smoking marijuana. This was part of his effort to restore authority to traditional Pueblo religious leaders. Collier fired him. Mirabel explained: "What I repeat at the [All Pueblo Council] meeting is purely instructions from my peoples not my own opinion." Collier took this as insubordination: "What you say and do as a member of the Pueblo is altogether your own concern, but I do not see how an Agency employee can be continued if he is stubbornly opposed to the Superintendent and to the Washington policies."

This precipitated a well-publicized controversy. Mabel Luhan opposed Mirabel's termination in the *New Mexican* and asked how it meshed with Collier's aim to hire Natives in the BIA "so they could learn to administer their own affairs." Writing to Collier, Mirabel challenged his boss's bestowal of self-determination on the "Indians": "If we supposed to manage our own affairs, how can we manage by keeping our mouth shut, for the sake of wages, And not do the duties of the peoples? My understanding was that we was to manage our own affairs through the Wheeler Howard Bill, but since the Govt. [*sic*] imployees [*sic*] have no voice for their peoples." Luhan then consolidated her break with her former ally in the *Albuquerque Tribune*: "Collier is enslaving [the Indians] to the wage system and is not carrying out his announced policy of making the Indians more self-governing."[59]

Collier's archive also contains some testy correspondence with Gertrude Bonnin and her husband Captain Richard Bonnin, who led the National Council of American Indians. In 1927 Gertrude Bonnin forwarded a check of $75 to support Collier's American Indian Defense Association's campaign to protect the Pueblos and she hailed him as "great friend of the Indian people." By 1932 Bonnin and her husband changed their minds. In their letter they recorded the details of their

disagreements with Collier about the timing of the circulation of a petition among Native tribes that denounced the policies of top BIA officials. They resented his "attack" on them for not advocating this measure in his time frame. The Bonnins suggested that Collier sometimes
strongarmed and misinformed "Indians" to get their backing so as to
make his own criticisms, proposals, or policies seem more authentic
("Indian" approved). They also implied that Collier was committed to a
racial hierarchy in "Indian" reform with Whites calling the shots. "We
do question the advisability of asking Indians to sign statements of
which they know little or nothing about," they objected. "We also believe it improper for anybody, like yourself, to write up inflammatory
statements and insist, almost to the point of coercion, upon Indians
signing it. If they don't sign it, you feel free to attack and denounce them
unfairly." They accused him of violating one of his own fundamental
social principles—cooperation. "If you are broad enough to have the
capacity to do great things for the Indians, you will be able to go on with
the work without annihilating us or even attempting to do so. . . . It takes
more than one to cooperate." Collier responded competitively to these
charges of attempted ventriloquism by clarifying that he represented as
many or more tribes than they did, and, "as your files can remind you, I
have been in greater or less measure your draftsman in making or elaborating statements which you have signed."[60]

The Native activist Ward Churchill (Creek, enrolled Keetoowah Band
Cherokee) has charged that Collier's reformist enthusiasms were informed by "the methodology of colonialist rule." And Patricia Penn Hilden (Nez Perce) has observed critically that "one of [Collier's] first acts
was to hire anthropologists who could tell the objects of Collier's attentions all about themselves."[61] Collier was not unfamiliar with similar
Native criticisms of his managerial policies in the 1930s and 1940s. Indeed, many Natives experienced problems with Collier's administration
that call to mind Lawrence's skepticism about Collier's "saviourism."

Despite the noncoercive intentions of the Indian Reorganization Act,
it attempted to reorganize the tribes into what Collier, the community
reformer, thought of as democratic or parliamentary bodies. Some of the
"tribes" that were affected were not even tribes in any political sense;
they were "bands" of Natives who were forced to form "tribal councils"
with other bands who spoke the same language and had a similar cultural background. That is, Collier's classificatory emphasis on tribes
initially overlooked the real day-to-day existence of working *communities*, especially the factor of clan autonomy.

Particularly by the 1930s, Natives subscribed to a wide spectrum of cultural and political values. Many were agitated both by Collier's plans and by his homogenizing (Puebloized) image of "Indians."[62] Traditionalists, often full-bloods, in many tribes did not favor the system of voting as a form of self-governance and saw it instead as a kind of democratic imperialism.[63] If Collier offended some traditionalists, his propensity to romanticize "Indians" as "changeless," the primeval tonic for Whites, enraged some Natives who had selectively assimilated over time. Some of these Natives had little interest in tilling communal farmland or playing "Indian" for the benefit of White consumers and tourists.[64] It may have been that Collier—who did not make helping more Natives gain access to college a prominent issue on his agenda—occasionally felt uncomfortable with some professional-managerial-class Natives who did not seem like the brand of authentic "Indian" from whom Collier derived therapeutic solace.[65] On the one hand, Collier's ethnoromanticism may have prevented him from apprehending just how ambitious and interested in social power many traditional and nontraditional Natives were on and off the reservations. On the other hand, he may have concluded that Native higher education, like the Court of Indian Affairs he initially lobbed for and gave up on, was not what Vine Deloria Jr. and Clifford M. Lytle have termed a "saleable" product within the ideological climates that prevailed in Congress and among some members of tribes.[66]

Collier claimed that the 1933 Native vote for the Indian Reorganization Act was a stunning victory for his democratic policies. Yet from certain perspectives it was anything but a clearcut affirmation of his vision of "Indian" renewal. "Although over two-thirds of the eligible tribes voted to come under the IRA," writes Robert Berkhofer, "this represented only 40 percent of the individual Indians voting in the special elections." About half of the tribes who voted in favor of the legislation established constitutions and governments as specified by the plan and few tribes formed corporations to bolster their economic position.[67]

Factional divisions within tribes, made more visible and aggravated by New Deal reorganization, included "full bloods versus mixed bloods; progressives versus conservatives; Catholic versus Protestant; Democrat versus Republican; Chiefs versus council."[68] "Indians" were not only far more diverse and complex in their social organization than Collier at first understood them to be, "the influence of [their] traditions and personal autonomy" made many refuse to conform to a Washington-imposed "reorganization" of their lives.[69] That is, "Indians" were in a sense too diversely *individual* to be Indianized as Collier thought best. Some Native critics of Collier's administration, like Robert Yellowtail, the first Crow superintendent of the Crows, employed the individualist language of "rights" to protest aspects of the Indian New Deal.[70] Natives learned to adopt "rights talk" in their many land claims disputes with the government and with corporations.[71]

In 1934 Secretary of the Interior Harold Ickes protested that "the basest misrepresentations are being circulated to try to defeat the measure. . . . aptly termed the Indian Bill of Rights." Whatever the causes, Collier's archive includes letters from tribal representatives dead set against this Bill of Rights. The Comanches of Fort Sill sent a Pratt-like protest in defense of policies that enabled them to "quickly merge into the white civilisation," have "property rights," and live off the reservation. The Kiowa council was terse: "260 against and 2 for." A Kiowa correspondent explained: "After having lived now for more than thirty-five years among white people, we do not think it is just and fair to our Indian race to be segregated or isolated from the white people; many of these white people have assisted us in farming, stock raising, etc., and have helped us in many other useful things as good neighbors." Tribal Business Committees for the Pawnee, Ponca, Kaw, Otoe, and Tonkawa tribes in Oklahoma voted unanimously against the Indian Reorganization Act's conception of "Indian Self-Government" and insisted that "our children who have had the advantage of our splendid boarding schools are more advanced and better prepared to take their places in the white community than children" at "Reservation public schools." The Oklahoma Arapahoe sent a resolution rejecting "the plan of SELF-GOVERNMENT" and disapproving the abolition of "the allotment act."[72]

Proassimilation Natives, especially those in the conservative American Indian Federation, went so far as to accuse Collier of trying to impose socialism on them and expressed anxieties that landowning Natives would be compelled to surrender land to the landless—something allegedly un-American.[73] In a 1934 press release Collier evenhandedly acknowledged that "the plan will run counter to the immediate, apparent individual selfish interests of a good many thousand of allotted Indians. . . . It is a corporate system, but not to the exclusion of individual ownership." His concluding sentence suggests the ideological Indianness he preferred: "It will free the Indians to be themselves, and many of the Indians thus freed will choose the Anglo-Saxon way, or the cosmopolitan way. Some will choose the ancient way, and that will be well."[74]

Collier ran into trouble when the Navajo stock reduction (by one third, 400,000 sheep and goats) for soil conservation issue boiled over in 1934. In some publications he represented the Navajos' ostensible willingness to volunteer—and pay for it—as a triumph of his reasonable administration: "The Navajos were expressly and formally told that compulsion would not be used."[75] But in a speech to the Navajos in 1935 he was more forthright about how he motivated reluctant Navajos to "volunteer" and gives some indication why he was not always trusted by his "wards" even as he sang hosannas to their spiritual depths. He remarked that in 1933 "I stated with all possible clearness that unless the further destruction of the soil by erosion, due to overgrazing, could be stopped, the Government would not be able to go forward with its investment of money on the Navajo Reservation. With much detail I stated that water development, irrigation, range improvements of all types, even the construction of new school buildings must stop, unless soil erosion were checked." He suggested that "it never will become necessary for the Government to use coercion in this matter" but cited the Secretary of the Interior's position that he "must use coercive authority if that is the only way. . . . [This is] authority in law."[76] And when in 1933 he addressed Navajo students who had returned to the reservation and exhorted them to support and help implement the reduction, he sounded much like Pratt in his invocation of "progress" (a discourse that he reviled elsewhere as the curse of "white civilization"): "It is true that you are the hope of your people, because you have been brought into contact with the modern sources of power—machinery, knowledge, science." Uneasy with this modernizing slant in 1942, when praising the Acomas' decision to "volunteer" for a radical stock reduction, he attributed it to their exercise of "ancient wisdom."[77]

During his administration the biweekly publication *Indians at Work* offered accounts of Natives engaged in Emergency Conservation Work on reservations. This important magazine reveals not only Collier's concepts of an enlightened "modern" but his plan for the *Indian modern.* Collier hails the New Deal not just as a "vast cooperative" experiment in planning the economy but as a departure from the "planless individualism" that has nearly destroyed Natives. He sees his Indian New Deal, and specifically the Emergency Conservation Work, as the crucial "planned community living" experiment within President Roosevelt's larger experiment: "The Indians and their lands can become laboratories and pioneers (not the only laboratories and pioneers) in this supreme American adventure."[78] As did American socialists and communists in their magazines, he tried to invest organizing—in place of individualism— with excitement. Of the Wheeler-Howard Indian Rights bill, he effused that it should leave one "breathless" to realize that "the statutory denial of tribal existence has been repealed, and that the denial of Indians of the right to organize, and to use that modern tool of power, the corporation, has been repealed." Now Natives can form "tribal corporations."[79] The magazine's articles retool self-help rhetoric as *collective self-help*, a self-help stimulated by the New Deal.[80]

As I contemplated the many articles and especially the before-and-after photographs that recount the agronomic battles against soil erosion (in place of Pratt's before-and-after being individualized photographs), it became clearer that Collier must have seen the erosion of reservation land as a metaphor for the erosive effects that individualizing (of land and humans) wreaked on Native communities and selves.[81] His Indian New Deal aimed to reclaim and conserve Native soil and cultures—*cultural agronomy*. Native workers established 4,745,000 acres of roadless areas on reservations. The photographs not only show Native communities laboring mostly outdoors to increase the value of their own land, as opposed to workshops lined with Carlisle worker-individuals; they exhibit Natives using their "modern"—a mix of tractors, horses, trucks, axes—in their own ways and remaining Natives. Neither the workers nor the schoolchildren photographed are uniformed. Collier consistently used the discourse of "racial consciousness," "racial genius," and "racial pride" to decree and justify Native group responsibility and relative autonomy.[82] His reassuring message was: "the modern" can be a tool for Native solidarity, not a threat. Ideally, New Deal Natives would not be modernized so much as they would Indianize the modern.

Yet this government-sponsored Indianizing had some restrictive contours and aims. Collier, in an *Indians at Work* piece titled "Indian Education Should Be Practical," apparently without irony quoted BIA Commissioner Leupp's comments, discussed in chapter 1, about why Natives, destined to be farmers, wagon-wheel menders, and so on, needed only minimal schooling that would enable them to "read the simple English of the local newspaper" and "write a short letter which is intelligible, though maybe mispelled." Leupp too was a defender of "Indian" "racial" "individuality" and used his evolutionary concept of this essence to assert that most "Indians" had substandard intellectual capabilities. Collier, after reprinting a good deal of Leupp's statement, commented, "His views on Indian education concur in part so interestingly with present policies that they are here reprinted after twenty-nine years."[83] He, like Leupp, had no qualms about constraining "Indians" range of access to "the modern." Collier approached such matters with the same confidence he brought to the soil-erosion disputes with Natives, some of whom came to see aspects of their New Deal "self-governing" as tantamount to No Deal governing. Collier's imagining of a government-sponsored Indianized "modern" was perhaps overly circumscribed by his imagining of "Indian."

Clyde Kluckhohn's and Dorothea Leighton's anthropological study *The Navajo* (1946), published just after Collier left office, presents an account of Natives at work much less upbeat than Collier's.[84] Some Navajos they describe who wound up working off-reservation had been involved in "soil conservation and livestock management" (173). Despite the fact that "Navajos are distinguished among American Indians by the alacrity, if not the ease, with which they have adjusted to the impact of white culture while still retaining many native traits and preserving the framework of their own cultural organization" (171), they tend to encounter difficulties in the market (they distrust fluctuating values) (172) and the workplace. The Navajos are "chiefly . . . unskilled workers" exploited by White employers who prefer to hire Natives not educated in BIA schools because they are less likely to accuse them of exploitation (169). Those dependent on working for Whites periodically risk their employers' retribution and abandon work to return to family and ceremonies so that they can regain the strength "to go back to their jobs. . . . the job to them was a way of earning necessary money, not a way of life" (167). Alienated proletarianization fuels hostility that is channeled into "factional quarrels," "aggression in family fights," or "fits of depression" (169). Those who "assimilate" rarely find satisfaction. "While as youngsters they are rewarded by school teachers and others for behaving like whites, as adults they are punished for having acquired skills that make them competitors of their white contemporaries." Students excited by their studies "are seldom received on terms of social equality, even by those whose standards of living, dress, and manners they have succeeded in copying almost perfectly. They learn that they must always (save within the Indian Service) expect to work for a salary at least one grade lower than that which a white person of comparable training and experience receives" (170).

Surely it would have been difficult to develop a Depression-era government-run educational system that would imaginatively train Native students to negotiate and resist such encompassing contradictions. Mostly to its credit, Collier's administration made Natives into one of the earliest large-scale experiments in what would now be recognized as multicultural, or bicultural, education.[85] It abolished some boarding schools, opened many reservation day schools, hired more Native teachers, deployed anthropologists to train teachers in Native cultures, and experimented with bilingual education and texts (which proved difficult to produce). Will Carson Ryan, a celebrated Swarthmore professor of education, accomplished much during his stint as BIA education director (1930–36). Ryan attempted to dismantle what was known as the Uniform Course of Study administered in all Indian schools and instead tried to take into account tribal individuality and cultural traditions. He stressed not the "three R's" or college preparation—curricula would become more academic in the 1950s—but rather community-oriented vocational training for rural occupations as well as instruction in artwork and craftwork. In the 1930s Chilocco Indian School pioneered a course in "Indian history and lore" but had difficulty finding materials.[86] Willard Thompson Beatty succeeded Ryan as director (1936–52). He advanced the protomulticultural initiative, particularly the production of bilingual textbooks (a short-lived project). Beatty, like Ryan painfully aware of the Depression, emphasized not academic training so much as coursework designed to address the "long range economic purposes of each reservation."[87]

Despite good intentions, the trend was more toward Collier's "paternalistic" style of self-government than truly community-based Native self-determination in education (this development would not gain significant momentum until the 1960s and 1970s).[88] Collier's protomulticulturalism never lost sight of Indian education as worker production. The New Deal BIA found that funds for educational innovation and support were harder to procure with the onset of World War II. The gains made were compromised and sometimes reversed by the conservative congressional backlash against the New Deal by the mid-1940s.[89] Only in the 1970s, Margaret Connell Szasz notes, would the BIA adequately recognize "the heterogeneity of the hundreds of Indian tribes that retain their identity within the predominantly non-Indian society" and establish contract schools shaped by the input of the community and parents.[90]

Collier's romanticism of the spirit blended strangely with his administrative pugnacity and egotism. A few weeks after he was in effect forced to resign in January 1945, Collier, depressed, sketched some self-analyses to try to pull himself together. In one piece he traced his combativeness back to a boyhood episode: a homeopathic doctor had improperly set the bones in his shoulder and arm after he had broken them, so a physician set them properly, but without giving him the relief of anaesthesia. The bones never healed correctly—something he compensated for by getting into fights and climbing great heights. Teased by his siblings for his minor deformity, Collier became the consummate oppositional individual, in the sense that he rejected their values and created his own. This led, in Collier's opinion, to his truculence (which he terms "indifference") in public life. For all his euphoric meditations on the Pueblos' "ancient" stability and therapeutic tranquility of spirit, he could write, in the personal and international distress of 1945, in words that might at first bring Pratt to mind more than himself, that this background had caused him to live with the "sentiment of the universe as a field of war."[91] He made diverse enemies in this war, while battling to change Indian policy in fundamental ways.

Pratt's approach to "Indians," as chapter 1 showed, was what might be described as a producer-culture ideology of *imposition*. "Indians" would be better off, in reformers' minds, by assimilating Carlisle's impositions: civilization, Americanization, individualism. Collier enunciated a more subtle, perhaps sometimes more insidious, therapeutic-culture ideology that claimed not to impose identities but to *discover* them. The diversity manager of the Indian New Deal convinced himself that he was simply *recognizing* "Indians" for who they were and acting on that recognition. Both Pratt and Collier felt as did a Euramerican eastern schoolteacher of Osages satirized by John Joseph Mathews (Osage) in his novel *Sundown* (1934): she taught "from the position of one who had been among the Indians and therefore knew them."[92] Collier, who could be as implacable as Pratt, did not want to entertain the possibility that his "discovery" was yet another Euramerican imposition of ideology on heterogeneous Natives. The history of the Indian New Deal suggests, however, that many different kinds of Natives considered what was built into Collier's ideological "recognition" and proposed "reorganization" of them and were not interested in all that he planned.

In 1943 Collier, in a self-congratulatory mood, reflected on why the Native death rate diminished under his administration: "Matching race against race, the Indian population is now growing some 50 per cent faster than the white." He acknowledged that improved medical service played a role. But the primary cause, he posited, was his program of self-government, a policy that produces what Pratt was attempting all along with his individualizing schemes: "In the past twelve years, the Indians individually and collectively have become tireless, joyous and competent workers." This has occurred, he added, in spite of the fact that "Indians" do not view work or economic advancement as a virtue or honor. Hard-working "Indians," he suggests, are healthy "Indians." Collier's therapeutic protomulticulturalizing, then, like Pratt's capitalist individualizing, was invented in part to workerize "Indians." Looking beyond World War II, he saw his innovative diversity reorganization of "Indians" as only a dry run for the diversity reorganization of the world:

"Our Indians today are furnishing a laboratory and a demonstration ground in behalf of the world's reorganization ahead."[93]

Detours from the Therapeutic:
La Farge's and McNickle's Fictions

Two novelists, Oliver La Farge (1901–63) and D'Arcy McNickle (Cree and Métis, enrolled as Salish) (1904–77), tried to write fiction that did not reinforce the White therapeutic ethos that was ideologically blanketing "Indians." After graduating from Harvard, La Farge became an expert anthropologist, archaeologist, and linguistic analyst of Southwestern and Central American Natives (especially the Navajos and Apaches), a Native rights activist (who often lived in Santa Fe), an advisor to Collier's Indian New Deal (as president of the American Association on Indian Affairs), and a novelist. His *Laughing Boy* (1929), the story of the union of two Navajos—Slim Girl, an Indian boarding school graduate, and Laughing Boy, a silversmith who sells his art to tourists—offers a critique of both Carlisle-style individualizing and the emerging consumer Indianism of the Southwest.[94]

Like so many boarding school students, Slim Girl has been educated to view her Native culture as "foreign." She is able to "sympathize with [the Navajo] spirit, but not enter into it" (107). As Eric Mottram phrases it, Slim Girl's "training" forces her to become something of a "tourist" in her own tribe.[95] La Farge narrates her emerging from her bicultural "struggle not American, not Indian, [but] mistress of herself" (46). Yet Euramerican culture has formed her obsession with empowerment and self-sufficiency. Slim Girl prostitutes herself not only to feed her seemingly insatiable possessive individualism—an appetite produced by the insecurity, not the ambition, inculcated in her by the boarding school— but also to retreat with Laughing Boy "back to the blanket." She yearns to escape with ample money to "the unmapped cañons, and the Indians who spoke no English," where, interestingly, money will have little value (47). Her Navajo allegiance is as unbending as her Euramerican acquisitiveness: "I am not a Navajo, nor am I American, but the Navajos are my people" (47). She pledges Laughing Boy "that our children [will] never go to school" (172).

Laughing Boy takes up "her ideas of amassing a fortune" (88), though on his own artistic terms. The unconventional "barbaric quality" of his silverwork catches "the tourist's eye" (79). Slim Girl strengthens "her husband in his natural reluctance to stamp shapeless strings of swastikas, thunder-birds, and other curiosities on his silver" (136), while he

Indians Inc.   211

introduces her to the potency of the land. For Laughing Boy, the land's
spiritual quality is enhanced by his craving for independence from Euramerican pressures. La Farge imagined Laughing Boy's spiritual connection to the land as culturally different from the White therapeutic
ethos that Indianizes depthscapes for tourists' ocular and photographic
consumption. Testifying to the land's empowerment of Navajo autonomy, Laughing Boy advises his wife: "Wait and look, by and by you grow
until you can take all this inside of you. Then nothing can make you
angry or disturb you" (101).

By chance, Laughing Boy discovers Slim Girl's prostitution, which to
her enacts her "revenge" on Whites. "It was just work" (169), she tells
him later. In his fury he kills the White rancher who hired his wife and
wounds her. La Farge gives Laughing Boy's swift retribution a symbolic
quality—his face "was hardly the face of an individual, rather, of a race"
(159). Just as they make their difficult peace with one another and ride
toward their "unmapped cañon," Slim Girl is shot by a jealous Navajo
named Red Man (curiously, this was the title of Carlisle's magazine).
Dying in her husband's arms, she feels some measure of ethnoredemp-
tion: "The Americans spoiled me for a Navajo life, but I shall die a
Navajo now" (177). Laughing Boy deposits their wealth on her grave and
reimmerses himself in Navajo culture.

La Farge's focus is on the Navajos, not on any Euramericans. Notwithstanding its occasional idealizing of ecological "Indian" spirituality, in
many respects the novel is antitherapeutic and critical of capitalist relations. It exposes some of the contradictions and painful dependencies
that many Natives who had been "educated" by Euramerican markets or
schools experienced even as they posed "authentically" for tourists'
cameras. La Farge remaps the Romantic Subjective Southwest con-
sumed by tourists as an often desolate site of systemic economic, cultural, and educational violence from which even the prospect of geographical evasion—Huck Finn's lighting out for the territory—provides
no real escape.

Laughing Boy won the Pulitzer Prize in 1930. Influential reviewers
romanticized it as both therapeutic and the genuine article. Mary Austin, for example, who was on the Pulitzer Prize committee, wrote a
review in which she celebrated the novel's impersonation of Indianness
("white thinking is a merely incidental intrusion"), its "primitive capacity for renewal," and its "authentic" status as a "story of primitive love."
Elizabeth Shepley Sergeant, another prominent member of the Santa Fe
and Taos art scene, likened it to "Cushing's Zuni reports" and praised its

"haunting strain of the Navajo night chant": "It will bring to many readers the kind of release that they have felt in the desert and lost in the railroad." Reviews often profiled La Farge as the Harvard blueblood who not only learned the Navajo culture and language but had the chameleon capacity to look Navajo. Advertisements staged La Farge as a Harvard tour guide. McNickle writes: "In one publicity picture [La Farge] is seated on a Navajo rug surrounded by a wealth of Indian crafts and dressed for a pack trip in Stetson hat, flannel shirt, riding breeches and boots." He quips: "And the face is still amiable."

In place of or in competition with the Fred Harvey Indian Detour that featured artisanal and dancing "Indians" off the beaten track (or railroad track), La Farge was lionized for offering readers a grittier, more "authentic," behind-the-scenes Harvard Indian Detour (his first archaeological trip to the Southwest was as a sophomore). La Farge, at least for some reviewers and readers, was like a Laughing Boy author whose literary silverwork destined for White middle- and upper-class homes had a "barbaric quality" unornamented with the stereotypically pretty tourist thunderbirds and swastikas.[96] Yet for his publisher's publicity department, some of his reviewers, and probably for many of his Euramerican readers, La Farge's more "authentic" Harvard Detour was taken as offering the same therapeutic effect as images of the Southwest from which Laughing Boy was supposed to have deviated in its pathbreaking "Indian" realism.

In Raw Material (1945) La Farge turned his critical eye on the novel that brought him fame and fortune in his late twenties.[97] He acknowledged that he wrote Laughing Boy under the romantic sway of the common "vanishing Indian" belief that Navajo lifeways are "inexorably doomed" to fall before the encroachment of "so-called civilization." From the vantage point of someone who got involved in legislative and administrative reform on behalf of Natives during the fifteen years after he won the Pulitzer, he lamented, "[Laughing Boy] might prove good publicity for the Navajos, but it could lead to no reforms" (177). As his activism developed, La Farge became more intrigued with making a different kind of subject matter literary—Natives "adjusting to a changing world which involves Hitler, soil erosion, and the conquest of ignorance and poverty." He regarded this approach as "a sort of antithesis of Laughing Boy" (189). As one character in La Farge's The Enemy Gods (1937) put it, "We have to learn to use the white man's knowledge, his weapons, his machines—and still be Indians."[98] Laughing Boy's love story, he regretted, participated overmuch in the exoticizing of "Indians." La Farge gradually turned down literary opportunities that would have channeled him into writing fiction for readers, editors, publishers, and reviewers who "like their Indians long-haired, beautiful, and 'unspoiled'" (189).

He broached these self-criticisms because he feared that his own love of "Indians" had been too therapeutically "escapist." *Raw Material* was partly La Farge's record of his critical "evolution" away from the "Western 'yearners'" intent on "avoiding reality" (153). He admitted: "The Navajos became for me a surer refuge from my troubles than any dream world could ever become" (157). For Whites use "Indians" to security-blanket themselves with amnesia: "To his lovers the Indian is in no small part a mechanism for forgetting the things which make them walk in fear" (155). He evinced skepticism even of the White yearners' reformism: "Because of the personal angle of approach, the fundamental quest for a satisfaction within themselves, there is always likely to be a distortion in their view, and when the text comes one can never be sure just who will think purely in terms of what will help the Indian" (155). Such reformers, he argued, suffer from a "messiah complex" often manifested as "monopolism," the conviction that they "know" "Indians" better than anyone and that they are destined to be their "saviour[s]."

In his critique of "saviours," La Farge dropped a tantalizing autobiographical hint: "Thank God, few white people ever get strong enough to be able to implement this craze, but it has happened, and to at least one fine tribe of my acquaintance it has done irreparable harm" (157). La Farge blasts the "Lady Bountiful[s]" who make "Indians" their pet projects, thus bringing to mind Luhan and Austin, among others. But he suggests that this role has also been played by "white men" (156). He strives to articulate what is wrong with this reformism even when in some material ways it has benefited the "Indians": the messiahs' "sense of superior wisdom" and "perhaps even racial superiority, does not conflict with their worshipful reverence for Indian wisdom and the beauties of Indian culture. In fact, it makes that reverence safe, freeing it from any dangerous tendency to put them in an inferior position" (156). This therapeutic impulse, even if it facilitates reform, can be self-servingly individualistic: "I have come to think that one of the prime tests of your real friend of the Indians as against those who are merely using Indians as a sort of ointment for the soul, is his willingness to admit superior information and to be corrected" (157). La Farge notes, furthermore, that some of these reverential-yet-condescending "Bountifuls" are wealthy and try to bribe "Indians" to like them.

La Farge's choice of the word *saviour* to describe these "messiahs" is the word Lawrence chose to characterize—demonize—Collier. Interestingly, La Farge lavished praise on the nomadic Navajos and Apaches for their commitment to freedom of choice and criticized the Pueblos for being village- and possession-bound. The Pueblos, of course, were the group most beloved and romanticized as "ointment for the soul" by Collier, Luhan, Austin, and others in the White Taos and Santa Fe community. Linking the production of "anxiety" to social structures that assign value to "the retention of possessions" (160), La Farge de-idealized the Pueblos (as did Marianna Burgess's *Stiya*): "The effort of life was for certainty. To achieve certainty one needed subordination. . . . Even today there are Pueblos in which it is possible for a man or woman to be tortured, not merely punished but tortured and possibly killed, for stepping out of line" (161).

It is tempting to read Collier into some of La Farge's criticisms of "saviours," and perhaps he is there in part. But La Farge repeatedly conveyed his tremendous respect for Collier, whom he disliked on first meeting him in the early 1920s and distrusted initially upon his appointment as BIA commissioner. Even before this appointment La Farge was impressed by Collier's knowledge of Native realities, bureaucratic affairs, and legalized entanglements. During La Farge's initial exchange with Collier, in Collier's capacity as commissioner, they agreed to disagree if necessary—coming from rival Native reform organizations—but quickly forged an alliance that La Farge considered a turning point in his ideological "evolution": "I count this meeting, too, as marking the end of Indians as an escape for me." It was not that earlier he had failed to recognize Native problems, it was that his perception of these problems and their implications was distorted by the therapeutic needs he imported to "Indians" (184).

He rated Collier as "beyond all comparison the best Commissioner we have ever had" (177). When La Farge edited *The Changing Indian* (1942), Collier wrote the introduction. Their essays complement and sometimes even read like one another (for instance, La Farge's applause for the Navajo stock reduction–soil conservation project). Demonstrating a pragmatic rather than a therapeutic approach to Native issues, La Farge lauded Collier's administration for its linkage of science and government, its initiatives to increase the employment of Natives in higher echelons of the BIA, and its efforts to help make Natives economically self-supporting, if not self-determining.[99]

For La Farge, Indianism had come to mean something like what it meant for Collier. La Farge referred to his political transformation with genteel restraint: "Since I left Harvard I have steadily become less conservative, reversing the usual process. I don't believe in Socialism, I have no use at all for Communism, but if, using the word within the American scheme of things, you want to call me radical and say it pleasantly I'll hesitate to deny it. This the Indians have done to me" (184). He invoked "simple Americanism" (189) as what motivated him to lend a hand in battles on behalf of Natives, and, by implication, redefined the Gilded Age Carlisle-style "Americanization" of the "Indian" as distinctly un-American.

McNickle's *Indian Man* (1971), his biography of La Farge, generously represented the achievement of *Laughing Boy* as one of cultural translation for Whites: "to project [Navajos] in their proper human form unencumbered by their habits of behavior and custom which made them picturesque but savage in the eyes of outsiders. . . . The blending was done so skillfully that the socialite sitting in her townhouse and the urban literary critic could read the narrative and have a sense of participation." He offered an example: when Laughing Boy and Slim Girl reconcile after he wounds her, the narrator comments, "He was very happy, it was like a second honeymoon." McNickle commends the translation: "La Farge has completed the illusion. The White reader had lived a Navajo's life without straying too far from his own experiences—no matter that the honeymoon is not a Navajo social custom." He gently addressed La Farge's blueblood discomfort with the incipient radicalism of *Laughing Boy*: "The protestation in his original Introductory Note, that the story was meant 'neither to instruct nor to prove a point, but to amuse,' is a bit of rhetoric carried over from Professor Copeland's classes at Harvard." The novel itself, he submits, differs from the author's reading of it: "The pages of *Laughing Boy* are . . . a sustained indictment of the society that produced the writer and would, unless tempered, destroy the Navajo world. He called himself an escapist later, perhaps because he could not think of himself as a propagandist or a reformer, but if escape was his purpose, he shot over his shoulder with telling effect as he ran."[100]

McNickle, three years younger than La Farge, was born on the Flathead (Salish) reservation in Montana. He sold his allotment to finance his education at the University of Montana, then Oxford, and later at the University of Grenoble. McNickle, like La Farge, was trained in anthropology and won distinction as a novelist. He worked as a freelance writer in New York City, an administrator and intellectual advisor to Collier in the Indian New Deal, the founding chair of the anthropology department at the University of Saskatchewan, and the founding director of the Newberry Library Center for the History of the American Indian (subsequently renamed the D'Arcy McNickle Center).[101] He also helped establish the National Congress of American Indians in 1944.[102]

As McNickle's correspondence with Collier, then his BIA boss, makes clear, he was a sophisticated and wide-ranging social theorist.[103] In *Indian Man* he expressed profound dismay that much support for the "Indian" cause dried up when many wealthy backers came to dread the New Deal. Collier fell prey to this predatory rightward turn: "And thereafter, wolves were in the land."[104] McNickle lamented in *Wind from an Enemy Sky* (1978), "A man by himself was nothing but a shout in the wind."[105] He was attentive to the ways in which social forces, sometimes through the process of individualizing, had contributed to making such isolation a general condition for Natives.[106]

McNickle's *The Surrounded* (1936) existed in different form as a complete novel as early as 1929. Despite some favorable readers' reports, it was rejected by more than a dozen publishers before it reached print. One evaluator who failed to convince the publisher to take a chance with it suggested, "I think we could work up a good ballyhoo for this novel, lining up such people as Oliver La Farge, Ruth Benedict, Blair Niles, John Collier, Robert Gessner, and others behind it." McNickle's substantial revisions included making his Salish-Spanish protagonist even more "surrounded" by Whites, like the rest of the Salish. Whether it was this alteration that made the novel seem more marketable to its eventual publisher is uncertain. In any case, it sold poorly.[107] La Farge's review praised the novel as a compelling fiction that educates the reader in the dynamics and struggles of Native life.[108]

The Surrounded narrates the story of Archilde Leon, his Salish mother Catherine, his Spanish father Max, and other members of the community on the Salish reservation in the Northwest. Archilde, like Alessandro in *Ramona*, is a violinist. He returns to the reservation as a young man and negotiates, among other things, the difficulties involved in his efforts to reestablish his connection with his Salish tribe. At his mother's feast he must perform Salish. "The deeper feeling was impatience, irritation, an uneasy feeling in the stomach. . . . He tried to play the part. But when he had devoured about a pound of roasted meat he began to feel sick" (62–63).

The novel's critical emphasis is its contestation of representations of Natives extant both in the Carlisle-era ideologies and in the newer therapeutic-period ideologies. Hence in reflecting on why he chose to settle with Natives, Archilde's Spanish father Max is aware that he "never thought the Indians were 'noble' or children of a lost paradise." Rather, they were "individuals [who] varied exceedingly. . . . There was no single trait he knew of to describe all Indians." They have different skin colors as well as characters. "The only thing he had never seen was a red Indian. There were shades of brown, some almost black ones, and a good many were as olive skinned as a Spaniard" (42–43). Salish solidarity is based on culture rather than pigmentation. Tribal dancing, as experienced anew by Archilde, made it seem "for a moment, as if they were unconquerable, and as if they might move the world were they to set their strength to it. They made one think of a wild stallion running free—no one could approach him, no one would ever break his spirit" (218). Mike, a Salish boy who has been cruelly punished by his White teacher, rebuilds his confidence when dancing with the elders. The major White objection to such dancing, which echoes the familiar BIA line, is not so much that it feeds tribal resistance—they are surrounded—but that it takes too much time from work (204).

An important leitmotif is the resilience of Salish agency and lifeways notwithstanding Euramerican efforts to manage them. Catherine, Archilde's Salish mother, recalls: "They would live on their allotment until they got restless; then they would take their tepee poles and travel to some relative's place or to some likely vacant site; later they would try still another place." She sees ostensible White independence as dependence: "With a white man you could not do that [move easily], she learned. Also, a white man went by the clock. . . . It made a man march around. A woman marched too" (172). Her school training in domesticity—dirt detection and the use of appliances—was something she was curious to learn but happier to ignore in her own homelife. "The cask butter churn dried up and fell apart, the washtub had long ago been battered into junk iron by her children, and what clothes she washed were just soaked in the creek and any dirt that could be shaken loose was carried off by the force of the stream" (171–72). Historically, the Salish were most interested in learning what gave the Whites power: they bought their guns (they had to, even to protect themselves from warring tribes armed by the Whites, 71) and were intrigued by their crucifixes ("We thought they would bring back the power we had lost—but today we have less," 74). Such antiromantic images of Natives ran contrary to Carlisle's representations of Whitened students, to the Santa Fe Railway's images of scenic artisanal natives, and to Lawrence's, Luhan's, Austin's, or even Collier's sketches of therapeutic rhythm-loving primitives.

McNickle's novel, like La Farge's, narrates the anger and resentment many Natives felt in response to Euramerican efforts to make them dependent. Catherine lives in sight of but apart from her husband Max in her log cabin as a daily repudiation of the power he would like to assert over her. Eventually her rage explodes. She kills a game warden immediately after he kills her other son Louis in the mountains for "illegal" hunting (in the presence of Archilde). Sheriff Quigley then enters the picture. Quigley is a walking stereotype of Old West rugged individualism: "He had read of those hard-riding, quick-shooting dispensers of peace, he had heard stories about them—and he was intent on being all of them in himself" (117). Suspecting Archilde's involvement in the game warden's demise, Quigley catches up with Archilde and his new romantic partner Elise, a cross-blood. He intends to arrest Archilde. Elise, like Catherine, is fed up with White men hunting Salish men under the cover of the law and retaliates. She uses the stereotypes of the passive "Indian" and woman to get near enough to Quigley to throw boiling coffee in his face and shoot him three times. "I said to myself that if Dave Quigley came for you I wouldn't let him take you. I did and I don't give a damn" (295). Archilde, who has still killed no one, reproves her, but then "kissed her and saw her smile" (295). Their evanescent kiss is interrupted by Parker, a Euramerican Indian agent, who is backed up by his Salish deputy. "It's too damn bad," Parker chides Archilde, "you people never learn that you can't run away. It's pathetic—" The final line of the novel follows: "Archilde, saying nothing, extended his hands to be shackled" (296–97). So the novel closes with a cocky Euramerican enunciation of the discourse of inevitability. The violinist is "surrounded."

Yet are he and the Salish defeated? In his reading of the novel, Louis Owens takes issue with critics who strain themselves to construe this as a wistfully happy ending or one that is buoyant about Native resistance. Owens cites several instances in the novel that form a disheartening pattern—things just seem to go wrong for the Salish. It is true that the two young boys, Mike (who had suffered the school punishment) and Narcisse, flee from the scene of Archilde's arrest undetected on their horses. But where will they go and for how long? Not much in the novel leads one to believe that they will be any less "surrounded" by institutions, stereotypes, and racism than Archilde. Owens concludes insightfully: "When Archilde extends his hands to be cuffed, the shackles are those of this national myth [of the subcivilized Indian]; he is imprisoned by America's image of the Indian. . . . McNickle does not appear to see a promising escape from this damning image."

I would add that Archilde is shackled by more than images, discourses, and stereotypes; he is handcuffed by the legalized colonial machinery of coercion that hunts him down in mountains the Salish regard as sacred. In fact it may be that Archilde is hunted because he has succeeded all too well in complicating White myths of what "Indians" are capable of doing and being, something perhaps close to McNickle's own experience out West and elsewhere. As Owens notes, McNickle's early versions of the novel have an ostensibly "happy" ending in which Archilde studies music in Paris, marries a beautiful White New Yorker, returns to the reservation and gets arrested, wins his defense in court, and lords over his new estate on the reservation much as his father did. Perhaps McNickle was afraid that this would be misread as a "happy" ending.

The Salish may not be defeated, but they surely—like many Native characters in later works by Native authors—are surrounded.[109] McNickle's denouement is not romantic, cute, therapeutic, sentimentally tragic, or multiculturally hopeful. It has none of the condescending charm of the Harvey Detour that would enchant tourist-readers. Seemingly, the novel would have the Salish submit neither to Euramerican pressures to be sub-White nor to inducements to be picturesquely cooperative as "Indians." It does not oversimplify the conflicts among and within cross-bloods, full-bloods and Whites. *The Surrounded*, more so than *Laughing Boy*, with its allure of "unmapped cañons," dispels the idea that Natives can any longer achieve simple geographical escape. Clearly, McNickle did not want the revised published version of his novel to seem as optimistic about Native-White relations as his BIA reform work with Collier, which conceptualized protomulticultural ways to bring Natives into capitalist versions of "the modern" while maintaining their cultural identities.[110]

In the 1950s McNickle experimented with ways of how best to encourage Natives (Navajos) to practice self-determination and "directed assimilation"—they would adopt only those aspects of "the modern" that would help them preserve essential aspects of their cultural lifeways. By the 1960s he became more politically interventionist and offered young Natives leadership seminars that included education in Native culture and heritage. Still, his final novel, *Wind from an Enemy Sky*, published posthumously in 1978, ends in a way that echoes *The Surrounded*, with the Native protagonist surrounded more by enemies than by hope.

Taos, Collier, and the Multicultural Containment of Critique

The European and later the American ideological tendency to represent "Indians" not simply as threats to "civilization" but as absorbing, albeit impractical, solutions to "overcivilization" has had a long and varied tradition that Taos artist colonizers modernized, psychologized, and anthropologized. Montaigne, Bishop Fénelon, the philosophes, European and American romantic authors, artists, and sculptors, among others, participated in producing a Noble Savagism that some of the most influential White Taos residents helped reencode as an Instinctual Indianism invested with the potential to unrepress Whites. One of the reasons this "modern" revision proved so ideologically fascinating, I have suggested, is that the sort of psychocultural critique that Whites used their reinvention of "Indians" to advance never really threatened to transform the U.S. socioeconomic and political system (after all, the Natives' own nineteenth-century martial resistance had proved futile). Bohemian professional-managerial-class artists could feel good about being critical of "the system" as "nonconformists"—in White Indianized ways that "the system" could tolerate and even support and commodify as (hegemonic) proof of its commitment to the freedom of individual and artistic expression.

The pragmatic control of "individuality" that Carlisle stood for and exhibited in its Indian education contributed to middle-class economic and ideological self-affirmation within the nineteenth-century producer-sentimental culture. Somewhat differently, the exotic release of "individuality" that Taos stood for and exhibited in "Indian" dances and artistic representations contributed to professional-managerial-class economic and ideological self-affirmation within the twentieth-century consumer-therapeutic culture. Without disregarding their considerable differences, to an extent Carlisle "Indian" reformism and Taos "Indian" reformism may be seen as two sides of the same ideological coin.

From the standpoint of cultural theory, Taos can be read as a hegemonic experiment in problem production, critique production, and fascination production. The problem that Taos literati sometimes used "Indians" to create as fascinating was indeed the problem of imperialist capitalism. But this problem, like the critique of it, was often psychologized and individualized as that of repression and inhibition. Taos literati whose self-imagining swerved in this ideological direction sometimes engaged in what Nathan Huggins derisively termed "soft rebellions"—limited, self-serving, feel-good rebellions that sponsored a "soft agency."[111]

Notwithstanding the communal or tribal aspects of Indianism that alienated bohemian and other professional-managerial-class Whites found therapeutic, the appeal of playing "Indian" for some may have been a protomulticultural form of playing "individual." Collier rebuked White Taos in "The Red Atlantis" (1922): "No, the colony is not a utopia, nor does it hint of the cooperative commonwealth. A rather severe individualism prevails; its result is to leave each several artist at the center of a wistful and socially undernourished solitude. . . . Their separateness from each other and from the Indians as human and social beings is distressing." He did, however, shower praise on a different body of artists who lived there. "The Taos art which is steadfastly great is the Indian art. The Indian artists are intensely social, they are, indeed, the community itself consciously living in beauty. The white colony fails altogether to learn this Indian secret of the Bluebird." Taos Euramerican individualism had economic implications: "At Taos one becomes a center of hostile criticism if he pays to an Indian a white man's wage for work equal to a white man's." A year later Collier lamented that the annual income per "Indian" in Taos was a mere $38, in the San Ildefonso and Tesuque pueblos less than $20.[112]

I have argued that the rise of Carlisle and of Taos was coextensive with the ascendancy of two significant modern productions of knowledge: personalizing "psychological" discourses that promoted the idea that definable "psychological" patterns were the primary cause of "the self" and the most riveting problem that should preoccupy "the self"; and diverse anthropological discourses, some of which studied the powers of cultures to shape humanity in profoundly different ways. Taos colonizers were influenced by both developments. At Taos the Euramerican acknowledgment of and respect for "Indian" cultural difference was in many respects a significant step toward cultural pluralism and relativism. However, the therapeutic redefinition of "Indians" as an ethnoracial resource for lost White "individual" essence suggests that these early protomulticultural gestures were still partly subordinated to the larger White goal of self-affirmation and class-affirmation, often class-affirmation disguised as or (mis)understood as simply self-affirmation.

Moreover, as authors, artists, the Santa Fe Railway corporation, and tourist businesses realized, the White Indianized critique of America could help sell novels, art, photography, advertising, tourism, and real estate. Taos and its "Indians" could be commodified profitably by corporate and bohemian protomulticulturalists as the "natural" American alternative to the mass-cultural, standardized, machine-made, often urban America that alienates Americans.[113] "Indians" were incorporated to make Taos into a center of the American *find "yourself"* industry. By 1956 Paul Horgan could write of Taos and Santa Fe: "What [visitors] find here now they can find . . . in almost any state. . . . Business, business, a lot of activity ending up in nothing."[114]

Collier was in some ways an exception to this professional-managerial-class Indianism, whose repression-model critique and multiethnic interests were often too ideologically contained and self-directed. "Collier was not the first non-Indian to appreciate Indian tradition," Deloria and Lytle acknowledge. But "he certainly was the first to understand, appreciate, articulate, and fight zealously for it." The 1928 Meriam Report, they add, "did not actually advocate, as he did, the 'restoration of Indian societies and culture'; it only sought a removal of restrictions on their activities." In his campaigning for the Indian Reorganization Act and in his publications, Collier usually went to conspicuous pains to emphasize Native diversity and tribal singularity by discussing specific tribal groups, not just "Indians" as a whole (even when his book titles still homogenized his subjects of study as "Indians").[115] When Congress reduced the funding of the Indian Reorganization bill, Collier resourcefully tapped other New Deal organizations, including the Soil Conservation Service, the Civilian Conservation Corps, the Works Progress Administration, and the Farm Security Administration to implement new BIA programs. Before Collier, Natives "had little in the way of formal organizations to express their wishes" to the government. His corporate charters "finally put an Indian tribe in the position where it could compete economically with its neighbors." The Indian BIA's efforts to hire Natives moved toward "self-management, if not self-government."[116]

In truth, Collier went beyond the limitations of the final version of the Indian Reorganization bill, Deloria and Lytle conclude, simply by "do[ing] as he wished." As congressional attention became centered on European crises, Collier cleverly and unconstitutionally invoked the principle of tribes' "inherent powers." Indeed, Senator Burton Wheeler tried to repeal the Wheeler-Howard Indian Reorganization bill just three years after he introduced it because he felt it violated "rugged individualism." Overall, Collier worked tirelessly—in opposition to proassimilation members of Congress who eventually held sway—to formulate and push through legal and bureaucratic reforms that would bring economic and political relief to Natives whose indigenous "cooperative," or even partly socialistic, socioeconomic ethos and social organizations he esteemed (figure 19).[117]

Yet if Collier was to a certain degree an exception to the bohemian professional-managerial-class Indianism of Taos, he could also be viewed as an apparent exception whose New Deal proved the rule. As I have observed, diverse Natives were critical of him and his rendition of an Indian New Deal, and they preferred to Indianize or to not Indianize themselves in their own nonuniform manner rather than accept his government-powered Indianizing of them. Many Natives recognized in his therapeutic "discovery" of them and "cooperative" "democratic"

19. John Collier in blanket and sneakers, retired at Taos, 1963, photographed by
C. J. S. Durham, John Collier Papers, Manuscripts and Archives, Yale University
Library

visions for them someone who represented still another colonial phase of their ongoing Euramerican top-down management problem.[118] If Collier can be regarded as a major contributor to the intellectual founding of U.S. ethnic studies (along with, for example, Carey McWilliams and Louis Adamic) and hemispheric studies, from another perspective he might also be seen more worrisomely as an early creator of aspects of what would later be known as diversity management studies.[119]

Diversity management is a term that refers to personnel practices that corporations developed in the 1980s and 1990s, a sign of the emergence of multicultural corporatism. In these decades many corporations endeavored to rework their public image and self-image as spaces that foster ethnoracial and other kinds of diversity and worker-individuality: "where decentralization replaces hierarchy; where diversity replaces homogeneity and legalistic affirmative action; where trust, freedom, and respect for the individual replace fixed work rules and a culture of managerial suspicion; where creativity, knowledge, and fun link human values to economic necessity in an economically and personally therapeutic fashion; and where activism and a commitment to shaping the corporate/social environment replace the postwar emphasis on white-collar obedience and conformity." Avery Gordon points out that diversity management "is opposed to assimilation in its cruder forms." At bottom, however, diversity management is a flexible personnel strategy designed to incorporate increasingly multiracial laborers and managers—a form of "liberal assimilationism." It workerizes—assimilates workers, sparks their incentive—ostensibly by allowing workers to "express" themselves. Yet the multicultural bottle contains the same old managerial wine: "Diversity management is, to state the obvious, capitalist management; it is not democratic self-governance and it does not even offer group-based autonomy."[120] Some of Collier's radical politics and programs that attempted to grant Natives more economic, political, and cultural independence substantively distinguish him from many corporate diversity-management practices and goals. At the same time, like some postmodern diversity managers, Collier saw the managerial efficacy of using the recognition of diversity to better form "modern" workers.

In closing I will argue that it is Taos, even more than Carlisle, that tells us about how "individuality" can be made to flow as a "psychological"—and multicultural—lubricant of modern American corporate-consumer-therapeutic capitalism. Undeniably, Carlisle taught "Indians" producer-culture values, feelings, fears, and ambitions that are perdurable even in the American production of possessive individualities today. Yet Carlisle used well-worn conventions of White Protestant "individuality" to digest and workerize "Indians," and in doing so ran the risk of making its stamp of "individuality" blatant as an ideological and emotional molding of laborers. For this reason, among others, Pratt favored the idea of the outing and letting the hegemonic culture at large—the family, the community, the workplace, the public school—individualize and workerize "Indians." And Pratt, intriguingly, despite the school's Indian extinction rhetoric, did not try fully to expunge Native identities in his individualizing and Americanizing program; even he recognized to some extent that Indianism could be a lubricant in structuring incentive and making worker-individuals. After Pratt's era ended, Carlisle made cultural pluralism a more overt component of its fabrication of incentive and worker-individuals.

But Taos was much more subtle, supple, and indirect in digesting Whites and "Indians" for use within the American marketplace. Its general psychologism and nascent cultural pluralism seemed less like a disciplinary system of digestion and more in tune with the philosophical tenets of an individualism that seemed to say to Whites and "Indians": it pays to *be "yourself."* Taos was equally understated in its workerizing dimensions: the entire community—whose economy, from a capitalist perspective, improved, especially for the corporations, companies, and artist colonizers—seemed to many Euramericans not to be about conventional incentive production or work but about something "deeper," the expression of "lost" "individuality."

The ostensibly "rebellious" thrust of the Taos and Santa Fe art scene was far more capitalist and what would now be termed *multiculturalist* than—what some feared—Bolshevist. When museums, galleries, and bookstores in Taos and Santa Fe were charged with promoting local artists' Bolshevist propaganda in the 1920s, poet and editor Alice Corbin Henderson contended that such artistic material was, in effect, multiculturalist; she defended "the contributions of alien races and cultures in favor of a political amalgamation which may leave only a colorless conformity in its wake."[121] At the conclusion of *Earth Horizon* (1932), Mary Austin again departed from her usual egotism to write that "in the deepest layers of ourselves we are incurably collective. At the core of our Amerindian life we are consummated in the dash and color of collectivity. It is not that we work upon the Cosmos, but it works in us."[122] Many artist-colonizers, like Austin, employed "Indians" colorfully to invest the very idea of collectivity not merely with political meaning but with therapeutic "depth"—"our [cosmic] Amerindian life." As I have argued, the very existence of the colony conspicuously testified to U.S. capitalism's ("democracy's") self-proclaimed tolerance of free "individual" expression. So being digested and workerized within corporate-consumer-therapeutic culture could seem liberating and invigorating to many Euramericans if it appeared to mean simply being "yourself" or recovering "yourself," psychologically and multiculturally.

The cultural efflorescence of Taos suggests that if one tendency of corporate-consumer-therapeutic culture was to assuage mounting insecurities about the erosion of self-making by psychologizing "individuality," desire, and incentive, another emerging trend was the therapeutic protomulticulturalizing of "individuality." Here racial "others" were exoticized as psychologically and aesthetically fascinating, far more so than economically and politically fascinating, in their *primitive noncon- formity.* The celebratory acceptance of a *plurality* of cultural groups, more than committed agitation to bring about the economic and political *equality* of cultural groups, could seem like a sufficiently noble bid to establish a fairer America. Thus the racial and ethnic "raw materials" that Pratt imagined as needing to be "fed" to the "civilizing mill" so that they would come out as well-mannered worker-individuals would in liberal corporate modernity be used increasingly to feed dominant White fascination with exploring "individuality" and "individual" "freedom," which in turn could be used as a powerful ideological and "psychological" lubricant to keep the American liberal corporate machine in fluid motion and seem, at its liberal best, multiculturally meaningful, inclusive, therapeutic, and relatively receptive to nonconformity.

Afterword

Diversity Incorporated and World Americanization

The great individualistic West is a lot of crap; it's an organized set-up.
—C. Wright Mills, letter, 1947

"I thought we broke that thing," Junior said.
"Nothing's broken yet," Thomas said.
—Sherman Alexie, *Reservation Blues*, 1995

security will never find it
they can't hear the clicking
of the gun
inside my head
—Joy Harjo (Creek), "I Am A Dangerous Woman," 1979[1]

If one wanted to make a case for the utility of "individuality" as a descriptive category, the lives of Pratt and Collier would be a rich resource. Both men are fascinating examples of multifaceted, contradictory, not easy to classify, not wholly governable individuals-in-action. One can identify ideological crosscurrents running through them, but the mix is complex—highly "individual." The Pratt who wrestled with government administrators for the welfare of his students, who insisted on retaining corporal punishment at Carlisle, who loved to mingle with wealthy benefactors, and who boasted that he had never owned land, and the Collier who wrote eloquently, movingly, and romantically of the social, subjective, and life-enhancing value of Native cultures even as he battled anyone, including Native allies, who got in his way, were both, to say the least, quirky, self-sacrificing, egotistical. At the same time, their careers illustrate some of the key ways in which the social meanings attached to "individuality" have changed in America and help us better understand how individuality ideologies have played significant, sometimes subtle roles in the establishment and exercise of economic, state, and cultural power.

In closing, I want to keep this historical complexity in mind as I posit ties between some inventions of individuality and of multiculturalism, both of which are vital machineries of subjectivity management and identity management within the American differentiation system. Much cultural and subjective good has come from the production of forms of individuality and of multiculturalism. But, as with my argument about the governmental, corporate, and cultural deployments of "individuality," I want to suggest that it is prudent to be wary about some of the uses to which versions of multiculturalism have been put in the last century.

As my research on this book progressed, the material I studied obliged me to expand my scope: I saw that my historical analysis of productions of forms of individuality had to encompass an analysis of multicultural modernizing. As top-down tactics within transforming power structures and bottom-up resistances became clearer, my subject matter compelled me to ponder not only changing forms and strategies of *individuality management*, but also developing forms and strategies of *diversity management*. (My reservation about using the word *management* is that it can make what was and is a struggle seem overmuch like what this management never was—a done deal, a one-way imposition of power to which groups submitted completely. The word can underplay the countervailing agents and organizations that make management exigent for those in power.)

Early in my research I formed a working hypothesis that at stake in my case studies was evidence of an important hegemonic shift. The movement begins with one cluster of related subjectivity and cultural formations—comprised of industrial-producer-sentimental culture, a popularized Protestant work ethic, melting-pot ideologies of the nation as culturally homogeneous rather than pluralist, mass-cultural constructions of character, self-making, and rugged individualism: *Americanizing often understood as individualizing*. This cluster unevenly but gradually appears to have taken on the outlines of another cluster—made up of corporate-consumer-therapeutic culture, emerging discourses on cultural relativism and pluralism (including some of the modernisms), Taos bohemian therapeutic Indianizing, Southwestern tourism organizations, Native arts and crafts institutions and networks, the Indian New Deal and the expansion of the corporate-liberal welfare state, therapeutic and consumer-culture concepts of psychological individuality and the worker who works to "express" himself or herself through consumption: *Americanizing conceptualized at times as multicultural modernizing.*[2] I never perceived these phases or clusters as wholly distinct. The Carlisle, assimilationist, melting-pot phase seemed to be dominant in the late nineteenth and very early twentieth century and to become somewhat residual by the Depression; but versions of this phase resurfaced with a post-Prattian vengeance in the postwar termination of tribes era. And one can see emerging signs of the ascendant 1920s Taos and 1930s New Deal phases in the publicity Frank Hamilton Cushing's work received in the Gilded Age, the booming Southwestern and Western tourism industry in the early 1900s, and the expanding welfare-state bureaucracy (particularly in Indian administration).

Yet as my research proceeded I came to recognize that this working hypothesis—Carlisle producer culture to Taos and New Deal therapeutic-consumer multiculture—is a little too pat to account for a hegemonic movement so dynamic, complex, and I am tempted to say *tactically contradictory.* It is noteworthy that both Carlisle and the Bureau of American Ethnology—which took rival stances toward Native cultures, though often informed by similar premises about evolutionary progress—were founded in 1879. One must not forget that both Pratt and Collier, even at the height of their influence, were regularly under fire— attacked by Natives, non-Natives, and bureaucrats for a variety of reasons. Bearing the relative constancy and acrimony of such struggles in mind, an alternative way to read this Carlisle to Taos and New Deal movement, the way I lean toward, is not oversimply as uneven progression from one loosely bounded hegemonic formation to another, but as a multiplicitous push-pull movement within one overarching yet ever-developing hegemonic formation that has featured this tension—typified best, perhaps, by the assimilation versus multicultural diversity binary opposition—as a means, albeit sometimes a risky means, of reproducing itself. Put crudely, as I read it, this capacious hegemony has developed in part through its tension management, which strives to circumscribe a basic push-pull movement of reform. If the hegemonic movement in recent times—the "culture wars"—is somewhat more in favor of the corporate, educational, and national multicultural—as I think it is, and in so many qualified ways am glad it is—it may be that this is partly because some forms of the multicultural are better able to serve some of the hegemony's developing reproductive needs that were served more overtly, even brazenly, in the assimilation and producer-culture phase.[3] (This summarizes the top-down dimension of my reading of this hegemonic dynamic; more on the bottom-up dimensions below.)

What remains consistent in the versions of hegemonic push-pull struggles—assimilation versus diversity—that have taken place over the past century is the ever-inventive reproduction of workers and classes. Pratt and Collier were both major contributors to what might be nominated *incentive studies*. In their own ways they tried to shape identities that would give workers—Native workers—the incentive to throw their energies into the "modern" (U.S. capitalism). What Pratt and Collier had in common was their desire to school most Natives to perform skilled and semi-skilled work. Of course, what they hoped these workers would do with their work sometimes differed immensely and this difference divides the two politically: Pratt's photographs in *Indian Helper* of Native students working show them preparing to work in shops for "number one"; Collier's *Indians at Work* exhibits workers working with and for their tribes on reservations. U.S. capitalism, especially in its corporate-consumer-therapeutic-culture phase, thrives on compensating many Americans, not all Americans, in varying degrees for its dramatically unequal distribution of wealth. Pratt tried to train Natives to accept "individuality" as a compensation and motive for working. Collier attempted to push "diversity," a term he used often, as a compensation and motive for working.

Based on my research, I recommend that Natives and non-Natives enmeshed in the current "culture wars" versions of the diversity versus assimilation tensions not allow their critical gazes to be deflected from the overall worker- and class-reproduction aims of this dynamic and productively contradictory hegemony.[4] The association of multiculturalism with worker and class reproduction—a central reproductive aim of pluralism management—has a history that precedes Collier's governmental uses of multicultural modernizing to persuade Natives to get excited about (some Euramerican constructions of) work. Capitalist forms of multiculturalism did not displace the popularizing of capitalist forms of individuality as contributors to incentive production in this history, rather these forms have often operated in tandem, yet also sometimes in friction, with one another.

In these final reflections I want to enlarge my focus on the history of some of the complex relationships between individualizing and multicultural modernizing strategies. I will move circumspectly toward this critique, however, by first reviewing a few of the reasons why certain forms of multiculturalism have been exigent for Natives to develop in response to the pressures and oppressions of the Carlisle and Dawes Act era. It is crucial to try to distinguish bottom-up uses of multiculturalism from top-down deployments, although the two have often been intertwined in the case of Natives. One of the most discerning spokespersons for bottom-up Native uses of multiculturalism is a former Carlisle student-turned-militant-multiculturalist: Luther Standing Bear.

In the mid-1930s Standing Bear mounted a forceful attack on the devastation that "civilizing" and "individualizing" had wreaked on Natives. Carlisle, he objected, was set up to transform Native youth into "the likeness of the invader." Natives, however, would not be *digested*: "The last drop of Indian blood will disappear in white veins before man can remake his brother man." The Citizenship Act of 1924, he protested, was "just another [government] hoax."[5] Reservations are "government prison[s]" that enforce the "slavery of the American Indian," destroy Native "incentive," deteriorate "spirituality," and diminish the power of traditional healers. He asked: "Has the white man's social order been so harmonious and ideal as to merit the respect of the Indian, and for that matter the thinking class of the white race?" And answered: "Regarding the 'civilization' that has been thrust upon me since the days of reservation, it has not added one whit to my sense of justice; to my reverence for the rights of life; to my love for truth, honesty, and generosity." Standing Bear invoked rights discourse in building his indictment: "[Whites] violated all of our rights as natives in our own land and as humans, and even the rights of creatures that we had so long protected." Casting Euramericans as "half civilized," he inverted hegemonic common sense: "Not until the hairy man from the east came and with brutal frenzy heaped injustices upon us and the families we loved was it 'wild' for us. When the very animals of the forest began fleeing from his approach, then it was that for us the 'Wild West' began." He concluded: "As long as [we] are in bondage I shall never cease to be a hostile—a savage."[6]

Collier voiced many of these ideas in the same period, though he was not such a "hostile." Standing Bear not only advocated institutionalizing multicultural education but, more so than Collier, envisioned the tactical utility of forming a Native university-trained professional-managerial class.[7] On his return from Carlisle, Standing Bear's brother asked the BIA commissioner for funds to attend a college in Chicago and was denied. The commissioner wrote that "if one boy be given such advantages, all Indian boys would want the same advantages" and that "tribal funds would not accommodate all the Indian boys who would at once crave a higher education." To this circumlocution Standing Bear retorted: "That is the most exalted opinion I ever heard an Indian Commissioner express on the educational aspirations of the Indian youth of the land, and I think his compliment was unintentional. Anyway, it was absurd, for in our Black Hills alone there was wealth enough not only to educate all the Lakota boys, but the boys of other tribes as well." Young Natives, he affirmed, "are capable of becoming doctors, lawyers, engineers, architects and road-builders on the reservations. Then too, they should be trained in the history and arts of their people; it is they who should perpetuate the native dances, songs, music, poetry, languages and legends, as well as the native arts and crafts."[8]

Standing Bear's proposals for educational reform resemble those that would soon be underway in the Indian New Deal. He identified education as part of a cultural front in the Native campaign to reshape "public conscience" and redefine the hegemony.[9] Native and White youth both, he underscored, need to be educated in Native histories, social values, and cultural achievements. "The history of this continent did not begin with the landing of the Pilgrims." White children must be disabused of racist stereotypes and Native youth need to be schooled to feel proud of their heritage and people.[10] Native education, he advised, drawing on his own experience as a reservation teacher, should be bilingual as well as bicultural. "With this sort of training the young Indian would be better able to cope with the discrimination he now encounters."[11]

Standing Bear articulated several dimensions of this emergent multicultural hegemonic trend. Natives more consciously organized not only around the establishment of cultural pride and new forms of education but around collective opposition to economic exploitation, political oppression, and discrimination. As many Natives sorted out not just the advantages but the disadvantages of Collier's protomulticultural ideas about what their "self-government" should be, they were better able to formulate what might best constitute their sovereignty in "modern" conditions.

Nonetheless, race pride—a concept vital to the multicultural idea of cultural sovereignty, like individualizing—has often been deployed on behalf of assimilation and worker reproduction, even in the writing of progressive critics, as I will show. In order to think critically about individualizing, the multicultural modern, and connections between them, these reproductive deployments of some versions of the multi-

cultural must be addressed. Below I begin to do so by considering historically some seminal discourses on multicultural subjectivity and citizen
formation.

At Carlisle "individuality" reigned as a formation of subjectivity, while
at Hampton "individuality," race pride initiatives, and cultural preservation ideologies were merged to shape worker incentives. Hampton endeavored to cultivate a compensatory racial identity not only so that its
Native students could better withstand the ravages of prejudice (no in-
significant feat, as Standing Bear notes), but so that they would have a
collective, as well as "individual," incentive to work within a system
geared to take advantage of them. The school's major publication (not the
special "Indian" publication) was aptly titled the *Southern Workman*.
Donal Lindsey has argued that while Hampton's late-nineteenth-century
protomulticultural accommodationism built "bridges for cultural understanding," it also supported "a rurally oriented, largely manual training that suited white supremacy."[12] Through its museum, publications,
and social studies classes, Hampton cultivated in its students a sense of
group tradition, group pride, and group individuality in part to motivate
them to get the job done. However digested they might feel at work, their
group individuality would presumably help them feel relatively undigested. Long before diversity became a national value, it was a Hampton value, a therapeutic aid to the inculcation of steady workers.

In 1916 Alain Locke, in four lectures delivered at Howard University,
and Randolph Bourne, in "Trans-national America" and his equally important essay "The Jew and Trans-National America," challenged monocultural "common sense" about the digestive destiny of minorities.[13]
Locke and Bourne, two progressive cultural critics, believed that the key
to America's democratic success as a national body resided in its capacity to allow and even assist its diverse racial and ethnic bodies to flourish culturally.[14] By the early twentieth century *ethnoracial difference*
was undergoing an ideological revision along the lines of *individual
difference*: henceforth there would be a hegemonic struggle to define
individual and ethnoracial difference not just as cultural and national
values but as principles of a more enlightened cultural, economic, political, and national assimilation process.

Locke, several years before he became a leading intellectual light of
the Harlem Renaissance, comprehended ethnoracial identity as a version of what Collier would later term "group individuality": "This race
pride or secondary race consciousness seems to be the social equivalent
to self-respect in the individual moral life."[15] In the late 1960s Stokely

Carmichael (now named Kwame Toure) and Charles V. Hamilton quoted a statement by the National Council of Churches to further develop this social logic and strategy: " 'We must not apologize for the existence of this form of group power [Black power], for we have been oppressed as a group and not as individuals.' " They concluded, more radically than Locke, that group power, identity, and pride are necessary to establish a strong "bargaining position."[16] Locke was not antiassimilationist. Indeed, at times, not so unlike the Hampton strategists, and quite unlike Toure and Hamilton, Locke envisioned the cultural encouragement of diversification and race pride as the key to a better lubricated assimilation: "Through a doctrine of race solidarity and culture, you really accelerate and stimulate the alien group to a rather more rapid assimilation of the social culture, the general social culture, than would be otherwise possible."[17]

World War I provoked Bourne's interest in contributing to the theorizing of identity diversity. Witnessing the upsurge of nativism and militarism at the outset of the war, he was afraid that the United States would continue to stress the formation of a cohesive Anglo-Saxon national-cultural identity and social ideals that would promote the ideological chauvinism exhibited by European nations then engaged in suicidal war. Bourne held that the United States was "the first international nation," that it had long been so, and that its cosmopolitanism was the source of its intellectual distinction and national power. He repudiated the equation of "Anglo-Saxonism" with modern diverse Americanism. U.S. cosmopolitans, Bourne warned, signaling his socialist bottom-up commitments, do not want a country that "is integrated only for domestic economic exploitation of the workers or for predatory economic imperialism among the weaker peoples." The transnational America he wanted to see come into being could do so only "when no national colony within our America feels that it is being discriminated against or that its cultural case is being prejudiced."[18]

But Bourne, like Locke, was not antiassimilationist. He understood how ethnoracial identity is akin to individuality and that the system that helps confer a compensatory sense of "individual" difference and singularity on its citizens (producing feelings of individual relative autonomy) can gain by supporting compensatory ethnoracial constructions of difference and cosmopolitan singularity (producing feelings of group relative autonomy).[19] Group individuality lubricates the "machinery" of assimilation: "All our elaborate machinery of settlement and school and union, of social and political naturalization . . . will move with friction just in so far as it neglects to take into account this strong, virile insistence that America shall be what the immigrant will have a hand in making it."[20] It also stimulates incentive: "The crusade against 'hyphenates' will only inflame the partial patriotism of transnationals, and cause them to assert their European traditions in strident and unwholesome ways."[21] In the forefront of his mind was his ideal model of the "assimilable" and ethnically "self-conscious" Jewish American.[22] While there is bottom-up radicalism in his insistence—"America is already the world-federation in miniature" (a League of Nations in and of itself)—nevertheless, he frames "trans-nationality" as an identity revitalization of a system that remains disturbingly fraught with socioeconomic contradictions ("economic imperialism").[23]

Without question Locke and Bourne cared not only about the continuance of the nation and the lubrication and reform of its assimilative "machinery" but about the groups, particularly (some of) the oppressed groups, who had struggled to survive and preserve their "cultural soul" within the nation.[24] Both intellectuals differ from Hampton's strategies in a crucial way: they did not wish to use pluralism to produce compliant workers. Locke and Bourne were more like ethnoracial union organizers.

Notwithstanding their bottom-up commitments, similar to Standing Bear's in the early 1930s, aspects of their theorizing seem to advocate a seemingly more enlightened inclusionary social-management practice. Their writings contain some elements of what Christopher Newfield and Avery Gordon call "assimilationist pluralism." Locke and Bourne move beyond a protomulticultural *exclusion* emphasis (asking who is excluded from the dominant culture and why) to a protomulticultural *inclusion* emphasis (theorizing how disparate groups might best be included in the national body). And both realize that ethnoracial or group individuality is capable not only of contributing to winning the consent of the governed but of stimulating their incentive. As the twentieth century progressed, this compensatory and perhaps consolatory ethnosubjectivity formation became so powerful that it, like the imagining of "individual" "depth," sometimes took the form of what might be labeled *ethnodepth*: one enacts oneself not only by "expressing" one's "inner" "individual" "psychological" self but by "expressing" one's seemingly essential group identity, one's group soul. Social powers—say, corporate powers—that recognize and capitalize on this development can be powerful indeed.[25]

Without in any way undervaluing Bourne's desire to empower the disempowered, he can be criticized for having concentrated only on European immigrants, with whom he engaged, to his intellectual delight, in the New York City that inspired Collier's early protomulticultural activism. Furthermore, he was incorrect in his prediction, couched in his mystifying passive construction, that the "Red Man" is "passing into oblivion. . . . There is no distinctively American culture." Sounding overmuch like a brash propagandist for the American settler colony, he declared: "We are all foreign-born or descendants of foreign-born. . . . [and] did not come to adopt the culture of the American Indian."[26] Waldo Frank, Bourne's confrère, also embraced U.S. diversity but advanced a more encompassing understanding of the social groups, such as Mexicans, that contributed to this multiplicity in *Our America* (1919). And Frank, unlike Bourne, celebrated the Natives' creative rather than possessive "cultural world" and their investment in "the business of beauty." Yet for all his support, Frank, like Bourne, issued the erroneous prognosis: "The Indian is dying and is doomed."[27]

Curiously, Bourne hinted at the emergence of a new world whose blueprint could be detected in the transnational United States. The American world traveler, he suggested, should "return with an entirely new critical outlook, and a sense of superiority of American organization to the primitive living around him." It is salutary when immigrants to America migrate back to their native lands, he added, because they will serve as emissaries of the new world (much as Carlisle students were schooled to return to the reservations and Americanize and individualize their tribes): "America is thus educating these laggard peoples from the very bottom of society up, awakening vast masses to a new-born hope for the future." Bourne seemed to be as much an Americanizer and incentive-builder as Pratt, except that his democratic Americanization was constituted through diversification and his transnational Americanization would eventually set the pattern for the rest of the world. If his principal aim was to conceptualize how American culture might best release *personality*, spiritualize *dual citizenship*, and repel the chauvinist nationalism that sanctions imperialism, along the way aspects of his thinking ran along the lines of what he took to be an enlightened diversity management.

Both Locke and Bourne acknowledged their debt to Horace Kallen's concepts of cultural pluralism, first published in *The Nation* in 1915.[28] Kallen elaborated his ideas in *Culture and Democracy in the United States: Studies in the Group Psychology of the American Peoples* (1924).[29] Like Locke and Bourne, he endeavored to reteach many Americans both how to value themselves and, citing John Dewey's plea for the addition of migration studies to the school curriculum, how to appreciate Americanness-in-movement (132). He argued that if the United

States identified its national singularity as its internationalism and let its diverse groups simply be themselves, then its manifold "peoples" would have more incentive and be more efficient (this will "eliminate the waste and stupidity of the social organization" [121]). Paradoxically, he suggested that bogus melting-pot Americanization fractures Americans, whereas a social policy that embraces diverse "cultural individualities" (131) unifies them (130, 132). Respect for pluralism, he contended, is tantamount to good old American respect for individuality, "the distinctive individuality of each *natio*" (124). Hyphenated Americans keep America "individual": "Race, in its setting, is at best what individualizes the common heritage, imparting to its presence, personality and force" (180). Thus to be American is to subscribe to individuality *and* to "group idiosyncrasy" (183)—the "group's individuality" (172).

Although Kallen was generally progressive, some of his pronouncements had a managerial accent. Kallen, like Locke and Bourne, framed pluralist ethnosubjectivity formation as the key to effective assimilation. The repeated "we" suggests his identification and perhaps his allegiance: "If we give the immigrants a favorable milieu, if we tolerate their period of adjustment, if we give them freedom to make their connections between old and new experiences, if we help them to find points of contact, then we hasten assimilation" (164–65). In this vision, while (almost) everyone's ethnoracial individuality is respected, socioeconomic relations do not undergo structural revision.

Kallen's views of "Indians" are far more disquieting than the comments of Bourne and Frank and display the limits and dangers of his Euro-supremacist pluralist assimilationism. American pioneers, he believed, encountered a "vacuum," an "empty" "American continent," "unconverted by the hand of man." The "Indians," he suggested, did not "signify" and "left no tracks" in "untamed" nature (211). He added, unreflectively, that Natives taught the early colonists how to feed themselves (214). The work of Bourne, Frank, Kallen, and Locke indicates how distinctive Collier's enlarged concept of ethnoracial groups was among non-Native pluralism theorists.[30]

Two years before Locke and Bourne considered the benefits of assimilation-through-diversity, and one year before Kallen previewed his pluralist assimilationism, Collier had published his study of juvenile crime in New York City, in which he held that Americanizing could be best accomplished by giving civic institutional support to immigrant cultures. Slightly over four decades later, in 1956, Collier, then a professor of sociology at the City University of New York, made yet another noteworthy contribution to the genre of national and transnational multicultural theorizing I have been tracing. By this date the Republican BIA had sought to overturn many of Collier's "un-American" policies and usher in the "termination" period, during which the government ended its legal recognition of numerous tribes so that it could justify selling tribal land. Collier described this new policy, which had brought about a "despair [that] must reach far beyond Indians," as *antimulticultural*: "The ideology or prepossession seems to be, merely, that cultural and social distinctiveness is offensive, and is contrary to the American way."[31]

What makes this postwar retrospective notable is Collier's explicit enunciation of his Indian New Deal policy of "indirect rule administration," that is, the winning of "consent" (his word) through "bilateral," or what would later more commonly be called "multicultural," exchange. Collier, despite his fall from power as a policymaker, had hopes that his idea would flourish. He laid out what was at stake in the development of new strategies: "The essence of indirect rule is mutual consent between the ruling power and the 'dependent' group. In indirect administration, events are composite or integrative—the purposes and necessities of the ruling group and the purposes and necessities of the dependent group are united into one flow, through cumulative empirical endeavor on both sides." Revealingly, he likened this rule to management tactics developed by modern personnel departments. Collier praised the model provided by Baltimore's McCormick Industry (a spice importer), "where, be it an active, conscious consent to suggestion from management or be it experimental innovation by the rank and file, the flow of decision and authority is from the local societies, and from the different levels of industrial employment, toward the summit, and not from the summit toward the lower levels and the local societies. . . . The principle of unanimity of consent has been found to be impressively productive, in terms of morale and of increased practical efficiency, in a competitive field of industry."[32] In the McCormick model the power structure's divisions and presumably its distribution of pay—"summit" to "lower levels"—remain intact. However, Collier assigned weight to the premise that company "morale" and "efficiency" had been revitalized by this ostensibly joyous marriage of bottom-up and top-down influence.

Indirect "bilateral" rule, "imperfectly achieved in Indian affairs," he acknowledged, is a U.S. experiment with postwar global implications: this management tool is "predictive of desirable futures all over the world." But desirable to whom? Its European application on "dependent people," he admitted, "has been uneven." But when it works it "release[s] . . . great and practicable energies among the dependent peoples."[33] Notwithstanding Collier's commitment to Native welfare, opportunity, and culture, and to democratic structures, what he proposes can be construed as a subtle form of hegemonic multicultural conquest. Indirect administration's bilateral means of securing consent will presumably help America not only "rule" Natives and stimulate Native "morale," "practicable energies," and "efficiency" but also transform the world. If Collier is a crusader for Natives, participatory democracy, and cooperative economic relations, here he also seems to adopt the role of enlightened transnational top-down multicultural personnel officer.[34]

Carey McWilliams is perhaps best known as a progressive man of conscience who brought his expansive sense of what constituted political issues to his editorship of *The Nation* for three decades after World War II. Before this phase, McWilliams, like Collier, whom he admired, was an intellectual founder of what is now nominated ethnic studies. His *Factories in the Field: The Story of Migratory Farm Labor in California* (1939) and *Ill Fares the Land: Migrants and Migratory Labor in the United States* (1942) focus on the struggles of Western migrant workers from several groups—Asian Americans, Mexicans, Filipinos, Armenians—to organize and press for economic and legal justice ("agricultural revolution"). McWilliams, like Bourne, placed his faith in marginalized groups, and, like Collier, he contributed to their empowerment from below. And at times, like Bourne and Collier, he seems to have considered what might best "hold people in line."

McWilliams's synoptic *Brothers Under the Skin* (1943) examined the position of numerous U.S. "minorities."[35] Beginning with Natives ("Indians now constitute our most rapidly growing minority" [72]), he scrutinized racial discrimination outside and inside the armed services and showed that the Axis forces were making good propaganda use of this injustice (4–5). Axis media, for example, portrayed the conditions on reservations (not unlike what Standing Bear described) to try to win the loyalty of the large Native population in South and Central America (22). This campaign was particularly embarrassing because the American media portrayed the war as "a clash between the idea of racial superiority (central to the Nazi doctrine) and the idea of racial equality (central to the concept of democracy)" (5). Racial injustice constituted a wartime personnel as well as public relations problem to "the extent that our minorities remain unconvinced that their interests are identified with those of the nation as a whole" (6). More boldly, he asserted, "When we say that imperialism must be banished from the postwar world, we forget that it must also be eliminated at home" (7).[36]

McWilliams took a transnational as well as national perspective in assessing the growing numbers and influence of people of color in the postwar world (16). Because "White peoples are a minority in the new world that is emerging from the war" (17), he pleaded, it is exigent to alter the pattern of "unequal rather than reciprocal" (18) relations between White cultures and peoples of color that have predominated in the international as well as national sphere. He cited estimates "that the white races, so-called, control 47,000,000 square miles of the earth's surface, or eight ninths of the land area, while the so-called colored peoples control 6,000,000 square miles or the remaining one ninth" (19). The population growth pattern, like the war itself, he counseled, presented the United States with a pivotal multicultural opportunity to revise its methods of governing. "We are a unique people" (3) *because* "the color of America has changed" (49).

Indian New Deal policies, McWilliams suggested, echoing Collier, offer a paradigm of policy change that the United States should experiment with in the future. "The new Indian policy represents in the words of a report of the National Resources Planning Board, 'the *first conscious official* attempt to preserve and creatively develop cultural traditions fundamentally divergent from those of the majority'" (76). Although Natives will continue to learn that "change is inescapable" and "that self-support implies successful competition" (75), under the new regime (he quotes Oliver La Farge) they will "'still be Indians'" (75). This seemingly bottom-up identity compensation, it appeared to McWilliams, would provide Natives with the motivation to adjust.

McWilliams, like Standing Bear, Locke, Bourne, and Collier, was resolutely committed to bottom-up multicultural democratic participation. At the same time, like Locke, Bourne, Kallen, and Collier, he asserted that multicultural identity production constituted a more efficient, flexible, and humane strategy of assimilation. "Paradoxically, it has been by reviving the best, the enduring, the indestructible elements of Indian life and culture that progress toward assimilation has been most rapidly effected. It seems impossible, in fact, to destroy an indigenous culture; to revive it, therefore, creates the most favorable prospect for acculturation" (74). Likewise, Louis Adamic, whose writings on ethnicity inspired McWilliams to write a book about him, advocated "exploiting diversity": all Americans should be encouraged to form a "firm *subjective* identification" with America that will incite them to contribute the full extent of their "talent and skills" to the nation.[37] The power structure that recognizes and sponsors cultural relative autonomy and ethnoindividualizing can more successfully (McWilliams quotes Collier) "'incorporate the group into the national system'" and "'reach the individual through his re-enfranchised group' " (77). Thus even McWilliams's (and Adamic's) thinking reproduced elements of assimilationist pluralism.

McWilliams saw Collier's advocacy of indirect administration, multi-cultural assimilation, and bilateral "consent" not simply as the strategy that America should adopt when working out its internal policies, but also as the U.S. strategy for the democratic assimilation of the world. He envisioned America as an experimental multiethnic " 'world labora-tory' " (15) that had the potential to resolve "similar [multiethnic] world problems" (78). Assimilation adjusts diverse minority groups not only to the needs of the nation, essential in wartime, but to what McWilliams calls the "modern" (73).[38] Again McWilliams quotes Collier to suggest not only a national but a transnational realization of a multicultural " 'modern' " " 'stability' ": " 'It is the problem of reconciling the rights of small groups of people to cultural independence with the necessity for larger economic units demanded by modern methods of production and distribution' " (78). The defense of small groups' cultural independence is laudable, but what McWilliams and Collier do not spotlight in these particular instances are the power relations reproduced by "modern methods of production and distribution."

The McWilliams who developed ingenious arguments against racism and the Collier who lobbied for pan-Indian unionization were in many ways robustly democratic. In much of their work what we currently term multicultural critique is the route to, not the evasion of, encompassing critiques of economic, legislative, and judicial as well as cultural oppres-sion. Yet, as the above quotations demonstrate, in some of their writings both seem to get excited about a hegemonic method of compensatory ethnoracial identity management—indirect administration or rule—that promises to produce an efficacious assimilation and "modernizing" not just of U.S. "minority" groups but of people of all colors throughout the world. In the work of Bourne, Collier, and McWilliams, efforts to imagine the bottom-up defense and empowerment of minorities are accompa-nied by a vision of a transformed multicultural America that represents, as Emerson put it, the "future of mankind."[39] Their antidiscriminatory and, especially in the case of Collier and McWilliams, antiracist radical-ism cohabits with a global vision of world Americanization (termed "modernization") that has numerous precedents in U.S. ideology. They sometimes replace American Protestant messianic evangelism with American multicultural messianic evangelism. Their America stands as the world's multicultural and multiethnic "city on a hill."

Bourne's, Collier's, and McWilliams's visions of an assimilation that moves perhaps democratically but also imperially from multicultural to transnational dovetails with what Brazilian political theorist Alfredo Valladão, writing in Paris in the 1990s, saw happening at the close of the twentieth century. Valladão argues that U.S. national identity has been busily transnationalizing itself in the twentieth century and what will appear more clearly in the twenty-first century is *World America*. America's "final frontier" is not space; its national goal is the management of "the internationalizing of the world." Valladão, like Bourne, Locke, Kallen, Collier, Adamic, and McWilliams, rejects the "melting pot" metaphor and puts in its place one more apt for U.S. cultural, subjectivity, and identity management in the twentieth century: the multiethnic "salad bowl," in which the savour of the American salad stems from the combination of ingredients all of which retain their own identities." He interprets America's (attempted) diversity production and administration of its increasingly multiethnic population of worker-individuals as its rehearsal for its twenty-first century bid to pull off its diversity management of the planet (what I imagine as the grand Caesar salad bowl). His summary of this elastic multicultural strategy of assimilation brings Collier, not Pratt, to mind: the "task of managing specific territories in the context of a universalist logic is only possible as long as there are living communities with enough autonomy to keep their art alive [as "data banks"]. . . . The American democratic empire has to reorganize its instruments of power to make it appear both the defender of specific identities and the site of their inevitable amalgamation." (I am reminded of Curtis's rumination in Garland's *Captain of the Gray Horse Troop* of 1901, quoted in chapter 3: "If I could, I would civilize only to the extent of making life easier and happier—the religious beliefs, the songs, the native dress—all these things I would retain.")

As corporate products surround the globe and its consumers (ostensibly "making life easier and happier"), the hegemonic theme encoding them will be imperial identity diversity as well as imperial "individuality." What will help establish the ideological appeal of the United States as the planetary diversity leader, Valladão suggests, is nothing less than its ideological promise of "individual" opportunity dating back to Benjamin Franklin and Horatio Alger: America "has succeeded in avoiding dismemberment and ruin by exalting individualism."[40] What Valladão, like Bourne, Locke, Kallen, Collier, Adamic, and McWilliams, is attuned to is the capacity of state, class, and corporate power to rule by not representing itself as a homogenizing or standardizing force.

Recent critics of corporate multiculturalism have identified connections between ideologies of individual differentiation and emerging strategies of multidisciplinary diversity management. "Corporate bodies have become racialized, gendered, and flexible enough to present both the local and global image, a place of belonging in diversity," writes Martin J. Beck Matustík. He profiles what might be called *corporate regionalism*: "[Eastern Europe's multinationals] have local poets, philosophers, and computer designers to help them create regionally appealing ad campaigns."[41] Henry Giroux quotes a Benetton (Italian clothing firm) advertisement that reassures its global consumers, "Diversity is good . . . your culture (wherever you are) is as important as our culture (wherever we are)." The corporate homogenization of aspects of daily life, Giroux argues, tries to succeed by investing in, acknowledging, and profiting from difference (*corporate relativism*)—"the move away from standardized markets and the intrusion of business into the postmodern world of plural identities."[42] Paul Gilroy dubs this "ethnomarketing."[43]

Many critiques of transnational corporate multiculturalism's identity management focus not so much on who gets excluded from the cultural scene—*exclusion studies*—as on how citizens get ideologically and institutionally included in identity formations—*inclusion studies* (of the kind I have offered in the preceding chapters).[44] If in the nineteenth century, American power structures primarily used discourses of character-building and self-making individualism to motivate worker-citizens, in the twentieth century, changing power structures learned how to use individuality (with its assurances of individual singularity, difference, dignity, relative autonomy, psychological depth) *and* ethnoindividuality (with its assurances of group singularity, difference, dignity, relative autonomy, collective depth) to structure incentive and promote the appearance of democratic inclusion. This trend has shaped new conceptions of what constitute pressing political contradictions and struggles. Nancy Fraser notes how terms such as *recognition, identity*, and *difference* have become popular rallying points in place of socialist terms such as *class interest, exploitation,* and *redistribution*. Fraser concludes, as did Sloan and La Farge in their work with Native artists, that "social justice today requires both redistribution and recognition."[45] The political valuing of difference, as Stanley Aronowitz observes, can block coalition organizing insofar as "the idea of difference becomes, in effect, the new universal that cannot be overcome but must, instead, be celebrated."[46] However, in some conditions the contextual recognition of difference has spurred an encompassing recognition of—and resistance to—oppression.

How, then, might Natives respond to these two historically interrelated hegemonic forces—formations of individualized and of multiculturalized identities? Natives have had plenty of practice in working this out. As the previous chapters have demonstrated, where Natives are involved, American hegemonic forces seem to have been astonishingly explicit about the strategies of cultural subjectivity formation—individualizing, diversifying—they have employed to try to reproduce themselves. To repeat what I said in my introduction, nothing I have studied has told me as much about how social and cultural institutions have tried to design "individuality," especially for the purposes of worker and class production, as the Carlisle publications, literature, and history. And nothing I have encountered has revealed so much to me about the roles that corporations, the government, and artists have played in efforts to establish linkages between individuality management and diversity management, affecting worker and class production, as the Taos and Indian New Deal publications, literature, and history. Some of the recent postmodern critiques of the corporate, national, and transnational deployment of multiculturalism I have discussed should sound familiar because, as we saw in chapters 3 and 4, elements of these corporate, national, and transnational diversity-management campaigns were tried out during the first half of the twentieth century.

The late-twentieth-century corporate commitment to accentuating and romanticizing difference was previewed in the advertising and public relations campaigns launched by the Santa Fe Railway and the Fred Harvey tourism, hotel, and transportation company. For these corporations the ethnomodernist romantic celebration of difference was not mainly liberatory; their aim was to develop Southwestern markets with global exports (markets that proletarianized many Natives, Hispanics, and Whites as cheap labor). As I have argued, in some respects this early corporate "recognition" of "Indian" identity was a sign of an emerging *be yourself* hegemonic style of economic and cultural internal colonialism. Then in the 1930s the Indian New Deal's heavily bureaucratized diversity management had wide-ranging economic, political, cultural, and educational effects on hundreds of thousands of Natives—a multicultural world unto themselves. This is the top-down picture; it must not be ignored.

But Natives and non-Natives who worked within and outside of topdown administrative and definitional structures also struggled to produce bottom-up initiatives, campaigns, constructions of incentive, and reorganizations of work and consumption. This bottom-up history also must not be overlooked, especially by Natives and non-Natives who might learn from it. Collier, Sloan, La Farge, Kabotie, McNickle, and others endeavored to turn the corporate media attention focused on

Natives and their work to Native advantage. The sale of high-quality Native artwork for fair prices to reeducated dealers and consumers, the restoration of some land to reservations (and the efforts to prevent more land theft), the inclusion of courses about Native cultures in schools, the hiring of more Native personnel in more positions of responsibility in the BIA, the establishment of credit for Native farmers, ranchers, and businesses, increased government acknowledgment of differences among and within tribes, and other cultural, economic, educational, and political issues were often parts of the overall picture discussed and debated by Natives and Whites. Modernist multiculturalists did not always succeed in achieving an effective redistribution of wealth, political power, or cultural access, or a commonly held recognition of racial equality, to say the least, but some of them frequently engaged the need for both redistribution and recognition. The Native experience in this early appearance of corporate and welfare-state protomulticulturalism is a particularly crucial one to reflect on in this millennium in part because many Natives *never* disconnected their conception of group identity from the political, economic, cultural, and educational issues and contradictions that entangled them.

In closing, here, as in the preceding chapters, I do not mean to suggest that Natives are in any way a monolithic group; yet it seems to me that there are at least three reasons why many Natives have been and are in a good position to think critically and strategically about how they might contend with the forces that would socialize them to be certain sorts of individuals, ethnoindividuals, workers, and, to quote Collier, "dependent" political subjects. As I review these reasons below, it is imperative not to forget the important point made by Sloan and La Farge: Natives, as their art makes evident, have long been transnational, transcultural, and modern. At the same time, it is also vital to keep in mind one implication of writings by Standing Bear, Eastman, Collier, La Farge, Martin, Churchill, and others: what was misnamed the New World was in many ways really the Old World, a world-in-change that was nevertheless enlivened by cultural ways of seeing, feeling, communicating, and relating that took thousands of years to develop and in the New World of Europe just hundreds of years to discard in the name of God or Reason or nationalism or Industrial Progress or corporate transnationalism.

First, in the twentieth century *self-determination*, not *individuality*, has been the keyword around which many Natives have organized. It conveys Native subjectivity and value, as well as cultural, educational, and political purpose and incentive. Self-determination and self-sovereignty are by no means synonymous with the individualistic self-help and self-making ideologies that have driven capitalist subjects. Natives have formulated self-determination not as an egoistic concept but as a relational concept that references a range of issues, concerns, conditions, and organizations including tribal and communal solidarity, economic well-being, Native-run political organization and advocacy, Native-influenced or Native-run education, cultural production and the marketing of cultural products, spiritual kinship. This term often encompasses Native commitments to their communities, lands, traditions, and collective as well as "individual" agency. The "self" in self-determination is the totality, past and present, of Native life, being, and survival. "The power to decide, or self-determination, is the fine line that separates cultural adaptation from cultural assimilation," Andrew Garrod and Colleen Larimore stress.[47] And self-determination, as Vine Deloria Jr. and Clifford Lytle insist, is *not* the same as being self-governed by U.S. policy.[48]

Second, traditionally Natives have cultivated what might be termed *kinship subjectivities.* As in the case of self-determination, one who understands kinship understands cultural subjectivity formation as encompassingly relational: one is part of one's family, one's clan, one's tribe, and one's nation, as well as kindred to nonhuman beings. Colonial forms of "individuality" production supplied Euramericans with the experience of being not only different from one another but also materially and spiritually different from plants and animals (objectified as "nature"). This colonial experience and imagination of difference could help naturalize or rationalize colonial attempts to conquer, transform, or kill others encoded as nonindividuals (or subindividuals) and nonhuman nature. Native diversity, as the Native authors I quoted described it in chapter 2, is intertribal, tribal-animal, tribal-bird, tribal-plant, tribal-rock, tribal-river. The traditional Native sense of totality far exceeds what many radical social theorists imagine even today. Both self-determination and kinship promote one's sense of responsibilities, not just rights. They make up a Native concept of citizenship that encompasses much more than social organization. These mutually reinforcing forms of cultural subjectivity formation get their power not by foregrounding difference (Dos Passos's snowflake individuality) or opposition (the Emersonian individual versus society paradigm, or human versus nature industrial-capitalist paradigm), but by highlighting connection, respect, and responsibility—what Jace Weaver calls "communitism."[49]

Third, many Natives aware of episodes in the history I have analyzed know the extent of what they (and many non-Natives with similar commitments) are up against. Deloria and Lytle, perhaps referencing the title of McNickle's novel *The Surrounded*, underscore that the political and legal circumstances that "have surrounded Indians for two centuries" have "made them understand the world in much different terms from any other group of American citizens." Natives have experienced forms not only of double consciousness but of "dual citizenship." They have had to gain critical insight into how Euramericans have been formed and how these formations have contributed to national identity.

Thus in *Ceremony* Silko reflects on the ideological impact that colonial soul-making had on Natives: "Christianity separated the people from themselves . . . [it encouraged] each person to stand alone because Jesus Christ would save only the individual soul."[50] Wendy Rose explains that she employs the word *whiteman* in her poetry to refer to "a way of life, a set of institutions, rather than to male human beings of European ancestry. . . . All of us, including such men, are victims of the 'whiteman.'" Jimmie Durham elaborates: "Wasicu is what the Sioux call white people. It means those who steal the best of everything for themselves, and it doesn't have any connotation of race or color."[51] Silko's medicine man Betonie views Whites as the creations of "witchery." Perhaps this witchery is simple witchery, or perhaps it is Silko's metaphor for an organization of life that even the word *capitalism* may not adequately describe. "If the white people never looked beyond the lie, to see that theirs was a nation built on stolen land, then they would never be able to understand how they had been used by the witchery; they would never know how they were still being manipulated by those who knew how to stir the ingredients together: white thievery and injustice boiling up the anger and hatred that would finally destroy the world." Silko implies that Natives and Whites must unite to resist that which formed such destructive—and, as Lawrence and Collier also saw, self-destructive—White subjectivities.[52] For many Native artists and social theorists, *decolonization*, imagined expansively, not multiculturalism, has been the principal concern.[53]

The gist of Standing Bear's final writings is not just that many Whites wanted Native land but that many were threatened by Native ways of producing life, value, desire, time, selfhood, and choice. He argues, as does Collier, that Natives were not only better at being more humane than Whites—to humans and nonhumans—but they were more successful at *being human*.[54] The implication of works by Standing Bear, Eastman, and Bonnin, as I held in chapter 2, is that many Native cultures have had a greater commitment to ensuring individual agency—freedom of movement and of time, for example—than did the capitalist "individuals" who sought to individualize "Indians." Collier, notwithstanding his homages to Natives' "group individuality," eventually learned that Native groups were too diversely individual to be bureaucratized, democratized, and Indianized as he thought best.

Natives have become used to Euramericans who have defined Natives (and Euramericans) as what, in Native eyes, they are not. Many Natives, like Standing Bear and Silko, have grasped connections between the production of particular subjectivities and the legitimation of land theft (for instance, the invention of White "rugged individualism"). For them subjectivity formation is not an arcane matter theorized by scholars; it is part of their history and struggles. Native cultural critique can be exceptionally sophisticated and encompassingly radical in its scrutiny of the ideologies, social structures, and organizations of life with which Natives have had to contend (see appendix). Many Native cultural critics and activists would happily undo a good deal of what has been done to this continent and the humans and nonhumans on it.

Durham predicts: "The world and its own history is catching up with the U.S. . . . Someday they must turn and face their terrible history, and ask the world if they can make a deal. Then we will have our chance, that so many Indians have sacrificed so much to insure." We are indeed at a historical juncture in which some of what Natives have negotiated, especially during the last century, should become increasingly germane to many non-Native as well as Native groups because versions of U.S.-based incorporated individuality.com and incorporated multiculturalism.com, as Valladão and others have suggested, are being exported with products around the globe (products including Indian curios and souvenirs in Europe, Asia, and elsewhere).[55] Critics of the digestive hegemonic forces, perhaps the "witchery," unleashed on Native America must be aware that versions of these hegemonic forces have transnationalized their scope.

"Indian," as many Natives (Standing Bear, Eastman, Weaver) and non-Natives (Collier, La Farge, Martin) have argued, signifies not just blood quantum. For them "Indian" also signifies the development of certain social values, relationships with "nature," and cultural forms of agency, beauty, and incentive and involves the recognition that the preservation of human and nonhuman life entails more than feeding narrowly conceived self-interest. Those who support the significance of these human developments, recognitions, and achievements have before them the challenge to try to transform what Standing Bear termed "public conscience." Collier, whatever his faults, realized this. To undertake this task, alliances make sense.[56] Requisite for the transformation of public conscience and imagination is a knowledge of the past that makes up the present (a present that was not inevitable), but more than that, a historically informed sense of cultural potentials, of what Natives and non-Natives may still *make* possible for humans and nonhumans in the future.

Appendix 1

Notes on Natives and Socialism

For more than a hundred years observers have perceived connections between Native critique and socialist critique. In chapter 1 I related numerous instances in which reporters, government bureaucrats (including BIA commissioners), and politicians vilified Natives as socialists and communists decades before they sought to turn the Bolshevist revolution, rather than U.S. social contradictions, into the major American problem. Both Natives and socialists have long advocated individual agency, common ownership of land, and social welfare—all of which has agitated U.S. capitalists dedicated to maintaining the premise that U.S. possessive individualism, the accumulation of private property, and the unequal distribution of resources are synonymous with independence.

As I noted in chapter 4, from the early 1920s through the mid-1940s Collier's critics painted his support for Natives socialist red. I have argued that there is a socialist side to his critiques, even before his advent as a Native rights advocate, and that his Indianism—his early protomulticulturalism—can be read partly as a redaction of socialism that would have a better shot at winning the American public's support. Indianism, after all, is indigenous, not Eurocentric. While in the 1920s there was a fierce government repression of U.S. socialism, at least some wealthy reformers felt good about backing Collier's protomulticultural Indianist activism. Collier's journal *Indians at Work* exhibits his efforts to help Natives become more economically self-sufficient (group-sufficient) in the "modern" world, something socialists would sympathize with even as they might evince some skepticism of this as preparation for proletarianization (still a major aim of many Indian schools). His protomulticultural hope, like La Farge's, was that Native identity would remain strong even while Natives worked for themselves—and capitalists—within the capitalist world.

One of the reasons Collier cherished this hope, however, is that he was conscious of some foundational differences between socialists' and Natives' values, goals, and desired subjectivity formations and on certain issues sided with the latter. "Liberals, socialists, cooperative commonwealth proponents, all believed in the same nature of man as did those who opposed their doctrines of human sameness, and all believed that the narrow segment of man they saw, or thought they saw—nineteenth-century western man—was universal man . . . the isolated, economic man."[1] Collier recognized that socialism—like what Marx considered its forerunner, capitalism—dwells on economic value and promotes a productionist concept of self that is determinately tied to laboring.

These differences are clues, perhaps, as to why many alliances of socialists and Natives do not seem to have occurred. The history of interactions between Natives and U.S. socialists from the late nineteenth century to the present has yet to be written. Here I offer only a few perspectives on that story to illustrate aspects of the radical range of Native critiques that must not be underestimated as resources for Natives and non-Natives.

In the first decades of the twentieth century, Native interest in socialism does not appear to have been commonplace. It is true that Oklahoma socialists vigorously opposed guardianship laws affecting Native children "through which lawyers, speculators, and oil prospectors expropriated lands under legal cover." But Oklahoma socialists found that many Natives largely distrusted White politics, as they did Whites, and that many were more preoccupied with their own tribal politics, which could be lively. Socialists in renters unions could resent having Native landlords, some of whom, like White landlords, were exploitative.[2] Racism accounts for, or at least describes, some socialists' hatred of or indifference to Natives. In addition, Natives and socialists could subscribe to contrary notions of what constitutes legitimate land rights and use. The Oklahoma Socialist Party platform of 1914, for example, states a commitment to enlarging the public domain and includes among its schemes to achieve this the "purchase of segregated and unallotted Indian lands." This if-you-don't-use-it (in approved ways) you-lose-it principle shows no acknowledgment of or willingness to guarantee the autonomy of tribal lands. In the mid-1920s the *Oklahoma Leader*, the prominent socialist newspaper in that area, hardly mentions Natives, despite growing class differences within Oklahoma Native communities. In one article about the lack of government funding for education, the author complains that "un-naturalized Indians . . . are not subject to taxation."[3]

A tale related by the famed Southwestern socialist organizer Oscar Ameringer elaborates Collier's perception of differences between socialism and Native cultures (notwithstanding some common agreement). In 1930 Ameringer chatted with a formerly wealthy "self-made" cattleman who, after going bust, heartily endorsed revolution. The cattleman advocated owning "our land and cattle and things in common like the Indians used to do before the government robbed them of everything by giving them title deeds." Ameringer concurred, but added, ever the loyal socialist, "provided we add railroads, banks, packaging plants and a great many other things to those you mentioned."[4] He wanted to "add" what even White capitalists would have embraced as signs of "progress."

If some Southwestern Natives had been present they might not have assented that such economic, technological, and bureaucratic developments, even if managed by utopian socialists, count as "progress." In the early 1980s several prominent Native intellectuals and activists gave vent to their disagreements with U.S. marxists and rejected the ideological tendency, patent in socialist as well as capitalist teleological schemes of "civilized" progress, to classify Native cultures as "primitive," "precapitalist," "preindustrial," or (by aspiring socialists) "presocialist." They assailed socialism as too much an ideological outgrowth of what it criticizes, too influenced by capitalism in imagining "what alternatives are actually viable," and too wedded to the "inevitability of industrialism."[5] The Native critics were more preoccupied with kinship concepts of relationship—what Euramericans more narrowly conceive of as "ecology"—than with making social advances in the operations of industrialism. Their notion of selfhood was not reliant on (socialist) concepts of the formative influence of modes and relations of production—the labored self. They tended to employ the category *Euramericans* rather than *capitalists* to represent the problem, while never overlooking the multiple dimensions of economic assault that Natives have withstood. Socialists who worry about the universalization of capitalism believe that this regionalizing of the forces that have oppressed Natives is off base and that capitalism is the problem everywhere. However much Native traditionalists and socialists might agree on the importance of community, the significance of welfare and an ethos of giving, the baneful effects of ideologies of possessiveness and egocentrism, and the limited individuality of capitalist subjects mass-labeled, or mislabeled, "individuals," still, their disagreements about what constitute problems and solutions are substantive.

More recently, Ward Churchill and Calvin Luther Martin, building on Vine Deloria Jr.'s analyses of Christian versus Native concepts of time and history, have contended not that history has left Natives behind but that Euramerican—capitalist and socialist—inventions of "history" have misrepresented Native organizations of life, value, and relationship as anachronistic nonoptions. Skeptical of socialist as well as capitalist saviourism, Natives "demand sovereignty and self-determination." Significantly, Churchill adds that Natives, knowing what they are dealing with and not needing socialists to " 'explain' it" to them, "cast about for the allies and alternatives of the sort marxists have often *claimed* to be."[6] Durham's efforts to establish hemispheric alliances underscore that this has not always been easy: "A progressive person from Brazil told me that since there are only a few thousand Indians remaining in Brazil, we were not important there; except in that we provided an example of workable communism." Still, he affirms: "I interpret the world through a Cherokee set of culture and language patterns. To me that means, necessarily, political involvement."[7] Thus some Natives contend not just that socialist critique's grasp of what needs to be transformed is not comprehensive enough in its range, but that it is an ideological carrier of aspects of the "modern" problem.

Appendix 2

A Proposal to Reopen Carlisle

A final consideration: In May, 2000, Natives from across the continent traveled to Carlisle to honor the students who lived and died there and to make Carlisle even more central to Native historical memory. Bearing in mind the complex roles Carlisle played in attempting to reproduce subordinate subjects for and to legitimate, in Silko's words, "a nation build on stolen land"—on Dos Passos's *elbow room*—one token reparation that the U.S. government might make is to relocate the army War College and Military History Institute that now occupy Carlisle's campus elsewhere and reopen Carlisle.

But this twenty-first century version of Carlisle could be symbolically, materially, and strategically different in structure and aim: run by Native teachers, amply and securely funded, consecrated to the study of Native cultures as well as other subjects, and dedicated to offering contemporary renditions of the leadership, activist, and incentive training that McNickle started to experiment with in the 1960s. A Native Carlisle might even be the center for the production of preparatory materials for Natives who are contemplating attending college. Native intellectuals, teachers, and leaders would work out the details of how the school might redefine education, and might draw on the inspiration of the dozens of tribal colleges, which teach mainstream and traditional Native productions of knowledge. This Native-made Carlisle could emblemize and teach self-determination, kinship, and critique rather than serve as a factory for the making of manual laborers trained to commit treason to their tribes, kill the "Indian" in themselves, embrace market dependencies as independence, and then anoint themselves "individuals."[1]

Abbreviations in Notes

I cite articles, reviews, letters, and notes with the abbreviations below in the endnotes. Sometimes reference data about material included in archives is not complete (for instance, publication data or date of composition). I present the reference data that is indicated in addition to relevant information about the material's location in the archives.

Archives of Individuals

JC   John Collier Papers, Manuscripts and Archives, Yale University Library

RHPP   Richard Henry Pratt Papers, Yale Collection of Western Americana, Beinecke Rare Book and Manuscript Library

Carlisle Industrial School for Indians Publications

AR   *The Arrow*, Microfilm, Sterling Memorial Library, Yale University

EKT   *Eadle Keatah Toh*, Yale Collection of Western Americana, Beinecke Rare Book and Manuscript Library

IBGF   *The Carlisle Indian Boys' and Girls' Friend*, Yale Collection of Western Americana, Beinecke Rare Book and Manuscript Library

IH   *The Indian Helper*, Yale Collection of Western Americana, Beinecke Rare Book and Manuscript Library

MS   *The Morning Star*, Yale Collection of Western Americana, Beinecke Rare Book and Manuscript Library

RM   *The Red Man*, Yale Collection of Western Americana, Beinecke Rare Book and Manuscript Library, and Sterling Memorial Library, Yale University

RMH   *The Red Man and Helper*, Yale Collection of Western Americana, Beinecke Rare Book and Manuscript Library

SN   *School News*, Yale Collection of Western Americana, Beinecke Rare Book and Manuscript Library

Other

IW   *Indians at Work*, Yale Collection of Western Americana, Beinecke Rare Book and Manuscript Library

Notes

Introduction

1. John Dos Passos, "A Question of Elbow Room," in *Essays on Individuality*, ed. Felix Morley (Philadelphia: University of Pennsylvania Press, 1958), 18, 16. Estée Lauder advertisement, late 1990s. Wendy Rose, "What My Father Said," in her *The Halfbreed Chronicles and Other Poems* (Los Angeles: West End, 1985), 19–20, see 19.

2. Terry Jones, of Monty Python, directed *Life of Brian*. I thank John McKay for suggesting that I see the film.

3. Jon Cruz, "From Farce to Tragedy: Reflections on the Reification of Race at Century's End," in *Mapping Multiculturalism*, ed. Avery F. Gordon and Christopher Newfield (Minneapolis: University of Minnesota Press, 1996), 19–39, see 23.

4. Herbert Hoover, *American Individualism* (Garden City, N.Y.: Doubleday Page, 1922), 36, 9, 63, 66.

5. For an analysis of the appeal that the Soviet Union held for some major African American intellectuals and artists, such as W. E. B. Du Bois, Claude McKay, Langston Hughes, and Paul Robeson, see Kate A. Baldwin, *Beyond the Color Line and the Iron Curtain: Reading Encounters between Black and Red, 1922–1963* (Durham, N.C.: Duke University Press, 2002).

6. Dos Passos, "Question," in *Essays on Individuality*, ed. Morley 13, 15, 26–27.

7. Ibid., 13, 18.

8. Steven Lukes, *Individualism* (New York: Harper, 1973), 18.

9. Joel Kovel, *The Age of Desire: Reflections of a Radical Psychoanalyst* (New York: Pantheon, 1981), 51, 58. The American sociologist Robert S. Lynd conceptualized cultural "individuals" as "private versions of the common culture" in *Knowledge for What? The Place of Social Science in American Culture* (New York: Grove, 1964 [1939], 154.

10. Quoted in Lukes, *Individualism*, 18.

11. Thoreau, "Civil Disobedience," in Henry David Thoreau, *Walden and Other Writings*, ed. William Howarth (New York: Modern Library, 1981), 635–59, see 647. George Kateb writes: "Someone with an individualist commitment has the state most in mind, the state as the formally vested agency of coercive power. . . . The state . . . must always

be kept under suspicion" (*The Inner Ocean: Individualism and Democratic Culture* [Ithaca, N.Y.: Cornell University Press, 1992], 1–2). F. O. Matthiessen's postwar perspective, shaped by his experience teaching in Prague, made him somewhat skeptical of Thoreau's performance of civil disobedience. Although it "sprang out of Thoreau's refusal to pay his poll-tax, as a protest against the slave-interests for waging the imperialist war against Mexico, I couldn't help feeling that Thoreau's defiance of the state must seem very innocent to those who had known the Nazis. [European] students had experienced something very different from the time and place where an Emerson could get his friend out of jail after one night. If you had made Thoreau's gesture, not in a New England village with a broad and still largely unsettled continent stretching westward beyond you, but in the hemmed-in Prague of 1939, you would have gone to a concentration camp and probably death" (*From the Heart of Europe* [New York: Oxford University Press, 1948], 130).

12. See Carla Kaplan, "Undesirable Desire: Citizenship and Romance in Modern American Fiction," *Modern Fiction Studies* 43 (spring 1997): 144–69. Also see Colin Morris, *The Discovery of the Individual, 1050–1200* (New York: Harper, 1972), 3. On individualist anarchism, see Stephen Pearl Andrews's mid-nineteenth-century writings, *Love, Marriage, and Divorce, and the Sovereignty of the Individual: A Discussion between Henry James, Horace Greeley, and Stephen Pearl Andrews and a Hitherto Unpublished Manuscript: Love, Marriage, and the Condition of Women*, ed. Charles Shively (Weston, Mass.: M & S Press, 1975), and Benjamin Tucker's 1897 tome, *Instead of a Book: By a Man Too Busy to Write* (New York: Haskell House, 1969).

13. Not everyone—for instance, some American socialists—had found the ideological elaborations of this snowflake premise either appealing or convincing. J. Edward Hall, a socialist organizer and former machinist in the United States, recognized Michelangelo Buonarroti's "genius" but doubted whether it would have taken the form it did in Peking or Madrid or in a different era. He held that "the individuality of a person, however strong it may be, is simply a reflex of the collective life by which he and his parents have been surrounded" ("The Place of Individualism in the Socialist System" [New York: New York Labor News Company, 1889], 10, 11). Similarly, Meyer Schapiro maintained that conventional assumptions about "genius" and "originality" overlook the underlying "socially organized relationships" that allow one to feel and cause one to want to feel "individual" in certain ideological ways. "Since [the artist] attributes his difficulties, not to particular historical conditions, but to society and human nature as such, he has only a vague idea that things might be different than they are; his antagonism suggests to him no effective action, and he shuns slogans of reform or revolution as possible halters on his personal freedom." "The Social Basis of Art," in *First American Artists' Congress* (New York: n.p., 1936), 35, 32, 36.

14. Quentin Anderson terms this the "imperial self" in *The Imperial Self: An Essay in American Literary and Cultural History* (New York: Knopf, 1972); see especially his discussion of Emerson, 3–58.

15. Emerson was influenced partly by Unitarianism's stress on self-culture and self-improvement. See Yehoshua Arieli, *Individualism and Nationalism in American Ideology* (Cambridge, Mass.: Harvard University Press, 1964), 256–57 (Unitarianism) and 277–85 (Emerson). Emerson was one of the nineteenth century's most popular "success" and "individuality" authors and lecturers. See Judy Hilkey, *Character Is Capital: Success Manuals and Manhood in Gilded Age America* (Chapel Hill: University of North Carolina Press, 1997), 70–71, 142, 162.

16. Ralph Waldo Emerson, "Self-Reliance," in *The Norton Anthology of American Litera-ture: Volume 1*, ed. Nina Baym et al. (New York: Norton, 1994), 1045–62, see 1059, 1049, 1046, 1062, 1048. See William Charvat's "American Romanticism and the Depression of 1837" (1937), in his *The Profession of Authorship in America, 1800–1870*, ed. Matthew J. Bruccoli (Columbus: Ohio State University Press, 1968), 49–67. For a brief discussion of Emerson's "blindness toward the reality of misery and social suffering," consult Arieli, *Individualism and Nationalism*, 285.

17. Lukes, *Individualism*, 73, 43.

18. C. L. R. James, *American Civilization* (Cambridge, Mass.: Blackwell, 1993), 40, 48, 102, 104. James's text was written in 1950 but remained unpublished until 1993, after his death. Beard exposed how corporations employ the discourse of individualism to lobby for the lifting of regulations that inhibit their profits, while they support other regulations that assure their wealth. Generally, he determined, "the creed, stripped of all flashy rhetoric, means getting money" ("The Myth of Rugged Individualism" [The John Day Pamphlets, no. 6] [New York: John Day, 1932], 18–19, 25). Dreiser argued in *How the Great Corporations Rule the United States* that "the wisest and greatest among the individualists" are those who see that corporations are transforming them into their "agent[s]" (Girard, Kansas: Haldeman-Julius, 1931, 9). Consult Alan Tractenberg's classic *The Incorporation of America: Culture and Society in the Gilded Age* (New York: Hill and Wang, 1982).

19. Matthiessen, *From the Heart of Europe*, 159.

20. Matthiessen, "Of Crime and Punishment," in *F. O. Matthiessen (1902–1950): A Collective Portrait*, ed. Paul M. Sweezy and Leo Huberman (New York: Henry Schuman, 1950), 21–36; see 32.

21. Matthiessen, *From the Heart of Europe*, 37, 89, 56, 90, 121, 133.

22. Lawrence Levine, *The Opening of the American Mind: Canons, Culture, and History* (Boston: Beacon, 1996), xv. Also see Stephanie Coontz, *The Way We Never Were: American Families and the Nostalgia Trap* (New York: Basic, 1992).

23. See Raymond Williams's definition of *individual*, in *Keywords: A Vocabulary of Culture and Society* (New York: Oxford University Press, 1976), 133–36.

24. See *individualize* in *The Oxford English Dictionary*. Individualizing was understood by several writers in midcentury to be a process linked favorably with epistemology, sympathy, and artistry but also with earthly self-imagining: "The natural effect . . . of pain and fear," wrote Rev. John Henry Newman in 1835, "is to individualize us in our own minds." In his reminiscences of England, *Our Old Home* (1863), Nathaniel Hawthorne politely lamented, "I a little grudged the tracts [of land] that have been filched away, so to speak, and individualized by thriving citizens."

25. Raymond Williams, *The Long Revolution* (London: Chatto and Windus, 1961), 72. In 1939 Robert Lynd also felt the need to enclose *individual* in quotation marks: "There are no Robinson Crusoes, no 'individuals' apart from other individuals, and it is a tautology to speak of 'the individual in society' " (*Knowledge for What?*, 153–54).

26. Niklas Luhmann, "The Individuality of the Individual: Historical Meanings and Contemporary Problems," in *Reconstructing Individualism: Autonomy, Individuality, and the Self in Western Thought*, ed. Thomas C. Heller, Morton Sosna, and David E. Wellbery (Stanford, Ca.: Stanford University Press, 1986), 313–25, see 313. Also see Niklas Luhmann, *Love as Passion: The Codification of Intimacy*, trans. Jeremy Gaines and Doris L. Jones (Stanford, Ca.: Stanford University Press, 1998 [1982]). Here Luhmann, sounding somewhat Emersonian, makes a distinction between "true individuality" and

the "culture of individuality": "A recognition of the single-mindedness of true individuality—or at least of every real individual, which includes failures!—has to assert itself against the culture of individuality." Yet he adds, "Both what a person expects in terms of recognition for his Self within personal relationships, and what he wishes to realize in terms of being able to speak freely about himself, do not involve something ideal, but rather something factual" (164). Moreover he hints that there may really be no "personal": "Today's society may perhaps be more accommodating as far as motivating the construction of a purely personal world is concerned, but one is also probably only just beginning to discover how improbable this is" (171).

27. Lukes, *Individualism*, 14, 22, 32, 34, 26.

28. Max Weber, *The Protestant Ethic and the Spirit of Capitalism* (New York: Scribner's, 1958), Winthrop, "A Modell of Christian Charity," in *The Puritans*, ed. Perry Miller and Thomas H. Johnson (New York: American Book Company, 1938), 195–99, see 198. On American Puritan subjectivity formations, see Merle Curti, *Human Nature in American Thought: A History* (Madison: University of Wisconsin Press, 1980), 44–69 (53 on Puritan notions of individual difference, 45–49 on depravity), and John Owen King III, *The Iron of Melancholy: Structures of Spiritual Conversion in America from the Puritan Conscience to Victorian Neurosis* (Middletown, Conn.: Wesleyan University Press, 1980), 13–82.

29. Peter Stallybrass, "Shakespeare, the Individual, and the Text," in *Cultural Studies*, ed. Lawrence Grossberg, Cary Nelson, and Paula Treichler (New York: Routledge, 1992), 593–610, see 593. Alan Sinfield, writing in *Alfred Tennyson* (Oxford: Blackwell, 1986) about eighteenth-century Britain, observes that the bourgeoisie used "the idea of the individual" to contest aristocratic authority. However, in nineteenth- and twentieth-century Britain and America, the bourgeoisie reconceived the "individual" "as the opposite of the social and the political, as a state of essential human values to which those 'public' discourses could contribute little and from which they might well detract" (66). In addition, see Nancy Armstrong and Leonard Tennenhouse, *The Imaginary Puritan: Literature, Intellectual Labor, and the Origins of Personal Life* (Berkeley: University of California Press, 1992), 17–18, 161–62, 171–72. Also consult Robert Bellah, Richard Madsen, William M. Sullivan, Ann Swidler, Steven M. Tipton, *Habits of the Heart: Individualism and Commitment in American Life* (New York: Harper, 1985): "Modern individualism emerged out of the struggle against monarchical and aristocratic authority. . . . In that struggle, classical political philosophy and biblical religion were important cultural resources. Classical republicanism evoked an image of the active citizen contributing to the public good and Reformation Christianity, in both Puritan and sectarian forms, inspired a notion of government based on the voluntary participation of individuals. Yet both these traditions placed individual autonomy in a context of moral and religious obligation that in some contexts justified obedience as well as freedom" (142–43).

30. Morris, *Discovery*, 2, 67, 74–75, 79, 87, 166. Also see Robert W. Hanning, *The Individual in Twelfth-Century Romance* (New Haven, Conn.: Yale University Press, 1977).

31. On medieval conceptions of authorship, see Terence Hawkes, *Semiotics and Structuralism* (Berkeley: University of California Press, 1977), 119–20.

32. Lee Patterson, " 'No Man His Reson Herde': Peasant Consciousness, Chaucer's Miller, and the Structure of the *Canterbury Tales*," in *Literary Practice and Social Change in Britain, 1380–1530*, ed. Lee Patterson (Berkeley: University of California Press, 1990), 113–55, see 125.

33. Stallybrass, "Shakespeare," in *Cultural Studies*, ed. Grossberg et al., 606, 610.

34. Quoted in Alain Renaut, *The Era of the Individual: A Contribution to a History of Subjectivity*, trans. M. B. DeBevoise and Franklin Philip (Princeton, N.J.: Princeton University Press, 1997), 29. For a comparison of European and U.S. constructions of individualism, see Arieli, *Individualism and Nationalism*, 183–86. Arieli argues: "The term [individualism], which in the Old World was almost synonymous with selfishness, social anarchy, and individual self-assertion, connoted in America self-determination, moral freedom, the rule of liberty, and the dignity of man. Instead of signifying a period of transition toward a higher level of social harmony and unity, it came to mean the final stage of human progress" (193). Yet Arieli also studies important nineteenth-century American critiques of individualism—for instance, the work of Albert Brisbane, Orestes Brownson, and William Henry Channing (235–45), and anarchist critiques by Josiah Warren, Stephen Pearl Andrews, and Benjamin Tucker (289–96). Lukes's *Individualism* contains chapters on French, English, German, and American constructions of individualism. Also see *The Status of the Individual in East and West*, ed. Charles A. Moore (Honolulu: University of Hawaii Press, 1968), and, on Japan, see Ralph Ketcham, *Individualism and Public Life: A Modern Dilemma* (New York: Blackwell, 1987), especially 143.

35. Lukes, *Individualism*, 75.

36. For a provocative critique of the relationship between privatizing family structures and the making of certain kinds of "individuals" and emotional dispositions, see Michèle Barrett and Mary McIntosh, *The Anti-Social Family* (London: Verso/NLB, 1982), especially 42–56: "Another twist of the screw of familialism and individualism is the way that being reared in an enclosed family, with one parent mainly responsible for the children, tends to produce a highly individualistic personality structure. . . . The typical personality of the normal successfully family-reared child may have its undesirable features: a need to form intimate one-to-one ties to the exclusion of a more diffused bond to a wider group, a tendency to go it alone as an individual and a lack of concern for group support and approval of group interests" (51–52).

37. Stallybrass, "Shakespeare," in *Cultural Studies*, ed. Grossberg et al., 612; Lukes, *Individualism*, 149.

38. On the American inventions and uses of the concept of "civilizing" from 1609 to 1851, see Roy Harvey Pearce's 1953 classic, *The Savages of America: A Study of the Indian and the Idea of Civilization* (Baltimore: Johns Hopkins University Press, 1965).

39. One exception is Neal Salisbury, "American Indians and American History," in *The American Indian and the Problem of History*, ed. Calvin Luther Martin (New York: Oxford University Press, 1987), 46–54.

40. S. Elizabeth Bird, "Introduction: Constructing the Indian, 1830s–1990s," in *Dressing in Feathers: The Construction of the Indian in American Popular Culture*, ed. S. Elizabeth Bird (Boulder, Colo.: Westview, 1996), 1–12, see 11.

41. Devon Mihesuah, *Cultivating the Rosebuds: The Education of Women at the Cherokee Female Seminary, 1851–1909* (Urbana: University of Illinois Press, 1993), 6.

42. Laura Wexler, "Tender Violence: Literary Eavesdropping, Domestic Fiction, and Educational Reform," in *The Culture of Sentiment: Race, Gender, and Sentimentality in Nineteenth-Century America*, ed. Shirley Samuels (New York: Oxford University Press, 1992), 9–37, see 15. Albert Memmi overgeneralizes: "The colonized is never characterized in an individual manner; he is entitled only to drown in an anonymous collectivity." *The Colonizer and the Colonized*, trans. Howard Greenfeld (Boston: Beacon, 1991 [1957]), 85.

43. Vine Deloria Jr., and Clifford M. Lytle, *The Nations Within: The Past and Future of American Indian Sovereignty* (New York: Pantheon, 1984), 244.

44. Leah Dilworth, *Imagining Indians in the Southwest: Persistent Visions of a Primitive Past* (Washington, D.C.: Smithsonian Institution Press, 1996), 169.

45. Patricia Penn Hilden, who is part Nez Perce, criticizes the efforts of art historian Sally Price to rescue the anonymous work of "primitive artists" by trying to identify their work: "Price intends to 'recuperate' the individuality of these overlooked individuals. But why?" Hilden notes "the very western privileging of the individual—especially 'geniuses'—in bourgeois society," observes that artifacts are valued more when individual identity can be ascribed to them, and concludes that the goal of Price's "recuperation is to make 'them' [the artists] . . . *just like us!*" See *When Nickels Were Indians: An Urban, Mixed-Blood Story* (Washington, D.C.: Smithsonian Institution Press, 1995), 42–43.

46. I discuss Krupat's earlier works on Native autobiography in chapter 2. See Arnold Krupat, *Ethnocriticism: Ethnography, History, Literature* (Berkeley: University of California Press, 1992), 201–31.

47. Krupat, *Ethnocriticism*, 204–10 (Krupat discusses Mauss's "evolutionary narrative" on 204).

48. Geertz is quoted in Jace Weaver, *That the People Might Live: Native American Literatures and Native American Community* (New York: Oxford University Press, 1997), 39.

49. Weaver, *People*, 39, 43, 39.

50. Owens is quoted in Weaver, *People*, 42.

51. See Andrew Garrod and Colleen Larimore, "Introduction," *First Person, First Peoples: Native American College Graduates Tell Their Life Stories*, ed. Andrew Garrod and Colleen Larimore (Ithaca, N.Y.: Cornell University Press, 1997), 1–19, see 6, 11, 15–16. I thank my colleague Ashraf Rushdy for telling me about this volume.

52. Marianne Chamberlain, "The Web of Life," in *First Person, First Peoples*, ed. Garrod and Larimore, 154–68, see 165.

53. Louise Erdrich, foreword, *First Person, First Peoples*, ed. Garrod and Larrimore, x–xi.

54. Oritz is quoted in Hilden, *When Nickels Were Indians*, 45.

55. Gary Witherspoon, *Language and Art in the Navajo Universe* (Ann Arbor: University of Michigan Press, 1977), 151, 152–53, 173.

56. On Native traders and the issue of who actually sailed across the Atlantic first, see Jack D. Forbes (Powhatan, Lenape, Saponi), *Africans and Native Americans: The Language of Race and the Evolution of Red-Black Peoples* (Urbana: University of Illinois Press, 1993).

57. Francis La Flesche, *The Middle Five: Indian Schoolboys of the Omaha Tribe* (Madison: University of Wisconsin Press, 1963 [1900]), 99. Eric Mottram, "The Red Bank: Indians in White Lives," in Eric Mottram and Philip Davies, *Culture and Technology in America: Three Essays* (London: Polytechnic of Central London, 1978), 17–37, see 18.

58. Robert F. Berkhofer Jr., *Salvation and the Savage: An Analysis of Protestant Missions and American Indian Response, 1787–1862* (New York: Atheneum, 1976), preface, n.p. This preface is not in the earlier edition. Also see John Collier, "The United States Indian," in *Understanding Minority Groups*, ed. Joseph B. Gittler (New York: Wiley, 1956), 32–51: Natives "developed, newly in the Western Hemisphere, languages numbering thousands" (34).

59. Quoted in Robert F. Berkhofer Jr., *The White Man's Indian: Images of the American Indian from Columbus to the Present* (New York: Vintage, 1979), 15.

60. See H. David Brumble III, *American Indian Autobiography* (Berkeley: University of

California Press, 1988): "Should we refer to Indians or Native Americans or Amerindians? I have chosen 'Indians': this is how most of the Indians I have met refer to themselves" (ix). He then points out, "The names of tribes differ, too, and more widely" (ix). Mihesuah also chooses to use the term *Indian:* "I prefer [it] over 'Native American,' which, in my mind, also applies to anyone born in the United States" (*Cultivating,* xii).

61. I discuss *Indian* and *Native American* below. Scholars have developed critical perspectives on commonplace words or terms such as *New World* (to *whom* was it new? why is the continent of Europe older than the Americas?), *discovery* (had not the indigenous inhabitants discovered this world before European colonizers?), *civilization* (civilization takes many cultural forms), *Western* (are the Americas' indigenous cultures not in the West, and does the term *Western civilization* recognize this?), *progress* (is progress a culturally and ideologically relative idea?), *primitive* (is primitive culturally inferior to "civilized," or simply culturally different?), *prehistory* (what could exist before history?), and *modern* (are there not different ways of being "modern"?). Calvin Luther Martin contrasts Natives' notions of themselves as being in kinship with animals and plants (who help humans survive) with the "fallacious cognitive inversion that the earth is 'the environment' for us to take care of": "both the earth and the concept of wildness have become cognitively trapped as 'the environment'—yet another thing for Homo to conserve and preserve" (*In the Spirit of the Earth: Rethinking History and Time* [Baltimore: Johns Hopkins University Press, 1992], 71). As for the notion of Euramerican "progress," Martin argues: "[Un-'discovered' Indians in the not yet new world] were feeding themselves just fine, and managing their relatively few indigenous diseases, and all in all were demographically stable before the Columbuses, Corteses, Drakes, Magellans, and James Cooks dropped anchor, with their swarms of pathogens, rats, and imperial mandates" (127). The category of "development" has been used to assert both that Natives have failed to "develop" their land "resources" and, in psychological discourse, as Hilden notes, to suggest that Natives have not achieved Euramerican standards of emotional "development"—for instance, when Native children have resisted Euramerican strictures at school with a silent, "potted plant" response. Hilden also foregrounds the idea of "Western" civilization as an ethnocentric construction. And she regrets that "the clear evidence of extensive farming by indigenous people did not prevent either land theft or its justification by this 'wilderness' designation" (*When Nickels Were Indians,* 80, 142, 236). Also consult Thomas C. Patterson, *Inventing Western Civilization* (New York: Monthly Review Press, 1997), especially "Inventing Barbarians and Other Uncivilized People," 87–115. In "Discovering America: An Introduction," Frederick Hoxie observes that Columbus's "discovery" misidentified the North American continent "as a new land, and cast its past into 'prehistoric' time" (*Journal of American History* [December 1992]: 835–40, see 835). Ward Churchill challenges the narrative of progress and assumptions about periodizing built into the term *preindustrial* and instead proposes *nonindustrial* ("False Promises: An Indigenist Perspective on Marxist Theory and Practice," in his *From a Native Son: Selected Essays on Indigenism, 1985–1995* [Boston: South End, 1996], 461–82, see 470). Against the assumptions built into the dominant Euramerican constructions of "modern," Luther Standing Bear writes: "White men seem to have difficulty in realizing that people who live differently from themselves still might be traveling the upward and progressive road of life." On the Euramerican category of "wild": "Since for the Lakota there was no wilderness; since nature was not dangerous but hospitable; not forbidding but friendly, Lakota philosophy was healthy." On "savage": "To make this label stick has been the

task of the white race" (*Land of the Spotted Eagle* [Boston: Houghton Mifflin, 1933], vi, 232, 251). In 1900 Francis La Flesche criticized the category of "wilderness": "The white people speak of the country at this period as 'a wilderness,' as though it was an empty tract without human interest or history. To us Indians it was as clearly defined then as it is to-day; we knew the boundaries of tribal lands, those of our friends and those of our foes; we were familiar with every stream, the contour of every hill, and each peculiar feature of the landscape has its tradition. It was our home, the scene of our history, and we loved it as our country" (*Middle Five*, xx).

62. Pratt, "Official Report of the Nineteenth Annual Conference of Christian Charities and Correction" (1892), in *Americanizing the American Indians: Writings by the "Friends of the Indian," 1880–1900*, ed. Francis Paul Prucha (Lincoln: University of Nebraska Press, 1978 [1973]), 261–71, see 261.

63. See Lorna M. Malmsheimer's seminal essay, " 'Imitation White Man': Images of Transformation at the Carlisle Indian School," *Studies in Visual Communication* 11 (fall 1985): 54–75. For reflections on the social construction of ethnicity, see Werner Sollors, "Introduction: The Invention of Ethnicity," in *The Invention of Ethnicity*, ed. Werner Sollors (New York: Oxford University Press, 1989), ix–xx, especially xiv.

64. Weaver, *People*, xiii.

65. Mather quoted in Ronald Takaki, "*The Tempest* in the Wilderness: The Racialization of Savagery," *Journal of American History* (December 1992): 892–912, see 910.

66. *Indianize, Oxford English Dictionary*.

67. Malmsheimer, " 'Imitation White Man' "; Karen Daniels Petersen, *Plains Indian Art from Fort Marion* (Norman: University of Oklahoma Press, 1971); Wexler, "Tender Violence"; Michael C. Coleman, *American Indian Children at School, 1850–1930* (Jackson: University Press of Mississippi, 1993); David Wallace Adams, *Education for Extinction: American Indians and the Boarding School Experience, 1875–1928* (Lawrence: University Press of Kansas, 1995). For the most thorough analysis of Carlisle, see Genevieve Bell's impressively researched, beautifully written, and subtly theorized study, "Telling Stories Out of School: Remembering The Carlisle Indian Industrial School, 1879–1918" (Ph.D. dissertation, Stanford University, 1998). Also see Everett Gilcreast, "Richard Henry Pratt and American Indian Policy" (Ph.D. dissertation, Yale University, 1967).

68. Also see Robert A. Trennert Jr., *The Phoenix Indian School: Forced Assimilation in Arizona, 1819–1935* (Norman: University of Oklahoma Press, 1988); K. Tsianina Lomawaima (Creek), *They Called It Prairie Light: The Story of Chilocco School* (Lincoln: University of Nebraska Press, 1994); Mihesuah, *Cultivating*; Delores J. Huff, *To Live Heroically: Institutional Racism and American Indian Education* (Albany: State University Press of New York, 1997); Brenda J. Child (Red Lake Ojibwe), *Boarding School Seasons: American Indian Families, 1900–1940* (Lincoln: University of Nebraska Press, 1998); *Away From Home: American Indian Boarding School Experiences, 1879–2000*, ed. Margaret L. Archuleta (Pueblo), Brenda J. Child, K. Tsianina Lomawaima (Phoenix: Heard Museum, 2000); Clyde Ellis, *To Change Them Forever: Indian Education at the Rainy Mountain School, 1893–1920* (Norman: University of Oklahoma Press, 1996); Scott Riney, *The Rapid City Indian School, 1898–1933* (Norman: University of Oklahoma Press, 1999).

69. See Barbara Ehrenreich and John Ehrenreich, "The Professional-Managerial Class," and "Rejoinder," in *Between Labor and Capital*, ed. Pat Walker (Boston: South End, 1979), 5–45, 313–34.

70. In the 1940s, contributors to *Common Ground*, a journal devoted to ethnic studies

founded by Louis Adamic and Margaret Anderson, use *multicultural* (according to Michael Denning)—along with the words *ethnic* (introduced by John Collier) and *diversity* (also often employed by Collier)—to describe the United States (Denning, *The Cultural Front: The Laboring of American Culture in the Twentieth Century* [New York: Verso, 1996], 448–49). Also see Christopher Newfield and Avery Gordon, "Multiculturalism's Unfinished Business," 76–115, in *Mapping Multiculturalism*, ed. Gordon and Newfield: "The word 'multicultural' had a fitful beginning in the World War II era, appearing in non-trendsetting situations such as a *New York Herald-Tribune Books* attack on prejudice on 27 July 1941, or, in 1959, a description of Montreal as multicultural (*Oxford English Dictionary*)" (94). Werner Sollors suggests that W. Lloyd Warner and Paul S. Lunt first used the word *ethnicity* in *The Social Life of Modern Community* (New Haven, Conn.: Yale University Press, 1941) in his introduction to *The Invention of Ethnicity*, ed. Sollors.

71. David Hollinger, "Cultural Pluralism and Multiculturalism," in *A Companion to American Thought*, ed. Richard Wightman Fox and James T. Kloppenberg (Cambridge, Mass.: Blackwell, 1995), 162–66, see 163–64. Also see Hollinger's chapter "Ethnic Diversity, Cosmopolitanism, and the Emergence of the American Liberal Intelligentsia," in his *In the American Province: Studies in the History and Historiography of Ideas* (Bloomington: Indiana University Press, 1985), 56–73, and his *Postethnic America: Beyond Multiculturalism* (New York: Basic, 1995). Jon Cruz contends that U.S. society "has always been 'multicultural,' but only recently has this been recognized and *named* as such in the context of the modern state's attempt to work with a politically pragmatic blend of cultural benevolence and statecraft to reconfigure its own legitimacy" ("From Farce to Tragedy," 28). But Adamic's *Common Ground* helped establish a national organization called the Common Council in the 1940s. See Louis Adamic, "This Crisis is an Opportunity," *Common Ground* (autumn 1940): 62–73. Its aim included: "A further revision of American history textbooks to give adequate recognition and space to the newer strains in our population" (71); "An ethnic encyclopedia or handbook of the American people" (71); an "information service" and "speakers' bureau" (70); efforts to use films, radio, magazines, newspapers, and foreign language presses to celebrate diversity (70). The Common Council also sought to aid in the formation of smaller local ethnic organizations "at whose meetings the cultural-racial situation in the U.S. is discussed, along with economic and political problems, critically but on a basis of acceptance" (71). Such "do-groups" would focus on matters of "discrimination and 'tolerance' toward the new-immigrant and Negro groups" (72).

72. A conceptual term, which I do not use here but which has influenced my thinking, is one devised by Michel Foucault: *governmentality.* Foucault conceptualizes governmentality as the "contact between the technologies of domination and those of the self." These cultural and institutional technologies attempt to govern "how an individual acts upon himself"—how he or she imagines, monitors, motivates, and individualizes himself or herself (Foucault, "Technologies of the Self," in *Technologies of the Self: A Seminar with Michel Foucault*, ed. Luther H. Martin, Huck Gutman, Patrick H. Hutton [Amherst: University of Massachusetts Press, 1988], 16–49, see 19.) Foucault understands the history of governmentality as a phase—beginning with the rise of the "Administrative State" in the fifteenth century—within the complex administrative history of subjectivity formation. His study of treatises on the pastoral "art of government" that emerged in the sixteenth to eighteenth centuries—which posited tactical interfaces among the government of the state, of the family, and of selfhood—sparked Foucault's

curiosity about the more modern expansion of state apparatuses and interventions geared to manage the political economy, the populations (in their "depths and details"), and the selves that would staff society and the economy. This modern "era of governmentality" features the governmentalized state and governmentalized "individuals" (Foucault, "Governmentality," *Ideology of Consciousness* 6 [autumn 1979]: 5–21. Also see *The Foucault Effect: Studies in Governmentality*, ed. Graham Burchell, Colin Gordon, and Peter Miller [Chicago: University of Chicago Press, 1991]). No other group in America has been so blatantly and continuously governmentalized as "Indians." If "Indian" reservations were often brutal experiments in governmentalizing populations, schools like Carlisle were somewhat more subtle institutional and cultural experiments in population formation and administration. Carlisle, as a government school, conspicuously governmentalized subjectivity in the form of "individuality." And the Indian New Deal—in the process of jettisoning many of Carlisle's monocultural premises and instituting the government's so-called self-government of "Indians"—governmentalized protomulticultural "individuality." The Bureau of Indian Affairs, in both phases, governmentalized "individuality," workers, and race. For some illuminating comments on the state's production and regulation of racialized identities and Carlisle, see Bell, "Telling Stories," especially 3–50.

73. In *British Cultural Studies: An Introduction*, Graeme Turner argues, "Hegemony is not maintained through the obliteration of the opposition but through the *articulation* of opposing interests into the political affiliations of the hegemonic group" (New York: Routledge, 1992, 212). Williams stresses, however, that new oppositional ideas and movements, even if "affected by hegemonic limits and pressures," can make "significant breaks" with the hegemony and reform it (*Marxism and Literature* [New York: Oxford University Press, 1977], 113–14, see 114). Also see Alan Trachtenberg's classic, *The Incorporation of America: Culture and Society in the Gilded Age* (New York: Hill and Wang, 1982).

1 Carlisle as Individualizing Factory

1. James Welch, *Fools Crow* (New York: Penguin, 1986), 180. N. Scott Momaday, *House Made of Dawn* (New York: Harper and Row, 1968), 102. Louise Erdrich, *Love Medicine* (New York: Bantam, 1989 [1984]), 252, 253.

2. Krupat too sees that "this is part of the Native American holocaust." Yet he also acknowledges that "some who went to the schools . . . felt they had learned things useful for themselves and for their people" (*The Turn to the Native: Studies in Criticism and Culture*, [Lincoln: University of Nebraska Press, 1996], 96). Similarly, Weaver cites stories of students having been "beaten or having [had] their mouths washed out with yellow cake soap for talking in their own tongues." But he also points out that boarding school was where some students learned other Native languages from their peers (indeed, sometimes they learned their own there) (*People*, 13, 13–14). Weaver also quotes Gerald Vizenor on the political and cultural significance that the learning of English—in schools—has had in the establishment of Native unity (15). See Leslie Marmon Silko on her relatives who attended Carlisle (3, 16) and her story about a Native girl's experiences in a government school (19) in *Storyteller* (New York: Arcade, 1981). On Natives, genocide, and cultural genocide, see David E. Stannard, *American Holocaust: Columbus and the Conquest of the New World* (New York: Oxford University Press, 1992), and Ward Churchill, *A Little Matter of Genocide: Holocaust and Denial in the Americas, 1492 to the Present* (San Francisco: City Lights, 1997).

3. Linda Hogan, *Mean Spirit: A Novel* (New York: Atheneum, 1990), 148. Another character, Ben, "had dreamed of the walls of Haskell [Institute] where he had gone crazy and removed his clothing and run away naked" (250).

4. Berenice Levchuk, "Leaving Home for Carlisle Indian School," in *Reinventing the Enemy's Language: Contemporary Native Women's Writings of North America*, ed. Joy Harjo (Creek) and Gloria Bird (Spokane), with Patricia Blanco, Beth Cuthand (Cree), and Valerie Martinez (New York: Norton, 1997), 175–86, see 179, 185.

5. Carlisle did in fact bear some resemblance to reform schools for juvenile delinquents. Donal F. Lindsey writes about the following response to Hampton Institute, which in 1878 began admitting Natives (in addition to African Americans): "John W. Cromwell, the militant editor of the Virginia Star, charged Armstrong with attempting to turn the institution into a reform school for Indian criminals" (*Indians at Hampton Institute, 1877–1923* [Urbana: University of Illinois Press, 1995], 32). Cromwell was referring to some of the Fort Marion prisoners whom Pratt got admitted to Hampton under his supervision. Also see Joseph Willard Tingey, "Indians and Blacks Together: An Experiment in Biracial Education at Hampton Institute," D. Ed. diss., Teachers College, Columbia University, 1978. On reform schools consult Anthony M. Platt, *The Child Savers: The Inventions of Delinquency* (Chicago: University of Chicago Press, 1977 [1969]).

6. Elaine Goodale Eastman, *Pratt: The Red Man's Moses* (Norman: University of Oklahoma Press, 1935), 8.

7. See Petersen, *Plains Indian Art from Fort Marion*, x (on the term *Florida boys*). Petersen's book contextualizes and reassesses the prisoners' plains drawings and offers biographies of eight of the artists. Some of these drawings were published, purchased, and exhibited in museums. About Pratt's use of the prisoners' drawings for "public relations," Petersen writes: "He sent a collection of drawings to the United States National Museum . . . and others to ranking army officers to demonstrate the industry of his men" (69). Petersen also discusses published reviews of the artists' work (71).

8. Robert Perkinson, " 'Within San Marco's Gloomy Walls': Performance and Cultural Exchange around the Indian Prison at Fort Marion, 1875–1878," unpublished manuscript (Yale University, June 1996), 12, 4, 9, 16, 15. In 1876 Pratt charged "50 cents for reserved seats; 25 for ramparts," and in one instance charged $1.00 for entrance to a fundraiser (36, 37).

9. K. Tsianina Lomawaima's study of Chilocco affirms that "no institution is total, no power is all-seeing, no federal Indian policy has ever been efficiently and rationally translated into practice, and much of the time produced unpredicted results anyway." She emphasizes that "Indian people at boarding school were not passive consumers of an ideology or lifestyle imparted from above by federal administrators" (*Prairie Light*, 164, 167).

10. Quoted in Curtis M. Hinsley, "Zunis and Brahmins: Cultural Ambivalence in the Gilded Age," in *Romantic Motives: Essays on Anthropological Sensibility*, ed. George W. Stocking Jr. (Madison: University of Wisconsin Press, 1989), 169–207, see 190.

11. Mark Twain, *A Connecticut Yankee in King Arthur's Court* (New York: Penguin, 1987 [1889]), 138, 189.

12. Coleman, *American Indian Children*.

13. Elaine G. Eastman, *Pratt*, 13–14.

14. He requested that his prisoners' families be permitted to accompany them, but his plea was denied. Later in life he acknowledged that his prisoners "were not tried" (Goodale Eastman, *Pratt*, 51). "The Constitution of the U.S. which provides that no man 'shall be

deprived of life, liberty and property without due process of law' was not observed in their case" (quoted in Lindsey, *Hampton*, 28). Actually, it was he who was commanded to draw up the list of those who would be incarcerated (the list was to include some whose attitude alone was resistant) (Perkinson, "San Marco's," 6).

15. On Stowe and the senator, see Lindsey, *Hampton*, 30, 28.

16. Perkinson, "San Marco's," 41, 42.

17. Lindsey, *Hampton*, 30.

18. Booker T. Washington, *Up From Slavery* (New York: Lancer, 1968 [1901]), 78, 24, 102. Lindsey writes: "*Up From Slavery* was read in many Indian schools and part of it was even translated into Lakota, in Santee Indian School's *Iapi Oaye*. Moreover, returned students at Lower Brule patterned an Indian Business League on the Tuskegeean's National Negro Business League" (*Hampton*, 269).

19. Lindsey, *Hampton*, 270.

20. Ibid., 180, 182. Lomawaima notes that Pratt "wanted no part of Armstrong's racial education" (*Prairie Light*, 4).

21. Pratt, from "Official Report," in *Americanizing*, ed. Prucha, 263.

22. Lindsey, *Hampton*, 181, 182, 176, 177.

23. Pratt suggested that Armstrong only grew interested in the "Indian" project when "he found the distinction of the people who were willing to pay for this education" (quoted in Lindsey, *Hampton*, 29). Yet Pratt too enjoyed showing off his individualized and Americanized "Indians" to rich people and supplicating them for funds.

24. See Lindsey, *Hampton*, 34, 30.

25. Coleman, *American Indian Children*, 38. The BIA, Coleman writes, only invested in the Indian education business when Congress allocated it $20,000 to do so in 1870, a figure that increased to "$3 million by 1900" (41). On the founding of Indian schools in the era, see Francis Paul Prucha, *American Indian Policy in Crisis: Christian Reformers and the Indian, 1865–1900* (Norman: University of Oklahoma Press, 1976), 265–91.

26. Coleman writes: "In 1893 Congress authorized the Secretary of the Interior to withhold rations and other annuities from parents and guardians who refused to send their children to school—but the next year partly backtracked and forbade the sending of children to off-reservation schools without parental or kin consent. Congress continued to pass laws of compulsion, and authorities on a number of reservations coerced children into school" (*American Indian Children*, 45). Fred Kabotie describes how Hopi tribal police were enlisted to force children to attend school in the early decades of the twentieth century. His uncle, deemed a "troublemaker," was exiled to Carlisle (Fred Kabotie with Bill Belknap, *Fred Kabotie: Hopi Indian Artist* [Flagstaff: Museum of Northern Arizona with Northland Press, 1977], 6). Pratt forced Jason Betzinez (Apache), at age twenty-seven, and other Apache prisoners to attend Carlisle. See Jason Betzinez with Wilber Sturtevant Nye, *I Fought with Geronimo* (Harrisburg, Pa.: Stackpole, 1959), 149.

27. See Elaine G. Eastman, *Pratt*. "Two boys . . . actually concealed themselves on the Missouri River boat as stowaways, and, when discovered, were not rejected" (80). She notes: "By the close of the first year, Carlisle had assembled nearly two hundred students from fifteen different tribes" (83). Yet she also acknowledges Carlisle's dismal graduation record (215). The average age of students was fifteen years (216). Clearly, Pratt wanted graduates—who had remained at Carlisle for five years—to return to their reservations as young and strong adolescent carriers of Carlisle ideology.

28. Coleman, *American Indian Children*, 43.

29. Twain, *Connecticut Yankee*, 161. Frederick Winslow Taylor, *The Principles of Scientific*

Management (New York: Norton, 1967 [1911]), 6, 73. See Twain's 1894 classic, *Pudd'n-head Wilson* (New York: Bantam, 1981), 26: *Puddn'head Wilson's Calendar* reads: "Training is everything. The peach was once a bitter almond; cauliflower is nothing but cabbage with a college education."

30. Pratt, "The Indian No Problem," *RMH* 5 (June 24 and July 1, 1904): 7–8, see 8.

31. "A Boy Like a Piece of Iron," *IH* 1 (March 26, 1886): n.p.

32. "Capt. Pratt Offered a Place," *IH* 7 (March 25, 1892): n.p.

33. "Twenty-Second Anniversary of the Arrival of Indian Students at Carlisle," *RMII* 2 (October 18, 1901): n.p.

34. Pratt, "Indian No Problem," 8.

35. General Armstrong came up with the theatrical idea to take and disseminate before-and-after photographs (see Lindsey, *Hampton*, 35).

36. The group photograph is shown in the film *In The White Man's Image*. On Yellow Robe's childhood, see Rosebud Yellow Robe, *Tonewaya and the Eagles and Other Lakota Indian Tales* (New York: Dial, 1979).

37. Pratt, "Official Report," in *Americanizing*, 261. In the mid-nineteenth century, Philip Schaff, a Swiss immigrant, had used death imagery to characterize the distinctiveness of American assimilation. He envisioned America enthusiastically as *"the grave of all European nationalities*; but a *Phenix grave*, from which they shall rise to a new life and new activity" (quoted in Arieli, *Individualism and Nationalism*, 255).

38. ["Written by one of our girls. . . . A Seneca Indian Student"], "The Senecas Past and Present," *IH* 6 (August 14, 1891): n.p.

39. Standing Bear, *Land*, 234. Also see Bell, "Telling Stories," 386–89.

40. "The Indian and How We Must Kill Him," *IH* 7 (April 8, 1892): n.p.

41. "From the Beginning," *RM* 15 (February and March 1899): 8–12, see 10.

42. Betzinez (with Wilbur Sturtevant Nye) asserts, "Pratt believed that discipline, kindness, and religion were the three foremost elements in rehabilitating these primitive children" (*I Fought with Geronimo*, 150).

43. Morgan, "A Plea for the Papoose: An Address at Albany," in *Americanizing*, ed. Prucha, 239–51, see 249.

44. *RM* 9 (February 1889): 4.

45. Dawes, from "Fifteenth Annual Report of the Board of Indian Commissioners," in *Americanizing*, ed. Prucha, 27–30, see 29. Elaine G. Eastman describes New York State's Six Nations as "an undigested mass" (*Pratt*, 143). Senator Q. C. Lamar of Mississippi compared the digestion of immigrants and African Americans to that of "Indians": "swallowing a camel and straining at a gnat" (quoted in Lindsey, *Hampton*, 40).

46. Lindsey writes: "Pratt could have been inspired by the similar practice of hiring out Indians on reservations. He had in fact found employment among whites for his St. Augustine prisoners in Florida, and a few of these Indians went to live with northern families while others were attending Hampton. The captain himself claimed the black experience of slavery as his model" (*Hampton*, 37). There was some dispute over whether Pratt or Hampton's superintendent Armstrong originated the concept. Lindsey concludes that it was probably Pratt's idea (36–38), but, as indicated above, he notes that the hiring out concept was not novel. Also consult Bell, "Telling Stories," 165–208.

47. Betzinez (with Wilbur Sturtevant Nye) complained, "After three long summers spent on a farm I realized that my education as well as my efforts to learn English were being retarded by being absent so long from school" (*I Fought with Geronimo*, 157).

48. Adams, *Extinction*, 157.

49. Richard Henry Pratt, *Battlefield and Classroom: Four Decades with the American Indian, 1867–1904*, ed. Robert M. Utley (New Haven, Conn.: Yale University Press, 1964), 312.

50. Pratt, "Official Report," in *Americanizing*, ed. Prucha, 268.

51. For example, see an anonymous, untitled article in *RM* 8 (May 1888): 4: "Telling the Indian in their homes what civilization is, is one thing. Taking them from their homes to civilization and soaking them with it is another, and the fruits of the processes are not to be compared with each other." On the absorption theme, see "Senator Teller's Views on the Sioux Bill as Recently Expressed in Congress," *MS* 6 (February 1886): 2: "Absorb the Indians into the body politic—to this end we must make haste shortly."

52. See William Cronon, *Changes in the Land: Indians, Colonists, and the Ecology of New England* (New York: Hill and Wang, 1983), especially his concluding chapter "That Wilderness Should Turn a Mart," 159–70.

53. Robert Utley writes of the Sioux and economic changes in the early nineteenth century, "Traders had become a necessary evil. The Indians had grown to depend on the goods they supplied, especially firearms and ammunition and metal tools, containers, and utensils. Life without them would be much more onerous, even fatal when confronting enemies equipped by firearms" (*The Lance and the Shield: The Life and Times of Sitting Bull*, [New York: Henry Holt, 1993], 39). Also see Frederick E. Hoxie, *Parading Through History: The Making of the Crow Nation in America, 1805–1935* (New York: Cambridge University Press, 1995), 26, 65, 78.

54. Theodore Dreiser, *Sister Carrie* (New York: New American Library, 1961 [1900]), 20–21.

55. Standing Bear, *Land*, 234–35.

56. Quoted in Utley, *Lance*, 190.

57. Harry Raven, "Speech By Harry Raven, Arapahoe, Entirely His Own," *SN* 3 (April 1883): n.p.

58. See *RM* 8 (May 1888): 4.

59. Quoted in Pratt, *Battlefield and Classroom*, 297.

60. *IH* 7 (October 2, 1891): n.p.

61. "Senecas Past and Present," n.p.

62. "The Earth How She Goes," *SN* 3 (April 1883): n.p.

63. Ralph I. E. Feather, "Dear Father," *EKT* 2 (February 1882): 6.

64. "Nellie Cary's Story," *MS* 2 (June 1882): n.p.

65. "The Prize Story," *IH* 2 (September 3, 1886): n.p.

66. Sam Townsend, "Do the Indians Want to Learn to Take Care of Themselves?" *SN* 1 (April 1881): n.p.

67. Elaine Goodale Eastman, "A Primitive Type of Womanhood," *RMH* 2 (December 6, 1901): n.p. Goodale Eastman edited the *Red Man and Helper* while her husband worked for the school as outing and recruiting agent in 1899–1900 (Raymond Wilson, *Ohiyesa: Charles Eastman, Santee Sioux* [Urbana: University of Illinois Press, 1983], 106).

68. Merrill E. Gates, "Proceedings of the Fourteenth Annual Meeting of the Lake Mohonk Conference of Friends of the Indian," in *Americanizing*, ed. Prucha, 331–44, see 336, 335.

69. Dawes, "Fifteenth," in *Americanizing*, ed. Prucha, 29–30.

70. See Berkhofer, *Salvation and the Savage*, 70–71. On Native agriculture Takaki notes that in 1616 "Captain John Smith sailed north from Virginia to explore the New England coast; again he found not wild men but farmers. The 'paradise' of Massachusetts, he reported, was 'all planted with corn, groves, mulberries, savage gardens.' 'The sea Coast

as you pass shews you all along large Corne fields.' Indeed, while the Abenakis of Maine were mainly hunters and food gatherers dependent on the natural abundance of the land, the tribes in southern New England were horticultural" ("*The Tempest* in the Wilderness," 904).

71. "Even now they are meateaters," Momaday observes of the Kiowas, in *The Way to Rainy Mountain.* "I think it is not in them to be farmers. . . . With the horse [the Kiowa] was transformed into the daring buffalo hunter, able to procure in a single day enough food to supply his family for a year, leaving him to sweep the plains with his war parties along a range of a thousand miles" (New York: Ballantine, 1970 [1969], 31, 82). The forced shift from hunting to farming that many tribes negotiated is a theme that has been taken up by many Native writers, from Christine Quintasket's early-twentieth-century *Mourning Dove: A Salishan Autobiography*, ed. Jay Miller (Lincoln: University of Nebraska Press, 1990), 3, 155, to Erdrich, *Love Medicine*, 11.

72. Carl Shurz, "Present Aspects of the Indian Problem," in *Americanizing*, ed. Prucha, 13–26, see 15. Charles Eastman observed that in order to enforce reservation administration and allotment, Natives' "food supply had to be ruthlessly cut off, and the buffalo were of necessity sacrificed" (*The Indian To-day: The Past and Future of the First American* [Garden City, N.Y.: Doubleday, Page, 1915], 63).

73. Morgan, "Plea for the Papoose," in *Americanizing*, ed. Prucha, 249. Disheartened by John Collier's New Deal efforts to regain land for Natives lost during the allotment era, Elaine G. Eastman, a diehard assimilationist, recycled the old disingenuous alibi for land theft: "Many tribes in their natural state made no use of the land except to hunt over it" (*Pratt*, 228). But she also quoted the missionary Fred B. Riggs on the disastrous effects that allotment and attempted farming had on the Sioux (tragically clear by 1935): " 'The much-lauded "Dawes Act" was a great blunder. Most of the land of the Sioux reservations is not fit for farms made in that way. The land as a whole not in separate parcels, is fit for cattle-raising' " (187). Of Dawes's own eventual criticism of allotment she writes, "The land, he felt, was too often '160 acres tied around an Indian's neck' " (237). Pratt objected: " 'I urged [Dawes] to make every subdivision of 160 acres a checkerboard, alternating the divisions in red and white, and having the Indians allotted the red divisions and the whites the white divisions. I have always believed that the Indian bureau killed this idea by claiming that the best lands could not under my plan be allotted to the Indians, and this enabled them to continue the old tribal system of segregation" (267).

74. Rosa Bourassa (Chippewa) argued for this position in a debate. "The Dawes Bill Discussed By Our Pupils: 'Resolved that the Signing of the Dawes Bill, February 8th, 1887, was the Emancipation of the Indians,' " *RM* 10 (March 1890): 7–8, see 7.

75. Lewis Merrill, "Is the Indian Doomed?" *RM* 11 (August 1892): 4.

76. "In the Indian Schools," one Carlisle article confirmed, "there is no more important task than the education of pupils to an understanding of the value and care of property." "The Sense of Ownership," *RMH* 1 (April 12, 1901), n.p.

77. Richard Henry Pratt, "The Indian Industrial School, Carlisle, Pa.," *Red Man Supplement* (December 1893): 1–5, see 5.

78. Armstrong, "Hampton Institute, VA.," *MS* 5 (June 1885): 7.

79. *RM* 9 (March 1889): 3. Reflecting on scholarship that studies Native land use in the early colonial period, Carey McWilliams suggests in *Brothers Under the Skin* (Boston: Little, Brown, 1943) that "although not 1 per cent of the immense area of agriculturally valuable topsoil, the virgin timber, and the mineral resources of the land was used intensively by

the indigenous Indian population. . . . from the Indian's point of view, however, the native population was making full use of its environment. Within the limitations of native technology, there was literally no room for additional people on the continent" (50–51).

80. See Salisbury, "American Indians and American History," in *American Indian*, ed. Martin, 53. Also consult John Mack Faragher's penetrating study, *Sugar Creek: Life on the Illinois Prairie* (New Haven, Conn.: Yale University Press, 1986), especially 10–36.

81. Letter from E. A. Hayt to Secretary of the Interior Shurz, in *Americanizing*, ed. Prucha, 79–82, see 80. Charles C. Painter, "Our Indian Policy as Related to the Civilization of the Indian," in *Americanizing*, ed. Prucha, 66–73, see 69.

82. Elaine G. Eastman, *Pratt*, 27. In 1871 General Francis Walker, then BIA commissioner, asserted, "When dealing with savage men as with savage beasts, no question of national honor can arise. Whether to fight, to employ a ruse, or to run away, is solely a question of expediency" (quoted in Collier, "United States Indian," in *Understanding Minority Groups*, ed. Gittler, 40).

83. "What Is Your Choice?" *IH* 2 (November 19, 1886): n.p.

84. Philip C. Garrett, "Indian Citizenship," in *Americanizing*, ed. Prucha, 57–65, see 63. On citizenizing strategies, see Prucha, *American Indian Policy*, 292–327.

85. "Recent Comments on Indian Matters: From Our Leading Papers," *RM* 9 (March 1889): 3, 6, see 3. In 1900 students pondered another reprint that criticized America for not nearly living up to the Christian connotations of the word *civilized*: "Civilization is a very elastic word, and we stretch it, or contract it, to mean almost anything we wish for the moment to put upon it" ("Civilization in the Making," *RMH* 1 [December 7, 1900]: n.p.). In contemplating U.S. attempts in the twentieth century to sever political connections with Natives, Deloria and Lytle point out that the government employed "citizenship as its excuse" (*Nations Within*, 4).

86. *MS* 5 (April 1885): 4.

87. "The Way to Civilize," *MS* 7 (1886): 2–3, see 2.

88. Pratt, "Indian No Problem," 8.

89. "The Wild Indian as Model," *MS* 7 (July 1887): 4. For brief biographical background on McGlynn, see *Dictionary of American Biography*, vol. 4 (New York: Scribner's, 1933), 53–54; *New Catholic Encyclopedia*, vol. 10 (New York: McGraw-Hill, 1967), 18–19; Charles Albro Barker, *Henry George* (New York: Oxford University Press, 1955), 483, 491–93, 513–14, 588–89, and on his vicissitudes as a political priest, see 464–65, 486–87, 489, 576.

90. Pratt, "Proceedings of the Ninth Annual Meeting of the Lake Mohonk Conference of Friends of the Indian," in *Americanizing*, ed. Prucha, 272–76, see 276.

91. Charles Kihega, "What Indians Must Have," *SN* 3 (February 1883): n.p.

92. "When We Came," *IH* 1 (October 7, 1885): n.p.

93. "The Way the Sioux City Journal Talks About the Indian Land Question," *IH* 1 (June 18, 1886): n.p.

94. *RM* 12 (December 1893): 1.

95. Kihega, n.t., *SN* 2 (May 1882): n.p.

96. "Can An Indian Stick to Business?" *IH* 5 (July 11, 1890): n.p.

97. "What Benjamin Franklin Did, and Indian Boy May Do," *IH* 2 (September 24, 1886): n.p.

98. *IH* 1 (June 4, 1886): n.p.

99. On Depew: "Let The Indians 'Tussle'!" *IH* 6 (April 17, 1891): n.p. On Vanderbilt: "What Cornelius Vanderbilt Has Done An Indian Boy Can Do," *IH* 2 (September 24, 1886): n.p.

On Geronimo: *IH* 2 (September 24, 1886): n.p. On stealing time: *IH* 7 (September 18, 1891): n.p. The ideology of "character" as capital, popularized in countless success manuals from 1870 to 1910, recycled preindustrial ideologies of thrift (from Cotton Mather, Benjamin Franklin, Thomas Jefferson) to take the sting out of the increasingly unequal class, racial, and gender distribution of capital and, even more boldly, to recast economic disadvantage and adversity as providential conditions for the self-production and accumulation of the most valuable capital—that of "character" (Hilkey, *Character Is Capital*, 140–41; also see 128–33, 137, 167).

100. "An Indian Woman Doctor," *IH* 1 (June 4, 1886): n.p.

101. "News Items Written By Members of the Junior Class," *RMH* 2 (October 4, 1901): n.p.

102. "Who Will Go to Oxford?" *RMH* 2 (April 11, 1902): n.p.

103. *IH* 1 (August 7, 1885): n.p.

104. *IH* 1 (December 11, 1885): n.p. Silko thematizes Euramerican constructions of Native self-blame (experienced by Pueblo World War II veterans): "They blamed themselves for losing the new feeling [of belonging to America as soldiers]; they never talked about it, but they blamed themselves just like they blamed themselves for losing the land the white people took. They never thought to blame white people for any of it; they wanted white people to be their friends." She also writes, "At home the people would blame the liquor, the army, and the war, but the blame on the whites would never match the vehemence the people would keep in their own bellies, reserving the greatest bitterness and blame for themselves" (*Ceremony*, 43, 253).

105. Washington, *Up From Slavery*, 46, 67.

106. "A Worthy Example," *IH* 5 (January 17, 1890): n.p.

107. "An Indian Boy of Spirit," *IBGF* 1 (July 31, 1885): n.p.

108. See Hoxie's discussion of the economic fate of the Crows in the early twentieth century in *Parading*, 273, 294, 305, 323–24, 366, 367.

109. La Flesche to Pratt, April 10, 1921, RHPP.

110. Pratt, "Official Report," in *Americanizing*, ed. Prucha, 269; Painter, "Our Indian Policy," in *Americanizing*, ed. Prucha, 73.

111. "The Farewell Meeting," *IH* 5 (August 1, 1890): n.p.

112. "Tents vs. Houses," *EKT* 1 (May 1880): n.p.

113. See Adams's discussion of what some returning students encountered, *Extinction*, 300–305.

114. Dennison Wheelock, "Is It Right for the Government to Stop the Teaching of Indian Languages in Reservation Schools," *IH* 3 (November 18, 1897): n.p.

115. The first author is Dessie Prescott; she writes to Uncle Willie. "Extracts from Home Letters," *MS* 2 (June 1882): n.p.

116. "How to Break Up the Medicine Dance," *MS* 7 (October 1886): n.p. "The Indians Are Beginning to Lose Faith in the Medicine Dance," *IH* 1 (July 20, 1886): n.p. "Medicine Dance," *IH* 1 (October 11, 1885): n.p. On medicine men as hinderances: "How Five Medicine Men Cured a Baby," *IH* 6 (July 10, 1891): n.p.

117. "A Big Job On Hand," *MS* 2 (May 1882): n.p.

118. Stephen R. Riggs as quoted (1894) in Berkhofer, *Salvation and the Savage*, 77. On treaty money see Coleman, *American Indian Children*, 39.

119. "When We Came," *IH* 1 (October 7, 1885): n.p.

120. "An Indian Boy of Spirit," n.p. One of Hank Morgan's great triumphs in sixth-century Britain, Twain indicates in *Connecticut Yankee*, was to manufacture and advertise soap (of course, it had to have a brand name, Persimmon's), because his commercial

"civilisation" could then be symbolized by "clean" bodies (the linkage of American capitalism with cleanliness). Commissioner Thomas Jefferson Morgan, whose thinking was clearly a product of this colonizing ideology, imagined "personal purity" as a basis of "social purity" and condemned tribal culture for "rejoic[ing] in the unclean" ("Plea for the Papoose," in *Americanizing*, ed. Prucha, 243).

121. Given to Pratt, January 4, 1888, RHPP.

122. Given to Pratt, June 24, 1904, RHPP.

123. "The Indians at Home," *IH* 3 (August 26, 1887): n.p. Also see the "Home Difficulties of a Young Indian Girl" series in *IH* September–December 1889, which forms the basis for Marianna Burgess's *Stiya, A Carlisle Indian Girl at Home.*

124. Ione L. Jones, "Home," *IH* 7 (March 4, 1892): n.p.

125. Dawes, "The Land in Severalty Bill Made Easy to Understand," *IH* 2 (May 6, 1887): n.p.

126. "Tents vs. Houses," n.p.

127. This Americanized response to camping is the inverse of what Walter Benn Michaels sees in Oliver La Farge's *Laughing Boy*, when Slim Girl, a Navajo, wants to go camping because Navajos encode camping as distinctively Navajo: "What this involves is the representation of your culture not as the things you love to do but as the things you love to do because they are your culture" (*Our America: Nativism, Modernism, and Pluralism* [Durham, N.C.: Duke University Press, 1995], 120). Of course, when one is faced with multiple or competing encodings of what one's *own* culture is supposed to be, one can more easily identify these constructions of one's culture as constructions, think critically about them as constructions produced by structures of power, and hence choose to adopt one of these constructions, a blend of these constructions, a revision of these constructions, or an identity that departs from—even as it is a response to—these constructions. Neither the Carlisle anecdote nor Michaels's interesting formulation represents how complex "your" identifications with what social forces try to define as "your culture" can be.

128. Berkhofer, *Salvation and the Savage*, 12.

129. Ibid., 70–71.

130. Lewis Henry Morgan, *Ancient Society, Or Researches in the Lines of Human Progress from Savagery Through Barbarism to Civilization*, ed. Eleanor Burke Leacock (Gloucester, Mass.: Peter Smith, 1974); henceforth all quotations from this book will be followed by page numbers in parenthesis in the text.

131. This emphasis on the educative incentive-building effects of property acquisition had some ideological roots in Protestant social logic. Praising the "love of property," the preacher, Yale College president, and grandson of Jonathan Edwards. Timothy Dwight, wrote: "The secure possession of property demands, every moment, the hedge of law; and reconciles a man, originally lawless, to the restraints of government. Thus situated, he sees that reputation, also, is within his reach. Ambition forces him to aim at it; and compels him to a life of sobriety and decency" (Dwight's *Travels in New England and New York, 1769–1815* is quoted in Arieli, *Individualism and Nationalism*, 252). For two classic socialist critiques of the historical roles that property has played in the production of consciousness and values—critiques influenced by the theorizing of Morgan and Karl Marx—see Friedrich Engels, *The Origin of the Family, Private Property, and The State: In Connection with the Researches of Lewis H. Morgan* (Peking: Foreign Languages Press, 1978 [1884]), and Paul Lafargue, *The Evolution of Property from Savagery to Civilization* (London: Swan Sonnenschein, 1890).

132. Gates, "Proceedings," in *Americanizing*, ed. Prucha, 343.

133. Schurz, "Present Aspects," in *Americanizing*, ed. Prucha, see 20.

134. Gates, "Land and Law as Agents in Educating Indians," in *Americanizing*, ed. Prucha, 45–56, see 51, 52.

135. Morgan, Report of October 1, 1889, in *Americanizing*, ed. Prucha, 74–76, see 75.

136. Gates, "Land and Law," in *Americanizing*, ed. Prucha, 50–51.

137. *IH* 1 (August 21, 1885): n.p. For insight into Theodore Roosevelt's use of masculinity to buttress his racializing of Natives, see Gail Bederman, *Manliness and Civilization: A Cultural History of Gender and Race in the United States, 1880–1917* (Chicago: University of Chicago Press, 1995), 181–83.

138. Pratt, "Official Report," in *Americanizing*, ed. Prucha, 261.

139. "Nowhere," wrote Charles Painter, "does the idea of the manhood of the Indian find place" ("Our Indian Policy as Related to the Civilization of the Indian," in *Americanizing*, ed. Prucha, 66–73, see 68).

140. "Neatness in Girls," *IH* 1 (January 8, 1886): n.p.

141. "The Sociable," *IH* 1 (January 8, 1886): n.p.

142. *IH* 7 (September 18, 1891): n.p.

143. A note that Embe is Marianna Burgess is inscribed in the Yale Sterling Memorial Library volume I perused. Barbara Landis, Indian School Research Specialist of the Cumberland Historical Society, has confirmed the link.

144. *IH* 6 (April 17, 1891): n.p.

145. The Pueblos' peaceful tribal ways were much publicized in the 1880s and commodified by the early-twentieth-century tourist industry. However, some students who returned to and rejected the Pueblos did in fact undergo severe public punishments (Adam notes this about the Pueblos in *Extinction*, 279). Stiya's anxieties about returning to her reservation resemble those of Polingaysi Qoyawayama (Hopi) of Sherman Institute and Annie Bender (Ojibway) of Lincoln Institute and then Hampton Institute. Irene Stewart (Navajo) explained that "having gotten used to living where there are hygenic facilities, it is very hard to live again in the old hogan." Helen Sekaquaptewa (Hopi) admitted, "I didn't feel at ease in the home of my parents now." Some students even "resisted kin demands to return to the people, and fled to a new school" (Coleman, *American Indian Children*, 158, 159, 179, 179, 61).

146. "How an Indian Girl Might Tell Her Own Story If She Had the Chance," *IH* 5 (September 20, 1889): n.p.

147. Ibid.

148. "How an Indian Girl," *IH* 5 (November 29, 1889): n.p.

149. [Burgess], *Stiya: A Carlisle Indian Girl at Home* (Cambridge, Mass.: Riverside Press, 1891), 89–90, 112.

150. Frances Sparhawk, *A Chronicle of Conquest* (Boston: D. Lothrop, 1890); henceforth all quotations from this book will be followed by page numbers in parenthesis in the text.

151. Sparhawk to Pratt, March 7, 1919, RHPP.

152. "What Michael Burns, An Apache Boy Thinks of the Indian Question," *SN* 1 (April 1881): n.p. Such views long predated the anthropological theory of Lewis Henry Morgan. Takaki, summarizing general trends, has compared the early-seventeenth-century ideological orientation present in colonial Virginia and also in colonial Ireland—that "savagery" is cultural and can be changed through education—to that prevalent in colonial New England—that "savagery" is racially inborn ("*The Tempest* in the Wilderness," see 904–12). "This social construction of race [in New England] occurred within the economic context of competition over land. The colonists argued that only those

who used the land were entitled to it. Native men, they claimed, pursued 'no kind of labour but hunting, fishing, and fowling.' Indians were not producers" (907). Carlisle linked elements of the early Virginia assumptions about the educability of "savages" to the producer ethos.

153. "From the Beginning," *RM* 15 (February–March 1899): 10.

154. *RM* 15 (December 1899): 1 and "Individuality Not Color," *RMH* 5 (May 20, 1904): n.p. For a far more politically and theoretically sophisticated version of this basic approach, see Paul Gilroy, *Against Race: Imagining Political Culture beyond the Color Line* (Cambridge, Mass.: Harvard University Press, 2000): "Until the color of skin has no more significance than the color of eyes, there *will* be war" (254).

155. *RM* 15 (December 1899): 1.

156. Douglass to Pratt, April 1, 1893, RHPP. Douglass intended to deliver his address on April 6, 1893. Mrs. Helen Douglass, his spouse, was invited to some of Carlisle's commencements after Douglass's death and had fond memories of "Mr. Douglass's pilgrimage to Carlisle and the beautiful and generous hospitality we there enjoyed." Her written opinion of Pratt was glowing: "How good a thing Captain Pratt that you were born and have come in time to help save a remnant of these people—our brothers and sisters—to themselves and to the world. May you and Carlisle live forever" (Mrs. Douglass to Pratt, February 2, 1899, RHPP).

157. "Do External Influences Make the Man?" *RM* 13 (February 1896): 3–6, see 4. On nineteenth-century popular discourses of self-making and success, see Hilkey, *Character as Capital*; John G. Cawelti, *Apostles of the Self-Made Man* (Chicago: University of Chicago Press, 1968); David Brion Davis, "Stress-Seeking and the Self-Made Man in American Literature, 1894–1914," in David Brion Davis, *From Homicide to Slavery: Studies in American Culture* (New York: Oxford University Press, 1986), 52–72; Irvin G. Wylie, *The Self-Made Man in America: The Myth of Rags to Riches* (New York: Free Press, 1954). For sophisticated anthropological approaches to self-making discourses, see Deborah Battaglia, ed., *Rhetorics of Self-Making* (Berkeley: University of California Press, 1995).

158. Quoted in Coleman, *American Indian Children*, 42.

159. On parallels between the colonization of Natives and the Irish, see Takaki, "*The Tempest* in the Wilderness." Some connections: "Initially, 'savagery' was defined in relationship to the Irish, and Indians were incorporated into this definition" (895). Sixteenth-century English "colonizers burned the villages and crops of the [Irish] inhabitants and relocated them on reservations" (894). "Sir Humphrey Gilbert, Lord De La Warr, Sir Francis Drake, and Sir Walter Raleigh—all participated both in invading Ireland and in colonizing the New World" (895). Commander John Mason, who with Captain John Underhill led the Puritans in the Pequot genocide, "conducted military campaigns against the Irish before he sailed for New England" (895).

160. "Indians versus Civilization," *MS* 6 (September 1885): 4. "Why They Were Civilized," *MS* 6 (September 1885): 4. "Where Are the Savages of the Nineteenth Century?" *RM* 11 (September 1891): 1. "Not All Savages Are Red," *RM* 15 (June 1899): 6.

161. "The Force of an Indian Arrow," *EKT* 1 (September 1880): n.p. "Indian Riders: Great Feats in Horsemanship—Scenes in an Indian Camp," *MS* 7 (August–September 1881): 3. "Names of States," *IH* 1 (October 7, 1885): n.p.

162. "Exploits of Spotted Horse: Almost in the Hands of the Enemy," *IH* 6 (May 29, 1891): n.p.

163. "Bad Indian Caught: The Famous Apache Kid Has Been Cornered," *RM* 12 (September–November 1894): 8.

164. See Phyllis de la Garza, *The Apache Kid* (Tucson, Az.: Westernlore Press, 1995), 4.

165. Letter from "W. Eagle Chief of the Poncas" to "Frank Eagle," *EKT* 2 (March 1882): n.p.

166. See C. Pinquodle (Kiowa) to Dear Friend Charles in "Extracts from Home Letters," *MS* 2 (July 1882): n.p., and Joseph Vetter to Samuel, *SN* 1 (June 1880): n.p. Also see Pratt's account of Spotted Tail's complaints about Carlisle in Pratt, *Battlefield and Classroom*, 237, 239.

167. Childers, "Ellis B. Childers' Speech," *MS* 2 (June 1882): n.p. Kendall, "Why Is It That Some of the Whites Hate Indians?" *MS* 3 (July 1883): n.p. "A Bit of History," *RM* 11 (September 1891): 8. See Carl Van Doren, *Benjamin Franklin* (New York: Viking, 1928), 209. "The African Problem—Just So About the Indians," *MS* 6 (July 1884): n.p. And the dialogue: "Only One Way of Playing It," *RM* 11 (September 1891): 1.

168. *RMH* 4 (January 22, 1904): n.p. "Is It Worth While to Educate Boys at Yale?" *RMH* 4 (January 29, 1904): n.p. On capital and labor: *IH* 1 (May 21, 1886): n.p.

169. Cornelious, Matlack, and Tyndall are quoted in "Resolved, That the Indian Should Be Exterminated," *MS* 7 (December 1886): 5, 8, see 8.

170. It is difficult to discern the tone and meaning of some of the outrageous positions taken in the debates. In 1873 DeWitt Clinton Duncan (Cherokee), an alumnus of the Cherokee Male Seminary and a member of the Cherokee National Council, represented the dominant position taken in the council in an article published in the *Cherokee Advocate*: "Can the mental wants of an Indian youth be satisfied . . . by resources less fruitful than that which caters to the Anglo-Saxon mind? The Cherokee language, at the present advanced period of their [Cherokee] civilization, can not meet the exigencies of our people" (quoted in Mihesuah, *Cultivating*, 81). Clinton, however, was advocating the absorption of aspects of "Anglo-Saxon" culture to enrich and strengthen the Cherokees as a tribe.

171. Hawkins and Kendall quoted in "Resolved, That the Indian Should Be Exterminated," 5, 8.

172. "She's An Indian," *RM* 11 (January–February 1893): 4–5, see 4.

173. See "Buffalo Bill Writes," *MS* 7 (August–September 1881): 3. On work: *IH* 2 (December 24, 1886): n.p. On London: *RM* 8 (March 1888): 4.

174. Pratt, *Battlefield and Classroom*, 121.

175. "Buffalo Bill's Wild West Show," *RM* 14 (June–August 1898): 1, 8.

176. See Barbara S. Lee's fascinating "Racial Resolutions in *Uncle Tom's Cabin* and *The Captain at Plymouth*: Acculturation through Drama at the Carlisle Indian Industrial School, 1909–1910" (M.A. thesis, Lehigh University, 1999). I am grateful to Barbara Landis, Cumberland County Historical Society, for sending me Lee's thesis.

177. E. G. E., "Two Indian Books," *RMH* 2 (October 9, 1901): n.p. (Elaine Goodale Eastman is the author of "Two Indian Books"). "More Renaissance of Indian Art: Apache Bead Work," *RMH* 4 (February 12, 1904): n.p.

178. *IH* 1 (May 21, 1886): n.p.

179. Consult Michael Oriard, *Reading Football: How the Popular Press Created an American Spectacle* (Chapel Hill: University of North Carolina Press, 1993), 233–47 (see 235 for the estimate that there were about 250 possible players out of the 1,000 Carlisle students). For a useful overview, see John Bloom, *To Show What an Indian Can Do: Sport at Native American Boarding Schools* (Minneapolis: University of Minnesota

Press, 2000), especially xi–xxi, 1–50. Also see John S. Steckbeck, *Fabulous Redmen: The Carlisle Indians and their Famous Football Teams* (Harrisburg, PA: McFarland, 1951); Joseph B. Oxendine, *American Indian Sports Heritage* (Lincoln: University of Nebraska Press, 1988).

180. Oriard, *Reading Football*, 235, 236.

181. "Yale 12, Carlisle 6," *Yale Daily News* 20 (October 26, 1896): 1–2.

182. *The Sun* quoted in "The Yale-Indian Football Game," *RM* 14 (November 1896): 1–5, see 2. *Journal* quoted in "The Harvard Game," *RM* 14 (November 1896): 5–7, see 5.

183. The *New York Journal* page containing Crane's review is reproduced in Oriard, *Reading Football*, 240 (the description quoted is by Oriard, 239).

184. "Harvard Game," 5, 6.

185. *World* (politeness) quoted in "Yale-Indian Football Game," 1. Albany *Argus* (roused) quoted in " 'Liners' from the Best Papers Upon the Playing of the Carlisle Indians, and Other Features," *RM* 15 (December 1898): 4–5, see 4. *Journal* (gentlemanly) quoted in "Harvard Game," 6. A few years later, under the guidance of their coach Glenn S. "Pop" Warner, the Carlisle players gained great notoriety for pulling stunts like wearing uniforms with footballs embroidered on them and (against Harvard in 1903) hiding the ball in the back of a player's jersey (Oriard, *Reading Football*, 243).

186. "The Football Banquet," *RMH* 3 (December 12, 1902): n.p.

187. See Hoxie, *Parading*, 58, 78–80, and Welch, *Fools Crow*, 4, 8, 177, 215, 314, 339, 383. Gilroy quotes Frantz Fanon's "observation" about how male Antilleans, in response to colonization, developed compensatory "fantasies of bodily potency" and dreamed of " 'muscular prowess,' " of " 'action,' " and of " 'aggression' " (*Against Race*, 255).

188. On the Harvard headline and the tendency of athletics to accentuate racial distinctions, consult Philip Deloria, " 'I Am of the Body': Thoughts on My Grandfather, Culture, and Sports," *South Atlantic Quarterly* 95 (spring 1996): 321–38, see 332, 329. Sometimes Natives mocked this positioning by performing—or hamming up—"Indian." Jim Thorpe was a member of the NFL Indian team the Oorang Indians. Some team members would "don blankets and headdresses" when they pulled into town to advertise their presence, as if they belonged to a Wild West show. During half-time, Deloria notes, team members would "perform Indian dances, as well as staging knife- and tomahawk-throwing contests, bear-wrestling exhibitions, and World War I 'Indian combat' re-enactments." Their athletic achievements and theatrics demonstrated "a certain bi-cultural sophistication." One quarterback commented that although Whites considered them " 'wild men,' " many players " 'had been to college and were generally more civilized than [White spectators] were' " (333).

189. Wheelock, "Should Football Be Abolished?" *RM* 14 (January 1898): 5–6, see 5.

190. As Hanay Geiogamah's (Kiowa) narrator puts it in his play *Foghorn*, in reference to the American Indian Movement's symbolic and physical *reoccupation* of land: "Thanksgiving Day, 1969. Alcatraz Island, San Francisco Bay. We are discovered, again. It was the first time that we have taken back land that was already ours. Indian people everywhere felt good about our having the island, about our determination." Geiogamah, *New Native American Drama: Three Plays* (Norman: University of Oklahoma Press, 1980), 45–82, see 54.

191. Oriard, *Reading Football*, 246–47.

192. Pratt, "Official Report," in *Americanizing*, ed. Prucha, 269, and on Pratt's dealings with the Sioux see Utley, *Lance*, 274.

193. Goodale Eastman, *Pratt*, 209. In his autobiography Asa Daklugie (Apache) claimed that

he threw Pratt on the floor when Pratt called him to his office and tried to whip him for his alleged classroom misbehavior. Pratt, once subdued, laughed, told Daklugie to sit down, heard his story, and advised that he be more respectful to his teachers. Coleman notes that this "picture of Pratt as a man who mixed strong convictions with a surprisingly tolerant sense of humor is consistent with other accounts" (*American Indian Children*, 151). There are other ways to read this episode. It may be that Pratt's seemingly benevolent sense of humor came to his rescue (saving face—and body) in those instances when he found that, notwithstanding his six-foot stature, he could not pull off the whipping.

194. "Colonel Pratt's Talk to the Students Last Saturday Evening, After the Cornell, 6—Carlisle, 10 Game," *RMH* 3 (October 24, 1902): n.p. Also see Pratt, *Battlefield and Classroom*, 317–18.

195. One Carlisle student wrote of Pratt: "He was over six feet tall, had broad shoulders, and stood erect. We greatly admired his military bearing" (quoted in Adams, *Extinction*, 262).

196. See Rosa La Flesche to Pratt, December 5, 1920, and April 10, 1921, RHPP, and Joshua Given to Pratt, June 24, 1904, RHPP.

197. Wheelock to Pratt, November 27, 1920, RHPP.

198. Gansworth to Pratt, June 16, 1897, RHPP.

199. Eastman, *Indian To-day*, 70, also see 71–72. Quoted in Goodale Eastman, *Pratt*, 110. She notes that Merrill Gates actually dubbed Pratt "Moses" (219) in a 1900 commencement address.

200. In particular see the letters of Thomas Sloan (who graduated from Hampton and through an apprenticeship became a lawyer) and Arthur Parker (a self-taught ethnologist and museum director whom Pratt originally steered away from Carlisle) to Pratt, RHPP. For example, see Sloan to Pratt, August 24, 1909: "You have more loyal boys among the Indians than any other person." Also see Parker to Pratt, September 19, 1913: "As I inquire I find that you have influenced the life action of more prominent ex-students of Indian Schools, than any other man who ever lived. And every student is loyal to you—'I am a product of the Pratt regime,' they say, 'therefore, I believe'—so—and so. Those who see things now say, 'the Indian students need a *father* like Gen. Pratt.'"

201. Pratt, *Battlefield and Classroom*, 231–35, 255, 282. Goodale Eastman, approving Pratt's willingness to stand up for what he believed was right or truthful, observes that the *Red Man* did publish a critical report of the massacre at Wounded Knee—"an instance of commendable courage in an officer of the regular army!" (*Pratt*, 184).

202. Morgan to Pratt, March 4, 1892, RHPP. On Pratt's struggles with the government, see Goodale Eastman, *Pratt*, 63, 82, 86.

203. Quoted in Goodale Eastman, *Pratt*, 149.

204. Goodale Eastman makes this point without developing the full political implications in *Pratt*, 264.

205. He wrote, for example, "The Catholic church wants the child for a priest. It takes him from his home and tribe, separates him absolutely, immerses him in the influence of the church for a long series of years until he is practically helpless for any other than priests' work, and then seldom, if ever, allows him to go back to family or tribe, but rather sends him to foreign and remote parts—for instance, Spanish and Italian priests to America, to boss us in Americanizing our Indians" (quoted in Goodale Eastman, *Pratt*, 126–27).

206. See Lindsey, *Hampton*, 27. In 1892 Pratt wrote that the Natives' "plane of life has always been above that of the African in his native state" ("Official Report," in *Americanizing*, ed. Prucha, 263).

207. Quoted in Lindsey, *Hampton*, 184, 25.

208. Interestingly, Krupat—a prominent non-Native Native American studies scholar—recognized this about himself: "It's only lately that I have begun to see class as having something to do with my attraction to contemporary Native American writers" (*Turn to the Native*, 110). For over a hundred years the U.S. government and economic forces have played key roles in transforming Natives into the working poor or unemployed. Also see Bell, "Telling Tales," 53.

209. Pratt's offspring to John Collier (unsigned copy of letter), June 21, 1934, RHPP.

210. See Oriard's astute remark: "Carlisle's games may even have represented class more than racial struggle: the underclass in competition with the privileged elite. . . . The more deeply considered racism in the football journalism of this period was found not in the daily newspapers but in the genteel periodicals" (*Reading Football*, 243).

211. Gates to Pratt, January 4, 1890, RHPP.

212. Morgan to Pratt, March 4, 1892, RHPP.

213. Pratt, "Proceedings of the Ninth Annual Meeting," in *Americanizing*, ed. Prucha, 276.

214. For examples of Pratt's correspondence with John Wanamaker, see Wanamaker to Pratt, June 30, 1913, RHPP; Wanamaker to Pratt, December 11, 1913, RHPP. Pratt certainly relished dropping names in his autobiography, *Battlefield and Classroom*; see, for instance, 309, 319. Washington wrote in 1901 that campaigns to persuade philanthropists to be philanthropic in one's cause give "one an opportunity to meet some of the best people in the world—to be more correct, I think I should say *the best* people in the world" (*Up From Slavery*, 184).

215. Adams, *Extinction*, 322.

216. Pratt, *Battlefield and Classroom*, 293. "After Col. Pratt's Scalp: Bureau of Indian Affairs Resents His Criticism of Its Actions," *RMH* 5 (1904): n.p.

217. See the statement (with no author indicated) in box 10, folder 344, RHPP.

218. On Carlisle as a "semi-military" outfit, see Pratt to Corbin, January 18, 1903, RHPP, and on his wish to resign his post as superintendent and lead Carlisle students and former students, see Pratt to the adjutant general, February 10, 1903, RHPP.

219. Pratt to Jones, January 19, 1903, RHPP.

220. Pratt, "American Indians; Chained and Unchained: Being an Account of How the Carlisle Indian School Was Born and Grew in Its First 25 Years," *RM* 6 (June 1914): 393–411, see 411.

221. Elaine G. Eastman, despite her assimilationist fervor, admits: "It is possible that Pratt underestimated the handicap suffered by the young Indian of only average ability and inadequate schooling, the great majority of whom left schools far short of a sound common school education. He himself had forced his way to the top, notwithstanding the lack of early advantage" (*Pratt*, 237).

222. Du Bois to Pratt, November 10, 1916, RHPP.

223. Pratt, *Battlefield and Classroom*, 223.

224. Pratt, "American Indians," 393, 394.

225. Quoted in Goodale Eastman, *Pratt*, 266, 271–72.

226. On Friedman and the investigations see Adams, *Extinction*, 323–25. During these years the young poet Marianne Moore taught composition at Carlisle. Her letters suggest that she found Friedman "incisive" but seemed afraid of him. She tried to keep her

distance from the investigation (which also involved Pratt's charges against Friedman) and preferred his successor. On Friedman's communication skills, see Moore to Mrs. Moore, July 21, 1912; on keeping distance from the "doomed" Friedman, see Moore to "Baby and Pidge," February 18, 1914; on Pratt's charges, see Moore to Puig (?), February 15, 1914; on Lipps, see Moore to Puig (?), March 9, 1914. Moore's correspondence is archived in the Rosenbach Museum and Library, Philadelphia. I am grateful to Evelyn Foldman, keeper of the Marianne Moore archive, for singling out the Moore letters related to Carlisle. For background on the four superintendents who ran Carlisle after Pratt, see Bell, "Telling Stories," 88–104.

227. See Harry Hemler's poem "Character," *The Arrow* 2 (December 8, 1905): n.p.: "C stands for Conscience./H stands for Honest./A stands for Ambition./R stands for Ready./ A stands for Aim in Life./C stands for Charity./T stands for Truthfulness./E stands for Energy./R stands for Righteousness." On self-support: "Lon Hill, Choctaw Millionaire," 4 *The Arrow* (April 17, 1908): n.p. On femininity: Elizabeth G. Bender, "Training Girls for Efficient Home Makers," 8 *RM* (January 1916): 154–56. On threat to close Carlisle: "Congressman Olmstead Favors Carlisle," *The Arrow* 3 (January 25, 1907): n.p.

228. "Success That Is Destructive," *The Arrow* 2 (September 22, 1905): n.p.

229. "Carlisle Penants and Novelties," *RM* 6 (June 1914): 426.

230. Sara J. Porter, "Native Art of the North American Indian," *The Arrow* 1 (November 3, 1904): n.p.

231. See *The Arrow* 4 (January 3, 1908): n.p.

232. See Robert Yellowtail, "The Indian and His Problem," *RM* 5 (May 1913): 412–16, silhouette is on 416.

233. Howard Fremont Stratton, "The Place of the Indian in Art," *RM* 7 (March 1910): 3–7, see 6, 4.

234. Emily S. Cook, "What's In a Name?" *The Arrow* 1 (September 22, 1904): n.p.

235. See Elaine G. Eastman, "In Memoriam: Angel DeCora Dietz," *The American Indian Magazine* 7 (spring 1919): 51–52, and Sarah McAnulty, "Angel DeCora: American Indian Artist and Educator," *Nebraska History* 57 (summer 1976): 143–99.

236. Angel DeCora, "Native Indian Art," *The Arrow* 3 (August 23, 1907): n.p.

237. Ibid.

238. Stratton, "Place of the Indian," 6, 5.

239. Francis E. Leupp, "Outline of an Indian Policy," *The Arrow* 1 (April 20, 1905): n.p.

240. One can see this hierarchical cultural relativism in Leupp's chapter "The Red Man as Teacher and Learner," in his *In Red Man's Land: A Study of the American Indian* (New York: Fleming H. Revell, 1914), 127–47. While acknowledging that the "caucasian race" and "American aborigines" have much to teach one another, he also asserts the evolutionary "superiority" of Whites (127).

241. Leupp, "Outline," n.p.

242. Leupp's views are in line with what Michaels terms nativist pluralism: "The Progressive commitment in Americanization, whether of Indians or aliens, is . . . repudiated by nativist pluralism, on the grounds that people cannot become what they aren't. But thus also, the commitment to the technologies of Americanization is preserved, on the grounds that people must become what they are" (*Our America*, 122). Once Leupp defined who Native Americans "were" with confidence, he could try to deprive them of land, education, funds, and, in general, the capacity to exercise self-determination. Such certitude would also ease his conscience.

243. Leupp, "Outline," n.p. See Donald L. Parman, "Francis Ellington Leupp, 1905–1909," in *The Commissioners of Indian Affairs, 1824–1977*, ed. Robert M. Kvasnicka and Herman J. Viola (Lincoln: University of Nebraska Press, 1979), 221–32, see 221.

244. See Leupp's chapter "Theory and Fact in Education," in his *The Indian and His Problem* (New York: Scribner's, 1910), 115–31, the quotation is on 121.

245. See Frederick E. Hoxie, *A Final Promise: The Campaign to Assimilate the Indians, 1880–1920* (Lincoln: University of Nebraska Press, 1984), 116–17, 108–11, 103–06.

246. Quoted in Hoxie, *Final Promise*, 97. The statement is made by Osborne Lawson, an ethnographer. See Hamlin Garland, *The Captain of the Gray-Horse Troop* (New York: Grosset and Dunlap, 1901), 56.

247. Robert G. Valentine, "The Big Job of Solving the Indian Problem," *RM* 4 (May 1912): 359–76, see 393, 395, 394, 396.

248. Hoxie, *Final Promise*, 177, 175, 206. See Diane T. Putney, "Robert Grosvenor Valentine (1909–12)," in *Commissioners*, ed. Kvasnicka and Viola, 233–42, see 233.

249. Arthur C. Parker, "Iroquois Hospitality a Matter of Record," *RM* 9 (September 1916): 18–23, see 20.

250. Thomas Sloan, "The Indian's Protection and His Place as an American," *RM* 4 (May 1912): 398–403, see 399.

251. Hoxie, *Final Promise*, 204.

252. Coleman, *American Indian Children*, 139.

253. Interestingly, the Native autobiographies that reflect on schooling which Coleman studies place "heavy emphasis on physical labor at the many government and missionary schools, but they rarely show that the autobiographers were themselves victims of racial prejudice." Coleman's argument conflicts with Hoxie's stress on the impact of changing racial ideologies in Indian school administration in *Final Promise*: "The narrators give little indication that they were markedly influenced by the changing educational controversies stirring in the decades around the turn of the century. Indian autobiographies demonstrate that a heavy manual labor element had been a feature of school life from the beginning of the period under review. And there is little evidence in these autobiographies of a discernible increase in racism—indeed of biological racism at all." Numerous autobiographers "noted that manual labor duties delayed their academic progress." Sometimes the incentive to work was fear, as James Whitewolf (Kiowa and Apache) acknowledged: "I didn't like the jobs they gave me. . . . But I knew that if I did them all right they wouldn't bother me. But if I didn't they might whip me" (*American Indian Children*, 47, 193, 113, 115). Workerizing dates back to Christopher Columbus, who realized immediately that Natives could be enslaved and forced to work in mines, and also to Governor Thomas Gates of Virginia, who in 1609 arrived "with instructions that the Indians should be forced to labor for the colonists and also to make annual payments of corn and skins" (Takaki, "*The Tempest* in the Wilderness," 902). In *Prairie Light*, a study of Chilocco, Lomawaima argues that "federal boarding schools did not train Indian youth for assimilation into the American melting pot, but trained them in the work discipline of the Protestant ethic, to accept their proper place in society as a marginal class" (99). This workerizing was one way schools staffed themselves: "The only employment available in domestic service for many young Indian women graduating from boarding schools was in the boarding schools themselves." Lomawaima sizes up this form of workerizing as "training in dispossession under the guise of domesticity" (86). She indicates that few Chilocco students

"continued their trade as an adult" (71). Yet some former students appreciated aspects of workerizing as an opportunity to develop "perseverance" (61).

254. See Goodale Eastman, *Pratt*, 241. Also see Bell, "Telling Stories," 199–202.

255. Here too I am in agreement with Coleman's assessment in *American Indian Children*: "One must not minimize the development of increasingly uneven power relationships" (195); students "were adjusting to the school, rather than the other way around" (196). But "symbiosis, mutual exploitation, characterized the whole school situation" (195). Coleman suggests that students expected nothing more than to gain access to "the knowledge of the white tribe" (197); they did not expect the classroom to be the site of multicultural learning (this sort of learning was more available outside class, especially in the interaction of students from different tribes).

256. Charles Eastman praised Carlisle but was critical of many other government schools and characterized student responses, "It is a case of serve the master and he will not bother you; all else is merely show." And he asserted, "The red man is a born actor" (*Indian To-day*, 78, 159). Tribal cultures may have given Natives sophisticated education in aspects of performance long before they arrived at Carlisle. In a 1983 interview, Momaday, in response to a query about the dearth of Native dramatists, said, "As far as I can see, the Indian has a very highly developed sense of the dramatic. It is present in virtually every expression of his life" (quoted in *Conversations with N. Scott Momaday*, ed. Matthias Schubnell [Jackson: University Press of Mississippi, 1997], 155). Contemplating masking, Momaday observes: "The masks anyone brings to a given situation are probably innumerable. I have acquired identities which are my masks. . . . One can mask the reality of something, but in the process another reality is presented, and very often it is a more appropriate reality for that moment" (Charles L. Woodward, *Ancestral Voice: Conversations with N. Scott Momaday* [Lincoln: University of Nebraska Press, 1989], xi).

2 School of Savagery

1. Silko, *Ceremony*, 94–95. Quintasket, *Mourning Dove*, 141, also see 30, 44, 117, 125, 127, 128. Jimmie Durham, *Columbus Day: Poems, Drawings and Stories about American Indian Life and Death in the Nineteen Seventies* (Minneapolis: West End Press, 1983), 84, 4.

2. Prucha, *American Indian Policy*, vi.

3. Krupat, *Turn to the Native*, 17. He also observes that "Native modes of knowing and understanding . . . have not been formulated *as* analytic or critical modes *apart* from the verbal performances they would know and understand" and that this is not a "deficiency . . . only a difference." Of course, the "Indian sense of self . . . is no more monolithic than any 'Western' sense of self" (*Ethnocriticism*, 44, 207).

4. Brian Swann and Arnold Krupat, "Introduction," in *I Tell You Now: Autobiographical Essays by Native American Writers*, ed. Swann and Krupat (Lincoln: University of Nebraska Press, 1987), xii. Also see *Native American Autobiography: An Anthology*, ed. Arnold Krupat (Madison: University of Wisconsin Press, 1994); Arnold Krupat's *The Voice in the Margin: Native American Literature and the Canon* (Berkeley: University of California Press, 1989), *Ethnocriticism*, and *Turn to the Native*; Brumble, *American Indian Autobiography*; and Hertha Dawn Wong, *Sending My Heart Back across the Years: Tradition and Innovation in Native American Autobiography* (New York: Oxford University Press, 1992).

5. Calvin Luther Martin has attempted to outline the kinds of Native subjectivities developed in Native cultures that believed in wide-ranging kinship relations (humans, animals, the earth). He argues that these subjectivities were informed by "an overarching cosmology, and worldview, seemingly distinctive to Native American societies—all of them." Still, Martin acknowledges that "the collective *Indian worldview* described in these pages is a convenient and candidly artificial abstraction, or distillation, of certain pivotal sentiments and a distinctive outlook on life shared by members of these legion societies" ("Metaphysics," in *American Indian*, ed. Martin, 34). Using the works of several Sioux authors and works by historians I too offer here a "candidly artificial abstraction, or distillation, of certain pivotal sentiments" that I hope will be useful in thinking about the sorts of cultural subjectivities that some—by no means all—Native students brought to Carlisle. Hilden occasionally tries to offer productive generalizations about "traditional Indians," yet she often circumspectly includes the modifier "most Native American tradition" (*When Nickels Were Indians*, 114, 108).

6. Coleman's analysis of Native autobiographies that recount responses to Euramerican schooling concludes that "no typical Hopi or Navajo or Sioux response to the school emerged" and that "we still know relatively little about how Indian school children themselves saw things" (*American Indian Children*, 194, x). Many Native cultures were complex and made it possible for students to react in diverse ways. Lomawaima's work on Chilocco (1920 to 1940) has led her to suggest that "fifty-one people [interviewed by her] have looked back on their lives and found meaning in fifty-one different ways" (*Prairie Light*, 160).

7. Wilson, *Ohiyesa*, 105–6.

8. Also see Zitkala-Ša, *Old Indian Legends* (Lincoln: University of Nebraska Press, 1985 [1901]). See Richard N. Ellis's useful introduction to the reprint of Standing Bear's *My People the Sioux* (Lincoln: University of Nebraska Press, 1975 [1928]), especially xiv–xv. Standing Bear refers to himself as an Oglala. But Ellis cites the research of George Hyde, which makes a strong case (based on Rosebud reservation records) that Standing Bear was a Brule. See George E. Hyde, *Spotted Tail's Folk: A History of the Brulé Sioux* (Norman: University of Oklahoma Press, 1962), 288.

9. See Clyde Holler, *Black Elk's Religion: The Sun Dance and Lakota Catholicism* (Syracuse, N.Y.: Syracuse University Press, 1995), 6–7, and Raymond DeMallie's indispensable introduction to his collection of the original interviews, *The Sixth Grandfather: Black Elk's Teachings Given to John G. Neihardt*, ed. and with an introduction by Raymond DeMallie (Lincoln: University of Nebraska Press, 1984), 3–99. DeMallie's introduction is itself a treasure-trove of insight into and information on Sioux culture and spirituality.

10. See Swann and Krupat, "Introduction," *I Tell You Now*, ed. Swann and Krupat, x; Krupat, *For Those Who Come After*, 29–30, 30–31.

11. Black Elk, *Black Elk Speaks: Being the Life Story of a Holy Man of the Oglala Sioux as Told through John G. Neihardt* (Lincoln: University of Nebraska Press, 1979 [1932]), 1.

12. Swann and Krupat, "Introduction," *I Tell You Now*, ed. Swann and Krupat, ix, xii.

13. Brumble, *American Indian Autobiography*; see Brumble's chapter on the former Carlisle student Albert Hensley (Winnebago), who was also a key figure in the ascendancy of the Peyote faith among the Winnebagos and in the establishment of the Native American Church, 130–46, especially 131 and 135.

14. Krupat, *For Those Who Come After*, 40. On sentimental privatization see Joel Pfister,

The Production of Personal Life: Class, Gender, and the Psychological in Hawthorne's Fiction (Stanford, Ca.: Stanford University Press, 1991).

15. Charles Eastman, *From Deep Woods to Civilization: Chapters in the Autobiography of an Indian* (Lincoln: University of Nebraska Press, 1977 [1916]), 188.

16. Standing Bear, *My People*, n.p. (preface).

17. On Eastman, see H. David Brumble's chapter "Charles Alexander Eastman's Indian Boyhood: Romance, Nostalgia, and Social Darwinism," in his *American Indian Biography*, 147–64; Wong, *Sending My Heart Back Across the Years*, 139–52, and David Reed's biographical overview of Eastman in *American Indian Intellectuals*, ed. Margot Liberty (St. Paul, Minn.: West, 1978), 61–74. Also consult Michael Elliott, *The Culture Concept: Writing and Difference in the Age of Realism* (Minneapolis: University of Minnesota Press, 2002), 89–160.

18. Frederick Hoxie maintains that Native authors—like Eastman, Standing Bear, Bonnin, Christine Quintasket (Mourning Dove)—"posed as bearers of an ancient spirit in the modern age." See "Exploring a Cultural Borderland: Native American Journeys of Discovery in the Early Twentieth Century," *Journal of American History* (December 1992): 969–95, see 981. Eastman learned about this typecasting in his efforts to establish a career as a physician: patients wanted him to practice exotic "Indian" medicine.

19. Standing Bear, *Land*, 107.

20. Eastman to Pratt, January 27, 1911, RHPP.

21. Eastman to Pratt, January 30, 1911, RHPP.

22. Charles Eastman, *Indian Scout Talks: A Guide for Boy Scouts and Camp Fire Girls* (Boston: Little, Brown, 1920), 188. To some degree Eastman labored to replace one stereotype with another: "No longer does the red man live alone in the blood-curdling pages of the sensational story-writer. He is the subject of profound study as a man, a philosopher, a noble type both physically and spiritually. . . . He is a true child of nature" (*Indian To-day*, 165).

23. Eastman, *Indian Scout Talks*, 188, 138–40, 69, 72, 25–33, 99, 100, 115, 133, 1, 189.

24. Charles Eastman, *Indian Boyhood* (New York: McClure, Phillips, 1902), 3, 10–11, 58–59. Eastman, *The Soul of the Indian: An Interpretation* (Boston: Houghton Mifflin, 1911), 10, 11–12, 35–36, 58–59, 88, 90, 91, 114–15. Eastman, *Deep*, 1, 38–39.

25. Standing Bear, *Land*, 149–50.

26. Eastman, *Soul*, 34–35. Also see Raymond J. DeMallie, "Kinship and Biology in Sioux Culture," in *North American Indian Anthropology: Essays on Society and Culture*, ed. Raymond J. DeMallie and Alfonso Ortiz (Norman: University of Oklahoma Press, 1994), 125–46.

27. See, for example, Hoxie's discussion of Crow tribal-family life, *Parading*, 169–92. On Native gender and sexuality constructions, see *Two-Spirit People: Native American Gender Identity, Sexuality, and Spirituality*, ed. Sue-Ellen Jacobs, Wesley Thomas, and Sabine Lang (Urbana: University of Illinois Press, 1997).

28. Standing Bear, *My People*, 29.

29. Eastman, *Soul*, 36.

30. Ella Cara Deloria, *Waterlily* (Lincoln: University of Nebraska Press, 1988), 64–65, 78, 163, 214–16.

31. See Utley, *Lance*, 8–9, 11–12, 70.

32. See John Demos, "Oedipus and America: Historical Perspectives on the Reception of Psychoanalysis in the United States," in *Inventing the Psychological: Toward a Cultural*

History of Emotional Life in America, ed. Joel Pfister and Nancy Schnog (New Haven, Conn.: Yale University Press, 1997), 63–78, especially 71–74.

33. Zitkala-Ša, *American Indian Stories* (Lincoln: University of Nebraska Press, 1985 [1921]), 9.

34. Yet, as Coleman notes, there were some parallels between the tribal and school authority structures that many students would have recognized: "Both systems assumed the importance of continual, incremental learning under the tutelage of adults. Both accepted the importance of spiritual knowledge, discipline and punishment, advance to higher status grades, the winning of particular prizes for tasks well performed, and the separation of the sexes." In some instances, Coleman also avers, parental disapproval of the school was precisely what made students determined to succeed there (*American Indian Children*, 53).

35. Eastman, *Soul*, 9.

36. Ibid., 10. On the one hand, Momaday, writing of the Kiowas in *Rainy Mountain*, recalls, "There were always dogs about my grandmother's house. Some of them were nameless and lived a life of their own. They belonged there in a sense that the word 'ownership' does not include" (25). Yet in his profile of the nineteenth-century Kiowas, he asserts: "Of all the tribes of the Plains, the Kiowas owned the greatest number of horses per person" (39). He adds: "The old men were the best arrowmakers, for they would bring time and patience to their craft. The young men—the fighters and hunters—were willing to pay a high price for arrows that were well made" (63).

37. Eastman, *Indian Scout Talks*, 189–90.

38. Eastman, *Deep*, 188.

39. Standing Bear, *My People*, 52–53.

40. Ibid., 275. Also see Zitkala-Ša on the responsibility to be generous, *American Indian Stories*, 162. Yet Robert L. Hall (Mohican) writes of Native "intellectual property": "Contrary to much popular and even some scholarly opinion, Indian property rights were well defined. A man might know every word of a song by heart yet be neither allowed nor willing to sing it himself unless he had purchased or earned the right along set guidelines. A person who repeated a sacred story to which he was not entitled was more than a literary thief subject to angry words and actions from his fellow tribesmen; he faced the prospect of supernatural retribution as well" (*An Archaeology of the Soul: North American Indian Belief and Ritual* [Urbana: University of Illinois Press, 1997], ix).

41. See Hoxie, *Parading*, 212.

42. See Adams, *Extinction*, 154.

43. Charles Eastman, *Indian Heroes and Great Chieftains* (Mineola, N.Y.: Dover, 1997), 39.

44. Utley, *Lance*, 12. Also see Adams, *Extinction*: "Tribal life was rooted in the idea that the welfare of the community depended upon the individual curbing material desires. Whereas a Protestant American measured an individual's worth by his capacity to accumulate wealth, an Indian did so by what he gave away" (122).

45. Eastman, *Deep*, 67.

46. Leupp, "Outline," n.p.

47. Eastman, *Deep*, 147–48.

48. Standing Bear, *Land*, 69. The aim was clear: "If a man were without a horse it was the chief's place to see that he got another; if a family needed a tipi it was the duty of all in the band to lend hands in getting another; and if a child became orphaned it received the care of everyone in the band. There was no possible excuse for hoarding; on the contrary

it stood for selfishness and lack of self-restraint, since all goods or accumulated property were tacitly for the purpose of distribution" (168–69).

49. Eastman, *Deep*, 194.

50. Eastman, *Soul*, 122.

51. Quoted in Eastman, *Indian Heroes and Great Chieftains*, 53.

52. Zitkala-Ša, *American Indian Stories*, 186.

53. Zitkala-Ša, *Old Indian Legends*, vi ("The old legends of America belong quite as much to the blue-eyed little patriot as to the black-haired aborigine."), 65, 27, 42.

54. Standing Bear, *Land*, 66, 166, 67, 124.

55. On rivalry and interdependence, see Standing Bear, *Land*, 135.

56. See James Welch's novel *Fools Crow* about the Pikunis in the 1860s and 1870s. Initially, Rides-at-the-door thinks the following about his son Running Fisher's pridefulness: "Rides-at-the-door had taken the young man's haughty attitude as a sign of strength, of youthful pride, the way it is when a youth is full of himself. Sometimes that is a good quality in a young man, for he marks himself as one who will stand out later in life. Many times that quality brings honor to the man's family as well as himself" (339). His older son is also ambitious. He was originally named White Man's Dog but is renamed Fools Crow for taking revenge on an important Crow chief. White Man's Dog wanted a repeating rifle: "Then he could bring about his own luck. He would have plenty of wives, children, horses, meat. He would have his own lodge, and his wives would cook boss ribs and black horn tongues while he smoked, told stories, recounted his war honors" (4).

57. Utley, *Lance*, 5–6, 14–15.

58. Standing Bear, *Land*, 233.

59. Standing Bear, *My People*, 138.

60. Eastman, *Soul*, 27.

61. Standing Bear, *Land*, 164. He also criticized the formation of an army whose soldiers were forced to fight (173).

62. Standing Bear, *Land*, 124, 125. He adds: "No Lakota chief ever dreamed of using the power of a judge in court, or a policeman on a street corner, for it was not a tenet of his society that one individual should account to another for his conduct" (132). On the role of the Fox Lodge in maintaining social order, see 143–44.

63. Eastman, *Indian To-day*, 10.

64. Adams, *Extinction*, see 210–38. Lomawaima, writing about Chilocco (1920–40), also records bootlegging as a form of (self-destructive) resistance (*Prairie Light*, 144). Coleman, *American Indian Children*, 153, 157. Coleman discusses various kinds of rejection—suicide (164), runaways termed "deserter[s]" (167), truancy and absenteeism (167), dissimulation (148), passive resistance or a refusal to learn (154), subcultural solidarity (155), parental withdrawal of students from the school (175). Also see Bell, "Telling Stories," 209–327.

65. Quoted in Adams, *Extinction*, 107.

66. Francis La Flesche describes the response of one student to his new school uniform: "He was delighted with his brand-new clothes, particularly with the long row of brass buttons that adorned the front of his jacket. When it came to the shoes, his grief for the lost scalp-lock was clean forgotten, and he strutted about to show the boys that his shining black shoes sang to his satisfaction" (*Middle Five*, 75–76). Coleman concludes his study of student autobiographies: "What should have emerged powerfully ... was the individuality of the Indian narrators responding to the school (not to mention their individu-

ality as reminiscing adults). . . . Each narrator responded with his or her own complex and shifting attitudes" (*American Indian Children*, 193). The autobiographers Coleman studies, of course, had varied responses to uniforms and drills (82, 88, 91).

67. Standing Bear, *My People*, 13, 25. Momaday celebrates the Kiowas' "old love of going" (*Rainy Mountain*, 12).

68. Quintasket, *Mourning Dove*, 20.

69. Standing Bear, *My People*, 26. Zitkala-Ša, *American Indian Stories*, 18.

70. Quoted in Utley, *Lance*, 247. One missionary wrote disapprovingly in 1827: "The Indian character is fond of roving about, upon foot or horseback, and dressed up finely, and do not regard working daily and all as they should do" (quoted in Berkhofer, *Salvation and the Savage*, 79).

71. There was a tradition of this Sioux cultural self-respect that justified the perpetuation of separate lifeways. In 1839 some Sioux responded ungratefully but tactfully to the missionaries' efforts to redeem them: "White men were made wearing clothes to work. It is proper for them [to] plough, build houses & c. But we were made naked to dance[,] hunt and go to war. If we should abandon the customs of our ancestors the Wakan would be angry at us and we would die" (quoted in Berkhofer, *Salvation and the Savage*, 107; also see 109).

72. Standing Bear, *My People*, 6.

73. Zitkala-Ša, *American Indian Stories*, 56, also see 49–50.

74. Ibid., 67. John Joseph Mathews (Osage) writes of his Osage protagonist in *Sundown* (Norman: University of Oklahoma Press, 1988 [1934]): "True to his heritage, he couldn't tolerate monotony and routine" (235).

75. "Zitkala-Sa Is in The Atlantic Monthly," *RM* 16 (June 1900): 6. Neihardt's Black Elk's "spiritual" concept of women, however, meshed with the patriarchal assumptions embedded in Carlisle's basic domestic training of females as character builders and purveyors of "influence": "behind the woman's power of life is the power of man" (*Black Elk*, 210).

76. See Rayna Green's (Cherokee) bibliographic work on writing by Native women, *Native American Women: A Contextual Bibliography* (Bloomington: Indiana University Press, 1983).

77. Utley, *Lance*, 7. See Quintasket's *Mourning Dove* for descriptions of the power Salishan mothers-in-law held as domestic managers (61), of the sacrifices mothers made for their family (121, 161), and of women abused by men and the drudgery of domestic labor (55, 56, 66). "Next to the dog," she writes, "the native woman had no equal in taking abuse from 'her man' " (56). For a critique of the positioning of women in Native cultures, see Paula Gunn Allen (Laguna and Sioux), *The Sacred Hoop: Recovering the Feminine in American Indian Traditions* (Boston: Beacon, 1986). Momaday observes that "in the Kiowa calendars there is graphic proof that the lives of women were hard" (*Rainy Mountain*, 79).

78. Standing Bear, *Land*, 83, also see 91, 90, 90, 127. In addition, "all the while [that Whites] were thinking that our women were slaves we felt that theirs' were. It may not flatter the white man, but the Lakota did not think him considerate toward his women" (172).

79. Eastman, *Indian Scout Talks*, 106, 109, 111.

80. Quintasket, *Mourning Dove*, 34, 39, 45, 82.

81. Standing Bear, *Land*, 140–41.

82. Coleman, *American Indian Children*, 24.

83. Ella Cara Deloria, *Waterlilly*, 59, 179–80, 63, 53, 137, 176, 179. On Salishan taboo systems (menstruation, pregnancy), see Quintasket, *Mourning Dove*, 67, 72.

84. BIA Commissioner William Jones, while lecturing Native students at Hampton in 1898, said to the females, "Much more depends upon you than upon the boys, and we look to you to carry home the refinement that shall really elevate your people" (quoted in Adams, *Extinction*, 175). In *When Nickels Were Indians* Hilden outlines some challenges faced by contemporary Native feminists: "One of the explanations for Native American women's more inclusive feminism may arise from their widespread awareness that certain gender relations were brought across the ocean from Europe and imposed on unwilling Native populations through overt government policies that always excluded women from decisionmaking processes whatever their traditional roles, and through the privileging of those Indian males" (160). She notes that some Native cultures treated women in oppressive ways and "in others, they inhabited a more egalitarian world." But she asserts that a phenomenon such as wife beating was a European import and that it is crucial "to distinguish between imported—and then imposed—European systems of gender relations and those which existed in indigenous societies through the period of the invasion" (246). Another challenge Native feminists negotiate is that some Native men have represented feminism as only "white and middle class, useless for the struggles of Indian women," claimed self-servingly and unhistorically that "indian women's roles (usually as subordinates, unpaid servants, to males) were prescribed by 'honored tradition,'" and informed women that "a separate women's movement would, in racist America, seriously weaken the larger—and by implication, more important—(men's) struggles" (168).

85. See Krupat, *Ethnocriticism*, 217. Also see Lee Irwin, *The Dream Seekers: Native American Visionary Traditions of the Great Plains* (Norman: University of Oklahoma Press, 1994).

86. Quoted in Adams, *Extinction*, 168–69.

87. Martin, *Spirit*, 80, 83. See Martin's thoughts on competing "thought-worlds" ("Metaphysics," in *American Indian*, ed. Martin, 33), anthropomorphism, "cultural achievement," and multispecies and other kinship relations ("Epilogue," in *American Indian*, ed. Martin, 192–220, see 201, 220, 215). Martin quotes one colonial-era Native who registered the changes his subjectivity had undergone: " 'Since prayer has come into our cabins, our former customs are no longer of any service . . . our dreams and our prophecies are no longer true,—prayer has spoiled everything for us' " (*Spirit*, 3).

88. On the power of medicine men, see Standing Bear, *Stories of the Sioux* (Lincoln: University of Nebraska Press, 1988 [1934]). Standing Bear writes that "the white race has come to fear nearly everything on earth—even his fellow being" (*Land*, 56).

89. See Calvin Luther Martin, *The Way of the Human Being* (New Haven, Conn.: Yale University Press, 1999), 69, 9, 159, 92, 199. On the notion of relatives, see Hilden: "Lakota tradition (like most Native American tradition) demands that individual Native people behave toward the whole world as though everything in it—a tree, a rock, a cloud—is a 'relative,' living, growing, existing as humans exist, following its/her/his path through life" (*When Nickels Were Indians*, 108). On empowerment, see Martin: "Humans learned their human powers and abilities from these other-than-human beings" (*Spirit*, 18). See Welch's *Fools Crow*—the protagonist's frequent interlocutor and advisor is a raven. Martin writes that the traditional Native "learned who he was by listening to the wisdom of the bear, the beaver, the eagle, the elements, and so forth.

Nature talked to him in a way we may never fully comprehend. . . . All were individuals who lived more or less in what we would call a mythic world" ("Metaphysics," in *American Indian*, ed. Martin, 30).

90. Martin, *Spirit*, 19, 86, 130. Also see Georges E. Sioui (Huron), *For an Amerindian Autohistory: An Essay on the Foundations of a Social Ethic*, trans. Sheila Fischman (Montreal: McGill-Queen's University Press, 1992), especially his chapter "The Amerindian Idea of Being Human," 20–38.

91. Martin, "Introduction" in *American Indian*, ed. Martin, 22. Martin, *Way*, 139, 194. Also see Shepard Krech III, *The Ecological Indian: Myth and History* (New York: Norton, 1999).

92. Martin, *Spirit*, 107, and Martin, *Way*, 201. He adds: "This is . . . what the current Native authors—Momaday, Silko, Erdrich, Welch, Vizenor, Alexie—are trying to say: that there is something intrinsically wrong with our story" (*Way*, 194). Martin elaborates the implications of barnyard mentality: "One can quite properly label the process [of domestication] detention, forced breeding, and patronization (fodder, shelter, and protection)—these constituting, of course, the precise terms of slavery, human slavery, down through the millennia since the neolithic. Small wonder that many scholars detect in animal domestication the ideological origins of human bondage, especially when the human victims could likewise be depersonalized and rendered as bestial, that is, inserted into the below-threshold category of animals, who long before had been imagined and spoken out of the realm of personhood (having volition and giving permission) by that clever speaker and artificer of creation" (*Spirit*, 58). I am not uncritical of Martin's work—his therapeutic wish to censor historical "horror" stories of what modern humans have done to one another (*Spirit*, 129), his almost New Age reverence for Natives whom he divests of social contradictions (akin to romantic and therapeutic images of nonindustrial Natives long sponsored by U.S. corporations and advertisers), his romantic propensity to cast genuine (too monolithic) Natives as "timeless," his representations of (too monolithic) Europeans and Euramericans and their interactions with Natives (he excises too many European and Euramerican self-critiques), his lack of interest in the ways in which some Natives *readily* picked up some European practices and values. In one passage, for example, he seems to know Indianness (which translates for him as preneolithic humanness) better than the Alaskan Yu'piks he lectures (and in the process he sounds like a "kinship" missionary). I sympathize with Martin's good intentions and see the force of his argument, yet I remain somewhat wary of his righteous stance and apocalyptic tone: "He [Oscar, a Yu'pik] and his people would become enslaved to these manufactures, and they would lose their old relationship, in truth with their powers, with the land and waters. I warned, too, that the game would not give itself so readily anymore—the Gift would likely disappear" (*Way*, 145). As Sherman Alexie, suspicious of New Age constructions of ostensibly "Indian" masculinity, insists: "A warrior does not necessarily have to scream to release the animal that is supposed to reside inside every man. A warrior does not necessarily have an animal inside him at all. If there happens to be an animal, it can be a parakeet or a mouse just as easily as it can be a bear or a wolf" (quoted in Hilden, *When Nickels Were Indians*, 190). Still, I admire Martin's attempts to reconstruct these earlier Native productions of relational subjectivity. His historical work on "traditional," biologically oriented Native subjectivity formation makes what for me is a persuasive case that existence should be imagined as more than human-centered: "Survival, life and death, were not oppressive, burning issues for them. They were epiphenomena: secondary issues growing out of a more

fascinating and engrossing, more important discourse with Nature. The issue, rather, was a life of appreciation, of affirmation, to keep the whole thing going. A life of responsibility of vigilance. A life committed to making the connections. . . . Humankind and Nature engaged in a living art" ("Epilogue," in *American Indian*, ed. Martin, 210). Ward Churchill's term *human chauvinism* conveys in part what Martin finds dangerous ("False Promises: An Indigenist Perspective on Marxist Theory and Practice," in his *From a Native Son: Selected Essays on Indigenism, 1985–1995* [Boston: South End, 1996], 461–82, see 479). I find even Martin's speculative work compelling, important, often radical.

93. Standing Bear tells the tale of a lost woman who dreams of wolves in a cave and wakes to find wolves who rescue her. In another tale two eagles save a young warrior by flying him to safety (*Stories of the Sioux*, 6, 24). He also notes in *My Indian Boyhood* (Lincoln: University of Nebraska Press, 1988 [1931]), "Life was a glorious thing, for great contentment comes with the feeling of friendship and kinship with the living things about you. The white man seems to look upon all animal life as enemies, while we looked upon them as friends and benefactors" (13).

94. Charles Eastman, *Old Indian Days* (Lincoln: University of Nebraska Press, 1991 [1907]), 59.

95. Charles Eastman, *Red Hunters and the Animal People* (New York: Harper, 1905), 234, 29, 31, 245, 244, vi, v.

96. Standing Bear observes: "Little animals . . . told us many things, so we watched them" (*My Indian Boyhood*, 62).

97. Standing Bear, *Stories of the Sioux*, 8.

98. Charles Eastman and Elaine Goodale Eastman, *Wigwam Evenings: Sioux Folk Tales Retold* (Boston: Little, Brown, 1925), 14, 24, 47, 30, 252–53, 188.

99. Black Elk, *Black Elk*, 204–5.

100. Ibid., 217.

101. On Native self-reliance, see Coleman, *American Indian Children*, 121.

102. Eastman, *Indian Boyhood*, 3–4, 18.

103. Eastman, *Deep*, 2, and Eastman, *Indian Boyhood*, 20.

104. Eastman, *Indian Boyhood*, 18. Curiously, Eastman eventually worked for the Boy Scouts. This organization regimented boys while exposing them to nature and training them in some of the skills Eastman was taught during his Sioux boyhood.

105. Standing Bear, *My People*, 3.

106. Eastman, *Deep*, 8.

107. See Coleman, *American Indian Children*, 68.

108. Martin tries to evoke the sense of time disrupted by European colonization: "Archaic societies maintain this strikingly vivid relationship with Nature because of their a priori commitment to living in mythic, rather than in historic time" ("Epilogue," in *American Indian*, ed. Martin, 268).

109. Eastman, *Deep*, 141, 193–94.

110. Ibid., 142, 143, 148. Standing Bear, *My People*, 122. Eastman, *Soul*, 24.

111. Eastman, *Indian Heros and Great Chieftains*, 104.

112. Eastman, *Deep*, 125, 165, 168, and *Soul*, 54.

113. On the devastating and exploitative effects of the bureaucratic domination of Sioux reservations, Eastman writes: "It was true that there had been a growing feeling of distrust among the Indians, because their annuities had been withheld for a long time, and the money payments had been delayed again and again. . . . The traders had given

them credit to some extent (charging them four times the value of the article purchased), and had likewise induced Little Crow to sign over to them ninety-eight thousand dollars, the purchase-price of that part of their reservation lying north of the Minnesota, and already occupied by the whites" (*Old Indian Days*, 117–18). Quintasket's *Mourning Dove*, in reference to the Salishan, also suggests that the hardship of life on reservations (175)—as well as interest in some White products, such as canvas tents (for use of sweat lodges, 138) and cowboy clothes (176)—promoted the Native adaptation of Euramerican ways. In addition, she describes the devastating impact that Euramerican mining (starting in 1896, [177]), homesteading (beginning in 1900, [180]), and allotment (183) had on the Salishan.

114. Black Elk, *Black Elk*, 215.

115. Eastman, *Indian Heroes and Great Chieftains*, 80, 78, 10, 105. On the "wily" (128) Little Crow, also see Eastman's *Old Indian Days*, 122–31.

116. Eastman, *Deep* 139, 195. Zitkala-Ša, *American Indian Stories*, 99. Eastman writes that the "Indian" has "resigned himself to the inevitable and [has] made up his mind to enter fully into membership in this great and composite nation" (*Indian To-day*, 3).

117. Eastman, *Deep*, 62, 72, 64–65.

118. Standing Bear, *My People*, 129. Zitkala-Ša, *American Indian Stories*, 48.

119. Standing Bear, *My People*, 55, 67. Eastman, *Soul*, 19, and *Deep*, 188.

120. Bonnin's political essay, "America's Indian Problem," is reprinted in Zitkala-Ša, *American Indian Stories*, 193.

121. Eastman, *Deep*, 155.

122. Philip Deloria, " 'I Am of the Body,' " 325.

123. Zitkala-Ša, *American Indian Stories*, 73. Some of Coleman's boarding school autobiographers, such as Dan Talayesva (Hopi), were similarly drawn to the status and style of having Euramerican clothing and uniforms, *American Indian Children*, 69–70. Coleman observes: "In the literature of Indian schooling, the term 'runaway' usually refers to those who absconded *from* the classroom, but a number of these narrators actually ran the other way" (70).

124. Zitkala-Ša, *American Indian Stories*, 85.

125. "The sign language, by the way, was invented by the Indian," Standing Bear noted. "White men never use it correctly" (*My People*, 143). Also see *My People*, 239, 144. Coleman writes: "At Carlisle, James Kaywaykla and other Apache children first learned the sign language—'which our people had never used'—a form of communication then becoming obsolete among the Plains Indians" (*American Indian Children*, 140). Standing Bear notes: "Those of us who knew the sign language made use of it, but imagine what it meant to those who had to remain silent" (*Land*, 242).

126. Standing Bear, *My People*, 70.

127. Clive Bush, *The Dream of Reason: American Consciousness and Cultural Achievement from Independence to the Civil War* (London: Edward Arnold, 1977), 280. Page 281 features a reproduction from Catlin's *North American Portfolio* (1844).

128. Hogan, *Mean Spirit*, 179.

129. Standing Bear, *My People*, 142, 192, 254.

130. See Arthur Kopit's play *Indians* (New York: Hill and Wang, 1969).

131. For Standing Bear's critique of White clothes and his exhortations to Natives to dress in traditional garb, see *Land*, 189–91, 233–35, 237.

132. Henry Wadsworth Longfellow, "The Arrow and the Song," in his *Poems* (Boston: Houghton, Mifflin, 1886), 90.

133. Standing Bear, *My People*, 141.

134. Wheelock to Pratt, RHPP, December 19, 1900.

135. See "James F. Thorpe," *Indians of Today*, ed. Marion E. Gridley (Chicago: n.p., 1936), 117. Also see Jack Newcombe, *The Best of Athletic Boys: The White Man's Impact on Jim Thorpe* (New York: Doubleday, 1975).

136. Eastman, *Indian Heroes and Great Chieftains*, 11, 12, 18. Eastman also hints that even Sitting Bull may have become too absorbed in strategic mimicry: "While among his own people he was always affable and genial, he became boastful and domineering in his dealings with the hated race. He once remarked that 'if we wish to make any impression upon the hated pale-faces, it is necessary to put on his mask'" (52).

137. Montezuma to Pratt, March 15, 1892, RHPP.

138. Montezuma to Roosevelt, June 29, 1904, RHPP.

139. Parker to Pratt, May 22, 1916, RHPP.

140. Parker to Pratt, April 2, 1914, RHPP.

141. Parker to Pratt, March 1, 1917, RHPP.

142. Sparhawk to Pratt, May 13, 1923, RHPP.

143. Pratt to Lyman Abbott, November 23, 1903, RHPP. Pratt to Fayette A. McKenzie, January 29, 1904, RHPP.

144. Pratt to Lyman Abbott, November 23, 1903, RHPP.

145. This profile of Quanah Parker is indebted to Hazel W. Hertzberg's discussion of him in *Search for an American Indian Identity: Modern Pan-Indian Movements* (Syracuse, N.Y.: Syracuse University Press, 1971), 241–45.

146. Holler, *Black Elk's Religion*, 213, 211. Utley observes that there is no word for "religion" in the Lakota language in *Lance*, 27. Also see Eastman, *Indian To-day*, 6.

147. Hilden recounts a story about a recent encounter between Episcopal Bishop Stephen Plummer (Navajo) and a British High Anglican professor at Emory University who questioned Plummer's fusion of Christian and Native spiritual beliefs: "'If you draw these comparisons in your theological teaching, how do you then distinguish between which version is true and which is myth?' The Bishop stared at him for a very long time, visibly perplexed. Finally, he said, 'But they are both true'" (*When Nickels Were Indians*, 56). On boarding school students' flexible, syncretic, inclusive belief orientations, see Coleman, *American Indian Children*, 119–22. Hoxie's research on the Crows also finds them uninterested in rigidly dividing "the world into believers and outcasts; they believed spiritual power might come to them from many sources." The Crows' appreciation of the *individual significance* of one's distinct spiritual vision and their cultural respect for *individual choice* far outweighed pressure on them to conform to any particular religious orthodoxy, and thus "Crow leaders were not inclined to reject missionary teaching out of hand; it deserved to be heard and evaluated." By the 1920s Crow "membership in a traditional ceremonial group or a peyote community could fluctuate, or individuals might shift their allegiances from one group to another." The Crows, like the Sioux and other tribes, were not wholly "assimilated" in some passive sense; their traditional cultural flexibility encouraged them to actively and selectively do what may have seemed (to Whites) like assimilating for their own good (*Parading*, 195, 196, 225).

148. Ohetoint's drawings are in the RHPP. For biographical information, consult Petersen, *Plains Indian Art from Fort Marion*, 161–70. In his farewell speech at Carlisle he said, "Do not walk in the Indian road any more" (166). Ohetoint's was "the only sketchbook stemming from Fort Marion and done at Carlisle" (164). Also see Mathews's *Sundown*

on the early-twentieth-century Osage reservation in Oklahoma: the young men "were now wearing 'citizens' clothes,' but clothes didn't seem to change them any" (68). Asa Daklugie, an Apache, encountered the same bells about which Bonnin's character complained, yet he claimed that his Apache training had been more "rigid" than what he encountered at Carlisle (quoted in Coleman, *American Indian Children*, 28).

149. La Flesche, *Middle Five*, xv.

150. Hoxie, "Discovery," 989–90, 992.

151. Lomawaima, *Prairie Light*, 28. Lomawaima quotes one Choctaw student's protest that the wearing of a uniform—"that damn G.I. issue striped denim drawers, gray sweaters"—had compromised her "individuality" (94). Student resistance to the forced wearing of bloomers, Lomawaima argues, demonstrated "student cooperation, ingenuity, and flamboyant display of individual identity" (96). She adds: "As tribal sovereignty was attacked on the political front, personal individuality was attacked in the dormitory and classroom" (99).

152. Quoted in Adams, *Extinction*, 157.

153. Lomawaima's *Prairie Light*, her study of Chilocco (1920–40), takes into account the many divisions among students: "intertribal" (155), "'eastern' versus 'western' tribes" (145), "skin color" (156), by age on entrance (157), "mixed blood versus full-blood" (145), gangs—"older students were at once the protectors and exploiters of the young" (113). Yet she also emphasizes that "schools often strengthened rather than dissolved tribal identity" (xiii). Moreover, "Daily student life was structured much more by students and school staff than by Circular Orders from Washington, and alumni reveal the limits of Central Office authority" (9). On bullying, also see Coleman, *American Indian Children*, 127, 129. In addition, Coleman stresses that students were used to maintain discipline in the school (127), to hunt "deserters" (135), to exhibit themselves to raise money for the schools (136). He also underscores that school staffs were by no means monolithic and that students had varying responses to them (97–99). On gangs in a Native school in Oklahoma, see Mathews's novel, *Sundown*, 28. And Francis La Flesche recalls that in his school, "The only distinction [students made among one another] was against cowardice; the boy who could not fight found it difficult to maintain the respect of his mates, and to get a place among the different 'gangs'" (*Middle Five*, 11). At school La Flesche helped form his gang—the "Middle Five" (36). His memoir chronicles some of their mischief and clashes with others.

154. Gerald Vizenor sketches the cultural significance of this boarding school project: "English . . . carried the visions and shadows of the Ghost Dance, the religion of renewal, from tribe to tribe on the vast plains at the end of the nineteenth century. . . . English, that coercive language of federal boarding schools, has carried some of the best stories of endurance, the shadows of tribal survivance, and now that language of dominance bears the creative literature of distinguished postindian authors in the cities" (quoted in Weaver, *People*, 15).

155. Adams also arrived at this conclusion in *Extinction*. Off-reservation schools, he noted, helped constitute "an enlarged sense of identity as 'Indians.' . . . Ironically, the very institution designed to extinguish Indian identity altogether may have in fact contributed to its very persistence in the form of pan-Indian consciousness" (336).

156. Coleman, *American Indian Children*, 184.

157. On the other hand, as Standing Bear maintained, schools cast the seeds of ideological divisiveness and conflicting notions of what "Indian" might signify in "modern"

times: "Many of the grievances of the old Indian, and his disagreements with the young, find root in the far-removed boarding-school" (*Land*, 252).

3 Modernist Multiculturalism

1. Ruth Benedict, *Patterns of Culture* (New York: Penguin, 1946 [1934]), 95–96, 238. Sherman Alexie, *Old Shirts and New Skins* (Los Angeles: American Indian Studies Center, University of California, 1993), 72–73, see 72. Frantz Fanon, *Black Skin, White Masks*, trans. Charles Lam Markmann (New York: Grove Weidenfeld, 1967), 151–52.

2. Warren Susman, *Culture as History: The Transformation of American Society in the Twentieth Century* (New York: Pantheon, 1984), 271–85. It is vital to point out, however, that the turn of the century is by no means a neat dividing line between producer culture and consumer culture. Writing about the mix of ideologies that motivated the well-known early-twentieth-century advertising executive and author Bruce Barton, Lears stresses: "Barton was genuinely divided between consumer and producer values. In one breath he praised personality and teamwork as agents of success; in the next, character and individual initiative." The P. T. Barnums of the nineteenth century knew a good deal about "personality" (a word current in that century) and the Dale Carnegies of the twentieth century were indebted to Franklin (even as they modified his maxims, individualized his civic sense of purpose, and failed to perceive his critical capacity for understated self-irony and even self-parody) (see Jackson Lears, "From Salvation to Self-Realization: Advertising and the Therapeutic Roots of Consumer Culture, 1880–1930," in *The Culture of Consumption: Critical Essays in American History, 1880–1930*, ed. Richard Fox and T. J. Jackson Lears [New York: Pantheon, 1983], 1–38, see 34). Also on therapeutic culture, see Christopher Lasch, *The Culture of Narcissism: American Life in an Age of Diminishing Expectations* (New York: Warner, 1979); Philip Rieff's *The Triumph of the Therapeutic: Uses of Faith after Freud* (New York: Harper and Row, 1966) and "Reflections on Psychological Man in America," in Philip Rieff, *The Feeling Intellect: Selected Writings*, ed. Jonathan B. Imber (Chicago: University of Chicago Press, 1990), 3–10; Richard Sennett, *The Fall of Public Man: On the Social Psychology of Capitalism* (New York: Vintage, 1978); Jackson Lears, *Fables of Abundance: A Cultural History of Advertising in America* (New York: Basic, 1994); Joel Pfister, "Glamorizing the Psychological: The Politics of the Performances of Modern Psychological Identities," in *Inventing the Psychological*, ed. Pfister and Schnog, 167–213.

3. Consult Pfister, *Staging Depth: Eugene O'Neill and the Politics of Psychological Discourse* (Chapel Hill: University of North Carolina Press, 1995), and "Glamorizing the Psychological," and Joel Pfister, "On Conceptualizing the Cultural History of Emotional and Psychological Life in America," in *Inventing the Psychological*, ed. Pfister and Schnog, 17–59, see 19–21.

4. Joseph Freeman, *An American Testament: A Narrative of Rebels and Romantics* (New York: Farrar and Rinehart, 1936), 159.

5. In "Glamorizing the Psychological," in *Inventing the Psychological*, ed. Pfister and Schnog, I have argued that the sexualization or "psychological" primitivizing of modern middle-class femininity brought with it the sexualization—in part a containment—of women's liberation, just at a moment, the years following 1910 when more women were working, graduating from college, and primed to agitate for the social and economic amelioration, not just the political alteration (getting the vote), of their status.

6. H. L. Mencken, *A Mencken Chrestomathy* (New York: Knopf, 1949), 624. In 1919
   Mencken painted puritans not only as "repressed," but as uncreative "materialists":
   "The great artists of the world are never Puritans, and seldom even ordinarily respect-
   able" (*Prejudices: First Series* [New York: Knopf, 1926], 198). In 1908 Van Wyck Brooks
   mocked "puritans" as founding Americans who regarded economic survival and prosperity as their primary virtue and raison d'être. He saw "modern" "puritans" as perpetuating this scheme of value long after the colonial battle for survival had passed (*The
   Wine of the Puritans* [London: Sisley's 1908], 14).

7. Randolph Bourne, "The Puritan's Will to Power," in *The Radical Will: Randolph Bourne
   Selected Writings 1911–1918*, ed. Olaf Hansen (New York: Urizen, 1977), 301–06, see
   301, 305. Of the puritan's intended converts (or victims), Bourne writes: "He first scares
   them into abandoning the rich and sensuous and expressive impulses in life, and then
   teaches them to be proud of having done so" (305). Bourne makes an interesting ideological point: "If there were no puritans we should have to invent them" (301). Other
   significant early-twentieth-century constructions of "puritans" include Waldo Frank,
   Our America (New York: Boni and Liveright, 1919). Subsequent scholarship on puritans
   suggests that Brooks, Bourne, Frank, Mencken, and others did exactly what Bourne
   suggested—*invented* their puritans—perhaps with some early ideological help from
   Nathaniel Hawthorne. See Edmund Morgan's early classic essay, "The Puritans and
   Sex" (1942), reprinted in *The American Family in Social-Historical Perspective*, ed.
   Michael Gordon (New York: St. Martin's, 1973), 282–95. Morgan's then-iconoclastic
   essay demonstrates that the puritans, "those bogeymen of the modern intellectual,"
   were not "squeamish" about sex (283).

8. Bourne, "Puritan's," in *Radical Will*, ed. Hansen, 302.

9. Ann Douglas, *Terrible Honesty: Mongrel Manhattan in the 1920s* (New York: Farrar,
   Straus and Giroux, 1995).

10. Carla Kaplan, "On Modernism and Race," *Modernism/Modernity* 4 (1997): 157–69, see
    165, 167.

11. Daniel Singal, "Modernism," in *Companion to American Thought*, ed. Fox and Klop-
    penberg, 460–62, see 460. For a more extensive discussion, see Astradur Eysteinsson,
    The Concept of Modernism (Ithaca, N.Y.: Cornell University Press, 1990).

12. Kaplan, "On Modernism and Race," 158.

13. See *Prehistories of the Future: The Primitivist Project and the Culture of Modernism*, ed.
    Elazar Barkan and Ronald Bush (Stanford, Ca.: Stanford University Press, 1995). Re-
    cently, scholars have complicated distinctions posited between modernism(s) and post-
    modernism(s) by identifying similar tendencies, epistemological approaches, and prob-
    lematics (Singal, "Modernism," 460, in *Companion to American Thought*, ed. Fox and
    Kloppenberg).

14. Kaplan points out: "What has escaped the notice of commentators of this period
    [1920s]—who tend to see its identity obsessions purely in terms of either melting pot or
    standardization and assimilation paradigms—is that a passion for social taxonomy is
    often janus faced. Alongside the attitude—exemplified by the Klan, the American Le-
    gion, and Justice Benedict—which seeks to root out difference so as to eradicate it, was a
    concomitant passion to root out difference so as to celebrate and exhibit it" ("Undesir-
    able Desire," 152).

15. Bourne, "Puritan's" and "Trans-national America" (248–64, see 261) in *Radical Will*, ed.
    Hansen.

16. Some modernists in the social sciences believed, as Dorothy Ross has phrased it, "that

no foundation for knowledge or value exists outside the meanings that human beings construct for their own purposes." This group included intellectuals such as the anthropologist Franz Boas and the sociologist John Dewey. Certainly cultural relativism influenced some of the reforms John Collier instituted in the BIA ("Modernism Reconsidered," in *Modernist Impulses in the Human Sciences*, ed. Dorothy Ross [Baltimore: Johns Hopkins University Press, 1994], 2). On modernism and relativism, also see Arnold Krupat, "Modernism, Irony, Anthropology," in his *Ethnocriticism*, 81–100, especially 85, 86, 89, 95, and Daniel Singal, *The War Within: From Victorian to Modernist Thought in the South, 1919–1945* (Chapel Hill: University of North Carolina Press, 1982), 261.

17. For instance, Collier's original version of the 1934 Indian Reorganization Act read: "It is hereby declared to be the purpose of Congress to promote the study of Indian civilization and preserve and develop the special cultural contributions and achievements of such civilization, including Indian arts, crafts, skills, and traditions" (Deloria and Lytle, *Nations Within*, 72).

18. Hamlin Garland, *The Captain of the Gray-Horse Troop* (New York: Grosset and Dunlap, 1901); henceforth all quotations from this novel will be followed by page numbers in parenthesis in the text.

19. Hamlin Garland, *Hamlin Garland's Observations on the American Indian, 1895–1905*, ed. Lonnie E. Underhill and Daniel F. Littlefield Jr. (Tucson: University of Arizona Press, 1976), 182, 167, 169, 173–74, 177.

20. "It is the White Man Who is the Savage," *RMH* 4 (March 18, 1904): n.p.

21. See Hoxie, *Final Promise*, 99.

22. Rev. George P. Donehoo, "The Soul of the Red Man—A Study—," *RM* 3 (April 1911): 317–22.

23. "Indian Blood," *RM* 8 (January 1916): 170. Arthur Parker deployed some of these changing White stereotypes to Natives' ideological advantage in his elaborately titled essay "Lure of the Woods: Joys of Camp Life on an Indian Reservation: Put your troubles in your pipe: Be an Indian, forget Work, Go Back to Nature and True Happiness" (1910). Parker offered not only therapeutic but evolutionary advice to "imported" readers: "It's nature to be an Indian in this country, so the scientists say, and the sooner imported Americans understand this the sooner the race will improve." Parker is quoted in Philip Deloria, *Playing Indian* (New Haven, Conn.: Yale University Press, 1998), 124.

24. Charles E. Waterman, "A Woman Without a Country," *RM* 8 (January 1916): 171–74, see 171. Patricia Penn Hilden, who is part Nez Perce, describes some non-Native responses to her nonconformity to standards of modern therapeutic intimacy: "Only occasional jarring incidents—when East Coast friends show hurt when one recoils, Indian fashion, from the hugging greeting *de rigueur* in New York, when women friends decide the friendship is unequal because one does not share intimacies—recall the presence of dissimilar inheritance" (*When Nickels Were Indians*, 2).

25. Zane Grey, *The Vanishing American* (New York: Grosset and Dunlap, 1925); henceforth all quotations from this novel will be followed by page numbers in parentheses in the text.

26. This stereotypical acknowledgment of "Indian" literary qualities can be contrasted with what the anthropologist Paul Radin admired so much about the Winnebagos—not their literary "souls" but their literary and intellectual skills as master storytellers. Storytelling in many Native groups had to be artful because tales and myths, along with rituals, were how beliefs in the sacred and supernatural were disseminated and perpetuated

(*The Culture of the Winnebago: As Described By Themselves* [Baltimore: Bollingen Foundation, Indiana University Publications, 1949], 10). On the dissemination of beliefs, see Holler, *Black Elk's Religion*, xvii.

27. Edgar Rice Burroughs, *The War Chief* (Chicago: A. C. McClurg, 1927); henceforth all quotations from this novel will be followed by page numbers in parenthesis in the text.

28. Edgar Rice Burroughs, *Apache Devil* (Tarzana, Cal.: Edgar Rice Burroughs Inc., 1933); henceforth all quotations from this novel will be followed by page numbers in parenthesis in the text.

29. See Hinsley, "Zunis and Brahmins," in *Romantic Motives*, ed. Stocking, 169–207.

30. See Mooney's (retitled by Dover) *The Ghost-Dance Religion and Wounded Knee* (New York: Dover, 1973), 657. For a brief overview of Mooney's interesting career, see Raymond J. DeMallie, "Introduction," in *The Ghost-Dance Religion and the Sioux Outbreak of 1890* (Lincoln: University of Nebraska Press, 1991), and for an in-depth discussion of Mooney's life and significance, see L. G. Moses, *The Indian Man: A Biography of James Mooney* (Urbana: University of Illinois Press, 1984).

31. For more textual and visual evidence of Cushing's sometimes histrionic self-Indianization (for example, an 1882 lithograph of Cushing in full dress as a Zuni war chief), see the compilation *Cushing at Zuni: The Correspondence and Journals of Frank Hamilton Cushing*, ed. Jesse Green (Albuquerque: University of New Mexico Press, 1990).

32. On professional-managerial-class rhetorics and narratives of confidence, see Richard Ohmann, *Selling Culture: Magazines, Markets, and Class at the Turn of the Century* (New York: Verso, 1996), especially the section "Fiction's Inadvertent Love Song," 287–337.

33. David Lubin, "Modern Psychological Selfhood in the Art of Thomas Eakins," in *Inventing the Psychological*, ed. Pfister and Schnog, 133–66, see 149–53 (his analysis of Eakins's painting of Cushing is on 151 and 153).

34. Hinsley, "Zunis and Brahmins," in *Romantic Motives*, ed. Stocking, 187.

35. Francis Parkman, *The Oregon Trail* (Garden City, N.Y.: Doubleday, 1946 [1849]), 2.

36. Sally Hyer, *One House, One Voice, One Heart: Native American Education at the Santa Fe Indian School* (Santa Fe: Museum of New Mexico Press, 1990), 5.

37. See Arrell Gibson, *Santa Fe and Taos Colonies: Age of the Muses, 1900–1942* (Norman: University of Oklahoma Press, 1983), 3, 6, 181.

38. For biographical background on Luhan, see Lois Palken Rudnick, *Mabel Dodge Luhan: New Woman, New Worlds* (Albuquerque: University of New Mexico Press, 1984), and Emily Hahn, *Mabel: A Biography of Mabel Dodge Luhan* (Boston: Houghton Mifflin, 1977).

39. Gibson quotes one observer of Taos in 1926: " 'No one among them ever said, come now, let us have a western Greenwich Village. Such an idea is, in fact, distasteful to them.' But as the author population of Santa Fe and Taos increased [in the 1920s], there occurred a concomitant increase of nonconformists—daring in dress, flaunting in lifestyle, several rated as 'kinky.' Gay status became a common and accepted form of sexual choice in both colonies, albeit a subject of continuing ridicule in the press" (*Santa Fe and Taos Colonies*, 198). Gibson also quotes artist John Sloan, who opined that Native art is "the only 100 percent American art produced in this country" (151). See Mary Austin's novel about Greenwich Village bohemian life in the 1910s, *No. 26 Jayne Street* (Boston: Houghton Mifflin, 1920).

40. On Greenwich Village and the bohemanizing of the Southwest, see George Stocking Jr., "The Ethnographic Sensibility of the 1920s and the Dualism of the Anthropological

Tradition," in *Romantic Motives*, ed. Stocking, 208–76, 219–20. On clashes between Native subjectivity formations and the therapeutic ethos, see Hilden, *When Nickels Were Indians*, 6, 80, 94, 97, 98, 234. There are provocative studies, however, of links between Native subjectivity formations and psychoanalytic assumptions: see, for instance, Anthony F. C. Wallace, "Dreams and Wishes of the Soul: A Type of Psychoanalytic Theory among the Seventeenth-Century Iroquois," *American Anthropologist* 60 (1958): 234–48, and George Devereux, *Ethnopsychoanalysis: Psychoanalysis and Anthropology as Complementary Frames of Reference* (Berkeley: University of California Press, 1978).

41. Consult Gibson, *Santa Fe and Taos Colonies*, 7, 58, 37–38. Yet Gibson adds that the artists were inspired by the cooperative model of the Pueblos and that they "developed a sense of community that tempered their individualism and competitiveness" (38). This led to political and economic support for the Pueblos in the 1920s.

42. On this matter, see Gibson, *Santa Fe and Taos Colonies*, 22, 31.

43. See T. C. McLuhan, *Dream Tracks: The Railroad and the American Indian, 1890–1930* (New York: Abrams, 1985), 11–37.

44. Here I am quoting Dilworth, *Imagining Indians*, 5, also see 16–18.

45. Quoted in Theodore S. Jojola (Isleta Pueblo), "On Revision and Revisionism: American Indian Representation in New Mexico," in *Natives and Academics: Researching and Writing about American Indians*, ed. Devon Mihesuah (Lincoln: University of Nebraska Press, 1998), 172–80, see 172.

46. Dilworth, *Imagining Indians*, 70–71, 131–33, 62, 169, 91–92, 156, 14, 147–50.

47. John Collier, "The Red Atlantis," *Survey Graphic* (October 1922): 15–20, 63, 66, see 16, JC reel 10, 326; Collier, "Address Delivered by John Collier at the Banquet of the Ninth National Conference of Camp Fire Girls Executives," April 12, 1930, 1–13, see 10, JC reel 10, 337.

48. "Report of the Committee on Indian Arts and Crafts," September 1934, JC reel 30, 529, 1–12, see 3, 3, 2, 5, 8, 10. Pratt was also critical of tourism's economic exploitation of Native artisans and of the tendency to instruct Natives in marketable "Indian" wares. Elaine G. Eastman writes about some of Pratt's complaints to the BIA in 1922: "When he discovered a 'New England schoolmarm' teaching 'Indian basketry' to a tribe which had never made baskets, the incident seemed to him a crowning absurdity" (*Pratt*, 197). Yet Pratt was not particularly keen on Natives who did make their own traditional baskets selling—and therefore perpetuating—"Indianness." He probably would not have objected, however, to the Irish—or Irish Americans—making Irish lace or the French—or French Americans—making wine.

49. Slavoj Žižek, "Multiculturalism, Or, the Cultural Logic of Multicultural Capitalism," *New Left Review* 225 (September–October 1997): 28–52, see 44.

50. Michaels, *Our America*, 119.

51. Dilworth, *Imagining Indians*, 187. Dilworth is referring to how ethnographers and modernist poets used "Indians."

52. Charles Briggs and Richard Bauman, " 'The Foundation of All Future Researches': Franz Boas, George Hunt, and Native American Texts, and the Construction of Modernity," *American Quarterly* 51 (September 1999): 479–528, see 483, 483, 519, 511, 520.

53. Kabotie with Bill Belknap, *Fred Kabotie*; henceforth all quotations from this book will be followed by page numbers in parentheses in the text.

54. Belknap writes: "Today, for instance, he might be sweating in his desert cornfield as his Hopi ancestors have for hundreds of years; tomorrow he could be jetting to New York in

his capacity as a trustee of the Louis Comfort Tiffany Foundation, deciding who will receive fine arts grants, and joining distinguished colleagues for dinner at the Century Club" (*Fred Kabotie*, xv).

55. Oliver La Farge et al., *Introduction to American Indian Art* (Glorieta, N.M.: Rio Grande Press, 1970 [1931]); henceforth all quotations from this book will be followed by page numbers in parenthesis in the text. On Sloan, Santa Fe, and his promotion of Native art, see Van Wyck Brooks, *John Sloan: A Painter's Life* (New York: E. P. Dutton, 1955), 153–67.

56. It was strategic for Sloan and La Farge to expand the popular White conception of Native "authenticity" at least in part because the category of authenticity was useful for helping prevent dealers from producing and selling art not made by Natives or made with only the exigencies of the mass market in mind. But the boundary between "modern" experimental and innovative arts and crafts and the pseudo "Indian" arts and crafts Natives were forced economically to produce is not always clear in Sloan's and La Farge's essay.

57. Sloan and La Farge combine racial essentialism with historical causation. Expressing beliefs similar to those of the Winnebago artist Angel DeCora, they write: "The American Indian race possesses an innate talent in the fine applied arts. The Indian is a born artist; possessing a capacity for discipline and careful work, and a fine sense of line and rhythm, which seems to be inherent in the Mongoloid peoples." Yet they also view this "innate" talent as a cultural achievement: "Such mastery does not spring up overnight out of nothing. Behind it is, not centuries, but thousands of years of development" (*Introduction*, 13, 17).

58. Spinden stupidly laments that the (mostly unarmed) Sioux who were killed (actually, massacred) in what he fallaciously terms the "battle of Wounded Knee" were mistaken about what they thought were "bullet-proof designs" on their shirts: "Foolishly or wisely, Indian art is filled with illusion and marked with the joy of supercraftsmanship" (*Introduction*, 72). Congressional medals of honor, Hinden notes, were awarded "by the handful to the mass murderers of Wounded Knee" (*When Nickels Were Indians*, 161).

59. For histories of Native artists, non-Native artists who supported their work, non-Native patrons, art schools for Natives, the exhibition of Native work in museums and galleries, and the development of markets for Native art, see J. J. Brody, *Indian Painters and White Patrons* (Albuquerque: University of New Mexico Press, 1971), and Robert Fay Schrader, *The Indian Arts and Crafts Board: An Aspect of New Deal Policy* (Albuquerque: University of New Mexico Press, 1983).

60. In modernism, Michaels holds, "the pathos of the vanishing race is preserved by being transformed to the vanishing culture" (*Our America*, 120). Michaels also argues that "in nativist modernism, modernization begins to be understood as racial betrayal" (113). This is not quite the case in the multicultural modernism supported by Sloan, La Farge, and Kabotie. Writing about the Navajos in Oliver La Farge's *Laughing Boy*, Michaels contends that they "understand their behavior not as constituting their culture but as representing it" (121). Sloan and La Farge suggested that many Native artists tended to grasp their practice both as constituting and as representing their Native cultures (through their uses of traditional aesthetics and their innovations). On the other hand, when Sloan and La Farge identify some Native mass-cultural productions (sombrero ash-trays, souvenir bows and arrows) as inauthentic, one can see, as Michaels notes, the deployment of the idea that one can "stray" from one's essential, authentic culture (*Our America*, 121). This sort of straying, according to Sloan and La Farge, was often forced on workers in sweatshops and poorly paid pieceworkers.

61. See Hyer, *One House, One Voice, One Heart*, 1–55.

62. On the issue of Hispanics (not exoticized and too proletarianized for tourism promotion), see Dilworth, *Imagining Indians*, 102, 150.

63. Mabel Dodge Luhan, *Lorenzo in Taos* (London: Martin Secker, 1933), 16. Luhan on Lawrence is quoted by Joseph Foster, *D. H. Lawrence in Taos* (Albuquerque: University of New Mexico Press, 1972), 37.

64. Luhan, *Lorenzo*, 18, 83, 51. One of two Danish artists who spent a considerable amount of time with the Lawrences at Taos, Knud Merrild, termed this the "gift of interest": quoted in Keith Sagar, *The Life of D. H. Lawrence* (Albuquerque: University of New Mexico Press, 1980), 149.

65. Foster, *D. H. Lawrence*, 141. D. H. Lawrence, *Studies in Classic American Literature* (New York: Viking, 1961 [1923]), 44.

66. Foster, *D. H. Lawrence*, 264; Luhan, *Lorenzo*, 142 (and see Luhan's long quotation from Lawrence's "We Need One Another," 142).

67. Luhan, *Lorenzo*, 71.

68. Luhan, *Lorenzo*, 28, 133, 28, 25. Years later, to help pay her psychoanalysis bills, Luhan sold the original manuscript of *Sons and Lovers* (1913) that Frieda Lawrence gave her (Sagar, *Life*, 170).

69. Luhan, *Lorenzo*, 132, 248. Lawrence, *Studies*, 85. On Lawrence's reworking of Freud, see Frederick J. Hoffman, "Lawrence's Quarrel with Freud," in his *Freudianism and the Literary Mind* (Baton Rouge: Louisiana State University Press, 1945), 149–80.

70. Lawrence, *Studies*, 39 and also 18–21, 101.

71. Luhan, *Lorenzo*, 17, 30, 143. Also see Waldo Frank, *Our America*: "In centers of the great Pueblo district of New Mexico, like Taos or Santa Fe, colonies of artists, seekers after the 'picturesque,' have gathered. They paint the Indians in costume, they collect blankets to decorate their walls. As an aesthetic force they are, in my judgment, beneath notice. They do not understand or absorb. Like all painters of the 'picturesque,' they are mere truants from reality" (116). More recently Hilden has criticized the tendency of modernist and postmodernist artists and academics to make "Indians" touchstones in the White "quest for that which could symbolize . . . 'alienated' modernist identity. . . . They want tribal people to move over a bit (sometimes quite a lot), so that they can share the cultural space they have defined (from a distance) as this strange condition called 'exile' " (*When Nickels Were Indians*, 204).

72. Luhan, *Lorenzo*, 55, 229, 255.

73. Ibid., 17, 122, 30, 143.

74. Ibid., 33, 197. Foster, *D. H. Lawrence*, 5. Red Fox noted in Gibson, *Santa Fe and Taos Colonies*, 240.

75. For a provocative discussion of Lawrence's uses of the discourse of primitivism (especially in regard to gender) in *The Plumed Serpent* and *Women in Love* (1920), see Marianna Torgovnick's chapter "Oh, Mexico! D. H. Lawrence's *The Plumed Serpent*," in her *Gone Primitive: Savage Intellects, Modern Lives* (Chicago: University of Chicago Press, 1990), 159–74.

76. Luhan, *Lorenzo*, 119.

77. Sagar, *Life*, 145. For earlier versions of Lawrence's chapters and some related unpublished material, see D. H. Lawrence, *The Symbolic Meaning: The Uncollected Versions of Studies in Classic American Literature*, ed. Armin Arnold (New York: Viking, 1964).

78. Luhan, *Lorenzo*, 180.

79. D. H. Lawrence, *Mornings in Mexico* (New York: Knopf, 1934 [1927]), 105. Sagar, *Life*, 142.

80. Lawrence, *Mornings*, 108, 106, 107, 118, 111.

81. Mary Austin, *The American Rhythm* (New York: Harcourt, Brace, 1923); henceforth all quotations from this book will be followed by page numbers in parenthesis in the text. See Esther Lanigan Stineman, *Mary Austin: Song of a Maverick* (New Haven, Conn.: Yale University Press, 1989) and Esther F. Lanigan, ed., *A Mary Austin Reader* (Tucson: University of Arizona Press, 1996).

82. Austin's letter is quoted in Gibson, *Santa Fe and Taos Colonies*, 206.

83. Quoted in Gibson, *Santa Fe and Taos Colonies*, 220.

84. See Gibson, *Santa Fe and Taos Colonies*, 248–50, 259, 152, 158–59, 149, 160, 215–17, 262, 200–201, 202–203. On Austin's correspondence with Wilbur about day schools, see Szasz, *Education*, 37.

85. Langston Hughes, *The Ways of White Folks* (New York: Vintage, 1990 [1933]), 69–98; henceforth all quotations from this book will be followed by page numbers in parenthesis in the text.

86. See Langston Hughes, "The Negro Artist and the Racial Mountain," in *Voices from the Harlem Renaissance*, ed. Nathan Huggins (New York: Oxford University Press, 1995), 305–309, see 305, 307, 306, 305.

87. Lawrence, *Mornings*, 112, 107–08, 108.

88. Ibid., 119, 118.

89. Luhan, *Mornings*, 59–60, 229. Historians such as Calvin Luther Martin, Ronald Takaki, and Richard Drinnon have proposed variations of this repression-model interpretation of the causes and dynamics of the White Euramerican colonization of Natives. Takaki argues: "Indians were allegedly dominated by their passions, especially their sexuality. Amerigo Vespucci was struck by how the natives embraced and enjoyed the pleasures of their bodies. . . . To be civilized, [Europeans] believed, required denial of wholeness— the repression of the instinctual forces of human nature" ("*The Tempest* in the Wilderness," 899). Drinnon's readings of Columbus's response to the Natives are informed by psychoanalytic concepts of denial, repression, and projection: "Those 'very handsome bodies with very fine faces' were stand-ins for the whole persons, for the soul *and* body persons buried in him and his crew under the armor of repressions. His first impulse was to enchain those bodies, just as he sought to subjugate the rest of nature—conquest of nature was always synonymous with conquest of the unconscious. . . . To have grasped their hands and entered their world, he would have had to become a child of nature. He would have had to see that the Other we negate is ourselves." He concludes, not unlike Lawrence, "We shall have to speak a new language, the secret language of the body" ("The Metaphysics of Dancing Tribes," in *American Indian*, ed. Martin, 106–13, see 112). At times Martin reads Natives as the psychological self modern Whites have lost; the New World (of Natives) is really the Older World. He seems to see Natives as versions of Chief Broom in Ken Kesey's repression-model novel, *One Flew Over the Cuckoo's Nest* (1962). Martin's "Indians" themselves are in danger of having their Indianness—a foundational form of relational humanness—repressed. "Historians might entertain the proposition that the world we have generated and defined for the Indian at large is also a kind of insane asylum in which he is more or less spiritually impotent, frustrating his efforts to communicate with either the mythic world or our Western world" ("Metaphysics," in *American Indian*, ed. Martin, 32).

90. Lawrence, *Studies*, 86, 105.

91. Lawrence, *Mornings*, 178–79. Foster, *D. H. Lawrence*, 103.

92. Lawrence, *Studies*, 35, 51.

93. Lawrence, *Studies*, 36, 51. Hilden has identified this White romantic fantasy about vengeful "Indian" blood as a literary and ideological trend. In reference to the vengeful Injun Joe's comment in Mark Twain's *The Adventures of Tom Sawyer* (1876)—"The Injun blood ain't in me for nothing"—Hilden notes: "Once most tribal people have been slaughtered, once all desirable land stolen, once the tiny remaining Native population has been successfully imprisoned on 'reservations,' the conquerors tell themselves that their victims will forever carry the memory of the terrible injustice—because they carry that memory in their blood" (*When Nickels Were Indians*, 58). Not in their minds or in their education, please note, but in their blood. Lawrence puts a spin on this pattern by situating the vengeful "Indian" not just in the "Indian's" blood but in White blood.

94. Lawrence, *Mornings*, 103. Lawrence, *Studies*, 33.

95. D. H. Lawrence, "The Woman Who Rode Away," in his *The Woman Who Rode Away and Other Stories*, ed. Dieter Mehl and Christa Jansohn (Cambridge: Cambridge University Press, 1995), 39–71, see 42, 49, 61, 65. On Lawrence showing the manuscript to Luhan, consult Mehl and Jansohn, "Introduction," xxi–lxv, see xxviii. I am grateful to Leonard Tennenhouse for suggesting that I read Lawrence's tale.

96. Lawrence, *Studies*, 119, 143. Foster, *D. H. Lawrence*, 326.

97. Lawrence, *Studies*, 176, 119.

98. See Mary Austin, *Earth Horizon* (Boston: Houghton Mifflin, 1932), 360–68; Gibson, *Santa Fe and Taos Colonies*, 223–24.

99. See Lawrence C. Kelly, *The Assault on Assimilation: John Collier and the Origins of Indian Policy Reform* (Albuquerque: University of New Mexico Press, 1983), 225.

100. Luhan, *Lorenzo*, 119. *Studies* vilifies a reformer who sounds much like Collier: "In the white man—rather high-brow—who 'loves' the Indian, one feels the white man betraying his own race. There is something unproud, underhand in it. Renegade." He also accuses the "Americanised Indian" of being renegade, thus conceiving of any significant ideological movement within or between the races as inherently suspect (51).

101. Quoted in Kelly, *Assault on Assimilation*, 225–26, 227.

102. Lawrence, *Studies*, 137. On the protest petition, see Kelly, *Assault on Assimilation*, 215. Mabel Luhan wrote Collier: "Lawrence's article, much cut, in Sunday Times very good really. . . . I am incapable of political articles even with masculine support." (Her self-assessment was not true.) Luhan to Collier, December 29, 1922 [?], JC reel 3, 90.

4 Indians Inc.

1. Sherman Alexie, *The Lone Ranger and Tonto Fistfight in Heaven* (New York: Atlantic Monthly Press, 1993), 107. Durham, *Columbus Day*, 84, 94.

2. John Collier, untitled paper on U.S. race relations for panel at Writers' Congress, Hollywood, California, typescript, October 1943, 1–5, see 1, JC reel 32, 630.

3. John Collier and Edward M. Barrows, *The City Where Crime Is Play* (New York: The People's Institute, 1914), 5, 9, 36–37. See Kenneth R. Philip, "John Collier, 1933–45" in *Commissioners*, ed. Kvasnicka and Viola, 273–82.

4. See Kenneth R. Philip's "John Collier and the American Indian, 1920–1945," in Jerome L. Rodnitzky, Frank Ross Peterson, Kenneth R. Philip, John A. Garraty, *Essays on Radicalism in Contemporary America* (Austin: University of Texas Press, 1972), 68; Philip, "John Collier 1933–45," in *Commissioners*, ed. Kvasnicka and Viola, 274.

5. Philip, "John Collier and the American Indian," 68.

6. Ibid.

7. Kelly, *Assault on Assimilation*, 219. Also see Lois Palken Rudnick, *Utopian Vistas: The Mabel Dodge Luhan House and the American Counterculture* (Albuquerque: University of New Mexico Press, 1996), 92.

8. John Collier, *The Entry to the Desert* (n.p.: privately printed, 1922); henceforth all quotations from this book will be followed by page numbers in parenthesis in the text.

9. Mabel Sterne [later Luhan] to Collier, November 21, 1922, JC reel 3, 90 (on her house and the tour East); Collier to Sterne [Luhan], January 2, 1923, JC reel 3, 90 (on Sterne staying away from Washington); Sterne [Luhan] to Stella Atwood, November 21, [1922?], JC reel 3, 90 (on Pueblo "slave labor," Pueblos as an "experiment," restricting Collier's interest to Pueblos); Collier to Sterne [Luhan], November 26, 1922, JC reel 3, 90 (on Collier's national ambitions).

10. John Collier, "Our Indian Policy," *Sunset Magazine* (March 1923): 13–16, 89–93, see 90, JC reel 10, 318; Collier, untitled typescript, n.d., 1–2, see 1, JC reel 32, 594.

11. John Collier, "Amerindians," *Pacific Affairs* (March 1929): 116–22, see 117, JC reel 10, 301.

12. John Collier, "Room for the Indians!," *The Woman Citizen* (March 8, 1924): 9–10, 26–27, see 9, JC reel 10, 329.

13. John Collier, "Are We Making Red Slaves?," *Survey Graphic* (January 1927): 453–55, 474–75, 477, see 454, JC reel 10, 303.

14. Collier, "Are We Making Red Slaves?," 455.

15. John Collier, "A Reply to Mrs. Eastman," *The Christian Century: A Journal of Religion* (August 8, 1934): 1018–20, see 1018, JC reel 32, 576; Collier, "Do Indians Possess Civil Rights?," *The Adult Bible Class* (June 1933): 259–61, see 259, JC reel 32, 577; Collier, "Indians, Inc.," *The Survey* (February 1930): 519–23, 548–49, see 519, JC reel 10, 312.

16. Collier, "Amerindians," 116.

17. Collier, "Amerindians," 119; Collier, "Address by Commissioner of Indian Affairs, at the Opening Session of the Institute on the Future of the Indian, Museum of Modern Art," March 4, 1941, 1–8, see 4, JC reel 32, 593.

18. John Collier, "Hammering at the Prison Door," *Survey Graphic* (July 1928): 389, 402–405, see 404, JC reel 10, 309.

19. John Collier, "Indians Come Alive," *Atlantic Monthly* (September 1942): 75–81, see 75, JC reel 32, 605.

20. John Collier, "America's Handling of Its Indigenous Indian Minority," radio address typescript, December 4, 1939, 1–13, see 12–13, JC reel 32, 565. On more enlightened policies in Mexico and Canada, see Collier, "The New Deal for the Indian," *Advance* (May 17, 1934): 136, JC reel 32, 620. "Their Indians are prosperous in reasonable proportion to the whites."

21. Collier, "Indians Inc.," 548.

22. John Collier, "The Vanquished Indian," *The Nation* (January 11, 1928): 38–41, see 38, JC reel 10, 335.

23. John Collier, "The World's Crisis and the Ancient Wisdom," typescript, 1942, 1–21, see 17, JC reel 32, 642.

24. John Collier, *From Every Zenith: A Memoir and Some Essays on Life and Thought* (Denver: Sage, 1963), 282, 433–34.

25. Karl Menninger to Collier, November 9, 1931, JC reel 3, 101; Collier to Dr. Manuel

Gamio, May 17, 1943, JC reel 31, 532. For the intellectual background of the larger psychological project planned for Mexico, see Laura Thompson to Dr. Juan Comas, December 17, 1942, JC reel 31, 532.

26. Collier, "The World's Crisis and the Ancient Wisdom."

27. Collier, *Zenith*, 435.

28. John Collier, *On the Gleaming Way: Navajos, Eastern Pueblos, Zunis, Hopis, Apaches, and Their Land, and Their Meanings to the World* (Denver: Sage, 1962 [1949]), 24, 7. Standing Bear, *Land*, 257.

29. Quoted in Gibson, *Santa Fe and Taos Colonies*, 158.

30. Collier, *Gleaming*, 15. John Collier, *Indians of the Americas: The Long Hope* (New York: New American Library, 1963 [1947]), 11.

31. Collier, *Zenith*, 248–49, 249.

32. Collier, *Gleaming*, 24, 33, 24. Collier, *Indians*, 99. For an astute discussion of Collier's ideological tendency to homogenize "Indians" to suit his own alienated, romantic needs, consult Giles Miller's chapter " 'Discovering' Pueblo Culture: John Collier and the Rhetoric of Indian Reform," 26–63, in his " 'Genuine' Culture and Consuming Personalities" (B.A. honors thesis, Wesleyan University, 1995), see 52, 60.

33. Collier, *Indians*, 11. Collier, "Memorandum to the Press," January 19, 1934, 1–4, see 4, JC reel 32, 600.

34. Collier, *Indians*, 136. Collier, *Gleaming*, 30. Robert Henri, the celebrated artist who migrated to Santa Fe, also reconsidered his assumptions about "genius" in *The Art Spirit* (1930). "We allot to some the gift of genius; to all the rest, practical business. Undoubtedly, in the ancient Indian race, genius was the possession of all; the reality of their lives. . . . Their work represents the pueblo and stands for their communal greatness" (quoted in Gibson, *Santa Fe and Taos Colonies*, 150).

35. Collier, *Indians*, 7. Collier, untitled typescript, n.d., 1–2, see 1, JC reel 32, 594.

36. Collier, *Indians*, 101.

37. Collier, *Zenith*, 464, 465, 466.

38. Collier, *Gleaming*, 155.

39. Collier, "Amerindian," 120; Collier, "Red Atlantis," 18.

40. Collier, "Address by Commissioner of Indian Affairs to Camp Fire Girls Over Columbia Network," c. 1936, 1–5, see 3, JC reel 32, 570.

41. Collier, "Our Step-Child, the Indian, III: His Religion," *Saturday Night* (September 18, 1926): 18, 20, see 18, 20, JC reel 10, 320; Collier, "Red Atlantis," 17; Collier, "Address . . . Camp Fire Girls," 3.

42. Collier, "Our Indian Policy," 13; Collier, "Taos—The Haunted," January 1921, 6, JC reel 10, 333; Collier, "Amerindians," 120.

43. Collier, "Does the Government Welcome the Indian Arts?" typescript, May 14, 1934, 1–7, see 7, JC reel 32, 575; Collier, "Address . . . Camp Fire Girls," 3.

44. Collier, *Indians*, 11, 102. Collier, *Gleaming*, 52. See Donald H. Parman's detailed account of the stock reduction episode, *The Navajos and the New Deal* (New Haven, Conn.: Yale University Press, 1976).

45. Parman, *Navajos*, 61.

46. Rudnick, *Utopian Vistas*, 16 (violence).

47. Ibid., 10.

48. Collier, *Zenith*, 190, 193. Collier on Indian Independence Day in Goodale Eastman, *Pratt*, 153.

49. Collier, *Zenith*, 149 and also see 150–52, 203.

50. Collier, *Indians*, 101, 104.

51. Collier, *Indians*, 150. On Moscow: "Pueblo Fly Refuses to Walk Into Commissioner Merritt's Parlor," *American Indian Life* 10 (October–November 1927): 7–12, see 11. Collier's essay "The Sacco and Vanzetti Horror" (1927) denounced the execution of the two Italian immigrant anarchists accused of murder and robbery ("They were condemned on a fiction") as well as the anticommunist and antisocialist paranoia fomented by the Red Scare and the Palmer raids ("The Sacco and Vanzetti Horror," August 10, 1927: 1–10, see 2, 3, JC reel 10, 329).

52. Collier, "Department of the Interior Memorandum for the Press," May 27, 1935, 1–5, see 1, JC reel 32, 567.

53. See Graham D. Taylor, *The New Deal and American Indian Tribalism: The Administration of the Indian Reorganization Act, 1934–45* (Lincoln: University of Nebraska Press, 1980), 141.

54. Elaine G. Eastman objected that "Mexican Indian schools, praised by Commissioner Collier as 'the best Indian schools in the world,' are frankly atheistic as well as communistic." She also protested against Collier's deliberate "plan to perpetuate the primitive communism of the Navajo, and even to extend it to other tribal groups" (*Pratt*, 148, 165).

55. Collier, *Indians*, 104, 185. Collier, *Zenith*, 188, 181, 123. Interestingly, James Watt, President Ronald Reagan's (disgraced) Secretary of the Interior, represented Native tribes as "socialism's failure" (quoted in Hilden, *When Nickels Were Indians*, 174).

56. Collier, *Indians*, 15. Collier, *Zenith*, 424, 466, 467.

57. Collier, *Indians*, 112–43. Collier, *Zenith*, 129, 130, 185. Collier, *Gleaming*, 38.

58. Robert Yellowtail to Collier, March 15, 1932, JC reel 4, 177; George H. Roberts to Collier, April 27, 1933, JC reel 16, 318; Chief Big Brave to Collier, n.d., letter received April 20, 1935, JC reel 16, 270; Antonio Lujan [Luhan] to Collier, November 10, 1927, JC reel 3, 89.

59. Antonio Mirabel to Collier, April 18, 1936, JC reel 16, 264; Collier to Mirabel, April 21, 1936, JC reel 16, 264; Mabel Dodge Luhan to editor of the *New Mexican*, May 5, 1936, JC reel 31, 534; Mirabel to Collier, May 9, 1936, JC reel 31, 534; Mabel Dodge Luhan, *Albuquerque Tribune*, May 11, 1936, JC reel 31, 534. On Mirabel and Aberle, also see Graham D. Taylor, *New Deal*, 47, 74.

60. Gertrude Bonnin to Collier, March 23, 1927, JC reel 1, 12; Richard Bonnin to Collier, March 3, 1932, JC reel 1, 12 (other criticisms include that of Collier's inflated sense of self-importance: "Nearly every time we attempted to confer with you you always appear to be in a great rush."); Collier to Gertrude Bonnin and Richard Bonnin, March 4, 1932, JC reel 1, 12.

61. Ward Churchill, "Marxism and the Native American," in *Marxism and the Native Americans*, ed. Ward Churchill (Boston: South End, 1983), 183–203, see 191. Hilden, *When Nickels Were Indians*, 243.

62. Pro-assimilationist Whites distressed by Collier cited homogenizing tendencies in his rhetoric that more typically marked their rhetoric during their long political ascendancy. Elaine G. Eastman complained: " 'The Indians,' says Mr. Collier, speaking of them as if they were a homogeneous racial group" (*Pratt*, 166).

63. Churchill, "Marxism," in *Marxism and the Native Americans*, ed. Churchill, 191. Krupat, *For Those Who Come After*, 107–08.

64. See Taylor, *New Deal*, xii (for a summary of Taylor's thesis) and especially 31–91. On Native factionalism, also see Deloria and Lytle, *Nations Within*, 169–70.

65. See Collier, untitled address to the National Conference of Social Work, typescript,

June 13, 1933, 1–13, see 5, JC reel 32, 617. In these remarks Collier does broach the issue of higher education: "To all of the Indians we have denied the opportunity for advanced professional, vocational and liberal education" (5). Also see Collier, "Memorandum, Talk By the Commissioner of Indian Affairs, John Collier, to the Returned Students of the Navajos at Program of the Returned Students, Fort Wingate, New Mexico," typescript, July 7, 1933, 1–3, JC reel 32, 632. Here he discusses education with the Navajo students but omits reference to higher education.

66. Deloria and Lytle, *Nations Within*, 153.

67. Berkhofer, *White Man's Indian*, 185–86. Also see Taylor, *New Deal*, 32. Deloria and Lytle point out that originally "all eligible voters who failed to vote would be counted as being in favor of adoption. For seventeen tribes, comprising a total population of 5,334, this voting reversed an otherwise negative vote" (*Nations Within*, 171–72). Later Collier changed the tabulation system so that nonvoters did not figure in the final tally (172).

68. Taylor, *New Deal*, 49. On factional divisions between full-bloods and cross-bloods in the early allotment era, see Mathews, *Sundown*, 45–46, 49–50, 57, 61–62.

69. Taylor, *New Deal*, 49.

70. Hoxie, *Parading*, 335–36.

71. Hoxie, "Exploring a Cultural Borderland," 989.

72. Harold L. Ickes, "Memorandum for the Press," March 22, 1934, JC reel 30, 509; "A Protest of Comanche Indians Against the Passage of the Wheeler-Howard Bill," March 12, 1934, JC reel 30, 508; "Minutes of the Kiowas Council," March 5, 1934, JC reel 30, 508; Jasper Saunkeah (Kiowa), n.t., n.d., JC reel 30, 508; Tribal Business Committees, n.t., March 17, 1934, JC reel 30, 508; Arapahoe, "Resolution," March 17, 1934, JC reel 30, 508. In his 1920s correspondence with the conservative Indian Rights Association, Collier was in effect accused of not seeing "progressive" or nontraditional Natives as bona fide Natives. Collier responded with a nuanced reading of the complexity of tensions— progressive versus traditional—in the Pueblos, but he revealingly labeled what had to take place as an "evolutionary process" of "adaptation"—"the acceleration could be faster . . . many good things of their past could be worked over into their future life." On this, see Herbert Welsh to Collier, November 3, 1924 (?), JC reel 3, 72, and Collier to Mathew X. Sniffen, October 1929, JC reel 3, 72.

73. Deloria and Lytle, *Nations Within*, 106, 169, 173.

74. Collier, "Memorandum to the Press," January 19, 1934, 1–4, see 3–4, JC reel 32, 600. Also see Collier, "Indians at Work," *Survey Graphic* 23 (June 1934): 261–65, 297, 299– 302, JC reel 32, 604. Collier explains: "Under the bill, individual allotted titles may be exchanged for equitable rights in a community title. Use of the land, ownership of the improvements, ownership of the rental value of the land, the right to use an equal area or value of land within the community estate, is safeguarded and made into an inheritable vested right" (297, 299).

75. Collier, "Indians at Work," 263. See Deloria and Lytle, *Nations Within*: although 400,000 sheep were slated for slaughter (109) and small herders were affected the most (185), this measure saved the soil from "total destruction" (185).

76. Collier, untitle remarks to the Navajos about stock reduction and soil erosion, December 6, 1935, 1–3, see 1–2, JC reel 32, 616.

77. Collier, "Memorandum, Talk . . . to the Returned Students of the Navajos," 2; Collier, "The World's Crisis and the Ancient Wisdom," 16.

78. Collier, "At the Close of Ten Weeks," *IW* (September 15, 1933): 1–5, see 1, 2, 3.

79. Collier, "Editorial," *IW* (July 1, 1934): 1–4, see 1.

80. Collier, "Editorial," *IW* (December 1, 1933): 1–4, see 1. Collier's original version of the bill contained long philosophical defenses of the Native right to self-government that Senator Burton Wheeler cut (Deloria and Lytle, *Nations Within*, 138).

81. For example, see *IW* (December 15, 1933), before-and-after erosion photographs—"Before IECH Road with Bad Crossings, Ft. Belknap" versus "After IECH Same Road, Crossings Eliminated"—on 21.

82. On the development of roadless areas, see Deloria and Lytle, *Nations Within*, 185. They also stress that the "New Deal sought to emphasize those activities that were native to the lands the Indians owned" (186). Collier, "Group Responsibility," *IW* (July 15, 1934): 4–6, see 5.

83. Collier, "Indian Education Should Be Practical," *IW* (September 15, 1934): 13–14.

84. Clyde Kluckhohn and Dorothea Leighton, *The Navajo* (Garden City, N.Y.: Anchor, 1962 [1946]); henceforth all quotations from this book will be followed by page numbers in parenthesis in the text.

85. Szasz, *Education*, 50, 69.

86. Ibid., 23, 34, 54, 4.

87. Ibid., 77, 65.

88. Szasz concludes: "The concept of direct Indian control over their children's schooling was not a viable issue" ("Path to Self-Determination," in Hyer, *One House, One Voice, One Heart*, 95). Szasz assesses Collier's administration as "paternalistic" (96). Krupat nicely summarizes some of DeLoria and Lytle's thinking on the distinction between Collieresque self-government—"a desire to extend Euramerican conceptions of civil rights and entitlements to Indians. . . . based on a mistaken understanding of the cohesive principles of Native American societies"—and Native self-determination—"Native societies conceive of themselves as nations, where the nation is not the modern nation-state but a synonym for the people (who have specific and concrete [rather than abstract] relations entailing responsibilities)" (*Turn to the Native*, 13–14). See Deloria and Lytle on the distinction between Native "nationhood" and U.S. government-mediated Native "self-government" (*Nations Within*, 14).

89. Szasz, *Education*, 77, 88.

90. Szasz, "Path," in Hyer, *One House, One Voice, One Heart*, 98.

91. Collier, untitled typescript, March 15, c. 1945, 1–3, see 3, JC reel 32, 650. He had written two self-analyses, which this not fully dated document seems to continue. See Collier, untitled, notes to himself about detecting the sources of his anxiety, ms., February 24, 1945, 1–3, JC reel 32, 650; Collier untitled, about his anxieties, ms., March 12, 1945, 1–3, JC reel 32, 650.

92. Mathews, *Sundown*, 27.

93. Collier, "What the Indians Will Do in the Future for Themselves and for Us," *Predictions of Things to Come Forecasts by Experts* (summer 1943): 92–97, see 92, 97, JC reel 32, 639.

94. Oliver La Farge, *Laughing Boy* (New York: Signet, 1971 [1929]); henceforth all quotations from this novel will be followed by page numbers in parenthesis in the text.

95. Mottram, "Red Bank," in Mottram and Davies, *Culture and Technology*, 24.

96. See Giles Miller, " 'Genuine' Culture and Consuming Personalities," 63–88. In his analysis of this therapeutic reencoding, Miller argues that the professional-managerial-class engagement with the "cultural Other" is here being "taken seriously as a new model for personal regeneration. . . . The sensation of humanity becomes an experience to be acquired by consuming cultural difference" (87). I am indebted to Miller's analysis of the novel's reception and for some of the ideological implications he draws from this.

Miller quotes from Mary Austin, "A Navajo Tale," *Saturday Review of Literature* (November 9, 1929): 362, and Elizabeth Shepley Sergeant, "A Navajo Novel," *New York Herald Tribune* (November 3, 1929): 7.

97. Oliver La Farge, *Raw Material* (Boston: Houghton Mifflin, 1945); henceforth all quotations from this book will be followed by page numbers in parenthesis in the text.

98. Quoted in D'Arcy McNickle, *Indian Man: A Life of Oliver La Farge* (Bloomington: Indiana University Press, 1971), 119.

99. *The Changing Indian*, ed. Oliver La Farge (Norman: University of Oklahoma Press, 1942), viii, ix, 167.

100. McNickle, *Indian Man*, 55, 56, 57, 56.

101. See Lawrence W. Towner, "Afterword," in McNickle, *The Surrounded* (Albuquerque: University of New Mexico Press, 1978), 299–305, see 304, 303.

102. See Louis Owens, *Other Destinies: Understanding the American Indian Novel* (Norman: University of Oklahoma Press, 1992), 78–79.

103. McNickle was interested in matters such as the radical implications of the category of democracy in the thinking of Samuel Adams and Tom Paine respectively, Robert Lynd's critique of capitalist power, Carey McWilliams's pathbreaking writings on the oppression and resistance of U.S. ethnicized and racialized groups, and how the gradual substantive—not just legal—emancipation of Natives in the United States might someday serve as a model for the liberation of postcolonial groups around the world. Authorship attributed to McNickle (addressed to Collier), "MEMORANDUM for the Commissioner," September 27, 1943, JC reel 15, 250; McNickle to Collier, "MEMORANDUM for Mr. Collier," November 6, 1942, JC reel 15, 250.

104. McNickle, *Indian Man*, 120.

105. Quoted in Weaver, *People*, 37.

106. Dorothy R. Parker, "D'Arcy McNickle: Living a Broker's Life," in *Between Indian and White Worlds*, ed. Margaret Connell Szasz, 240–54, see 242, 251, 252.

107. See Owens, *Other Destinies*, 60–62, 78.

108. D'Arcy McNickle, *The Surrounded* (Albuquerque: University of New Mexico Press, 1978); henceforth all quotations from this novel will be followed by page numbers in parenthesis in the text.

109. In subsequent decades Native authors developed the theme of being "surrounded." For instance, in Hogan's *Mean Spirit* a Native character reflects on the inability of Oklahoma Euramericans to realize the danger even of sending Native children to school: "These people [Euramericans] had no sense of the danger, that surrounded, even suffocated, the lives of the Indians" (120–21). Natives who were educated or successful sometimes became targets: "Whenever an Indian didn't fit their vision, the clerks and agents became afraid" (58).

110. On Owens's critique of other critics (72–73), his discussion of things that go wrong for the Salish (65–66, 70, 73), and his appraisal of earlier versions of the novel (74–77), see *Other Destinies*. Owens also observes: "While his non-fiction does indeed argue for Native American cultural survival in convincing and confident terms, McNickle's fiction does not fully support such optimism" (72).

111. Nathan Huggins, *Harlem Renaissance* (New York: Oxford University Press, 1971), 91. Josh Morgenstein, "Agency Studies" (Wesleyan University, May 1999). Inspired by Huggins's term, Morgenstein developed the term *soft agency*.

112. Collier, "Red Atlantis," see 15–16, 19; Collier, "Our Indian Policy," see 93.

113. Writing of the commercial alliance between Taos and Santa Fe artists and the tourist

industry, Gibson notes that Santa Fe Railway and Fred Harvey Enterprises' "advertising [using Taos and Santa Fe artworks] invited tourists to escape the stress of city life, as the artists and writers had done, and join them in 'Nature's Hideouts' in northern New Mexico" (*Santa Fe and Taos Colonies*, 250–51).

114. Horgan is quoted in Gibson, *Santa Fe and Taos Colonies*, 271.

115. Deloria and Lytle, *Nations Within*, 46, 59, 107. Michaels notes of early-twentieth-century pluralism: "The technologies of assimilation are reimagined as technologies of racial identification" (*Our America*, 116). The multicultural modernism of Collier's New Deal regime can be read as a complex diversity-management approach to the national digestion of diverse groups as workers. But Michaels's framing of this pluralist approach to "assimilation" does not indicate that diversity production and management *can* facilitate programs that seek to politically, economically, and culturally empower *disenfranchised* groups.

116. Deloria and Lytle, *Nations Within*, 175, 184, 47, 144, 146.

117. Deloria and Lytle, *Nations Within*, 168, 188, 178. I concur with Coleman's assessment of the Indian New Deal's achievements, notwithstanding Collier's "top-down" efforts to renovate what he thought of as bottom-up tribal self-government: "It was a far cry from the absolutist programs of the previous three centuries. And this new approach survived for less than a decade in the BIA. By the end of World War II the cycle had turned again; not quite back to intolerance for all things Indian, but away from such open respect for tribal culture. By the 1950s a fresh call for assimilation arose, now encapsulated in the idea that the government should 'terminate' its responsibility for tribal affairs and thus 'free' the Indian for participation in American life" (*American Indian Children*, 52).

118. As Deloria and Lytle note, New Deal Native self-government was subject to "ideological guidelines" set by the Secretary of the Interior and the Commissioner of Indian Affairs (*Nations Within*, 170). Deloria and Lytle also lament that Collier "ensured the passage of the Indian Arts and Crafts Board, which for most of its existence has been a sinecure for non-Indian art hobbyists and buffs and has encouraged both Indians and non-Indians to think of culture as primarily the artifacts produced by the ancestors of today's Indians" (250). More generally: "Self-government was not wrong; it was simply inadequate" (14).

119. For other early contributions to hemispheric studies, see Waldo Frank, "The Two American Half-Worlds," *Common Ground* (spring 1942): 63–70, and his *America Hispana: A Portrait and a Prospect* (New York: Scribner's, 1931), and also Konrad Bercovici, "You and I, and the Hemisphere," *Common Ground* (spring 1941): 73–83.

120. Avery Gordon, "The Work of Corporate Culture: Diversity Management," *Social Text* 13 (fall/winter 1995): 3–30, see 6, 12, 18.

121. Quoted in Gibson, *Santa Fe and Taos Colonies*, 265.

122. Austin, *Earth Horizon*, 368.

Afterword

1. Mills to Ruth Harper, June 2, 1947, in *C. Wright Mills: Letters and Autobiographical Writings*, ed. Kathryn Mills with Pamela Mills (Berkeley: University of California Press, 2000), 104. Sherman Alexie, *Reservation Blues* (New York: Atlantic Monthly Press, 1995), 28. Joy Harjo, "I Am a Dangerous Woman," in her *What Moon Drove Me to This?* (New York: I. Reed Books, 1979), 19.

2. Edward Berkowitz, *America's Welfare State, from Roosevelt to Reagan* (Baltimore: Johns Hopkins University Press, 1991).

3. Christopher Newfield and Avery Gordon argue: "Pluralism remains something like a majority ideology in the United States" ("Multiculturalism's Unfinished Business," in *Mapping Multiculturalism*, ed. Gordon and Newfield, see 102). Also see A. R. Lategola, "Public Policy and Multiculturalism in America: Educational Rhetoric and Urban Realities," and Rajeswari Mohan, "Multiculturalism in the Nineties: Pitfalls and Possibilities," in *After Political Correctness: The Humanities and Society in the 1990s*, ed. Christopher Newfield and Ronald Strickland (Boulder, Col.: Westview, 1995), 297–312, 372–88. In addition, consult George Lipsitz, *The Possessive Investment in Whiteness: How White People Profit from Identity Politics* (Philadelphia: Temple University Press, 1998).

4. On the "culture wars," see Levine, *Opening of the American Mind*, and James Davison Hunter, *Culture Wars: The Struggle to Define America* (New York: Basic, 1991).

5. Standing Bear, *Land*, 230, 68, 245, 244.

6. Luther Standing Bear, "The Tragedy of the Sioux," *The American Mercury* (November 1931): 273–78, see 276, 277, 278. Standing Bear, *Land*, 251, 258, 227, 38.

7. Standing Bear writes: "The Sioux have been disinherited" ("Tragedy," 275–76). As their statements in *The Red Man* make plain (quoted in chapter 1), Robert Yellowtail and Thomas Sloan supported this position.

8. Standing Bear, *Land*, 240. Standing Bear, "Tragedy," 278.

9. Standing Bear, "Tragedy," 278.

10. Standing Bear, *Land*, 228; also see 236, 252, 254.

11. Standing Bear, "Tragedy," 234, 241, 278.

12. Lindsey, *Hampton*, 179; also see 176, 177, 182–84.

13. Other texts that explore pluralist perspectives in this period include Frank, *Our America*; Horace J. Bridges, *On Becoming an American: Some Meditations of a Newly Naturalized Immigrant* (Boston: Marshall Jones, 1918); Issac B. Berkson, *Theories of Americanization: A Critical Study* (New York: Arno, 1969 [1920]). Citing the "cosmopolitanism" of Floyd Dell, Alvin Johnson, Hutchins Hapgood, and Edmund Wilson in these years, David Hollinger notes that Bourne was not alone in his consciousness of the cultural and political importance of nurturing diversity (*American Province*, 59–60).

14. Intellectuals who helped popularize versions of pluralism in this period also include John Dewey and Jane Addams.

15. Alain Locke, *Race Contacts and Interracial Relations: Lectures on the Theory and Practice of Race*, edited and with an introduction by Jeffrey C. Stewart (Washington: Howard University Press, 1992), 97.

16. Quoted in Newfield and Gordon, "Multiculturalism's Unfinished Business," in *Mapping Multiculturalism*, ed. Gordon and Newfield, 100, 101. On similar matters raised by Locke, Toure, and Hamilton, see Kwame Anthony Appiah, *In My Father's House: Africa in the Philosophy of Culture* (New York: Oxford University Press, 1992), 28–72.

17. Locke, *Race Contacts*, 97.

18. Bourne, "Trans-national America," in *Radical Will*, ed. Hansen, 258, 260. On the development of Anglo-Saxonism in the early and mid-nineteenth century, consult Reginald Horsman, *Race and Manifest Destiny: The Origins of American Racial Anglo-Saxonism* (Cambridge, Mass.: Harvard University Press, 1981).

19. See Horsman's *Race and Manifest Destiny* on the relationship between the nineteenth-century emergence of racial classifications and the "Romantic interest in uniqueness" (4).

20. Bourne, "Trans-national America, 259, 249.

21. Ibid., 263.

22. Randolph Bourne, "The Jew and Trans-National America," *The Menorah Journal* 11 (December 1916): 277–84, see 280.

23. Bourne, "Trans-national America," 258.

24. Bourne, "The Jew and Trans-National America," 279.

25. Michaels describes aspects of this development in subjectivities formations in his reading of Nella Larsen's *Quicksand* (1928). The "transcendence of the 'personal' by the 'racial,'" he suggests, "is not a simple replacement of an individual by a collective identity." He sees race, in Larsen's novel, as coming to "occupy the site of individuality" to which race—a group identity comprised of group expectations about behavior, thought, and feeling—initially "had seemed to be opposed." The heroine Helga, a mulatto expatriate in Denmark, gradually believes that she experiences a compelling racial essence, what I term an *ethnodepth* or *ethnoaura*, "'something deep down inside me.'" Michaels, however, points to the historical and ideological situatedness of this experience and imagining of depth or aura: "Although it is Negroes, not America, that she misses, the Negroes she misses can exist only in America; only under American laws of racial identity can the thing that's 'deep down inside' of Helga be her race; only in America can she be herself by being Negro." This logic of race—also held by racist nativists such as Lothrop Stoddard—operates along lines similar to what Joan Scott calls the "logic of individualism" ("Multiculturalism and the Politics of Identity," *October* 61 [summer 1992]: 12–19, see 17). For Michaels this logic of race is illogical, a mistake— there is no inherent racial depth or aura. Cultures—for instance, Native cultures, the Southwestern tourist industries—*constitute* rather than simply *represent* this depth or aura. "Cultural identity," Michaels objects, becomes imagined and experienced erroneously as "a form of personhood" (for instance, to be and express "Native" by acting and speaking "Native") and forms an authenticity armor (*Our America*, 115–16, 116, 138). Yet it might be argued that cultural producers, such as Larsen, Eastman, and Bonnin, contrived and disseminated discourses of ethnodepth not because they had a yen for what some might think of as illogical racist formulations, but because these discourses helped their respective already racialized groups produce meaning, significance, and incentive within social structures that legitimated the unequal distribution of political, economic, cultural, and subjective power. Locke too comprehended "race" and thus "race pride" as fabrications, but also as inventions made requisite and advantageous as strategies of group organizing, resistance, survival, value production, and incentive production (tactical ethnosubjectivity formation). The weakness of Michaels's "logic" approach is that he seems not to view politics, organizing, survival from the bottom up. Philosophically, Michaels tends to be a pragmatist—this leads him to ask how someone can identify with a place and a culture that he or she has not experienced first-hand (Africa, in the case of Helga). Nonetheless, he does not appear to recognize the pragmatic side of adopting racial identification for social and psychic survival and resistance in oppressive conditions. Gordon and Newfield fear something that does not seem to be a pressing concern for Michaels: "American society declares itself postracist and blames all racializing stigma on its targets, declaring exclusions to be the benefits of a common culture while managers supervise a self-perpetuating political and economic process in the name of diversity" ("Introduction," in *Mapping Multiculturalism*, ed. Gordon and Newfield, 1–16, see 10).

26. Bourne, "Trans-national America," in *Radical Will*, ed. Hansen, 256, 249.

27. Frank, *Our America*, 106, 114, 116, 115.

28. For a critique of Kallen, see Werner Sollors, "A Critique of Pure Pluralism," in *Reconstructing American Literary History*, ed. Sacvan Bercovitch (Cambridge, Mass.: Harvard University Press, 1986), 250–79.

29. Horace Kallen, *Culture and Democracy in the United States: Studies in the Group Psychology of the American Peoples* (New York: Boni and Liveright, 1924); henceforth all quotations from this book will be followed by page numbers in parenthesis in the text. Several times Kallen pays homage to Bourne's analysis of "trans-national America" (131, 232)—Bourne had died in 1918.

30. Locke concentrated on African American but offered Collier his "deep personal appreciation" for Collier's "kind and helpful contribution" to Howard University's "Minorities Problems" conference in 1935 (Locke to Collier, April 18, 1935, JC reel 15, 230).

31. Collier, "United States Indian," in *Understanding Minority Groups*, ed. Gittler, see 49, 51, 50. For an overview of the ruthless termination phase in which the federal government sought to terminate the special legal status of tribes, transfer their administration to the states, and further disenfranchise Natives of their land and relocate them in cities, see Donald Fixico (Sac and Fox, Seminole, Muscogee Creek), *Termination and Relocation: Federal Indian Policy, 1945–1960* (Albuquerque: University of New Mexico Press, 1986), and James S. Olson and Raymond Wilson, *Native Americans in the Twentieth Century* (Urbana: University of Illinois Press, 1984), 131–56. On Collier's development of the Institute of Ethnic Affairs and contributions to a nascent ethnic studies after he stepped down as Indian Commissioner, see Collier, *Zenith*, 324–403.

32. Collier, "United States Indian," 44, 45–46. Collier goes on to compare indirect rule with Kurt Lewin's concept of "patient-centered therapy" and "group dynamics and social action research" (46). Deloria and Lytle praise many of Collier's accomplishments but are critical of his notions of "indirect rule" (*Nations Within*, 188–89).

33. Collier, "United States Indian," 44, 44–45.

34. For perspectives on the history of the managerial development of personnel departments in the 1920s and 1930s see Elton Mayo, *The Human Problems of an Industrial Civilization* (Salem, N.H.: Ayer, 1992 [1933]), Loren Baritz, *The Servants of Power: A History of the Use of Social Science in American Industry* (Westport, Conn.: Greenwood, 1977), and Richard Gillespie, "The Hawthorne Experiments and the Politics of Experimentation," in *The Rise of Experimentation in American Psychology*, ed. Jill Morawski (New Haven, Conn.: Yale University Press, 1988), 114–37.

35. McWilliams, *Brothers Under the Skin*; henceforth all quotations from this book will be followed by page numbers in parenthesis. His cultural autobiography, *The Education of Carey McWilliams* (New York: Simon and Schuster, 1979), refers to Natives in passing only a handful of times. See Denning's astute comments about his significance in *Cultural Front*, 260–67, 449–52.

36. McWilliams had ideological allies. In 1940, in the inaugural issue of the multicultural *Common Ground*, his friend Louis Adamic, the journal's editor, also admonishingly cast Naziism as parasitic assimilationism (62) (its "frenzy for uniformity and regimentation, and for stamping out diversity" and its social production of "inferiority" [65]) and framed the war as America's opportunity to embrace its diversity ("real Americanization" [64]), to become truly democratic, and to repel Nazi efforts [quoting Paul Joseph Goebbels] to exploit U.S. "'social and racial tensions'" [63]. For a time, then, the Nazi threat partly shifted some American critical attention away from class and economic exploitation to the effects of the production of racial difference as an urgent locus of

concern. "The future, ours and the world's," Adamic held, "is in unity within diversity, in making civilization safe for differences" ("Crisis" 67).

37. Adamic, "Crisis," 65, 67, 63. Adamic is as interested in "common ground" and national unity as he is in securing national respect for diversity, and so he counsels Americans to "curb our individual and group egoism" (66). Carey McWilliams, *Louis Adamic and Shadow-America* (Los Angeles: Arthur Whipple, 1935).

38. Deloria and Lytle quote something similar from the Meriam Report, though the report's authors usually prefer to use the word *modern* rather than *dominant*: " 'The poverty of the Indians and their lack of adjustment to the dominant economic and social systems produce the vicious circle ordinarily found among any people under such circumstances' " (*Nations Within*, 44).

39. Quoted in Arieli, *Individualism and Nationalism*, 289, also see 253–54, 255, 284.

40. Alfredo Valladão, *The Twenty-First Century Will Be American*, trans. John Howe (London: Verso, 1996), 3, 195, 65, 64, 62, 188. Michaels describes the early-twentieth-century "Progressive commitment to Americanization": "Making Americans into Americans takes its place alongside making Negroes into Negroes and Navajos into Navajos" (*Our America*, 122). Israel Zangwill's long play *The Melting-Pot: Drama in Four Acts* (New York: Macmillan, 1912) helped popularize the term.

41. Martin J. Beck Matustík, "Ludic, Corporate, and Imperial Multiculturalism," in *Theorizing Multiculturalism: A Guide to the Current Debate*, ed. Cynthia Walker (Malden, Mass.: Blackwell, 1998), 100–17, see 102–03, 104.

42. Henry Giroux, *Disturbing Pleasures: Learning Popular Culture* (New York: Routledge, 1994), 4, 14. "Capital has fallen in love with difference; advertising thrives on selling us things that will enhance our uniqueness and individuality," Martin Davidson maintains. "From World Music to exotic holidays in Third-World locations, ethnic TV dinners to Peruvian knitted hats, cultural difference sells." Davidson's *The Consumerist Manifesto: Advertising in Postmodern Times* (New York: Routledge, 1992) is quoted in Giroux, 12.

43. Gilroy, *Against Race*, 254; also see his remarks about "the corporate pimping of black culture" (264).

44. For an excellent example of the critique of multiculturalism driven by multiculturalism's exclusion emphasis, see Scott Michaelsen, *The Limits of Multiculturalism: Interrogating the Origins of American Anthropology* (Minneapolis: University of Minnesota Press, 1999). For instance, Michaelsen writes: "The thinking of multiculturalism in even its most advanced, progressive formations is inherently shot through with hierarchies and exclusions" (1). Hilden criticizes both a "laundered" multiculturalism (Disney's commercial multiculturalism or the dehistoricized and depoliticized celebrations of Cinco de Mayo in Los Angeles) and a liberal multiculturalism that lumps together the traditions of various groups under one rubric (*When Indians Were Nickels*, 22, 33; on other civic and corporate uses of "Indians," see 51, 194, 200).

45. Nancy Fraser, "From Redistribution to Recognition," in *Theorizing Multiculturalism*, ed. Walker, 19–49, see 19, 20.

46. Stanley Aronowitz, "Reflections on Identity," *October* 61 (summer 1992): 91–103, see 101. Also see Stanley Aronowitz, *The Politics of Identity: Class, Culture, Social Movements* (New York: Routledge, 1992). In addition, Jon Cruz warns: "The multiplication of identity formations can also purge the desire for something bigger, and *bigger for all*. As localized identities become more numerous and compressed, the capacity to achieve a larger social identity appears to be compromised" ("From Farce to Tragedy," in *Mapping Multiculturalism*, ed. Gordon and Newfield, 35).

47. Garrod and Larrimore, "Introduction," *First Person, First People*, ed. Garrod and Larrimore, 16.

48. Deloria and Lytle, *Nations Within*, 213. Also see Robert A. Nelson and Joseph F. Sheley, "Bureau of Indian Affairs Influence on Indian Self-Determination," in *American Indian Policy in the Twentieth Century*, ed. Vine Deloria Jr. (Norman: University of Oklahoma Press, 1985), 177–99.

49. Weaver, *People*, xii–xiii, 39, 43.

50. Deloria and Lytle, *Nations Within*, 2, 3. Silko, *Ceremony*, 68.

51. This is Rose's explanatory note for her poem "Naayawva Taawi," *Halfbreed Chronicles*, 35. Durham, *Columbus Day*, 85. Deloria and Lytle write: "Many Indian nicknames spoke derisively of the whites as 'people who take orders,' or 'people who march in a straight line'" (*Nations Within*, 9).

52. Silko, *Ceremony*, 191, 204. On the witchery that created Europeans and Whites ("The world is a dead thing for them"), also see Silko, *Storyteller*, 130–37, 133. But she also expresses some degree of hope. Of her White "great-grandpa Marmon" she writes: "I see in his eyes / he had come to understand this world / differently" (*Storyteller*, 256). Frank, *Our America*, 107. See Richard Slotkin's monumental trilogy that analyzes dimensions of the centuries-long destruction to which Silko, Durham, Rose, and Frank refer: *Regeneration Through Violence: The Mythology of the American Frontier, 1600–1860* (Middletown, Conn.: Wesleyan University Press, 1987 [1973]); *The Fatal Environment: The Myth of the Frontier in the Age of Industrialization, 1800–1890* (Middletown, Conn.: Wesleyan University Press, 1986 [1985]); *Gunfighter Nation: The Myth of the Frontier in Twentieth-Century America* (New York: Atheneum, 1992).

53. As Newfield and Gordon acknowledge: "Although some nationalist thought is separatist *and* militantly antipluralist, this usually follows from its regarding pluralism as an instrument of supremacism." M. Annette Jaimes Guerrero (Yaqui and Juaneño), "Academic Apartheid: American Indian Studies and 'Multiculturalism,'" 49–63, see 49–50 (decolonization), and Newfield and Gordon, "Multiculturalism's Unfinished Business," 99, both in *Mapping Multiculturalism*, ed. Gordon and Newfield.

54. Standing Bear, *Land*, 56, 170.

55. Durham, *Columbus Day*, 95. Also see Thomas King (Cherokee), *Medicine River* (New York: Penguin, 1995 [1991]), 9–10 (Indianness and mass culture), 174 (international fetishization of traditional Indianness).

56. On alliances, see Georges Sioui, "Rebuilding First Nations: Ideological Implications for Canada," *Center for the Study of Canada* 9 (February 1997): 1–6. On matters of identity, see Arnold Krupat, *Red Matters: Native American Studies* (Philadelphia: University of Pennsylvania Press, 2002).

Appendix 1

1. Collier, *Zenith*, 64.

2. James R. Green, *Grass-Roots Socialism: Radical Movements in the Southwest, 1895–1943* (Baton Rouge: Louisiana State University Press, 1978), 109, 265–66, 109–10, 109–10. Also on the socialist battle against guardianship, see Angie Debo, *And Still the Waters Run: The Betrayal of the Five Civilized Tribes* (Princeton, N.J.: Princeton University Press, 1991 [1940]), 185–86.

3. "Platform and Campaign Book: Socialist Party of Oklahoma 1914," n.p. (Tamiment Li-

brary, New York University), 23. "Many Elements Combine to Cheat Oklahoma Farm Children of Their Educational Heritage," *Oklahoma Leader* 6 (March 27, 1925): 5.

4. Oscar Ameringer, *If You Don't Weaken: The Autobiography of Oscar Ameringer* (New York: Henry Holt, 1940), 452.

5. Ward Churchill, "Marxism," in *Marxism and the Native Americans*, ed. Churchill, 184, 188, 187. See Winona LaDuke (Anishinabe), "Power Is In the Earth," in South End Press Collective, *Talking About a Revolution* (Cambridge, Mass.: South End Press, 1998), 67–79. She observes: "Capitalism and communism are really much more about how the wealth is distributed, if it trickles down or is appropriated at the beginning to those who have worked for it. But, you know, someone has to question where the wealth came from. What right does society have to the wealth? What is the relationship between that society and the land from which it got its wealth?" (75). In 1930 John Dewey contrasted "the 'corporatization' of American life" with bygone "pioneer individualism," and in the following year Norman Thomas similarly compared pioneer "rugged individualism" with an unfree corporate world of "chain banks and stores, of trusts . . . and holding companies!" Unfortunately, Dewey's and Thomas's nostalgia for the rugged individualism that occupied the allegedly unoccupied "wilderness" overlooks how imperial individualism was devised in part to expunge the Natives who inhabited the so-called wilderness. Yet Dewey suggested that America has yet to see egalitarian individuality: "A stable recovery of individuality waits upon an elimination of the older economic and political individualism, an elimination which will liberate imagination and endeavor for the task of making corporate society contribute to the free culture of its members." And Thomas advocated cooperation and cooperative individuality rather than competition and possessive "individuality"—and bourgeois psychologized "individuality." See Dewey, *Individualism Old and New*, 48, 36, 72, and Norman Thomas, *Socialism and the Individual* (Girard, Kansas: Haldeman-Julius, 1931), 12, 20. Algernon Lee, president of the socialist Rand School of Social Science (principally for workers in New York City), also contended that the "individualistic democracy" of the village blacksmith had been wrecked by the wage slavery instituted by corporations. Lee, like Dewey and Thomas, romanticizes the individualism that Americans expressed by going West; he too fails to examine this as colonial or imperial individualism. Lee, "On to Social Democracy! 'Rugged Individualism' Out of Date—Dictatorship Even Worse Than Capitalism—We Must Socialize Our Democracy" (n.p., 1939, Tamiment Institute Library).

6. Churchill, "False Promises," in *From a Native Son*, 468, 478. Martin, "Introduction," in *American Indian*, ed. Martin, 11–14. Vine Deloria Jr., *God Is Red* (New York: Grosset and Dunlap, 1973), especially "The Concept of History," 111–28, and "The Spatial Concept of History," 129–50.

7. Durham, *Columbus Day*, 3, 6. He adds: "Every year we lose more land. Every year we get poorer and more desperate. Every year more Indian young people commit suicide or are committed to prisons. Yet we are exploited by every 'movement' and cause, from the political parties to the hippies to the ecologists, and this has always been true" (4).

Appendix 2

1. See Barbara Landis, "Remembering Carlisle Indian School," *News From Indian Country* (May 2000): 13b. See *Tribal College Journal of American Indian Higher Education* (1989–).

Index

anthropology: commodification of Native
art and, 160–66; of the person, 16–17;
therapeutic ethos and, 152–53
anthropomorphism, Native Culture and,
112–13, 293n.87
Apache Devil, 149–50
Apache Kid, exploits of, 68–69
Apache tribe: beadwork of, 74; communalism in, 200; La Farge's involvement with,
211, 215; Southwest artists and, 159
Arapahoe tribe, 205
Arieli, Yehoshua, 265n.34
Armstrong, Samuel Chapman (General),
38–39, 51, 272n.23, 273n.35, 273n.46
Aronowitz, Stanley, 245
Arrow, The, 36, 86–88
art and aesthetics: government preservation
of Native arts and crafts, 199–211; Native
concepts of, 18, 36–37, 68–70, 88–93,
142–45; of Southwest Natives, commodification of, 152–66, 246–51,
303n.48; in Taos native art, 222–27. *See
also* cultural theory; Native culture
assassination metaphor, assimilation and
use of, 42–49
assimilationism: agricultural policies and
food distribution and, 50, 275n.73;
"assimilationist pluralism," 237–38,
242–45; dilution of Native culture and,
115–19, 295n.113; diversity management
vs. 224, 239–51; ethnoracial identity and,
234–39; faking Indian and, 126–27;
ideology of individuality and, 12–13;
incorporation of diversity and, 231–51;
Indian Reorganization Act and ideology
of, 205–11; as individualization, 41–49;
literature of, 62–65; modernism and,
140–41, 300n.14; "parasitic" assimilation
of Nazism, 317n.36; Pratt's naïveté concerning, 84–85, 284n.221; in Southwestern Native art, 161–66, 304nn.56–
57; subjectivity construction and, 139–
41
Atlantic Monthly, 99, 101, 110
Atwood, Stella, 186–87
Austin, Mary, 14, 24; on collectivity, 226–
27; commodification of Native art and,
166; native dancing discussed by, 173–

77, 183; protomulticulturalism and, 136;
on Pulitzer Prize committee, 212; "saviourism" and, 214–15; Taos colony and,
194, 198; therapeutic ethos and, 153
"authenticity" of Native art, 161–63,
304n.56
autonomy, individualism and, 4–5

Barrett, Michèle, 265n.36
Barrows, Edward M., 186
Battlefield and Classroom, 82, 284n.214
Bauman, Richard, 160
Beard, Charles, 6–7, 263n.18
Beecher, Henry Ward, 43, 46
Be Glad You're Neurotic, 138
Belknap, Bill, 160, 303n.54
Bell, Genevieve, 268n.67, 270n.72, 273n.39,
46, 284n.208, 285n.226, 287n.254, 291n.64
Bellows, George, 156
Benedict, Ruth, 135, 217
Berkhofer, Robert, 19, 204, 311n.67
Betzinez, Jason, 43, 272n.26, 273n.42,
273n.47
be-yourselfism, individuality as, 4
biblical images: Native agricultural
development and, 50, 274n.70; Native
civilizing using, 56–57
Bird, S. Elizabeth, 15
Bisch, Louis (Dr.,), 138
Black Elk, 14, 99, 113; assault on Native
culture and, 115, 127; religious conver-
sion of, 127, 297n.146
Black Elk Speaks, 99, 113, 116, 292n.75
Block, Ernest, 156
"blood" psychology, Lawrence's concept of,
168–72, 178–83, 194
Board of Indian Commissioners, 50
Boas, Franz, 160
Bolshevism, Southwest artist colonies
accused of, 226–27
Bonnin, Gertrude Simmons (Zitkala-Ša),
14, 23, 39, 80, 290n.40; on assault on
Native culture, 115–19, 249–50; *Atlantic
Monthly* writing, 99, 101–4; Collier's cor-
respondence with, 202–3, 310n.60; cul-
tural identity issues and, 316n.25; on
Native culture, 101–4, 106–13
Bonnin, Raymond T., 99, 202–3

Carlisle Kid (Nah-deiz-az), 58

Carmichael, Stokely, 235–36

Cary, Nellie, 48

Catholic Church: Black Elk's conversion to, 127; Pratt's criticism of, 81–82, 125, 282n.205

Catlin, George, 120–21

Caveman Within Us: His Peculiarities and Power; How We Can Elist his Aid for Health and Efficiency, 138

Century of Dishonor, 51

Ceremony, 249

Chamberlain, Marianne, 18

Changing Indian, The, 215

Channing, William Henry, 265n.34

"character" ideology: Carlisle's embrace of, 54–55, 277n.99; Native culture in context of, 89–93; paradigm shifting concerning, 136–41

Charcot, Jean Baptiste, 186

Chaucer, Geoffrey, 10

Cherokee Female Seminary, 15

Cherokee Male Seminary, 281n.170

Childers, Ellis B., 69

Chinese, American atrocities against, 67

Chippewa tribe, 200

choice, Native concepts of, 23, 113–15

Christianity, Native attitudes concerning, 112, 114–15, 126–27, 249, 297n.147. *See also* religion; spirituality

Chronicle of Conquest, A, 64–65, 155

Churchill, Ward, 203, 247, 256, 267n.61, 295n.92

citizenship: citizenizing of Natives, 52–53, 118, 276n.85; individual rights as cornerstone of, 4; White concepts of, 12

Citizenship Act of 1924, 233

City Where Crime Is Play, The, 186

civil disobedience, individualism and, 4, 262n.11

civilization: assault on Native culture by, 115–10; Christian connotations of, 276n.85; Eastman's discussion of, 106–13; "Indianness" as retreat from, 146–52; of Natives, Carlisle policies for, 52–78; White concepts of, 12

class issues: diversity vs. assimilation and, 232–51; football at Carlisle and, 284n.210; land seizures from Natives as safety valve for, 51–52; in multiculturalism, 245–51; Native culture's response to, 92–93, 106; Pratt's attitude concerning, 81–85, 284n.208. *See also* middle class; professional-managerial class; working class

cleanliness, individualization associated with, 58–59, 277n.120

Cody, Buffalo Bill: Pratt's criticism of, 71–72, 74; Standing Bear's appearance with, 121

Cold War, ideology of individuality during, 2–3

Coleman, Michael: assault on Native culture discussed by, 296n.123; on Carlisle school, 37, 109, 290n.34, 291n.66; on Indian New Deal, 314n.117; on intertribal divisions at Carlisle, 298n.153; on native autobiographies, 288n.6; on Native education as exploitation, 94, 286n.253, 287n.255; on Native sign language, 296n.125; on tribal compared with school structures, 291n.64

collective incentive concept, Native culture in context of, 91–93

Collier, John: assimilationism criticized by, 275n.73; commodification of Indianism and, 24–26, 222–27, 246–51; Howard University and, 317n.30; incentive studies influenced by, 232; Indian New Deal and, 185, 223–27, 314n.117–18; Indian Reorganization Act and, 199–211; "indirect rule administration" concept of, 240–41, 317n.32; individualization theories of, 13, 229–30, 249; La Farge and, 211, 214–16; Lawrence's criticism of, 182–83, 214–15, 307n.100; McNickle and, 217–20; multiculturalism advocated by, 233–34, 242–45; Native criticism of, 202–11; Navajo stock reduction program and, 205–6, 311n.75; Pratt compared with, 80, 209–11; primitivism and, 144; protomulticulturalism of, 136, 185–86, 192, 197–99, 238–39; Pueblos and, 171, 186–89, 193–202, 209–11; Santa Fe Indian School and, 164; "saviourism" of, 185, 189–92; self-analysis by, 211, 312n.91; socialist influences on, 200–

Dawn Man, Austin's concept of, 173–76
death imagery, assimilation and use of, 42–
    49, 273n.37
Debs, Eugeve V., 106
DeCora, Angel, 88, 106
Deloria, Ella Cara, 14, 104, 111
Deloria, Philip, 118–19, 282n.188
Deloria, Vine, Jr.: Indian New Deal dis-
    cussed by, 16, 223, 314n.117–18; Indian
    Reorganization Act discussed by, 204;
    kinship networks discussed by, 248;
    Native concepts of time and history dis-
    cussed by, 256; on Native educational
    policies, 312n.88; on pluralism and
    assimilation, 314n.115, 318n.38
Deloria, Vine, Sr., 118–19
DeMallie, Raymond, 288n.9, 302n.30
"depth," cultural concept of, 137–42, 167–
    77, 194–99, 237–38
Dewey, John, 3, 238, 315n.14, 320n.5
Dickinson College, 43
difference: commodification of, 245–51,
    318n.42; ethnoracial concepts of, 235;
    individuality and, 4–5; modernist con-
    cepts of, 140–41, 300n.14
"digestion" metaphor of Native assimila-
    tion, 41–49, 250–51; hegemonic theory
    and, 43, 46–49, 273n.45; racial identity
    and, 235; therapeutic ethos, 142–45
Dilworth, Leah, 16, 158–60
disease metaphor, assimilation and use of, 43
diversity management: corporatist incor-
    poration of, 227, 229–51; multicultural
    corporatism and, 225, 244–45; racial
    identity and, 235, 315n.13
Dixon, Edward, 124
domesticity, middle-class cult of, 8, 59, 61–
    62
Donehoo, George P. (Rev. Dr.), 145
doom metaphor, Native culture in context
    of, 151–52, 171–77, 238
Dos Passos, John, 1–8, 10–11, 27, 63, 248,
    257
Douglas, Ann, 139
Douglass, Frederick, 23, 66–67, 280n.156
drama and dramatics: at Carlisle, 72–76;
    Native use of, 121–32; tribal culture of,
    287n.251

Dreiser, Theodore, 6–7, 47, 263n.18
Drinnon, Richard, 306n.89
Du Bois, W. E. B., 23, 83–84, 140
Dunn, Dorothy, 164
Durham, Jimmie, 14, 97, 185, 249–50, 256,
    320n.7
Durkheim, Emile, 9
Dwight, Timothy, 278n.131

Eadle Keatah Toh, 36, 59
Eakins, Thomas, 151–52
Eastman, Charles (Ohiyesa): assault on
    Native culture discussed by, 115–19,
    249–51, 295n.113, 296n.116; biographies
    of, 116–19; Carlisle School and, 39, 47,
    80, 274n.67; on commodification of
    Native culture, 23; cultural identity
    issues and, 14, 316n.25; on faking Indian-
    ness, 123–24, 297n.136; observations of
    Native culture by, 103–15; as physician,
    118, 289n.18; Pratt and, 283n.201; work-
    erizing policy at Carlisle criticized by,
    287n.251; writings by, 98–103, 275n.72,
    289n.22
Eastman, Elaine Goodale: agricultural pol-
    icies criticized by, 275n.73; on assimila-
    tion, 273n.45, 284n.221; Carlisle dis-
    cussed by, 49–50, 272n.27; Collier
    criticized by, 310n.54, 310n.62; on Native
    arts and crafts, 303n.48; Native culture
    discussed by, 113
ecological "spirituality": Native culture as
    key to, 145–66, 193–94, 212; and
    "environmental" Indians, 145–52
economic inequality: assimilation and,
    318n.38; Emerson's indifference to, 5,
    263n.16; land seizures from Natives as
    safety valve for, 51–52; of Native artists at
    Taos, 162–66, 222; thrift ideology as
    response to, 277n.99
Education for Extinction, 93–94, 298n.155
education of Native students: Collier's
    views on, 207–11; for extinction or
    exploitation, 93–95, 286n.253; history of
    individualizing in, 14–28; individualism
    through, 66–74, 279n.152; Native com-
    munity control over, 209–11, 312n.88;
    Native concepts of, 103–13; as Native

route to power, 92–93. *See also* higher
education

"elbowing," individuality and, 6–7

Eldridge, Harry C., 72

Ellis, Havelock, 186

Emerson, Ralph Waldo, 4–5, 8, 243, 248,
262n.15, 263n.16

Enemy Gods, The, 213

England: colonization of Ireland by, 67;
individualism in, 9, 264n.29

English language, Native empowerment
through, 128–29

Entry to the Desert, The, 187

environmental Indians, 145–52

Erdrich, Louise, 14, 18

Etahdleuh, 39

ethnic studies: Collier's contributions to,
224, 240, 317n.31; ethnoracial identity
issues and, 235–36; McWilliams's influence on, 241–45; terminology of, 269n.70

ethnocriticism, 16–17

ethnodepth concept, 237–38, 316n.25

ethnomodernism, 140–41; Southwest
Native art and, 166–77

etiquette of Natives, 104–13

Europe, ideology of individualism in,
265n.34

evolutionary ideology: "digestion" management of Natives and, 142–45; Native culture in context of, 90–93; therapeutic
value of "Indianness" and, 301n.23

exploitation, education of Natives for, 94–
95

Exposition of Indian tribal Arts, 160–64

extermination of Natives, Carlisle debates
concerning, 70–71

Fabian Society, 175

faking Indian at Carlisle, 120–32

family structures: Carlisle's deliberate break-
down of, in Native families, 56–57, 65–68;
consumer-therapeutic culture and, 137–
41; in Crow tribe, 289n.27; individualism
and, 10–11, 265n.36; in Native culture, 17,
103–13; repudiation of Native forms of,
48–49, 279n.145; of Sioux, 103; White perception of Native family bonds, 59–62. *See
also* kinship values

Fanon, Frantz, 135, 282n.187

femininity: consumer-therapeutic cultural
concept of, 137–41, 299n.5; White concept of, imposed on Natives, 62–65

feminism: in Native culture, 110–11,
293n.84; primitivism as response to,
137–41, 299n.5

Fénelon, François (Bishop), 221

Fielding, William J., 138

Final Promise, 286n.253

firearms, White-Native trading of, 46–47,
274n.53

First Person, First Peoples, 17–18

Flintstone cartoon, 7–8

Foghorn, 282n.190

food supply, Native coercion through management of, 50, 274n.72

Fools Crow, 291n.56

football at Carlisle, 74–78, 281n.179,
282n.185, 282n.188, 284n.210

Forbes, Jack D., 266n.56

Ford, Henry, 94

Forest and Stream, 145

Fort Marion prison camp, 31–32, 37–38,
271n.5, 271n.14; employment among
whites for inmates of, 273n.46; Indianizing performances at, 72

Foster, Joseph, 167, 198

Foucault, Michel, 17, 269n.72

Franchise Day, 50

Francis, John, Jr., 86

Frank, Waldo, 170, 238–39, 305n.71

Frank Hamilton Cushing, 151–52

Franklin, Benjamin, 54, 69, 114, 136–37,
244, 277n.99, 299n.2

Fraser, Nancy, 245

Fred Harvey Company, 156–60, 166, 187,
246, 313n.113

Fred Harvey Indian Detour, 158, 213

Freeman, Joseph, 137

French Revolution, ideology of individualism in, 8–9

Freud, Sigmund, 140, 168, 174–75, 186,
193

Friedman, Moses, 85, 284n.226

Friends of Carlisle, 36–37

Friends of the Indian, 49–51, 61, 97,
135

munalism in, 200; snake dance of, 158,
178–79
Hopper, Edward, 172–73
Horgan, Paul, 222
Howard University, 235
*How the Great Corporations Rule the
United States*, 263n.18
Hoxie, Frederick: Native exploitation dis-
cussed by, 94, 286n.253; on Native heal-
ing practices, 289n.18; on Native naming
customs, 128, 267n.61; tribal family
structure described by, 289n.27
Huggins, Nathan, 221
Hughes, Langston, 14, 176–78
human chauvinism concept, 295n.92
hunting, Natives' attitudes concerning, 50–
51, 112–13, 275n.73
Huxley, Aldous, 3
Hyde, George, 288n.8

Ickes, Harold, 205, 311n.72
identity formation, Native concepts of, 23,
245–51, 318n.46
*Ill Fares the Land: Migrants and Migratory
Labor in the United States*, 241
immigrants: Collier's work with, 186; ethnoracial identity issues and, 237–38;
land seizures from Natives as safety valve
for, 50–51; Natives compared with, 52–
53
"imperial self" concept of individuality,
262n.14
incentive studies: ethnoracial identity and,
236–37; theoretical principles of, 232–51
incorporated individuality concept, 27
Indian Arts and Crafts Board, 160, 314n.118
Indian Arts Fund, 175
"Indian Blood," 146, 301n.23
Indian Boyhood, 98
Indian Boys' and Girls' Friend, The, 32–33,
36
Indian Business League, 272n.18
Indian Craftsman, The, 36, 86
Indian Helper, The, 53, 59, 71, 74, 86;
Native culture in, 36; Native femininity
depicted in, 62–63; promotional photo-
graphs in, 40–41, 232
Indian Heroes and Great Chieftains, 116

Indianization: of Carlisle students, 71–78;
commercialization of Native literature as,
100–103; Indian New Deal and, 207–11;
Lawrence's discussion of, 179–83; Native
initiatives in, 132; by Natives, 21–22; in
Native student literature, 98–119; as pre-
cursor to individualization, 20–22; ster-
eotyping through, 41–49
Indian Man, 216
Indianness: Carlisle's commodification of,
23, 32–34, 86–87; Collier's romanticism
concerning, 194–211, 309n.32; commodification of, 152–66, 222–27, 246–
51, 313n.113; cultural pluralism and, 94–
95; ethnomodernist encoding of, 170–77;
faking at Carlisle, 120–32; fictional
Native characters as departure from,
211–20; ideological resignificance of,
136–83; La Farge's view of, 214–20;
Native autobiographies as, 100–103;
Native exploitation of, 124–32; New Age
philosophy and, 294n.92; Taos artist
colony's attitudes concerning, 221–27;
therapeutic ethos and, 145–52, 221–27
Indian New Deal, 185; assessment of, 223–
27, 314n.117–18; Collier and, 185, 223–
27; education programs of, 234; governmentalizing function of, 200–211,
270n.72; historical background to, 13,
26–28; "indirect rule administration" of,
240–41, 317n.32; La Farge's involvement
with, 211; land theft and, 275n.73; legacy
of 209–11; McNickle's involvement with,
216–20; McWilliams's assessment of,
242; Native-White power struggles and,
16; pluralism and, 141–42, 314n.115;
protomulticulturalism and, 136; soil and
agricultural policies in, 207–11,
312n.81–82
"Indian Problem": Carlisle students' perceptions regarding, 69–70; Native culture
in context of, 91–93
Indian Reorganization Act, 191–92,
301n.17; Collier's work with, 199–211,
223; governmental support for, 205,
311n.72; Native support for, 204,
311n.67; self-help philosophy in, 206–7,
312n.80

Moore, Marianne, 284n.226

Morada, 153

Morgan, Edmund, 300n.7

Morgan, J. P., 101

Morgan, Lewis Henry, 50, 53, 55, 60, 62, 67, 80, 279n.152

Morgan, Thomas Jefferson, 43, 278n.120

Morgenstein, Josh, 313n.111

Morning Star, The, 36, 53–54, 67

Morris, Colin, 9–10

Morris, William, 186

mortality rates, as Native schools, 42

Mottram, Eric, 19, 211

Mourning Dove, 109, 292n.77, 296n.113

Mr. Man-on-the-band-stand icon at Carlisle, 42–43, 55, 62, 71, 120

Mr. See All icon at Carlisle, 32–34, 36–37, 62, 120

multiculturalism: changing definitions of, 26, 268n.70, 269n.71; commodification of, 245, 318n.42; corporatist "diversity management" and, 225; critique of, 245, 318n.44; expansion of minority influence and, 241–45; individuality and, 230–51; McWilliams's theory of, 241–45; modernist concept of, 25–26, 135–40, 163–66, 304n.60; Natives' view of, 249–51, 319n.53; protomulticulturalism and, 141–42; Southwest artist colonies and, 158–66, 226–27

Museum of Modern Art, 160

Museum of New Mexico, 193

My Indian Boyhood, 295n.93

My People the Sioux, 99, 101

naming customs of Natives: American place names based on, 68; colonial Whites' usurpation of, 19–20; cultural attributes of, 107–8, 127–28; White support for, 87–88

Nampeyo, 16

National Council on American Indians, 202

Nations Within, 314n.115, 314nn.117–18

Native American Church, 288n.13

Native Americans, application of term, 19–21, 267n.61

"Native Art of the North American Indian," 87

Native autobiographies: commodification of, 100–103; cultural diversity of, 98, 288n.6; ideology of individuality in, 14, 16–18; reflections on education in, 286n.253; Southwestern Native art depicted in, 160; subjectivity formation in, 98–119; theme of assault on Native culture in, 119, 296n.123

Native culture: animals in, 112–13, 294n.92, 295n.93; Apache beadwork, 74; as artifacts, 314n.118; assault on, by "civilization," 115–19, 296n.114; campaigns for survival of, 191–92; in Carlisle publications, 36–37, 68–70; Collier's defense of, 222–27; Collier's theories concerning, 193–99, 203–11, 310n.62; commodification of, 86–93, 159–66, 303n.48; diversity of, 98, 287n.3; education and extinction of, 93–95; faking Indian by Natives and, 120–32; at Fort Marion prison camp, 38, 271n.7; Garland's discussion of, 142–45; government role in preservation of, 199–211; individualism vs. multiculturalism in, 245–51; missionaries' support for, 81; Natives' pride in, 88–93; ownership issues in, 103–13; performance aspects of, 287n.251; religion and the sacred in, 104–5; ritual in, 151–52; role of women in, 110–13, 292n.75, 292n.77, 293n.84; Southwest artist colonies' marketing of, 156–66; storytelling in, 301n.26; subjectivity formation and, 98–132, 288n.5; superiority to Whites in ideology of, 109–10; at Taos, 222–27; tradition vs. individuality in work of, 16, 266n.45; "vision quests" in, 111–12; White mythologization of, 151–52

Native language: eradication of, in Carlisle students, 57–58, 77–78; missionaries' support for, 81; sign language, 120–21, 296n.125

Native populations, statistics on, 191

Natives: governmentalizing of, 270n.72; ideology of individualism and history of, 13–28; individualization campaigns for, 12–14; nineteenth-century writings of, 14; origin and application of term, 21; psychoanalysis and cultural encoding of, 24

Buffalo Bill Cody criticized by, 71–72; as Carlisle superintendent, 20, 22–23, 36, 41, 43, 46–49, 273n.42; class and race attitudes of, 78–85, 91–93; coercion of Native children into schools, 39–40, 272n.26; Collier compared with, 210–11; conflicts with government of, 80–85; corporal punishment used by, 79, 282n.193; corporate capitalism and, 135–36; criticism of, 88–93; Dawes act criticized by 275n.73; Douglass's assessment of, 280n.156; early life of, 37; Eastman's correspondence with, 101–3; educational policies of, 68–78, 81–85, 198; exploitation of Native culture criticized by, 303n.48; faking Indian at Carlisle fostered by, 125–32; football at Carlisle and, 76–79, 81–82; as Fort Marion prison camp director, 31–32, 37–38, 128; Garland in contrast to, 144–45; at Hampton, 38–39, 272n.23; incentive studies influenced by, 232; Indianness opposed by, 146, 151; individualization theories of, 51–56, 170, 178–79, 191–92, 226–27, 229–30; lobbying activities of, 82–85; Montezuma's correspondence with, 124; Native communalism opposed by, 105–6; photograph collection of, 71–76; Puritanism and ideology of, 138–39; reservations opposed by, 53–54, 56–57, 81–85, 125–26; Sparhawk and, 64–65; Standing Bear and, 99, 121–22; students' regard for, 79–85, 283n.195, 283n.200; treason to parents and tribe fostered by, 104, 117; writings of, 86

Prescott, Dessie, 58, 277n.114

primitivism: in Garland's work, 144–45; McNickle's fiction as response to, 218–20; modernism and, 137–42, 299n.5; Native writers' concept of, 117–18; therapeutic ethos and, 145–52

Problem of Indian Administration, The, 190–91

production, White vs. Native concepts of, 60

professional-managerial class: commodification of Native artwork by, 160; concept of primitive in, 138–41, 173–77; cultural "Other" concept among, 213, 312n.96;

Indian New Deal and, 223–27; Natives' entry into, 92–93, 204, 233–34; perceived alienation of, 152; self-affirmation of, 221–27

property ownership: assault on Native culture and concept of, 115–19; Carlisle student debates over, 70–71; White vs. Native concepts of, 50, 60–62, 105–13, 278n.131, 290n.44; 290n.48

Protestantism: ideology of individualism and, 9; property ownership concepts in, 278n.131, 290n.44

"Protest of Artists and Writers Against the Bursum Indian Bill, The," 183

protomulticulturalism: Collier's concept of, 185–86, 192, 197–99, 238; emergence of, 26–27; exclusion vs. inclusion in, 237–38; governmental adoption of, 136–83; at Hampton Institute, 39; modernist version, 141–42; racial identity and, 235; Southwest Native culture and, 164–66; in Taos colony, 221–27

Prucha, Francis Paul, 94, 97

pseudoindividuality concept, 27

psychoanalysis: Collier's discussion of, 186, 193–99; "depth" concept and, 137–41; ethnomodernism influenced by, 167–77; influence in Southwest artists' colonies of, 153–66; modernist multiculturalism and, 135–41; "racial individuality" concept and, 178–83; repression model of Native colonization, 306n.89; Taos therapeutic ethos and, 24, 221–27

"psychological" as cultural category, 25, 137

public schools, Native enrollment in, 46

Pueblo tribe: artist colonies' perceptions of, 159–66, 170–77; capitalist commodification of, 157–66; Collier and, 186–89, 193–202, 209–11; communalism and individualism of, 303n.41; factionalism in, 204–5, 311n.72; La Farge's view of, 215; land theft from, 182–83; Luhan's relations with, 187, 189; tribal customs of, 63, 279n.145

Puritanism: ideology of individualism and, 9–11, 179, 264n.29; primitivism and, 138–41, 300nn.6–7

"Puritan's Will to Power," 139

Joel Pfister is a professor of American Studies and English at Wesleyan University. He is the coeditor of *Inventing the Psychological: Toward a Cultural History of Emotional Life in America* (1997), and author of *Staging Depth: Eugene O'Neill and the Politics of Psychological Discourse* (1995) and *The Production of Personal Life: Class, Gender, and the Psychological in Hawthorne's Fiction* (1991).

Library of Congress Cataloging-in-Publication Data
Pfister, Joel.
Individuality incorporated : Indians and the multicultural modern / by Joel Pfister.
p. cm. — (New Americanists)
Includes index.
ISBN 0-8223-3254-X (cloth : alk. paper)
ISBN 0-8223-3292-2 (pbk. : alk. paper)
1. Indians of North America—Cultural assimilation. 2. Indians of North America—History—Sources. 3. Whites—Relations with Indians. 4. Individualism—United States. 5. Indians in literature. 6. Indians in popular culture. 7. United States—Race relations. 8. United States—Politics and government. I. Title. II. Series.
E98.C89P45 2004   305.897'073'09—dc22   2003016059